RETHINKING THE MASTERS OF COMPARATIVE LAW

Rethinking the Masters of Comparative Law

Edited by

ANNELISE RILES
Northwestern University School of Law

·HART·
PUBLISHING

OXFORD—PORTLAND OREGON
2001

Hart Publishing
Oxford and Portland, Oregon

Published in North America (US and Canada) by
Hart Publishing c/o
International Specialized Book Services
5804 NE Hassalo Street
Portland, Oregon
97213-3644
USA

Distributed in the Netherlands, Belgium and Luxembourg by
Intersentia, Churchillaan 108
B2900 Schoten
Antwerpen
Belgium

Hart Publishing Ltd is a specialist legal publisher based in Oxford, England.
To order further copies of this book or to request a list of other
publications please write to:

Hart Publishing Ltd, Salter's Boatyard,
Folly Bridge, Abingdon Road, Oxford OX1 4LB
Telephone: +44 (0)1865 245533 or Fax: +44 (0)1865 794882
e-mail: mail@hartpub.co.uk

British Library Cataloguing in Publication Data
Data Available
ISBN 1 84113–289–6 (cloth)
1 84113–290–X (paper)

Typeset in Sabon 10pt
by Hope Services (Abingdon) Ltd.
Printed in Great Britain on acid-free paper
by Biddles Ltd, Guildford and King's Lynn

Contents

Part IV Mid-Century Pragmatism

List of Illustrations

Acknowledgments

The essays in this collection were first presented at the second annual Faculty Conference of the Northwestern University School of Law in March, 2000. We are grateful to the Law School for hosting this conversation and for assisting with the preparation of the volume , and we thank the commentators and the audience for the spirited discussion that ensued, as well as Elizabeth Olds for coordinating the conference. This project is also the artifact of a remarkable friendship with Jane Campion, whose creative eye, editorial skill and generous spirit guided us through the final stages of revision. Among her many contributions, I want to acknowledge her work in collecting many of the portraits in the book from archives around the world, and her creation of the artwork that appears on the cover. Finally, I wish to thank Bryant Garth, David Gerber, David Kennedy, Hiro Miyazaki and David Van Zandt, as well as my students in Comparative Law at Cornell Law School in the Spring of 2001 and Richard Hart at Hart Publishing, for their criticism and assistance of many kinds.

AR
Ithaca,
April 15, 2001

About the Authors

Jorge L. Esquirol is Assistant Professor at Northeastern University School of Law. He was the academic director of Harvard Law School's Graduate Program from 1992 to 1997. He received his juris doctor degree from Harvard Law School and his undergraduate degree from Georgetown University. Professor Esquirol writes in the area of Latin American law and focuses on legal theory and constitutional law. His recent article, "The Fictions of Latin American Law," analyzes René David's contribution to the formalist paradigm of Latin American legal thought. Professor Esquirol has researched extensively at the Colombian Constitutional Court and also teaches at Los Andes University in Bogotá.

Vivian Grosswald Curran teaches comparative law at the University of Pittsburgh, where she also has founded a program to teach foreign languages in a legal context. She has published articles and chapters in numerous law journals and books in the areas of comparative law, and law and semiotics; is the author of two books, "Learning French Through the Law" (1996), "An Introduction to Comparative Law" (forthcoming); and is translating into English Bernhard Grossfeld's "Kernfragen der Rechtsvergleichung" (1996). She received her Ph.D. in French Literature and Romance Philology and her J.D. from Columbia University.

David J. Gerber is Distinguished Professor of Law and co-director of the International and Comparative Law Program at Chicago-Kent College of Law. He has been a Visiting Professor of Law at Northwestern University School of Law, the Universities of Freiburg and Munich in Germany and the University of Stockholm in Sweden. His most recent book is *Law and Competition in Twentieth Century Europe: Protecting Prometheus* (1998).

Robert Launay is Professor of Anthropology at Northwestern University. He holds a doctorate in anthropology from Cambridge University. He has conducted extensive field research among Muslim traders in Cote d'Ivoire and is the author of *Traders Without Trade: Responses to Change in Two Dyula Communities* (1982), and *Beyond the Stream: Islam and Society in a West African Town* (1992), as well as numerous articles. He is currently working on a book manuscript on the "prehistory" of anthropology entitled *Savages, Despots and Romans: The Urge to Compare and the Origins of Anthropology*.

Ugo A. Mattei is Alfred and Hanna Fromm Professor of International and Comparative Law at the University of California (Hastings), and Professor Ordinario di Diritto Civile at the University of Torino, Italy. He is an associate member of the International Academy of Comparative Law and occasionally teaches at the Faculté International de Droit Comparé in Strasbourg. He is the author of several books and law review articles, including *Comparative Law and Economics* (1997) and "Three Patterns of Law: Taxonomy and Change in the World's Legal Systems," *American Journal of Comparative Law* (1997).

Annelise Riles is Professor of law at Northwestern University School of Law and a Research Fellow at the American Bar Foundation. She received a doctorate in social anthropology from Cambridge University in 1996 and a juris doctor degree from Harvard Law School in 1993. Her recent publications include *The Network Inside Out* (2000), "Wigmore's Treasure Box: Comparative Law in the Era of Information," *Harvard Journal of International Law* (1999), and "Infinity within the Brackets," *American Ethnologist* (1998).

Amr A. Shalakany is a legal advisor to the Palestinian Negotiating Team in the final status peace negotiations with Israel. He is a Visiting Lecturer at Bir Zeit University Law School in Palestine. He received his doctor of juridical science degree from Harvard Law School in 2000. From Cairo University, he received a Licence de Droit, a Diploma in International Trade and Investment Law, and a Diploma in Private Comparative Law. He was senior fellow at Harvard University's Islamic Jurisprudence Workshop. He has also served as a legal counselor and researcher at the Cairo Regional Centre for International Commercial Arbitration. Professor Shalakany is the author of "Between Identity and Redistribution: Sanhuri, Genealogy and the Will to Islamise" *Islamic Law and Society Journal* (Winter 2001), "Arbitration and the Third World: Bias under the Scepter of Neoliberalism" *Harvard International Law Journal* (April 2000), "Disempowering the National: The Contribution of Arbitration," in *Third World Approaches to International Law Reader* (1999), and "Transfer of Risk in Sale of Goods Contracts: A Comparative Study of the Civil and Common Law Systems in Relation to International Trade Law," *Cairo Law Faculty Journal* (1995).

Ahmed White is Assistant Professor at the University of Colorado School of Law. He graduated from Yale Law Schol in 1994, where he was essays editor for the Yale Law Journal. From 1997 through 1998 he served as legislative counsel with the Louisiana State Senate. Professor White's scholarship focuses on the Rule of Law ideal and, especially, on the historical contingency of its normative program. As such, his work has entailed extensive study of Western Marxism and its encounter with the liberal legal system. He is author of "Victims Rights and the Rule of Law: The Threat to Liberal Jurisprudence," *Kentucky Law Journal* (1999).

Hitoshi Aoki is Associate Professor of Comparative Law at Hitotsubashi University in Tokyo. Prior to that position, he taught criminal law for four years at Kanto Gakuin University and held a research fellowship at the Japan Society for the Promotion of Science. Professor Aoki received his master of laws degree at Hitotsubashi University in 1986. His recent works in comparative law include *A Comparative Study of the Legal Concept of Cruelty to Animals: France and Japan* (1998) and *The Impossible Attempt: France and Japan* (1995) – both studies of the reception of Western legal thought in Japan – and *Nobushige Hozumi and Sir James George Frazer* (1996).

Introduction:
The Projects of Comparison

ANNELISE RILES*

"These men were neither heroes nor villains nor anonymous citizens. They were pragmatic technicians seeking to find scientific and practical solutions to public problems in times of crisis: hence they qualify as intellectuals."[1]

"we should look not at whether this or that person could conceive of other cultures in this or that way . . . but at the effectiveness of the vision, the manner in which an idea was implemented."[2]

FROM TYPOLOGIES TO ALLEGORIES

Comparison, as a creative or scientific, pragmatic or utopian act, a method and a project, is one of the most ubiquitous and yet undertheorized dimensions of modern knowledge. One dimension of comparison is its uses as a tool for thinking about legal problems. This book reflects on the effects, consequences and uses of the modern comparative project in the pocket of legal studies known as comparative law.[3]

 * Research and writing of this introduction as well as chapter four was supported by grants from the American Council of Learned Societies, the Social Science Research Council, the Howard Foundation, the National Endowment of the Humanities and the American Bar Foundation.

 [1] Paul Rabinow, *French Modern: Norms and Forms of the Social Environment* (Cambridge, 1989) (writing about the protagonists in the modern discipline of urban planning).

 [2] Marilyn Strathern, "Out of Context: The Persuasive Fictions of Anthropology" 28 *Current Anth*. 84, 251 (1987).

 [3] For general discussions of modernism in legal studies, see David Luban, *Legal Modernism* (Ann Arbor, 1997); J. M. Balkin, "What Is a Postmodern Constitutionalism?," 90 *Mich. L. Rev*. 1966, 1990 (1992); Nathaniel Berman, "Modernism, Nationalism, and the Rhetoric of Reconstruction," 4 *Yale J.L. & Human*. 351, 380 (1992); Peter Fitzpatrick, *The Mythology of Modern Law* (London, 1992); David Kennedy, "The Move to Institutions," 8 *Cardozo L. Rev*. 841 (1987); Pierre Schlag, "Cannibal Moves: An Essay on the Metamorphoses of the Legal Distinction," 40 *Stan. L. Rev*. 929 (1988); Gunther Teubner, *Law as an Autopoietic System* (Oxford, 1993); Thomas C. Grey, "Langdell's Orthodoxy," 45 *U. Pitt. L. Rev*. 1 (1983); Duncan Kennedy, "Toward an Historical Understanding of Legal Consciousness: The Case of Classical Legal Thought in America, 1850–1940," 3 *Res. L. Soc*. 3, at 89 (1980). For intellectual histories of comparative law in the modernist era, see generally Marie-Claire Belleau, "Les Juristes Inquiets: Legal Classicism and Criticism in Early Twentieth-Century France," 1997 *Utah L. Rev*. 379 (1997); Jorge Esquirol, "The

The questions here are as consequential as they are diverse. How did comparative law come to represent a discipline apart from jurisprudence or international law on the one hand, and from the social sciences and the humanities on the other? How were the tools of the comparative lawyer's toolbox created and honed? What are the consequences of the intellectual and practical choices comparativists have made over the decades and the centuries? Each of the essays in this volume confronts these questions with reference to the life and work of a figure exemplary of a particular moment in the discipline. These include its prehistory (Bodin, Montesquieu), its roots in nineteenth century liberalism (Weber), its associations with the critique of "legal classicism" (Wigmore, Kantorowicz), the introduction of social science in legal scholarship, twentieth century projects of modernization (Hozumi, Rabel), of decolonization (Sanhuri), of rebuilding after and laying blame for fascism (Kantorowicz, Sacco), of fighting the cold war (David, Schlesinger).

This book is a product of its intellectual moment, a moment defined by an expanding interest in comparative law among scholars and practitioners outside the traditional community of comparativists on the one hand and, paradoxically, a waning of interest in mid-century methods of comparative law among comparativists on the other. In many parts of the world, comparative law is now taken as newly relevant to projects of constitution and code-drafting or the harmonization of laws. Even the American courts, last bastions of parochialism, have begun to consider the value of comparative materials in decision-making. Unlike other paragons of modernism from architecture to social science that seem to inspire only quaint nostalgia girded by a collective loss of faith in underlying projects and methods, then, modernism in comparative law is more contemporary than ever.

At the same time, however, by now, certain paradigms, critiques, and questions about the state of the discipline are universally accepted among its members. First, everyone is now a critic of the typologies of legal systems and traditions that characterized mid-century comparative legal scholarship.[4] Second, and very much related to the first, everyone is a methodologist—to be a comparativist today is to worry about the proper terms, categories, scale, methods, and data to be used in comparison.[5] Third, the consensus about the

---

Fictions of Latin American Law," 1997 *Utah L. Rev.* 425 (1997); Mitchel Lasser, "'Lit. Theory' Put to the Test: A Comparative Literary Analysis of American Judicial Tests and French Judicial Discourse," 111 *Harv. L. Rev.* 689 (1998); Annelise Riles, "Wigmore's Treasure Box: Comparative Law in the Era of Information," 40 *Harv. Int'l L.J.* 221 (1999).

[4] *See, e.g.,* F. H. Lawson, *The Comparison: Selected Essays 2* (Amsterdam, 1977) ("the word "comparative" suggests universality, and nowadays to be universal means to be superficial"); Mathias Reimann, "Stepping Out of the European Shadow: Why Comparative Law in the United States Must Develop Its Own Agenda," 46 *Am. J. Comp. L.* 637 (1998) (critiquing "the classical edifice" of mid-century comparative legal scholarship); William P. Alford, "On the Limits of "Grand Theory" in Comparative Law," 61 *Wash. L. Rev.* 945–956 (1986).

[5] *See, e.g.,* Alan Watson, *Legal Transplants* (Athens, 1993) (focusing on the proper method of comparative legal research); Lawson, *supra* note 5, at 104–80 (discussing questions of scale in comparative law); John C. Reitz, "How to Do Comparative Law," 46 *Am. J. Comp. L.* 617–18 (1998) ("Most of us who reach and write in the field of comparative law however were not taught formally how to do comparative law. Rather, we have for the most part worked out our own methods based on an amalgam of the scholarship we thought effective for our particular purposes at that time.")

discipline's identity is that comparative law is, or should be "an academic discipline"[6]—a pocket of legal scholarship devoted to the larger questions of law in which research questions are defined in relation to certain internal debates such that a body of knowledge of some kind might ensue. Yet finally, this conception of the project also produces a certain ubiquitous angst about the disciplinary identity of comparative law today—a lingering question about what makes comparative law unique vis à vis other academic disciplines, from the anthropology or sociology of law to comparative politics, or jurisprudence,[7] and a sense of being at a loss about the way forward.

What might come after this critique of modernist models, then? How to break open the debates that have stymied the discipline, to go beyond simply intervening in them? The authors of these essays have sought to understand the relationship between the person and the project, not just the method and the model. The title of the book is meant, somewhat tongue in cheek, to reflect the discipline's own view of its founding figures and to break out of the fashionable urge simply to critique old methods. The subjects of the chapters were chosen in the following way: we simply asked one another whose life and work we might like to devote a year to learning more about. It is from one point of view an ad hoc selection, not at all a scientific sample of the canon, therefore. But from another point of view the volume is well-suited to answer the question of what this tradition means for us now.[8] The subjects of each chapter emerge as the authors of academic and institutional projects, as exemplary proponents of epoch-making theories and ideas, and also as legacies reimagined by succeeding generations towards their own ends. Ultimately, we aim to develop a certain curiosity for and about this discipline by confronting others' curiosity about it. We acknowledge that there are dangers in such a move, from the possibility that one might find nothing of present value, to the possibility of slipping into nostalgia for a simpler, transdisciplinary past.[9] Nevertheless, our hope is that by revisiting the orthodoxy surrounding these

[6] Watson, *supra* note 6, at 1; Pierre LeGrande, "John Henry Merryman and Comparative Legal Studies," 47 *Am. J. Comp. L.* 3, 4 (1999) (quoting Merryman: "There are professional activities for which rule-comparison is directly useful, but scholarship is supposed to have larger concerns"); David Kennedy, "New Approaches to Comparative Law: Comparativism and International Governance," 1997 *Utah L. Rev.* 545 (1997).

[7] *See, e.g.*, Watson, *supra* note 6, at 4–9 (formulating a methodological proposal explicitly aimed at differentiating what comparative lawyers do from the work of sociologists); James Gordley, "Is Comparative Law a Distinct Discipline?," 46 *Am. J. Comp. L.* 607 (1998).

[8] At the conference and in subsequent conversations among the authors, there was spirited discussion around the question of whether this collection makes a canonical statement and what consequences might ensue. Some emphasized that certain figures had been included who were not acknowledged "masters," while others who should have been included were not, and that we should perhaps entitle the volume, rather, "some masters" to acknowledge this fact. This provoked further strong objections from some that the authors of these chapters should define our own canon, and take responsibility for doing so.

[9] On the subject of nostalgia for modernism, *see* Marilyn Strathern, "Nostalgia and the New Genetics," in Debbora Battaglia (ed.), *Rhetorics of Self-making* (Berkeley, 1995); Stephen A. Tyler, *The Unspeakable: Discourse, Dialogue, and Rhetoric in the Postmodern World* (Madison Wis., 1987). We are grateful to Bonnie Honig for raising the problem of nostalgia at the conference.

figures and emphasizing multi-faceted readings of their texts we might trans-
pose the question of "the canon" of comparative law into another kind of
inquiry altogether.

Although the subject matter concerns the discipline's history, this is first
and foremost a volume about our present, then. The authors' contemporary
theoretical and political commitments are vital to their reading of the figures
they write about. For some, the retracing of an academic lineage is intended
allegorically to create a space for a different kind of work. Other authors
address the way figures such as Sanhuri in the Islamic world, or Kantorowicz
in Europe and the United States, have become sites of political confrontation
today—how, as Shalakany aptly puts it, "the debate about Sanhuri is not a
debate about Sanhuri at all." Still other authors, such as White and Esquirol,
pursue exactly the opposite goal, that is, they seek to render figures such as
David and Weber as sites of contemporary politics in precisely the way
Shalakany and Curran lament that Sanhuri and Kantorowicz have become.
Still others, such as Launay, seek to trace the intellectual origins of issues of
contemporary political contestation such as the problem of relativism in comparative law. Some authors draw an explicit parallel between their subject's
predicament and their own; others do not. In all these ways, the book is an
investigation of, and engagement with what has been at stake in doing comparative law and what is at stake in doing it now.

By framing our intervention in these debates as a matter of disciplinary history, we are opting for a rehearsed genre. There have been many histories of
the discipline of comparative law. Indeed, the recounting of the discipline's history, from its birth at the International Congress of Comparative Law in 1900
to the present, is a classical trope in comparative legal scholarship.[10] Yet it is
perhaps not surprising, given the importance of demonstrating that this fledg-
ling discipline had a history, that this has been in the main a history of the pro-
gression of models, not a critical history of persons and projects. One element
that is consistently left out of such accounts, for example, is the relationship
among the particular individuals who made this history.[11] Collectively, these
chapters trace a rich network of intellectual, personal and institutional influences: The early twentieth century French comparativist Edouard Lambert
emerges as a figure in constant dialogue with Egyptian leftists such as Sanhuri
on the one hand and American rightists such as Wigmore on the other.
Wigmore in turn borrows his theories of comparative law from the Japanese
student of James Frazer, Nobushige Hozumi, on the one hand, and the
American devotee of modernist social science, Roscoe Pound, on the other.
Kantorowicz is deeply engaged with the American realist movement during his

[10] For a classical performance in the genre, *see* H. C. Gutteridge, *Comparative Law: An
Introduction to the Comparative Method of Legal Study & Research* (Cambridge, 1949) 11–22. *See
also* Konrad Zweigert & Hein Kötz, *Introduction to Comparative Law* (Tony Weir trans., 3rd ed.
Oxford, 1998) 48–62 .

[11] *Cf.* Yves Dezalay & Bryant G. Garth, *Dealing in Virtue: International Commercial Arbitration
and the Construction of a Transnational Legal Order* (Chicago, 1996).

years in exile through his personal friendship with Pound, and in Germany he also influences Rabel, who in turn comes to shape the American post-realist orthodoxy through students such as Max Rheinstein. A generation later, René David claims the mantle of Lambert to establish himself as France's leading comparativist, and in turn has a deep influence on Sacco, Italy's leading comparativist.

Finally, a note for an interdisciplinary audience. For students of modernism more familiar with the arts, social sciences or humanities the problems will seem both intimately familiar and oddly off-key. Figures such as Montesquieu or Weber are shared icons of law and social science; the methods of the comparativist, likewise, will remind anthropologists of a tradition that only lost out to ethnography after the Second World War.[12] What are the consequences of the intellectual and practical choices comparativists have in their intellectual, political and institutional lives? The initial familiarity of the problems— the collapse of confidence in evolutionary theory, or debates about the functions and contexts of law ironically shield this constellation of ideas and practices from view by rendering them open to interpretation as just another version of conversations disciplines from jurisprudence to anthropology might think they know.

What makes this project unusual is the unique position of the authors vis à vis this modernist tradition, and hence the way the "double alienation" (Shalakany) or "antinomies" (White) of the comparative lawyer are very much also our own. Precisely because the modernism of comparative law has a future, not simply a past, so to speak, the re-evaluation of this history has special purposes and effects.

Taken as a whole, then, the essays provide a vivid picture of the intellectual and personal milieu of the modern comparativist. In the remainder of this introduction, I take the opportunity these rich essays afford to read the papers collectively against the received understanding of comparison and comparative law in the discipline today. I hasten to add that this reading is only my own; it is not the product of any consensus among the authors and I can only hope that it will challenge further uses and readings. The history of modernist comparative law, I argue, is not principally a history of comparison per se at all. In this sense, readers should not be misled into taking current debates about methodology

---

[12] For an illuminating introduction to the differences between mid-century legal, anthropological and sociological approaches to the terms of comparison, *see* Sally Falk Moore, "Legal Systems of the World: An Introductory Guide to Classifications, Typological Interpretations, and Bibliographic Resources," in L. Lipson and S. Wheeler (eds), *Law and the Social Sciences* 11 (New York, 1986). Moore exemplifies the anthropological view of comparative law when she criticizes comparative lawyers for their blindness to legal pluralism in their discussion of legal systems, their lack of attention to non-Western societies, and for their crude distinctions between the "good" of modern Western law and the "bad" of pre-modern and non-Western law. Moore describes the difference between comparative lawyers and anthropologists in part in terms of the former's preference for library research and the latter's preference for fieldwork. *Id*. at 32. Moore does point out, however, that Marxist anthropology is very much like comparative law in its cross-cultural and historicist claims. *Id*. at 30.

and disciplinary identity too literally. Rather, the history of comparative law is a history of the emergence, and ultimate exhaustion, of what I will call Projects. Where in anthropology, for example, the holism of social context emerges as the dominant trope to replace the historicism of nineteenth century evolutionary theory, in comparative law we will see that it is Projects that take history's place. This Project is sometimes critical, sometimes utopian, and most often one of mundane institution building, and it is these different possible modalities that give the discipline its depth and texture.

FROM SCIENCE TO POLITICS

A reader of the essays that follow cannot help but be struck by the similarities in background and predicament of these "masters". The comparativist emerges as a person who is, and who consciously strives to be, both an insider and an outsider in virtually every domain. Many were born within a few years of one another, and are literally or figuratively persons from the nineteenth century speaking to the twentieth, as Kantorowicz put it (see Fig. 1). Many knew each other personally. For the most part, the bright, successful sons of bourgeois families, some were initiated into comparative law through their early travels—Hozumi to England for studies, Sanhuri to France, Wigmore to Japan. Others found travel, and comparative law, forced upon them by the events of World War II.

The masters also share an ambivalent relationship to the legal academy. At times, they emphasize their alienation from other jurists. At other times, they actively campaign to become a part of the mainstream academy and its curriculum. Both academics and amateurs, at times political radicals and at others conservative, figures caught between familiar and distant legal worlds, these comparativists seem defined by a constant task of translation—to themselves as much as to others. Debates in legal theory often provide a foil to work against, as much as a source of engagement, as in Kantorowicz' critique of American Legal Realism. It is no surprise, then, that the community of comparativists, the sociality of the discipline, emerges as vital to its members.

One of the odd features of this "discipline" is the absence of the debates that typically constitute academic communities (Riles, chapter 4). True, many of the figures discussed in this book make proposals about the direction and methods of the discipline. But from reading the texts comparative lawyers produce, it is difficult to identify explicit fault lines or factions.[13] And then one notices that, curiously, this discipline can peg the very date of its birth—to the International Congress of Comparative Law held in Paris in 1900.

[13] One interesting exception is Max Weber's scathing critique of the "historicism" of Lambert and Eurlich (and one must assume Weber would have included Eurlich's colleague Kantorowicz in this group as well). *See* Max Weber, *Max Weber on Law in Economy and Society* (Max Rheinstein, trans., Cambridge, Mass., 1966). One can read Weber's entire project as a rehabilitation of formalism from the damage these scholars had done.

1721	Publication of Montesquieu's *Lettres Persanes*.
1734	Publication of Montesquieu's *Considérations sur les Causes de la Grandeur des Romains et de leur Décadence*.
1748	Publication of Montesquieu's *De l'Esprit des Lois*.
1855	Birth of Nobushige Hozumi.
1863	Birth of John Henry Wigmore.
1864	Birth of Max Weber.
1866	Birth of Edouard Lambert.
1870	Birth of Roscoe Pound.
1874	Birth of Ernst Rabel.
1877	Birth of Hermann Kantorowicz.
1894	Publication of Weber's *Habilitationshrift*.
1895	Birth of Abdel-Razzak Al-Sanhuri.
1897	Publication of Wigmore's "The Pledge Idea: A Study in Comparative Legal Ideas."
1899	Nobushige Hozumi presents "Ancestor-Worship and Japanese Law" at the International Congress of Orientalists in Rome
1900	First *Congrès International de Droit Comparé* is held in Paris.
1902	Publication of Lambert's *La Fonction du droit comparé*.
1904	Nobushige Hozumi presents "The New Japanese Civil Code as Material for the Study of Comparative Jurisprudence" at the International Congress of Arts and Science.
1906	Edouard Lambert is appointed dean of Khedivial Law School in Cairo. Birth of René David.
1907	Publication of Kantorowicz's *Der Kampf um die Rechtswissenschaft*.
1909	Birth of Rudolph Schlesinger.
1920	Death of Max Weber.
1921	Edouard Lambert becomes head of the *Institut de Droit Comparé*.
1923	Birth of Rudolf Sacco.
1925	Posthumous publication of Weber's *Wertschaft und Gesellschaft*.
1926	Death of Nobushige Hozumi.
1934	Publication of Kantorowicz's *Some Rationalism About Realism*.
1936	Publication of Wigmore's *Panorama of the World's Legal Systems*.
1940	Death of Hermann Kantorowicz. Publication of Wigmore's *A Kaleidoscope of Justice*.
1943	Death of John Henry Wigmore.
1964	Death of Roscoe Pound.
1971	Death of Abdel-Razzak Al-Sanhuri.
1990	Death of René David.
1996	Death of Rudolph Schlesinger.

Fig. 1. Timeline

The masters' extensive personal correspondence covers questions of method and doctrine, but also much more mundane and practical questions about funding arrangements, conference programs and pedagogical methods. Those who do not participate in this internal conversation, whether because they write before the discipline's founding moment or because their academic community is elsewhere, are not truly recognized as comparativists: to comparativists, Montesquieu, Maine, Weber or Frazer are mere forefathers; they exist only as texts and not as *participants* in the institutions and the social practices that define the discipline. One gains an initial clue, then, to the significance of institutions and relations over models and arguments in this discipline.

This brings us to what is most unique about comparative law, as against other disciplines that have claimed comparison as their field of expertise. I have in mind the foregrounded quality of a particular, very explicit kind of politics—which I will refer to as the Project—that on the face of things displaces and directs the theoretical and political questions we more readily associate with modern scholarship and the late modern predicament more broadly.[14] Weber finds himself at the center of a debate about the merits of imperialism. Rabel confronts the task of rebuilding Vienna in the aftermath of the devastation of the First World War. Hozumi and Sanhuri draft their nations' legal codes. Some of these figures—Lambert or Rabel, for example—are gifted institution builders and institutional players while others—Kantorowicz or Hozumi, for example—are not. Shalakany puts it well when he emphasizes that "legal reform" is to be understood as one register for the double alienation that has characterized the encounter with modernity.[15]

Science

This volume begins with Launay's re-evaluation of what he aptly terms the prehistory of comparative law and anthropology in the figure of Montesquieu,[16] as an initial reflection on the implications and consequences of the quite recent separation of comparative thinking about law into a discipline apart. Montesquieu, it turns out, has his own antecedents and prehistories (here in the figure of Bodin) which he recovers for particular political purposes and to brilliant effect. Launay offers this story as a warning about claims of grand epistemic shifts, modern revolutions, or the newness of particular ideas. Indeed, we will see that Hozumi is not, as it turns out, the first modernizer of Japanese law; nor are Lambert and Sanhuri the first to bring the science of modern Western law to Egypt. Launay suggests rather that we consider the uses of comparative typologies and investigations which, in Montesquieu's case, ironically turn out to be

---

[14] Jean Comaroff & John L. Comaroff (eds), *Modernity and its Malcontents: Ritual and Power in Postcolonial Africa* (Chicago, 1993); Anthony Giddens, *The Consequences of Modernity* (Cambridge, 1990); Julia Kristeva, *Strangers to Ourselves* (Leon S. Roudiez trans., New York, 1994).

[15] *Cf.* Nathaniel Berman, " 'But the Alternative is Despair': Nationalism and the Modernist Renewal of International Law." 106 *Harv. L. Rev.* 1792, 1793–1903 (1993).

[16] *See, e.g.,* Gutteridge, *supra* note 11, at 12 ("Montesquieu the founder of comparative law since it is he who first realized that a rule of law should not be treated as an abstraction, but must be regarded against a background of history and of the environment in which it is called upon to function.")

the furtherance of a very local argument about the place of the aristocracy in France. Collectively, the essays demonstrate how the harnessing of typologies and historical claims in the service of present political goals has a robust tradition in the discipline.

The story of comparative law, as defined by its adherents, however, begins elsewhere, with a moment of abandonment—the rejection, or at least the backgrounding of a scientific conception of the comparative project. In the second half of the nineteenth century, enthusiasts of evolutionary theory had sought to trace the origins of legal institutions through the application of "the comparative method."[17] In this, the comparative study of law was a relative late-comer among the new disciplines of comparative philology, comparative anatomy, comparative biology, comparative politics, comparative religion, and so on.[18] Comparative law was without a doubt a science, albeit a nascent and underdeveloped one, and it was this scientific hope that provided the excitement and motivation for the discipline.

This scientific orientation and self-image at once set comparative law apart from and provided a shared orientation with the legal academy as a whole. The chapters by Riles and Curran capture a taste of the orientations of comparative lawyers around the time of the discipline's founding. Kantorowicz and Wigmore shared some of the positivist philosophical premises and the assumptions about the independent character of legal knowledge prevalent in the wider legal academy on both continents, although they adamantly opposed others. They approached comparative research as a method for demonstrating and building on these assumptions by adding to the theories a greater level of *factual detail*. It is precisely because science was so highly valued in the legal academy of the late nineteenth and early twentieth centuries that comparativists could find a certain caché in the claim that their work was more scientific than that of their colleagues, and it was the intersection of evolutionary theory and legal classicism that provided the justification for the distinct identity of the subdiscipline and the ambition for their collective project. Yet although the nineteenth century comparativist was firmly rooted in the legal academy, this did not require him to imagine the evolution of law as a subject apart. On the contrary, the nineteenth century comparativist borrowed freely from work in other fields, from history to ethnology to the classics.

The tacit rejection of evolutionary theory that coincided with the establishment of an independent discipline of comparative law emerged primarily through the discipline's contacts with jurisprudence rather than the social sciences. Shalakany alludes to the uses of comparative materials in the critique of the classicist Ecole de l'Exégèse in France by Edouard Lambert and other young jurists who were first and foremost legal theorists, and only secondly comparativists. Mattei describes Sacco's mid-century battles with Italian formalism in

---

[17] *See* Henry Maine, *Ancient Law* (London, 1861).
[18] *Cf.* Jerome Hall, *Comparative Law and Social Theory*, 4 (Baton Rouge, 1963); Gutteridge, *supra* note 11, at 16.

similar terms. For theorists such as Roscoe Pound in the United States, Edouard Lambert in France, Rudolfo Sacco in Italy and others, the new model for legal scholarship that would replace the biological sciences was to be the social sciences, and they imparted this model to comparative law. The role of comparison in these early jurisprudential critiques of classicism has been largely forgotten by comparativists themselves.

If comparative law was vital to the critique of legal classicism, however, by the same token, many of the received insights about the character of modernism in legal studies will seem to get it all wrong for the field of comparative law. Unlike other legal fields, for example, over the course of the twentieth century comparative law moves towards a more radical separation from other disciplines, their methods and their work. From the 1930s forward, the ideal reader of twentieth-century comparative legal scholarship is the law professor and, even more importantly, the bureaucrat or the judge, not the social scientist.

This separation is a matter of method as much as of audience. The social sciences which have served as a model for legal studies in the twentieth century are characterized for the most part by the absence of broad comparative brush strokes, by the backgrounding of explicit comparisons between societies, in favor of a more tentative, implicit comparison of foreign materials. As the historian of anthropology Adam Kuper puts it, "Obviously the more one stresses the inner character of a culture, the more difficult it is to move on to comparison and generalization."[19] The emphasis is on empirical research rather than on the juxtaposition of historical and other materials.

Comparative law evolved in precisely the opposite direction: J. H. Wigmore is a far more committed empiricist than is René David, for example. Likewise, the cross-cultural typologies of Weber become relevant to comparative law at precisely the moment at which they are exposed to vehement critique in the social sciences. Throughout the period covered by the chapters in this book (and largely to the present day) comparativists explicitly compare the law (or legal system, or norm, or legal culture) of a singular State A with that of State B. There is very little that is tentative about the project.

Indeed, comparative lawyers have often described their work as a response to the impasses of legal and social scientific modernism as much as a continuation of those movements. As Curran points out, this critical perspective is enabled in part by the different epistemologies and aesthetics of law prevalent on the Continent and in the Anglo-American academy. Kantorowicz, for example, writes explicitly against the Realists from a civilian point of view; conversely many American comparativists are motivated by a desire to expose the parochial, inward turn that accompanied the realist revolution.

---

[19] Adam Kuper, *Anthropology and Anthropologists* 194 (London, 1987).

Projects

Social science was not the only, or even the dominant model to displace evolutionary science in the legal academy, then, nor was the revolt against classical legal scholarship the only concern. Indeed, the founding moment of comparative law was also a moment of acknowledgment that comparative law is (only) a "method," not a science.[20] Equally important to the comparative lawyer from the outset were the *projects* comparative law as a discipline might serve—the unification of law, the development of a "universal common law" for transnational business and other relations, the uses of comparative information about foreign legal systems for legal reform projects.[21] From this point of view, the uniqueness of comparative law resides in its applications to real problems in the world. For example, Sanhuri confronts an endemic modernist problem of the Arab intellectual's alienation from both East and West. Yet Sanhuri experiences this as a problem of how to draft a project of code in the service of anti-imperialist modernization.

The comparative lawyer is a person who engages comparison for a *purpose*, in other words, whether it is to find a model for modernization, or to harmonize legal regimes. The chapters in this volume offer a catalog of some of the purposes that have animated the comparative project in the twentieth century:

- *The Colonial Project.* Beginning with Weber, the necessities of colonial administration figure prominently in the rationale for comparative law. Lawson, for example, writes that

  "[C]olonial governments, particularly in Africa, cannot allow innumerable systems of native law to develop in higgledy-piggledy fashion without guidance. . . . The comparative lawyer may thus be able to lend a helping hand in moulding what may prove to be new national systems of public and private law in what are now our colonial territories."[22]

---

[20] Hall quotes Frederick Pollock's early assertion to this effect at the first International Congress of Comparative Law held in Paris in 1900. *See* Hall, *supra* note 19, at 7.

[21] Gutteridge emphasizes that the conflict between programmatic and historical visions of the discipline was already there at its founding moment:

"For some the value of comparative legal studies consisted in their practical aspect, the underlying assumption being that a nation can profit from a careful study of new legislation enacted by foreign countries, and that the knowledge thus acquired can be turned to good account in the reform and development of the law . . . Another view was that comparative legal research has as its object the discovery of the abstract notions which underlie all systems of law and can be utilized to build up a common system of jurisprudence. . . . For others, comparative studies were only of value in a historical sense as illustrating the tendencies which mould the growth of the law in all systems or as casting light on the development of a national system in its earliest stages—But it was held that on a broad view of the matter the objective of comparative lawyers should be the ultimate unification of private law, and the creation of a form of international common law." Gutteridge, *supra* note 11, at 18.

[22] Lawson, *supra* note 5, at 17.

At the same time, the Egyptian Sanhuri and the Japanese jurist Hozumi exemplify the uses of comparative law as what Aoki terms a "weapon" against foreign imperialism and a "tool" of decolonization.

- *Modernization and Reconstruction.* This nascent discipline would come to stand for and to address the equally "new" modernizing projects of the day. The rebuilding of Europe, the evolution of the common law, the drafting of legal codes all stood to benefit from comparative expertise, while these projects in turn provided a purpose and an organizing frame after the dissolution of the evolutionary paradigm. The epistemology of evolutionary theory is not so much discredited, then, as *transposed* into a project of modernization.
- *Internationalism.* The chapters in this volume illustrate that one of the most important projects of comparative law is the promotion of universalism at every level, from battles with parochialism within national legislatures to legal unification projects, the development of ties among foreign scholars, and the evolution of international institutions. The international Project that garners the greatest dedication, however is comparative law itself. From Rabel's efforts to found a professional field through the institutions he directed and the committees on which he served, to Sacco's careful nurturing of a generation of disciples, comparativists emerge as skilled and committed institution builders. One cannot read Shalakany's essay without pausing to marvel at the mixture of Orientalist fantasy, humane concern and sober networking that animated Lambert's commitment to the Egyptian students he trained first in Cairo and then in Lyon.
- *Institution Building.* What makes this modern institution-building unique is that it is inseparable, in its practitioners' own conception, from theories, methodologies, or data gathering. Although earlier figures such as Wigmore, Pound or Weber were institutional players, their institutional politics was a step removed from, something of a different order than, their scholarship. For mid-century figures such as Rabel and David, compromises but also possibilities, and Esquirol and Gerber emphasize the institutional side of comparative law comes to shape the theoretical paradigms.

One indication of the distance of this mid-century discipline devoted to Projects from the more theoretical critiques of jurisprudence of earlier comparativists such as Kantorowicz, Wigmore or Lambert is the different kind of ancestry it now claimed. This lawyerly genre of comparison, at once located in the world and bringing it forth, championed a different comparative tradition, the tradition of Max Weber. Weber's use of comparative law as an argument for the liberal state and its imperialist ambitions becomes the archetype of the modern comparative Project. Weber's framework, likewise, which through its rational deployment of categories defends the possibility of formalism in new, modern terms was also well-suited to a discipline centered around questions of modernization. Weber is utterly absent, in contrast, in the work of Wigmore or Hozumi, for whom Henry Maine and James Frazer were the models,[23] or Kantorowicz and Lambert, for whom Weber's dogged defense of legal formalism was precisely the enemy.

Contrary to the academic aspirations of today, the early modernist comparative lawyer is best understood, in other words, as a kind of independently operating bureaucrat. Like urban planners, for example,[24] intellectual work entails a specific engagement with the world. The masters go far beyond the usual modernist faith in the transformative power of knowledge: their ideas *create* a world—they don't just "reflect" or "influence" it. The relation between knowledge and social facts is literal, not just metaphorical.[25] In this sense, the Project is Messianic, as Gerber puts it, although it is also highly mundane.

What I mean when I characterize the Project as mundane is that the Project will strike today's comparativists, like their social scientific colleagues, as at once something patently obvious about the practice of comparative law and impervious to analysis or critique. What defines the comparative law of Projects is its politics, by which I mean its very surface-level politics of modernization, institution-building, colonial administration and decolonization, not the kind of hidden politics late modern cultural critics are skilled at discovering in the margins of the text. The Projects, in contrast, leave nothing to uncover or discover. In fact, this bureaucratic politics—following Weber, let's call it Rationality—is so much on the surface that it may not fit our definition of politics at all: anthropologist Sally Falk Moore is not alone when she critiques "the Euro-Anglo-centered form of classification of legal systems" for being "much less political and much more technical in its concerns" than anthropological arguments.[26] Ironically, in such conditions of over-explicit politics, the pressing task for the authors of this volume becomes to recover the latent person and the knowledge in the politics rather than the politics of the person or the knowledge: Esquirol, for example, powerfully describes René David's careful erasure of his own intellectual contribution in order to portray his ideas as mere common sense so that they could garner wider support in contentious times.

This is not to suggest that Projects definitively conquered science as the singular defining identity of the discipline in the twentieth century. The evolutionary science that had appealed to nineteenth century scholars persisted as a dominant trope—but it was now subsumed in a new kind of practical emphasis such that one could talk of modernization itself as a science.[27] Hozumi, for example,

---

[23] Mid-century comparative lawyers were fond of pointing out that even Henry Maine viewed his work principally as a tool of legislative policy rather than a contribution to the advancement of science. *See, e.g.,* Hall, *supra* note 19, at 16; Gutteridge, *supra* note 11, at 27.

[24] *See* Rabinow, *supra* note 1.

[25] For a discussion of the metaphorical relations between social facts and analytical categories in modernist social science, *see* Marilyn Strathern, "The Relation: Issues in Complexity and Scale," 6 *Prickly Pear Pamphlet* (1995).

[26] Moore, *supra* note 4, at 13.

[27] H. C. Gutteridge divides comparative legal scholarship into "descriptive comparative law" and "applied comparative law" and it is clear that the latter is the more sophisticated and significant in his view. Rabel divided the field into three distinct kinds of projects. A somewhat technical

appropriates the nineteenth century evolutionary theories of James Frazer, as a blueprint for a project of modernization. What is at stake here is not a simple contrast between one set of modernist paradigms and epistemologies suited to "the real world" and its modern problems and another outdated, nineteenth century set that is not: where Hozumi chooses the nineteenth century ideas of Frazer as the talisman of modernization, Sanhuri chooses the twentieth century ideas of Lambert and the social scientific tradition for the very same purpose. What has shifted in the twentieth century in comparative law, what now matters, in other words is not the theory, or the epistemology, but the purpose of scholarship.

It should be noted that as organizing tropes Projects have never been as coherent and rhetorically engaging as nineteenth century historicism. Where the evolutionary paradigm dictated a precise research problem—the tracing of the origins and evolution of specific legal institutions—and also a method (the discovery of facts about primitive or ancient legal institutions), the purpose and methods of modern comparative law were far more murky and multiple. Again, however, where in other disciplines the consequences of the failure to find a paradigm for the twentieth century as engaging as evolutionary theory was for the nineteenth century take the form of philosophical or political *critique*—of debates among scholars about theoretical method—in comparative law, they take the form of engagement with, and even responsibility for, the world and its projects. The most powerful example in this book is Curran's account of how Kantorowicz' concept of Free Law actually came to be blamed for the decisions of Nazi judges. If the comparativist's ideas could build a world, they could also be held to have destroyed it, it seems.

This also implied that events in the world would have a direct impact on the methods and purposes of comparative law. One of the consequences of the fact of the War, of course, is its impact on the society of comparativists. Enter a new class of émigrés (in this volume represented by Kantorowicz and Schlesinger), upon whom comparison is forced as a livelihood, rather than chosen either as an intellectual interest (Wigmore) or a political weapon (Sanhuri). In David, Schlesinger, Sacco, and above all Kantorowicz, one can see how the fact of the Second World War shakes the foundation of the Project and transforms it from a cause of institution building to one of discourse—of *convincing* an audience of the unity and equality of human kind. The émigrés' personal and intellectual problem is suitably modernist—how to make an audience appreciate another world, how to develop a tolerance for foreignness when all that one has at one's disposal is the language of the audience. This is very different from the earlier generation of modernizers who looked to other societies as *models* and who

---

set of positions have evolved on the question of whether comparative law is one discipline or actually two or more "subdisciplines" devoted to science, projects, and in some cases, social science. *See, e.g.*, David Gerber, "System Dynamics: Toward a Language of Comparative Law?," 46 *Am. J. Comp. L.* 719, 724 (defining three objectives of comparative law—"One is 'scientific' and seeks new knowledge about how legal systems work. A second is practice-related by which I refer broadly to the application of legal knowledge for legal practice or policy purposes. Related to both of the above is a third, which involves the transmission of information about legal systems.")

hence did not confront this problem of description. Yet although comparative law consequentially becomes far more discursive in the second half of the twentieth century, I want to emphasize that language remains a Project of its own. Even where Kantorowicz or Sacco deploy the linguistic tools of semiotics, structuralism or hermeneutics, *their* semiotics is in the service of a goal, in the world, of building a consensus, of *solving*, rather than simply analyzing, the problem of difference.

In sum, what we demonstrate collectively in this volume is that "comparison" per se was never the core of what modern comparativists stood for. What sets the discipline apart is neither its international orientation nor the act of comparison per se, then. From this point of view, the categories and typologies of twentieth century comparative law so frequently critiqued in the literature today can be understood as a kind of afterthought. In the remainder of this introduction I want to reflect on the consequences of the supremacy of Projects for the methods and models of comparative law.

AESTHETICS OF RATIONALITY

I have tried to describe the comparative lawyer as a practical intellectual—a person motivated above all by the *effect* of finding certain similarities and differences in the world. The notion that the act of comparison is an act in the world, of the same order as the founding of an institution for example, is a unique and fascinating dimension of the comparative legal ethos. This motivation has consequences, in turn, for the aesthetics of comparison, that is, the parameters, categories or bases of comparison scholars adopt. I will shorthand the conceptual and rhetorical tools of the modernist comparative lawyer as the aesthetics of rationality.

W.T. Murphy has recently argued that the terms of reference and paradigms of modernist sociology are largely borrowed from legal knowledge, whose essence he describes as "a certain skepticism combined with a certain decisionism. Lawyers both want proof and need decisions, and tend to tailor the character of the proof they seek or want to the need for those decisions."[28] What the emerging social science borrowed, he argues, was not the categories of the lawyer but something more subtle:

> "In Weber's case, it is essentially the *attitude* of the lawyer, including the importance to lawyers of classification (so as to render matters susceptible to proof and amenable decision), which is the basis of the elaboration of his 'sociology."[29]

Murphy captures here the conditions and consequences of the comparativist's approach to his or her task. Modern comparison is enabled only by the bridging of cultural particularities, in two senses. First, the problem of cultural difference,

---

[28] W. T. Murphy, *The Oldest Social Science? Configurations of Law and Modernity*, 38 (Oxford, 1997).
[29] *Id.*

or of national particularity that animates comparative law, emerges precisely because of the loss of faith in a universal science or logic in its strong nineteenth century form. Yet in a second and related sense, modern comparison is enabled because it is *useful* in overcoming these particularities, in harmonizing laws or modernizing customs. The very possibility of comparative law, and indeed of the management of difference within the state, then, depends on a notion of legitimate practice that is also outside and beyond the particular. It is here that comparative law borrows most explicitly from the kinds of arguments that animate Weber: for comparative law, the answer to both these questions—the methodological and the programmatic—has been the notion of rationality. In this sense, comparative law cannot exist, that is, it cannot *work*, without this idea.

Consider, for example, the act of comparing traditional and modern legal systems, of comparing stages of modernization. It is the rationality of the comparison—by which I mean here the Weberian notion of a clearly elaborated analytical process and a set of well-defined categories—that overcomes the particularity of the comparativist's perspective on such a contentious issue. Lambert and Sanhuri's method of code-writing has three steps, Shalakany tells us: first they investigate the content of Islamic law; second, they compare this content with modern law, finally, they reconstruct the former along scientific lines. What renders the particularities of the Egyptian case open to a general solution in this conception is the universal rationality of science. We are far away, by now, from Montesquieu's assertion that the law suitable to one people is probably not suitable to another.

Curran offers another example of the workings of this mechanism in her discussion of Kantorowicz' concept of Free Law. Having participated in the deconstruction of the legal classicism that had served as a strong justification for universals, Kantorowicz was consumed by the question of how to recreate a more modest and honest universalism—and he was equally consumed, Curran points out, by his desire to fight back against the urge of some American realists to take his insight as an assault on the possibility of rational law. How to turn critical insights into a positive, even moderately utopian program? Kantorowicz hits upon the image of the rational judge, a new kind of bureaucrat through whose mental operations it becomes possible to recognize, and then rationalize, the irrational.

The consequences of this orientation are expansive and diverse. For example, the method of modern comparative law is often bureaucratic at a most practical level. Mattei describes Schlesinger's "common core project" as an elaborate structure of committees that drafted and ultimately responded to questionnaires about the nature of law in different jurisdictions. Academic work emulates conference work here. Bureaucracy, in the sense of committee work such as Schlesinger's, but also of missions, evaluations, or the production of documents is often comparative.[30] The rationality of the bureaucrat as scholar, likewise, is predicated on a certain practical commitment to universals. We can trace comparative lawyers'

---

[30] For a discussion of the comparative quality of modern bureaucratic knowledge, *See* A. Riles, "The Transnational Appeal of Formalism: The Case of Japan's Netting Law," *available at* http://www.ssrn.com.

focus on attaining a new kind of universalism through elaborate conventions and committees to the "common concept of the 1900 Congress."[31]

Where the goal is a rational and bureaucratic universalism, the methodological complexities of data, and the details of questions of method necessarily become secondary. It is no surprise that comparative law did not follow its social scientific siblings in the direction of modern empiricism, in other words, nor is it surprising that there is little method to the method, as Gerber puts it in this critique of Rabel's work in this volume. "Science" here is a purposeful and practical commitment, not a method in itself. This bureaucratic mode of scholarship also gravitates toward particular kinds of arguments and claims. It is much better suited to demonstrating (or rather, negotiating) underlying commonalities (common cores) than to challenging or critiquing paradigms, for example. Hence the distance between bureaucratic "functionalism" that is the dominant method of modern comparative law and the functionalism of modern social science: Rabel's comparison of the functions of rules arises directly out of the needs of his institutional project.

CONCLUSION

"The belief in progress, so characteristic of 1900, has died. World wars have weakened, if not destroyed, faith in world law."[32]

"Such questions as these will arise: does a given problem of law lend itself to comparative investigation? Where are the relevant rules of foreign law to be found? What weight is to be attributed respectively to statute law, customary law, judge-made law and the opinions of legal text-book writers? What means can be adopted to ensure that the literature which is available gives the actual state of the law and is not obsolete or otherwise misleading? Are there special features of the foreign laws about to be examined which if not known to him, might lead an English lawyer astray?"[33]

In an important recent article, Vivian Curran critiques post-war American comparative law for focusing on the discovery of similarities across legal systems at the expense of difference. Drawing on linguistic theory, Curran argues that all acts of knowledge are inherently comparative, and that cognitive acts of comparison always entail both the elucidation of similarities and the elucidation of differences.[34] In explaining the universalist bias in post-war comparative law as an artifact of a generation of émigrés' attempts to find a role for themselves in the American academy and to come to terms with the consequences of the war,

---

[31] *See* Hall, *supra* note 19, at 44.

[32] Zweigert & Kötz, *supra* note 11, at 3.

[33] Gutteridge *supra* note 11, at 72.

[34] Vivian G. Curran, "Cultural Immersion, Difference and Categories in U.S. Comparative Law", 46 *Am. J. Comp. L.* 43–92 (1998). Curran treats comparison as a synonym for metaphor or analogy, as used in linguistic theory to speak of the universal and innate dimensions of human cognitive experience. For the present purposes, I limit the meaning of comparison to what comparative lawyers would understand as comparison, that is, a particular and specialized kind of comparative exercise.

Curran nicely illustrates the effects of Projects—of the modern comparativist's focus on the effects of scholarship in the world—on aesthetics, that is, the nature of the comparative act. In her emphasis on difference, Curran also speaks for the current mood of the discipline, with its loss of faith in commonalities and its desire to reinvigorate the discipline with infusions of theories from the outside.

From this point of view, what I have described in this introduction may seem too mundane to be of interest. The Project I have described is exhausted, today's comparativists will say; the discipline's technocratic devotion to universalism is something of an embarrassment. The real ambition now is to construct an autonomous and respected academic discipline—to present comparative law as the future vanguard of legal theory.[35]

In some respects, comparative lawyers' recent turn to method and their efforts to recreate comparative law as an academic discipline recalls the "academic discipline" of pre-modernist comparative law. At the same time, the loss of grand ambitions for the discipline separates the present moment from both its nineteenth and mid-twentieth century past.

Ironically, however, the current surge of interest in comparative law among mainstream legal scholars results from their engagement with a new set of mid-century Projects—the writing of the constitutions of emerging states or the resolving of trade disputes, for example. For these new converts to comparative law, of course, the methodological angst that now plagues the discipline is as irrelevant as it was to an earlier generation of Project proponents.

This would suggest that the problem now facing the discipline of comparative law is not how to articulate a new set of methods as how to articulate (to the discipline's most recent converts) the basis of our collective exhaustion with the Projects that are now once again proliferating in the legal academy. Ironically, our experience with the fantasies, and ultimate failures of Projects may be the relevance and enduring legacy of modernist comparative law at this juncture. The review of the history of the discipline we have undertaken in this volume suggests that if one redefines the status of the Project the categories will follow.

---

[35] I myself have recently made such a suggestion. *See* Riles, *supra* note 3.

Part I

Founding Moments

MONTESQUIEU.

Né en 1689, mort en 1755.

C'est un homme impossible à remplacer.

Paroles de Louis XV.

Burdet sculp

Fig.1 Charles-Louis de Secondat, Baron de Montesquieu
(Reproduced by kind permission of The British Library,
from *Deuvres de Montesquieu* (Paris, 1819))

1

Montesquieu: The Specter of Despotism and the Origins of Comparative Law

ROBERT LAUNAY

Emile Durkheim, in his Latin dissertation of 1893 on *Montesquieu's Contribution to the Rise of Social Science*, asserted that "It was he, who, in *The Spirit of Laws*, laid down the principles of the new science [of sociology]."[1] This view, that Montesquieu was not simply a forerunner but literally the founder of modern sociology, has since been repeated time and again, notably by Louis Althusser,[2] Raymond Aron,[3] and E. E. Evans-Pritchard.[4] The sociological aspects of the book are listed systematically by Evans-Pritchard:

> ". . . the insistence on the scientific, comparative study of society, the use of the data of as many societies as possible; the inclusion of primitive societies as examples of certain types of social systems; a need to start with a classification or taxonomy of societies based on significant criteria . . . ; the idea of inter-consistency between social facts (social systems), and that any social fact can only be understood by reference to other social facts and environmental conditions, as part of a complex whole; and the idea of this interconsistency being of a functional kind."[5]

I suspect that Evans-Pritchard, as an anthropologist, was somewhat over-eager to stress the importance of Montesquieu's inclusion of "primitive" societies, or rather, as Montesquieu and his contemporaries called them, "savages." In fact, "savages" per se are for the most part conspicuously absent from the pages of *The Spirit of Laws*, though other examples of non-European societies figure very prominently indeed. Be this as it may, the work remains remarkable for the range of social phenomena which it attempts to analyze—law, government, marriage, economy, religion, population, warfare—as well as for the broad spectrum of societies—past and present, European and non-European—cited as examples.

---

[1] Emile Durkheim, *Montesquieu and Rousseau: Forerunners of Sociology*, 1 (Ann Arbor, 1960).
[2] *See* Louis Althusser, *Montesquieu: La Politique et l'Histoire* (Paris, 1959).
[3] *See* Raymond Aron, *Les Etapes de la Pensée Sociologique* (Paris, 1967).
[4] E. E. Evans-Prichard, *A History of Anthropological Thought* (London, 1981).
[5] *See id.* at 11.

Montesquieu's comparative and "sociological" approach is explicitly predicated on the principle of legal relativism, formulated at the end of Book I in no uncertain terms:

> '[Laws] should be so specific to the people for whom they are made, that it is a great coincidence if those of one nation can suit another. They should be relative to the physical qualities of the country; to its frozen, burning or temperate climate; to the quality, location, and size of the territory; to the mode of livelihood of the people, farmers, hunters, or pastoralists; they should relate to the degree of liberty which the constitution can admit, to the religion of the inhabitants, to their inclinations, to their wealth, to their numbers, to their commerce, to their mores, to their manners . . ."[6]

In fact, Montesquieu's radical relativism is, in the final analysis, itself quite relative. It is hardly a disinterested stance. On the contrary, as we shall see, comparisons are constructed with a specific political agenda in mind. This does not, of course, vitiate the very real and radical achievements of Montesquieu's *demarche*, but rather puts them in their proper perspective and can, in addition, help to answer the question: why did Montesquieu find it necessary to elaborate the kind of comparative, relativistic approach he adopted?

In fact, neither Montesquieu's broad comparative scope nor his legal relativism were entirely novel; both flourished among legal and historical scholars in France, especially in the sixteenth century, only to fall in relative abeyance during the next century. A brief comparison of Montesquieu's approach to those of his immediate as well as his somewhat more distant predecessors sheds light on his choice to resurrect, rather than to invent, a comparative stance.

The remarkable development of a comparative perspective in sixteenth century France grew out of the humanist critique of scholastic jurisprudence.[7] Initially, humanist scholars had been concerned with challenging interpretations of Justinian's legal code on philological grounds, but the code itself and the way in which it had been compiled quickly fell prey to criticism on similar grounds. While the aim of early critics, particularly in Italy, was to perfect the Roman code, such a critique ultimately challenged the universal authority of the code itself, notably in France, where the persistent application of common law in many domains called into question the relevance of Roman law for French jurisprudence.

Such issues of jurisprudence were in fact directly relevant to the deep religious and political divides which split France in the sixteenth century. Most obviously, Huguenot intellectuals were particularly receptive to challenges to the

---

[6] Charles-Louis de Secondat, Baron de Montesquieu, 1 *De l'Esprit des Lois*, ch. 3 (Paris, 1979) (1748). All citations are my own translation.

[7] For accounts of the development of the comparative approach in sixteenth century French law and history, *see* Julian H. Franklin, *Jean Bodin and the Sixteenth-century Revolution in the Methodology of Law and History* (New York, 1963); George E. Huppert, *The Idea of Perfect History: Historical Erudition and Historical Philosophy in Renaissance France* (Urbana Il., 1970); Donald R. Kelley, *Foundations of Modern Historical Scholarship: Language, Law and History in the French Renaissance* (New York, 1970).

universal authority of Roman law, just as they refused to accept the universal authority of the Roman Catholic Church. Moreover, Catholics in France were also deeply divided amongst themselves, with the ultra-Catholic League under the leadership of the Duke of Guise eventually entering into an open revolt against the monarchy. Intellectuals loyal to the monarchy, especially those who were attempting to broker a compromise between Protestants and Catholics, were equally drawn to Gallican ideas of French legal specificity which would limit, without denying, the authority of the Church, especially in the legal and political domain.

At least three key elements of Montesquieu's *The Spirit of Laws* were directly formulated by sixteenth century French thinkers: the doctrine of legal relativism; the historical quest for the origins of the French monarchy and its legal basis; and the comparative study of legal and social institutions, explicitly including those of non-Europeans. Legal relativism was most clearly enunciated by François Hotman, one of the most radical Huguenot critics of the Justinian code:

> "The learned men of every age have observed and voiced approval of the rule that the laws should be accommodated to the form and condition of the commonwealth, not the commonwealth to the laws . . . consequently, the laws of one monarchy are often useless to another, just as medicines are not all suitable to all men whatsoever without consideration of their sex, their age, and nationality."[8]

Etienne Pasquier pioneered research into France's medieval history, in the process rejecting out of hand the myth of the Trojan origins of the French monarchy, based on the rather dubious claim that the Franks were originally descendants of refugees from the sack of Troy (like Aeneas, of course, but also Brutus, the legendary Trojan founder of Britain according to Geoffrey of Monmouth). The discovery that the Franks were actually Germans and consequently that the origins of French "feudal" law were more Germanic than Roman further undermined the authority of Rome and of Roman law. Most ambitious of all was Jean Bodin's project of a universal history that would encompass the histories of the Chaldaeans, Assyrians, Phoenicians, Hebrews "in such a way as to grasp the principles of their political organization rather than those of their religion,"[9] the Medes, the Persians, the Hindus, the Scythians, the Greeks, Italians, Celts, Germans, Arabs, Turks, Tartars, Muscovites, Americans, and Africans, among others. Bodin's aims were no less than to lay the foundations for understanding the principles underlying the rise and decline of states and civilizations, but also to discern universal principles[10] transcending the apparent variability of forms of social and political organization.

---

[8] François Hotman *cited in* Franklin *supra* note 3, at 46–7.

[9] Jean Bodin *cited in* Huppert *supra* note 3, at 101.

[10] The most notable example being his exposition of the modern notion of sovereignty in Jean Bodin, *Les Six Livres de la Republique* [The Six Books of the Republic] (1577).

These three key elements—relativism, historicism, and comparativism—
were, by way of contrast, far more marginal if not absent from seventeenth century thought. In some instances, sixteenth century ideas were deliberately
suppressed; in 1714, Nicolas Fréret was actually sent to the Bastille for disput-
ing the Trojan origins of the French monarchy.[11] None of these principles
appealed to absolutist monarchies, anxious to justify their rule on universal
principles. At the same time, the Cartesian emphasis on deductive reason was
hardly compatible with the messy inductivism typifying comparative or historicist approaches to social, political, and legal theory. Obviously, advocates of
the Divine Right of Kings, such as Bossuet or Filmer, were opposed to relativism
on principle; but so were their polemical opponents, those who, like Locke or
Hobbes, argued for one or another variety of social contract theory.

In one sense, Montesquieu's *The Spirit of Laws* marked the decisive swing of
the pendulum back in the direction of sixteenth century thought, in sharp contrast to the style and content of his immediate predecessors. But why, all of a
sudden, this return? The answer is in part that *The Spirit of Laws* is a thinly
veiled critique of monarchical absolutism. Even so, while it is easy to understand
the absolutist penchant for universal principles of legitimacy, it is equally true
that absolutism can just as easily be challenged in the name of universal principles; Rousseau is the most obvious example of such a critique. If Montesquieu
eschews such a strategy, it is because his argument is aimed at advocating what
he considers the best policy for France in particular, and perhaps more generally
for modern Western Europe, but decidedly not for human society in the
abstract. Paradoxically, it was Montesquieu's very Gallican concern for the
specificity of France which led him to return to an earlier relativist, historicist,
comparative perspective which had also been staunchly Gallican, though for
ideologically very different reasons and in the context of very different political
controversies.

The controversies in question were those that opposed the French *parlements*
to the monarchy.[12] The *parlements*, of which there were twelve in all (the largest
in Paris and the others in the provinces) were in principle judicial bodies,
although by the eighteenth century they played an important political role in the
kingdom. Offices were either inherited or sold; indeed, Montesquieu inherited
the office of *president à mortier* of the Parlement of Bordeaux in 1716, only to
sell it ten years later.[13] Despite the sale of offices, the overwhelming majority of
magistrates in the *parlements* were, like Montesquieu, members of the aristocracy. Not surprisingly, their opposition to the monarchy tended to coincide
with any measures that might be construed as an attack upon their privileges.
Such measures included the monarchical proclamation of the Papal Bull
Unigenitus, with harsh anti-Jansenist provisions, as French law. The issue was

[11] *See* Huppert *supra* note 3, at 73.
[12] *See* Jean Egret, *Louis XV et l'Opposition Parlementaire 1715–1774* (Paris, 1970) for a detailed account of the struggles of the French monarchy and the *parlements* in Montesquieu's era.
[13] *See* Robert Shackleton, *Montesquieu: A Critical Biography*, 15–20, 82–84 (London, 1961).

hardly one of deep religious conviction for most magistrates, but rather the defense of the Gallican prerogatives of the Catholic clergy in France. In particular, the *parlements* regularly opposed attempts to abrogate aristocratic exemptions from taxation, as means to rationalize the finances of France and to pay for its European wars. It would be a gross over-simplification to depict the quarrels between the *parlements* and the monarchy as pitting the interest of the "aristocracy" and the "bourgeoisie." Indeed, the divide between them was highly permeable, and the aristocratic magistrates themselves tended to be of relatively recently ennobled bourgeois stock. The fact that such differences were more akin to modern party politics than to class warfare did not prevent participants from adopting impassioned political stances.

Montesquieu carefully and subtly frames his defense of the *parlements* and of the aristocratic interests which they represented by comparing France and, more generally, Western Europe to other societies and forms of government, either in the European past or in the rest of the world. His first and no doubt most crucial step is to propose a typology of forms of government: republics, monarchies, and despotisms. Durkheim[14] among others noted Montesquieu's debt, but also his distance, from Aristotle's typology of constitutions in terms of rule by one (monarchy or tyranny), the few (aristocracy or oligarchy), or the many (polity or democracy).[15] Montesquieu's originality is that he bases his typology, not on the number of rulers, but rather on the principle which underlies each form of government: republics are animated by "virtue," monarchies by "honor," and despotisms by "fear." This classificatory shift is animated by a different set of preoccupations than those of his predecessors in classical antiquity. Aristotle's most critical concern is whether the polis is governed for the common good or for the exclusive benefit of the ruler or ruling party; Polybius attributes the stability and military successes of Rome to its mixed constitution, with elements of monarchy, aristocracy, and democracy judiciously combined. Montesquieu's preoccupation is with the historical uniqueness of the Western European (and a fortiori the French) monarchical system. The central question is: what sets modern "monarchies" apart, either from republics or from despotisms. The typology itself, as well as the examples Montesquieu chooses to exemplify non-monarchical forms of government, is specifically geared to answering this question.

A "monarchy," for Montesquieu, is a regime where "one lone person governs, but by fixed and established laws."[16] In this respect, it shares features with both despotism (one sole ruler) and republics (the rule of law). But what is to prevent

---

[14] *See supra* note 1, at 8–9, 24–35.

[15] This tripartite division derives from Aristotle, *The Politics*, 101–48 (T. A. Sinclair trans., Harmondsworth, 1962), but was also adopted by Polybius, *The Rise of the Roman Empire*, 302–52 (Ian Scott-Kilvert trans., Harmondsworth, 1979). Polybius's importance for Machiavelli (who in turn heavily influenced Montesquieu's thought) has been amply discussed by Pocock. *See* J. G. A. Pocock, *The Machiavellian Moment: Florentine Political Thought and the Atlantic Republican Tradition* (Princeton, 1975).

[16] Montesquieu *supra* note 2, bk. 2, ch. 1.

the lone ruler from subverting the rule of law? According to Montesquieu, the answer lies in the existence of "subordinate and dependent intermediary powers,"[17] most notably the aristocracy. In other words, the "honor" which underpins the monarchical system is an explicitly hierarchical system of status honor, where each rank is intensely jealous of its privileges and prerogatives. By responding vigorously to any real or perceived threat to such hereditary privileges, the nobility constitutes an effective check on arbitrary royal power. This is not to say that Montesquieu paints an idealized portrait of the aristocracy. On the contrary:

> "Ambition with indolence, pettiness with pride, the desire to get rich without work, the aversion for truth, flattery, treachery, perfidy, abandoning all one's commitments, the contempt for the duties of a citizen, the fear of the prince's virtues, the expectation of his weaknesses and, more than all this, the perpetual ridicule cast upon virtue form, I believe, the character of the greater number of courtiers in all places and at all times."[18]

Indeed, Montesquieu hastens to add (perhaps not entirely convincingly) that in this passage he does not intend to satirize monarchical government.

Montesquieu's paradoxical contention that the monarchical system works by means of, rather than in spite of, the very moral failings of its protagonists draws heavily on Bernard Mandeville's delightfully cynical *Fable of the Bees*.[19] The motto of Mandeville's book is "Private Vices, Publick Benefits." Its argument is that England owes its prosperity, not to the moral virtues of its people, but on the contrary to their failings. Mandeville's argument rests on a sort of moral psychology that, as far as intentions are concerned, equates "virtue" with "reason" and "vice" with "passion." Most human actions, Mandeville contended, are motivated by emotions—"passions"—rather than by "reason," a view that was to find consistent echoes in eighteenth century theories of morality, for example in Adam Smith and David Hume.[20] On one hand, Mandeville mercilessly lampoons the pretensions of the "respectable," most of whom are, he suggests, motivated by a vain desire for praise and more generally that others think well of them; even those few who may behave virtuously outside of the public eye are more often concerned with maintaining their own good opinion of themselves than with a truly disinterested concern with public welfare. Given such a bleak assessment of human nature, it is hardly surprising that he concludes that ". . . unhappy is the People, and their Constitution will be ever precarious, whose Welfare must depend upon the Virtues and Consciences of Ministers and Politicians."[21]

---

[17] *Id.* at bk. 2, ch. 4.

[18] *Id.* at bk. 3, ch. 5.

[19] Bernard Mandeville, *The Fable of the Bees* (Oxford, 1924) (1714). Montesquieu cites *The Fable of the Bees* in a footnote to bk. 7, ch. 1, so there can be no doubt, not only that he had read the book but that he kept it in mind while writing *The Spirit of Laws*.

[20] *See* Adam Smith, *The Theory of Moral Sentiments* (Indianapolis, 1976) (1759); David Hume, *A Treatise of Human Nature* (Oxford, 1888) (1739–1740).

[21] Mandeville *supra* note 15, bk. 1, at 190.

Mandeville's paradox, however, as the motto of his book puts forth, is that the unintended consequences of self-interested actions may be highly beneficial. Mandeville delights in arguments that egregious immorality may be in the public interest. Prostitution, for example, by providing an outlet for the sexual urges of rakes, may help to preserve the chastity of "proper" young women. The apparently wasteful desire for frivolous and expensive luxuries on the part of the rich provides much needed work for the masses of the poor. What is more, such wealth would hardly be available for the wasting were it not for the unscrupulous avarice of their forbears. Thrift and moderation, however virtuous in the abstract, are bad for the economy!

Montesquieu's disabused portrait of courtiers is entirely in the spirit of Mandeville. Even more important, his whole conception of "honor" as the key principle of the monarchical system is equally Mandevillian. Every individual, at least every "noble," is concerned with maintaining if not improving his rank. (It must be borne in mind that, since the sixteenth century at least, the upper strata of the bourgeoisie had been consistently ennobled; the kind of ambition that Montesquieu had in mind was hardly the monopoly of the hereditary aristocracy.) "It is true," he notes, "that, philosophically speaking, it is a false honor which directs all parties to the State: but *this false honor is as useful to the public as a true one would be to those particulars who might possess it.*"[22] One could hardly imagine a more emphatic formulation of the principle of "Private Vices, Publick Benefits."

Yet the thrust of Montesquieu's argument is ultimately very different from Mandeville's. For Mandeville, the principle of "Private Vices, Publick Benefits" is rooted in human nature, in the view that humans are essentially selfish and self-interested, perpetually concerned with seeking gratification of one sort or another, such that their contribution to public welfare must rest on the unintended rather than the intentional consequences of their actions. Montesquieu, on the contrary, relativizes such a principle, limiting it in space and time to the monarchical systems of government characteristic of modern Western Europe. Republican as well as despotic systems are characterized by a different calculus of virtues and vices. The motto for a "republic" in Montesquieu's scheme would be "Private Virtues, Public Benefits"; for "despotism," "Private Vices, Public Failings." In republics and despotisms alike, private morality and public welfare go hand in hand, for better or for worse. Only monarchies constitute an exception.

Not surprisingly, Montesquieu's paradigmatic examples of both republican and despotic governments are in one sense or another "distant" from modern Western Europe, either in time (Rome furnishing the principal models of republican government) or in space (examples of despotism primarily associated with Asian societies). *The Spirit of Laws* is abundantly footnoted, and it is consequently easy to determine both Montesquieu's preoccupations and his source materials. Out of a total of 667 citations, no less than 204 are from ancient

---

[22] Montesquieu *supra* note 2, bk. 3, ch. 7 (my emphasis).

Rome.[23] A few poets aside, the bulk of these refer to Roman historians, most notably Tacitus, Livy, and (somewhat more unconventionally) Denis of Halicarnassus. Montesquieu's sources for his account of classical antiquity reflect the standard humanist education of the time, including its distinctive Latin bias. However, no less than 213 citations—a very substantial proportion—refer to the non-European world and demonstrate Montesquieu's considerable interest and familiarity with the rapidly growing corpus of travel literature. The vast bulk of these citations (165) concern Asia: 51 for Turkey and Persia; 22 for India and Siam; 72 for China; and 20 for Japan. (To these I would be inclined to add the 17 references to Russia and "Tartary.") By way of comparison, sources on Africa are cited only 8 times, and only 18 for the Americas. Such a strong Asiatic bias reflects, but only partly, the travel literature available to Montesquieu at the time. Out of some 805 "geographical" books on the non-European world published in France in the 17th century, some 218 (27%) are about the Americas; 127 (16%) about Africa; 428 (53%) about Asia; and 32 (4%) about the Pacific.[24] Clearly, Africa and the Americas are underrepresented in *The Spirit of Laws*, and are only very marginally the focus of Montesquieu's attentions.

Montesquieu's apparent disinterest in America and fascination with Asia reflects the structure of his argument, and not simply his personal tastes in the literature of exploration. Both American "savagery" and Asian "despotism" constitute plausible antitheses of Europe.[25] However, the contrast of American "savagery" to European "civilization" is totally unsuitable to Montesquieu's purpose. On one hand, "savagery" had served Hobbes as an example of humanity in a "State of Nature," in order to argue that government—*any* government—was preferable to anarchy, an argument which runs absolutely counter to Montesquieu's. On the other hand, "savages" had been used to devastating effect by Montaigne and, much closer to Montesquieu's time, by the Baron de Lahontan as a vehicle for criticizing the moral bankruptcy of contemporary France. Such critiques were admittedly closer in tone and in spirit to Montesquieu's thought. Indeed, Montesquieu's first and highly successful literary venture, the *Persian Letters*, presents a sardonic vision of French society through the eyes of two fictional Persian travelers, much as Lahontan's fictional dialogue with Adario, "un sauvage de bons sens qui a voyagé [a savage of good sense who has traveled]" mercilessly satirizes the pretensions of

---

[23] For a careful analysis of Montesquieu's sources on which I have based the following discussion *see* Paul Vernière, *Montesquieu et l'Esprit des Lois ou la Raison Impure*, 40–8 (Paris, 1977).

[24] These figures are taken from William B. Cohen, *The French Encounter with Africans: White Response to Blacks 1530–1880*, 7 (Bloomington IN., 1980). I have omitted from the calculation those works dealing with Europe or classed as "general." Incidentally, Cohen's tabulations demonstrate that proportionally fewer books were published about Asia in the eighteenth century; to the extent that most of Montesquieu's sources are drawn from the late seventeenth and early eighteenth centuries, the seventeenth century figures are perhaps more representative.

[25] By Montesquieu's time, there was an extensive literature in French on American savages, given the extent of French colonial interests in North America as well as missionary enterprises, especially on the part of the Jesuits; *see* Gordon M. Sayre, *Les Sauvages Américains: Representations of Native Americans in French and English Colonial Literature* (Chapel Hill NC, 1997).

"civilization."[26] Lahontan, like Montaigne, extols the virtues of the "savages" as opposed to the vices of "civilized" Europe. For these authors, "savages" are "naturally" good and Europeans "unnaturally" depraved. Montesquieu, on the contrary, maintains a critical distance from his Persian protagonists and, even more important, has no interest whatsoever in depicting Persia as a model society compared to France.

In *The Spirit of Laws* even more than in the *Persian Letters*, Asiatic "despotism" constitutes an anti-model, an entirely negative vision of government as well as of society. Again, such a vision reflects, but only partly, Montesquieu's sources. If, all in all, he cites 24 different sources on Asia, the lion's share of these citations (105 out of a total of 165) derive from only four sources. Admittedly, two of these are anthologies: the *Lettres Edifiantes et Curieuses* [Edifying and Curious Letters[27]] (cited 20 times) regularly edited by the Jesuits as part of the propaganda campaign for their overseas missions, and which also constituted a major source of ethnographical and historical information; and the *Recueil des Voyages qui ont servi à l'établissment de la Compagnie des Indes* [Anthology of Voyages which contributed to the establishment of the [Dutch] East India Company][28] (cited 25 times). The other two principal sources are Jean Chardin[29] (cited 20 times), a French Huguenot jeweler whose account of his travels through Turkey and Georgia to Persia in the late seventeenth century originally inspired the *Persian Letters*; and Father Du Halde (cited 40 times), whose *Description de l'Empire de la Chine* [Description of the Chinese Empire][30] compiled from accounts of his fellow Jesuits "became the standard authority on matters Chinese for much of the eighteenth century.[31]

Chardin's depiction, though by no means invariably negative, of the Persian court provides ample fodder for Montesquieu's composite portrait of Asiatic "despotism." On the other hand, Jesuit depictions of China were, for the most part, highly adulatory, especially as compared to descriptions, not only by Protestants but also by representatives of rival Roman Catholic missionary orders.[32] As Vernière[33] points out: "Montesquieu insists on counterbalancing

---

[26] *See* Charles-Louis de Secondat, Baron de Montesquieu, *Lettres Persanes* (Paris, 1964) (1721); Louis-Armand, Baron de Lahontan, *Dialogues Curieux entre l'Auteur et un Sauvage de Bon Sens qui a Voyagé et Mémoires de l'Amérique Septenrionale* (Baltimore, 1931) (1703).

[27] *Lettres Edifiantes et Curieuses, Ecrites des Missions Étrangeres Par Quelques Missionnaires de la Compaigne de Jesus 1702–1776* (34 volumes) (Paris).

[28] *Recueil des Voyages Qui Ont Servi à l'Établissment de la Compagnie des Indes* [Anthology of Voyages Which Contributed to the Establishment of the [Dutch] East India Company] (Amsterdam, 1710).

[29] *See* Jean Chardin, *Travels in Persia 1673–1677* (New York, 1988) (1686).

[30] Father Du Halde, *Description de l'Empire de la Chine* [Description of the Chinese Empire] (1735).

[31] P. J. Marshall and Glyndwr Williams, *The Great Map of Mankind: Perceptions of New Worlds in the Age of Enlightenment*, 84 (Cambridge Mass., 1982).

[32] On Jesuit descriptions of China, see L. Etiemble, *L'Europe Chinoise, T. 1: De l'Empire Romain à Leibniz*, 241–307 (Paris, 1988); Donald F. Lach and Edwin J. Van Kley, *Asia in the Making of Europe: A Century of Advance*, 168–200; 222–269; 1564–1571 (Chicago, 1993).

[33] *See* Vernière, *supra* note 19, at 47.

the optimistic vision of the Jesuits with the hostile testimony of the Dutch [in the *Recueil des Voyages*] . . . the Englishman Anson, and the Russian ambassador Lange." Fair and equitable treatment of the Chinese is hardly the issue; in spite of the overwhelmingly favorable treatment characteristic of the sources he relies on most heavily, Montesquieu paints a bleak picture of Chinese "despotism" which corresponds to his discussions of Turkey, Persia, and India. Etiemble[34] lays the blame on one Father Foucqet, an ex-Jesuit with an axe to grind against his erstwhile order, and who was able to appeal to Montesquieu's anti-Jesuit sentiments in order to cast grave doubts about their portrayal of China. Be this as it may, in his determination to oppose a model of Asiatic "despotism" to European "monarchy," Montesquieu was quite willing to overlook the attitude of authors he cited when they ill suited his purpose.

The composite picture of "despotism" which Montesquieu constructs from— or against—his sources is of a society where ". . . one person alone, without law and without rule, decides everything according to his will or his caprices."[35] The portrait is unambiguously and entirely negative: ". . . despotism does frightful damage ['cause . . . des maux effoyables'] to human nature."[36] The construct of "despotism" is in effect Montesquieu's answer to Hobbes, a combination of sovereign authority and a society "without law and without rule," akin to Hobbes' State of Nature.[37] Chardin's description of the Persian court is Montesquieu's paradigmatic example, though, even here, he exaggerates his sources for polemical effect. For instance, citing Chardin, he baldly states that

> "In Persia, when the king has condemned someone, one cannot speak anymore about him, nor ask for his pardon. If he were drunk or out of his senses, the order of execution should be carried out in any case; otherwise, he would contradict himself, and the law cannot contradict itself."[38]

Indeed, Chardin relates several incidents where the Persian king loses control of his temper in fits of drunkenness. For example, he tells the story of how the king, in a drunken rage and annoyed that a lutenist has not played to his taste, orders the player's hands cut off.[39] The king's favorite, expecting the king to calm down, lets the lutenist off with a reprimand. However, on awakening, the king is so furious to find the lutenist's hands intact that he orders his favorite's hands cut off as well, and when the Lord Steward attempts to intervene, condemns all three. But, at last, the king is persuaded to relent . . . a detail that flatly contradicts Montesquieu's assertion of the irreversibility of the despot's verdicts.

If Montesquieu uses Persia as his prototype of Asian despotism, Japan is depicted as the most extreme case, an arch-despotism among despotisms, perhaps because the Japanese are symbolically the easternmost of "eastern" peoples,

---

[34] *See* Etiemble, *L'Europe Chinoise, T. 2: De la Sinophilie à la Sinophobie,* 50–72 (Paris, 1989).

[35] Montesquieu *supra* note 2, bk. 2, ch. 1.

[36] *Id*. ch. 4.

[37] Thomas Hobbes, *Leviathan* (Harmondsworth, 1968) (1651).

[38] Montesquieu *supra* note 2 bk. 3, ch. 10.

[39] Chardin *supra* note 23, 7–8.

but also, no doubt, because the expulsion of missionaries and repression of Christianity earned them the hatred of the Jesuits, while Dutch merchants, the only Europeans with any access at all to Japan, were unsympathetic to Asians of any sort. Montesquieu's vision of Japan is of a nation where laws are so severe that they are paradoxically ineffectual:

> "One punishes almost all crimes with death, because disobedience to so great an emperor as Japan's is an enormous crime . . . These considerations are drawn from slavery ['servitude']; and stem most of all from the fact that, since the emperor is proprietor of all goods, almost all crimes directly contravene his interests . . .
>
> It is true that the astonishing character of this opinionated, capricious, determined, bizarre people, who brave all perils and all misfortunes, seems at first sight to absolve legislators of the atrocity of their laws. But, for people with a natural contempt for death, who rip open their stomachs on the slightest pretext, are they corrected or stopped by the continual sight of executions? and don't they become accustomed? . . . The atrocity of the laws thus prevents their execution. When the penalty is without measure, one is often obliged to prefer impunity."[40]

The play of public and private virtues and vices that characterize Mandeville's scheme applies as well to Montesquieu's depiction of "despotism." If evil in the public domain stems from the submission of the entire nation to the caprices of a single individual, a condition which Montesquieu considers equivalent to universal slavery, its private analogue is the harem, where everyone—not only wives but also the eunuchs who guard them—are similarly reduced to "domestic slavery" (the precise term Montesquieu uses in Book XVI to characterize polygamy) by submitting to the caprices of the master of the household:

> "As concerns polygamy in general, independent of the circumstances which can render it slightly tolerable, it is of no use to the human race, nor to either of the two sexes, that which abuses and that which is abused.[41]
>
> . . . the slavery of women is very consistent with the spirit of despotic government, which likes to abuse everything. Thus we have seen, at all times, *in Asia* [my emphasis], domestic slavery go hand in hand with despotic government."[42]

If Montesquieu's characterization of "despotism" allies private and public vices, his model of republican government has "virtue" as its central governing principle. Admittedly, he repeatedly insists that he means *civic* virtue, the commitment of citizens to uphold and defend their system of government, and not "morality" per se. However, such pleas are partly disingenuous. Not only might the blanket claim of the moral superiority of republics to monarchies be considered politically seditious, but it would be doubly offensive to the Church. In the first place, it would suggest that morality depended more on the proper form of "government" rather than on the proper religion; second, readers could not help but notice that, in the mid-eighteenth century, the most obvious and

---

[40] Montesquieu *supra* note 2, bk. 6, ch. 13.
[41] *Id.* bk. 16, ch. 6.
[42] *Id.* bk. 16, ch. 9.

successful examples of republican government in contemporary Europe, Holland and Switzerland, were Protestant and not Catholic. Montesquieu had good reason to wish to avoid unnecessarily offending the religious authorities. His nomination to the French Academy in 1727 had very nearly been stymied, according to Montesquieu himself, by the objections of a Jesuit priest to the ideas expressed in the *Persian Letters*.[43] His anxieties were far from groundless; in spite of a vigorous defense on his part against charges that the book was irreligious, it was placed on the Index of Forbidden Books in 1751.[44]

Montesquieu's undisguised admiration for the "ancient" model of republican government had already been propounded in a treatise, published in 1734, *Considerations of the causes of the greatness of the Romans and of their decadence*[45]; the "decadence" in question was not so much the fall of the Roman Empire but rather of the republic. In *The Spirit of Laws*, Montesquieu's assertion of the moral superiority of "ancient" republicans to "modern" monarchists is abundantly clear:

> "Most ancient peoples lived in governments whose principle was virtue; and, while it remained in force, they accomplished things which we no longer see today, and which astonish our small souls."[46]

If monarchies are characterized by the ambitions of their subjects, republics depend on the equality of their citizens. Luxury and ostentation are central to monarchies, frugality to republics.

Nowhere does Montesquieu more forcefully expose his views on the relationship between form of government and private morality than in a short chapter[47] on "The condition of women, under diverse governments:"

> "Women have little restraint in monarchies; because the distinction of ranks summons them to the court, they find there the spirit of liberty which is, more or less, the only one tolerated. Each one uses her charms and her passions to further her fortune; and since their weakness permits them no pride, but only vanity, luxury reigns everywhere among them.
>
> In despotic States, women introduce no luxuries, but are themselves an object of luxury. They must be extremely enslaved . . . Their quarrels, their indiscretions, their repugnancies, their leanings, their jealousies, their outbursts, this art which small souls have of making themselves interesting to great ones, cannot be of no consequence . . .
>
> In republics, women are freed by laws, and captive of mores (*"moeurs"*); luxury is banished, and, with it, corruption and vices.
>
> In Greek cities . . . the virtue, the simplicity, the chastity of women was such that one has scarcely ever seen a people who have maintained, in this respect, better control."

---

[43] Shackleton *supra* note 9, at 85–89.

[44] *Id.* at 356–377.

[45] *See* Charles-Louis de Secondat, Baron de Montesquieu, *Considérations sur les Causes de la Grandeur des Romains et de Leur Décadence* (Paris, 1968) (1734).

[46] Montesquieu *supra* note 2, bk. 4, ch. 4.

Mandeville, it is true, had anticipated the argument that ancient republics were characterized by virtue, but only to satirical effect:

> "I have heard People speak of the mighty Figure the Spartans made above all the Commonwealths of Greece, notwithstanding their uncommon Frugality and other exemplary Virtues. But certainly there never was a Nation whose Greatness was more empty than theirs: the Splendor they lived in was inferior to that of a Theatre, and the only thing they could be proud of, was, that they enjoy'd nothing."[48]

Englishmen, he sardonically retorts, would hardly wish to trade places with the Spartans. There is no trace of such irony in Montesquieu but, on the contrary, a sense of nostalgia that such virtues are almost beyond the comprehension of the "small souls" of the present.

In any case, Montesquieu is ultimately more preoccupied by the menace of despotism than by the ideal of a virtuous republic. The whole of Book VIII is concerned with "The corruption of the principles of the three governments." The inclusiveness of the title is deceptive; "despotism" is not subject to the same risk of corruption as republics or monarchies. Rather, "the principle of despotic government is ceaselessly corrupted, because it is corrupt by its very nature."[49] Monarchies and republics, on the other hand, run the real risk of turning into despotisms. Montesquieu hazards a despairing metaphor: "Rivers run into the sea; monarchies lose themselves in despotism."[50] It would seem as if monarchical absolutism was, virtually inevitably, turning France into another Persia. Indeed, Montesquieu had already (albeit obliquely) suggested as much in the *Persian Letters*; writing of Louis XIV, Usbek the Persian suggests that ". . . of all the governments in the world, that of the Turks or of our august sultan would please him most (Letter XXXVII)." (The *Persian Letters*, it should be noted, were published a safe six years after Louis XIV's death!) If Louis XIV represented the "arch-Orientalizing" French monarch, it hardly followed that, after his reign, France was safely back on the path of "moderate" government: "Most of the peoples of Europe are still governed by their mores (*"moeurs"*; one might say "customs" or even—anachronistically—"culture"). But if, by a long abuse of power, if, by a great conquest, despotism were at one point to establish itself, neither mores nor climate would impede its establishment; and, in this fair part of the world, human nature would suffer, at least for a while, the insults it bears in the three others."[51]

But why, if "Asiatic" despotism constitutes the supreme political evil, is not the establishment of a "Roman" republic the antidote? Herein lies the crux of Montesquieu's argument, and its subtlety. A binary contrast of "republican" to "despotic" government would, of course, be entirely consistent with an argument

---

[47] *Id.* bk. 7, ch. 9.
[48] *See* Mandeville *supra* note 15, at 245.
[49] *See* Montesquieu *supra* note 2, bk. 8, ch. 10.
[50] ch. 17.
[51] *Id.* ch. 8.

from universal principles, typical of one or another seventeenth century theorist. Precisely because Montesquieu is arguing that a republic, however, ideal in the abstract, is not a workable solution to France's political ills does he need to resort to a relativistic argument. Depending on a multiplicity of factors—climate, terrain, customs, history, size—one or another form of government is appropriate. Size is particularly critical: ". . . it is the natural property of small states to be governed as republics, middle-sized ones to be subject to a monarch, great empires dominated by a despot."[52] Montesquieu, in his *Considerations*, had already attributed the demise of the Roman republic to Rome's acquisition of a great empire. Clearly, Montesquieu saw France's territorial ambitions, in Europe and abroad, as a threat to liberty.

The political point of the argument is that, *for France* (though not necessarily in the abstract), a republican government is not a plausible option. Its history, its customs, its size, all militate against a republican solution, one that seemed to Montesquieu (can one blame him?) frankly unrealistic in the mid-eighteenth century. Consequently, he argues, the only *plausible* defense against the "tide" of despotism is the aristocracy, as imperfect (if not morally bankrupt) as it might be. This explains why Montesquieu includes such a long section at the end of the book where he develops the thesis of the Germanic (and feudal, i.e., aristocratic) origins of France. His plea for the maintenance of aristocratic privileges cannot logically rest on an argument like Mandeville's from "human nature," for clearly many societies around the world maintain no such privileges; nor can it rest on the argument that this is by any stretch of the imagination an ideal form of government. Only a relativistic argument can hold: it is the best that France can manage for the time being. It is, implicitly, more important to stave off the real threat of despotism than to attempt to institute an ideal, but implausible, republic.

Montesquieu's contrast of French "monarchy" to distant paradigms of "Asiatic" despotism or "ancient" republicanism is, itself, partly a cautionary measure. Examples existed far closer to home. Montesquieu very clearly regards Spain and Portugal as anti-models, monarchies perhaps but that border on despotism, not least because of the size of their empires. Indeed, in his discussion of the relationship of the size of polities to the nature of government, Montesquieu very ironically cites Spain as the exception that proves the rule: "To hold on to America, it did what even despotism does not do; it destroyed its inhabitants,"[53] and then proceeds to point out Spain's failure to impose despotic rule over the Netherlands. Spain and Portugal are cited as noteworthy examples of religious intolerance.[54] Montesquieu's suggestion[55] that the power of the clergy in Iberia constitutes the only real check on the despotic authority of the monarchy again provides a parallel between Spain and "Asiatic" despotisms, for

---

[52] *Id*. ch. 20.
[53] *Id*. ch. 18.
[54] *See e.g., id*. bk. 25, ch. 13.
[55] *Id*., at bk. 2, ch. 4.

which religion also constitutes, in his analysis, the principal moderating force. Holland, on the other hand, represents an equally appropriate example of a republic, not least by its small size. However, as eloquently as Montesquieu denounces the evils of the Spanish crown (especially in the New World), he remains curiously silent about the republicanism of Holland. Admittedly he points out, without giving specific examples—but they were no doubt unnecessary—that Catholicism is more suited to monarchies and Protestantism to republics,[56] not least because of "the spirit of independence and liberty" which, he suggests, characterizes the peoples of northern as opposed to southern Europe. It would certainly not have been politic of Montesquieu to idealize Holland, and would hardly have served his case for maintaining aristocratic privilege. However, the Dutch case would have made it clear to Montesquieu's contemporary readers that republican government did not in any sense contradict human nature, nor was it impossible to establish in modern Europe.

In short, relativism, comparativism, and historicism served Montesquieu, as they had served his sixteenth century predecessors, as a means of asserting the specificity of the French case in order to argue for a particular (and partisan) political agenda. In the sixteenth century, the argument for French legal and political particularism served as a means of asserting independence from "Roman" hegemony, not only for Huguenots but also for supporters of a French monarchy in open conflict with the ultra-Catholic party. For Montesquieu, it allowed him to argue, along with the *parlements*, for the maintenance of aristocratic privilege, in contradistinction to the (incipient) despotism of Spain or the open republicanism of Holland. In other words, from its very origins, the comparative perspective has been formulated in terms of specific Western European political debates and discourses. Needless to say, this is equally true of various universalist theories, framed in terms of invariant "human nature."

Be this as it may, *The Spirit of Laws* is much more than a highly sophisticated (and, arguably, sophistical) defense of the privileges of the French aristocracy. This is no doubt because of the unresolved tension in the book between the absolute and the relative senses of "best government." In absolute terms, Montesquieu's idealization of republican government, especially of Rome, is transparent and sincere. The relativist argument that different types of government are appropriate for different societies is much harder to make if one is ultimately suggesting, as does Montesquieu, that one's own society must settle for what is after all, in the abstract, only second best. It is this very tension that drives the (anachronistically speaking) sociological and functionalist tenor, not to mention the vast scope, of the work.

Paradoxically, the logical needs of Montesquieu's ideologically charged argument do not require, in and of themselves, such a broad horizon in space or time. Contemporary Western European regimes, from Spain to Holland, provided the range of examples which Montesquieu needed, and were in important respects

---

[56] *Id.* at bk. 24, ch. 5.

more directly relevant instances than Asia or the ancient world. But it was pre-cisely the spatial and temporal distance of Persia or the Roman republic that allowed Montesquieu a certain degree of latitude; their apparent irrelevance for contemporary France made them safer examples to choose. Moreover, Muslim Persia (unlike Catholic Spain) and pre-Christian Rome (unlike Protestant Holland) could safely be denigrated or idealized without antagonizing the Church too flagrantly. Not incidentally, the virtues of Rome or the vices of Asia could easily be exaggerated for polemical purposes without ruffling any feath-ers; we have already seen how Montesquieu systematically represented Asian regimes in a less favorable light than did some of his sources. Ultimately, in Montesquieu's scheme, Asia and Rome were not necessarily important in and of themselves, but constituted ways of categorizing European politics.

Despite the systematically negative depiction of Asia in *The Spirit of Laws*, Montesquieu's representation is markedly different from more modern versions of "Orientalism."[57] Montesquieu may indeed assert the political, if not moral, superiority of Western Europe, but hardly as an invitation for domination. On the contrary, exaggerated territorial ambitions are the hallmark of "despotism." The Spanish conquest of America, Montesquieu insists repeatedly, was disast-rous for Spain as well as for the Americas, and he would certainly have looked askance at attempts to achieve similar dominion over Asia or Africa. (In fact, in the mid-eighteenth century, European colonies in Africa and Asia were virtually all limited to coastal enclaves, geared to establishing and maintaining a mono-poly over sea transport but not at all towards subjecting the populations of the interior.)

In any case, Montesquieu's contemporaries were not all convinced by his unflattering portrait of "Asiatic despotism." Voltaire, who considered himself a victim of aristocratic privilege and consistently supported the monarchy against the *parlements*, was hardly attracted to Montesquieu's particular political views.[58] Not surprisingly, his depiction of Asia was equally antithetical to Montesquieu, idealizing China in particular but other Asian regimes as well.[59] The Physiocrat François Quesnay wrote a long essay in 1767, *The Despotism of China*,[60] which, in spite of its title, is entirely laudatory and explicitly seeks to refute Montesquieu's claims. These depictions of Asia, too, positive as well as negative, can only be understood in terms of specifically Western European political discourse. "Asia," in these writings, stood more or less for the French monarchy, not necessarily for the non-European world.

---

[57] *See* Edward W. Said, *Orientalism* (New York, 1978).

[58] For Voltaire's involvement in the controversy between the monarchy and the *parelements, see* Peter Gay, *Voltaire's Politics: The Poet as Realist*, 87–143, 309–33 (Princeton, 1959). Voltaire pub-lished an astute critique of *The Spirit of Laws* in 1768 as part of a series of dialogues, "L'A, B, C," Voltaire, *Dialogues Philosophiques*, 253–345, especially 256–66 (Paris, 1966), later expanded in 1777 as a *Commentaire sur l'Esprit des Lois*, 35 Voltaire, Oeuvres Complètes de Voltaire, 3–109 (Kehl, 1785).

[59] Etiemble *supra* note 27, 207–306.

[60] François Quesnay, *Ouevres Economiques et Philosophiques*, 562–660 (Paris, 1888)

Even so, the inclusion of Asia within a broad comparative perspective had implications, perhaps unintended, which went beyond purely European political controversies. Specifically, if one were to accept the functionalist logic of Montesquieu's argument that different political regimes were suited to different times, places, and peoples, why then should "despotism" be suited—and, worse, suitable—to Asia? *The Spirit of Laws* includes extensive discussions of the effects of various factors—climate, geography, history, religion, custom— which may simultaneously account for, mitigate, or for that matter exaggerate the effects of one or another form of government. Montesquieu clearly asserts that republics and monarchies are to be found only in Europe; despotisms rule the rest of the world. This is not meant at all as a complacent assertion of European superiority, but on the contrary as a cautionary statement of the despotic menace that forever lurks beneath the surface of political life. However, it is hard, following Montesquieu, to escape the conclusion that there is something about non-Europeans, especially Asia and Asians—their climate, their culture, their character—that calls for despotic rule, that forms of government unsuitable for "us" are perfectly adequate, perhaps even salutary, for "them." Ironically, Montesquieu's suggestion that "despotism" was in some way suited to Asia would provide the ideological justification for a European imperialism which Montesquieu never envisioned and which he would certainly have opposed.

Fig. 1 Max Weber
(Reproduced by kind permission of AKG London)

2

Max Weber and the Uncertainties of Categorical Comparative Law

AHMED A. WHITE

I. INTRODUCTION

Without question, Max Weber is a giant figure in the development of modern social theory. After a century or so, his basic concepts and insights remain highly influential among scholars in all the social disciplines, including law. Of particular importance to comparative law scholars is Weber's methodology. Weber offers a lucid, distinctly typological approach to the problems of legal comparison, one that many comparative law scholars have either appropriated outright for contemporary problems or replicated in important respects. The practice of appropriating Weber is particularly evident in the methodologies of traditional, "categorical" comparative law, especially the framing of comparative debate around "legal families," "legal traditions," and other types.

Regardless of how directly comparative law scholars appropriate Weber, in doing so they risk incorporating an inner logic of his approach that tends in a very insidious way to be quite conservative, even reactionary. This logic encompasses neo-Kantian assumptions that in Weber's case have a propensity to "reify" and ultimately validate the conflicts and contradictions of modern capitalism and *fin-de-siècle* German imperialism. Of particular relevance in this regard is the grounding of Weber's comparative framework in philosophical dualism and formal rationalism. These elements of Weber's methodology, in particular, threaten to exert an insidious influence in modern comparative law scholarship.

This chapter is both a critique of Weber's methods of legal comparison, as well as an attempt to uncover in this critique some of the implications of categorical comparative law. I develop the first of these contentions in three stages: first, by uncovering the methodological substance of Weber's comparative law; second, by assessing its logical (and to some extent, biographical) underpinnings; and third, by considering how Weber's inner logic tends to form an organic connection between his comparative methods and his political position. The second contention I develop by exploring the replication of elements of Weber's inner logic among the methods of traditional comparative law and the implications of this. Finally, in a brief conclusion, I identify aspects of Weber's approach that remain more or less incontestably valid for comparative law scholarship.

In order to develop this argument, a brief overview of Weber's comparative project is probably in order.[1] Weber's contributions to comparative legal discourse are almost entirely couched within his writings on legal sociology, which themselves are contained in key chapters of his *Economy and Society*. Weber's foray into legal sociology is motivated ostensibly by a straightforward ambition to explain the ascendancy of the West and to anticipate the normative limits of western society and its modernist fate. Accordingly, on the broadest plane, Weber's legal sociology is an inherently comparativist attempt to understand the causal interface between law and social development across societies. As such, his attention to comparative law develops in parallel with his more familiar efforts to explain the European origins of capitalism and modernism in terms of unique cultural and religious formations. This is a project famously centered, of course, on the ethic of Calvinist Protestantism.[2]

Like his general sociology—and to an extent that becomes very important to the present argument—the particulars of Weber's legal sociology rest on his understanding of the nature of rationality. Weber distinguishes at least four "ideal types" of legal systems on the basis of the character of legal thought that

---

[1] At the outset it should also be noted that Weber is a famously difficult thinker whose writings on almost every topic steadfastly defy straightforward interpretations. In the words of one of his most sympathetic intellectual biographers, Reinhard Bendix, "The plain fact is that Weber's work is difficult to understand." Reinhard Bendix, *Max Weber: An Intellectual Portrait*, 18, 27 (Garden City, N.Y., 1960). In fact, practically every academic who encounters Weber, including Weber's main biographers, characterizes him not only as difficult, vague, or ambivalent, but also as given to irreconcilable and contradictory claims. *See, e.g.*, Marianne Weber, *Max Weber: A Biography* (New York, 1975); John Patrick Diggins, *Max Weber: Politics and the Spirit of Tragedy*, xii–xiv (New York, 1996).

Weber's legal writings are almost universally regarded as at least as short on clarity and rife with internal contradictions as any other area of his work. Indeed, the foremost American exponents of Weber's legal thought, including Anthony Kronman and David Trubek, make this point quite explicitly. Kronman, although he begins his monograph on Weber with an appeal to the "overarching conceptual unity" of Weber's project, and repeatedly avers to its "surprising consistency and unity of purpose," finally concludes that, "There is . . . something in Weber's writings that can almost be described as an intellectual or moral schizophrenia, an oscillation between irreconcilable perspectives that helps explain why he has found supporters as well as detractors on both the Left and Right." Anthony Kronman, *Max Weber*, 167, 185 (Stanford, 1983). David Trubek, "Max Weber on Law and the Rise of Capitalism," 3 *Wis. L. Rev.* 720 (1972). For an anomalous, contrary interpretation of Weber, *see, e.g.*, Sally Ewing, "Formal Justice and the Spirit of Capitalism: Max Weber's Sociology of Law," 21 *Law & Society Rev.* 487 (1987).

[2] On the place of Weber's legal thought relative to his overall comparative thought and to Marxism, *see, e.g.*, Max Rheinstein, "Introduction" in *Max Weber on Law in Economy and Society*, vii (Max Rheinstein trans. & ed., Cambridge Mass., 1966). *Cf.* Roger Cotterrell, "Legality and Political Legitimacy in the Sociology of Max Weber" in *Legality, Ideology and the State*. 69 (David Sugarman ed., London, 1983).

underlies each system: formal-rational; substantive-rational; formal-irrational; and informal-irrational. Weber conceives of rational legal systems as grounded in general, unambiguous norms, and irrational legal systems as based on arbitrary, often ad hoc norms. Formal legal systems, he submits, are based in externally derived norms, while informal legal systems derive rules on the basis of factors internal to the specific legal issue. Weber further distinguishes legal systems on the basis of the political system to which they conform, and specifically the mode by which authority is legitimated in such a system. To this end, Weber identifies three types of authority: traditional; charismatic; and rational. By overlapping these two typologies, one based on the character of legal thought and the other on the mode of legitimation, Weber compiles a matrix that comprises the essential structure of his legal sociology and his comparative framework.[3]

Weber uses this typology to speak to practical questions about social development. According to Weber, a key evolutionary advantage of the West from a legal standpoint was the early development in European societies of formal-rational legal systems juxtaposed with rational systems of political authority. For the West, the prevalence of formal-rational norms and rational modes of authority provides, Weber believes, a constellation of structures and norms consistent on a functional level with the development of capitalism: for example, a predictability of sovereign authority consistent with capitalist accounting and planning, and a minimum of equality among private actors vis-à-vis the state consistent with the wage-labor contract. Conversely—and this is of particular relevance to comparative law discourse—Weber explains the relative stagnation of other civilizations in part by the underdevelopment of their legal systems and authority structures—by, for example, the prevalence of informal or irrational legal norms, or traditional authority structures. Indeed, for Weber every non-European society—Persia, India, China, various African societies, Arabia, Russia, and so on—is characterized by a distinct *legal* impediment to optimal social development along western lines. Needless to say, this project dovetails neatly with Weber's familiar claims about the unique evolutionary advantages enjoyed by the West in more spiritual, cultural, and material quarters, and with his overarching desire to explain social development on the bases of non-universal, non-economic processes.[4]

III.   NEO-KANTIANISM IN WEBER'S COMPARATIVE LAW

It is axiomatic that Weber was a neo-Kantian thinker. That Weber evidences strongly neo-Kantian tendencies is not at all surprising in light of his intellectual

---

[3] *Max Weber on Law in Economy and Society* (Max Rheinstein trans. & ed., Cambridge Mass., 1966), (a distillation of the legal components of Weber's *Economy and Society*).

[4] Perhaps the best short summary of Weber's views on comparative law in English remains David Trubek, "Max Weber on Law and the Rise of Capitalism" 3 *Wis. L. Rev.* 720 (1972).

heritage. By age twenty three, according to his widow, Weber had embraced the key tenets of the neo-Kantian framework: "Weber had long since fought his way to a recognition of the limits of intellectual power and had for the time being cast anchor in a silent veneration of the unexplorable."[5] As a mature scholar, Weber was utterly immersed in a Kantian renaissance then sweeping through continental academe. Of particular significance was Weber's relationship to the so-called Baden or Southwest German School of neo-Kantianism, and especially its representatives, Wilhelm Dilthey, Emil Lask, Heinrich Rickert, and (indirectly) Wilhelm Windelband.[6] Despite numerous differences, Weber clearly shares with these figures several signature intellectual traits, including an intense skepticism about universalism and foundationalism and a reluctance to assimilate natural and social inquiry. Still more revealing than these traits are two others: a commitment to philosophical dualism; and an attachment to a formal rationalism and its dim implications for the prospects of resolving social, political, and legal conflicts.[7] A closer inspection reveals the fundamentality of these latter two traits to Weber's typological framework.

Weber's dualism seems to have some basis in his personality, for Weber was much given to contradictions and inconsistencies. As Weber's biographers have recognized, such tendencies are hardly the products of a lazy intellect, but rather reflect the depth of his antinomic character, his unshakable view of the world as fraught with irreconcilable oppositions.[8] According to his widow, Weber "regarded it as his task to endure the antinomies of existence."[9] Indeed, according to another of Weber's biographers, Arthur Mitzman, the whole of Weber's

---

[5] Weber, *Max Weber*, *supra* note 1, at 104.

[6] Guy Oakes, "Max Weber and the Southwest German School: the Genesis of the Concept of the Historical Individual" in *Max Weber and his Contemporaries*, 434 (Wolfgang J. Mommsen & Jurgen Osterhammel eds., London, 1987).

[7] *See, e.g.*, Richard Bendix, "Max Weber and Jakob Burkhardt," 30 *American Sociological Rev.* 176 (1965); Fritz Ringer, *Max Weber's Methodology: The Unification of the Cultural Social Sciences*, 36–52 (Cambridge Mass., 1997).

Taking its cue from Kant's own distinctions between phenomena and *noumena*, pure and practical reason, ontology and epistemology, the philosophical dualism of neo-Kantianism manifests itself in the embrace of a number of conceptual antinomies that, as Hegel anticipated, are but various incarnations of the more fundamental antithesis of subject and object. *See, e.g.*, G. W. F. Hegel, *The Encyclopaedia Logic*, 48, 91 (T. F. Geraets et al. trans., Indianapolis, 1991).

Hence, at the methodological core of neo-Kantian thought are vigorous oppositions of theory and practice, nature and society, and especially fact and value, for example. Much more so than Kant himself, the neo-Kantian tradition made clear its regard for these antinomies, however articulated, as just that: fundamental, ultimately irreconcilable statements about the nature of existence itself. Thus, for neo-Kantians, dualism must motivate every effective intellectual project; fact and value distinctions must not only be recognized *within* a scholarly contribution, they must characterize the life and work of the scholar herself. For neo-Kantians, too, the *ultimate content* of reason, along with any deep notion of philosophical truth must lie beyond the aptitude and concerns of genuine scientific inquiry. In a more fundamental way, neo-Kantianism evidences its impoverished grasp on reason in the way it reduces reason to a primarily epistemological construct with rather impotent ontological implications. It is this tendency that underlies the formal and subjective rationalism associated with the Baden School of Neo-Kantianism.

[8] *See, e.g.*, Diggins, *Max Weber*, *supra* note 1, at xii–xiv.

[9] Weber, Max Weber, *supra* note 1, at 678.

life, intellectual and otherwise, can be explained in terms of an antinomic dis-
position rooted in his upbringing and in the everyday contradictions of his
class.[10] Notably, this antinomic attitude clearly extends from Weber's day-to-
day affairs, which he consistently managed with a curious mixture of decisive-
ness and hesitation,[11] to Weber's political attitudes, which are laden with all
sorts of contradictions and paradoxes.[12]

In addition to underlying his basic ideal-typical approach,[13] dualism provides
a theoretical basis for Weber's well-known embrace of value-neutral methods.[14]
For Weber, the sociology of law, properly undertaken, must set aside ethical or
moral judgments, and focus instead on the factual, objective, and empirical
aspects of the subject.[15] Only then, as Anthony Kronman so clearly notes, does
Weber believe legal sociology is able to distinguish itself from the intrinsic distortions of "dogmatic" and "moral" jurisprudence.[16]

Weber's value-neutrality does not entail a complete abdication on subjective
questions of value, ethics, morals, and the like. As is widely recognized by his
supporters and critics alike, Weber tends to segregate such questions from the
purer stages of scholarly inquiry while maintaining their ultimate relevance; he
bookends objective inquiry temporally between subjective judgments. In this

[10] Arthur Mitzman, *The Iron Cage: An Historical Interpretation of Max Weber* (New York, 1970).

[11] Weber, *Max Weber, supra* note 1, *passim*.

[12] Wolfgang J. Mommsen, "The Antinomian Structure of Max Weber's Political Thought," 4 *Current Persp. in Soc. Theory* 289 (1983).

[13] Piers Beirne, "Ideology and Rationality in Max Weber's Sociology of Law," 2 *Research in L. & Soc.* 103, 125 (1979) (Bierne argues that the ideal-type serves Weber as a way of avoiding the epistemological difficulties inherent in Weber's underlying dualism.)

[14] Leo Strauss offers a well-known conservative critique of Weber along these lines. Leo Strauss, *What is Political Philosophy, passim* (Glencoe Il., 1959).

[15] *See, e.g.,* Max Weber, *On the Methodology of the Social Sciences* (Edward A. Shils & Henry A. Finch trans., Glencoe, Il., 1949). *Cf.* Talcot Parsons, "Value-Freedom and Objectivity," in *Max Weber and Sociology Today* 40 (Otto Stammer ed., Oxford, 1971); W. G. Runciman, *A Critique of Max Weber's Philosophy of Social Science*, 40–47 (Cambridge, 1972). On the relationship between this perspective and Weber's attitude towards the world more generally, *see, e.g.,* Weber, *Max Weber, supra* note 1, at 315–22.

[16] Kronman, *Max Weber, supra* note 1, at 6–22. Moreover, for Weber the category of "formal rational" legal thought crucial to his comparative project—itself derives meaning from the segregation of facts and values. Indeed, according to Kronman, *all* of the vital aspects of Weber's legal sociology, including his crucial conception of authority types as well as his distinction between archaic and modern contractual regimes, rest ultimately on his conception of value. *Id.* at 42–43, 50–56, 86–87, 107–08. Kronman writes, for example, that for Weber

"Legal-rational authority rests on the epistemological assumption that values can only be established in [deliberate, willful acts of norm creation], and thus rejects the fundamental premise of all traditional domination that there are certain facts which have an independent ethical meaning of their own, a meaning that has not (indeed, could not have) been given them *by* men but which, quite to the contrary, is given *to* men by their ineluctable fate. Traditional authority presupposes the essential identity or continuity of "is" and "ought"; legal-rational authority, by contrast, severs the connection between these two domains in a principled way by tracing the legitimacy of every binding norm back to its deliberate enactment its imposition, by human beings, on an otherwise morally neutral world."

Id. at 53 (emphasis in original).

respect, Weber was committed to value-neutrality but not in the strictest sense of the word. Put another way, Weber's value-neutrality was a matter of internal methodology and not overall intellectual interest.[17]

Value-neutrality represents by no means the only reflection of dualism in Weber's comparative law project. Dualism also inheres in the manichean categories of legal rationality that comprise the substance of his comparative typology: substantive reasoning versus formal reasoning, rationality versus irrationality, and ultimately substantive rationality versus formal rationality. While his use of this is more sophisticated than many commentators suggest, Weber ultimately viewed these categories in mutually exclusive terms.

Weber's neo-Kantian character reveals itself yet more thoroughly in the normative stance that underlies Weber's overall understanding of these categories. As Herbert Marcuse argues, a deep political conservatism inheres in Weber's ostensibly descriptive, neutral uses of the concept of reason. Marcuse points to several interconnected ways in which, when Weber speaks of formal rationality, in particular, the "Ought shows itself in the Is." One feature is the closed hierarchy of rationality peculiar to his scheme, which tends to foreclose the more nuanced notions of reason that are integral to more radical perspectives. Another related feature is Weber's preemptive attribution of one or another of his categories of rationality (legal or otherwise) to every attempt to transcend existing forms. Such is Weber's view of socialism, for example. A third feature, also related to the others, is Weber's repeated appeals to "fate" and other pessimistic notions in his erstwhile neutral descriptions of these categories, an appeal that again confirms the impossibility of transcending existing rational forms. Together these themes deny in a very normative way the possibility of transcending the limitations of formal rationalism in law and in social organization more generally.[18] A rather similar, although more generic, critique of Weber's concept of reason is made by Max Horkheimer, who argues that Weber's overall grasp of the nature of reason is rooted in a subjectivist conception that utterly forecloses his grasp, let alone acknowledgement or embrace, of any radical notions of reason. Further, Horkheimer argues, Weber's dualism presupposes such a subjectivist conception in the first place.[19] Taken together, Marcuse's and Horkheimer's critiques qualify Weber's overall theory in two ways. First, for Weber there can be no deeper rationalities lurking hidden or latent within legal forms and no prospect of developing a truly dynamic, historical perspective on the evolution of legal forms and legal regimes. All of this is consistent with Weber's ultimate view that the future of human civilization and law in particular can hold little but tragedy, decay, and regression from an already imperfect condition. But second, neither is Weber able with this

---

[17] On this aspect of Weber, *see, e.g.,* Maureen Cain, "The Limits of Idealism: Max Weber and the Sociology of Law," 3 *Research in Law & Sociology* 53, 63–65 (1980).

[18] Herbert Marcuse, "Industrialization and Capitalism in the Work of Max Weber," in *Negations* 201 (1968).

[19] Max Horkheimer, *The Eclipse of Reason*, 1–12 (New York, 1947).

framework to divulge the full import of irrationality among legal and social forms even in a purely descriptive vein, as his relatively anaemic conception of rationality offers an excessively myopic view of the issue.[20]

IV. THE INNER LOGIC OF WEBER'S COMPARATIVE LAW AND ITS UNDERPINNINGS: LUKACS AND MOMMSEN

It is easy, and for that reason quite tempting, to imagine that intellectual frameworks, even if they do not fall out of thin air, are ideological in the crudest sense of the word. It is tempting, for example, to see such constructions as either consciously devised to serve some specific agenda or, with only a little more sophistication, as simple mirror images of a thinker's class, race, or gender. Unfortunately, such assumptions are usually worthless for understanding sophisticated intellectual contributions. This is especially the case with Weber, who so adamantly denied that his intellectual project possessed any internal value-orientation. With Weber as with perhaps most important intellectuals, the content of theory is surely influenced by social context, but the mechanisms behind these influences are invariably complicated, indirect, and subtle.

In the view of Georg Lukacs, the Hungarian Marxist philosopher, the rise of neo-Kantian scholarship, including Weber's, can only be understood as products of the complex interrelationship between intellectual consciousness and the practical realities and material culture of mature capitalism and *fin-de-siècle* imperialism. Lukacs sheds considerable light on the nature and origins of Weber's inner logic, for he sees both the tendency to embrace dualism and the affinity for formal conceptions of reason as products of the inability of the "bourgeois" intellect itself to really transcend or even elude the (relative) irrationalities of the real, practical world. For Lukacs, the embrace of both dualism and formal rationalism represents modern intellectuals' betrayal of the critical tendencies inherent in the concept of reason and the Enlightenment more generally. In his view, this betrayal (of which the neo-Kantian tradition is only the most salient representative), arises not from the crude reduction of intellectual problems to this or that set of interests, but instead involves, first, the "reification" of intellectual consciousness by a logic peculiar to modern market society: abstract valuation, blind objectification, equivocation, and permanent contradiction. Second, this process involves the re-articulation of philosophy and social theory, and the re-definition of reason in particular, in conformance with this reified consciousness.

Lukacs strives to demonstrate the origins of this reifying process in the facility for the commodity structure "to penetrate society in all its aspects and to remold it in its own image," to "subjugate" human consciousness to its form.[21]

---

[20] *Weber on Law in Economy and Society, supra* note 3, at 301–20. *See also,* David Trubek, "Weber's Tragic Modernism and the Study of Law in Society," 20 *Law & Society Rev.* 573, 589–93 (1986).

[21] Georg Lukacs, *History and Class Consciousness*, 85 (Rodney Livingstone trans., London, 1923).

More specifically, Lukacs, building on Marx's well-known determinations, proposes that through the mediation of "abstract labor" the commodity form stamps itself into the structure of modern consciousness. Like Marx, Lukacs believes that extension of commodity production necessarily purges labor, the broad capacity for the practical transformation of nature and society, of its erstwhile intrinsic particularity, and purges as well the capacity of the laborer to exert conscious, intellectual control over her own works and thus to transcend subject-object oppositions. As this process extends itself across society, as abstract labor and the commodity form become ubiquitous, so do the conceptual dualisms, or as he puts it "antinomies," that are consistent with the segregation of the practical (objective) and intellectual (subjective) sides of labor, seem to correspond to the "true" structure of society. In Lukacs' terms, the decisive intellectual product of the maturation of commodity production is then the "fragmentation" and "atomization" of social being. *Clearly following Weber*, Lukacs argues that "rationalisation" under capitalism breaks down the erstwhile organic structure of economic production, which "turns into the objective synthesis of rationalised special systems whose unity is determined by pure calculation and which must therefore be arbitrarily connected with each other."[22]

Rather than challenge this distorted, reified state of affairs, neo-Kantian thought acquiesces. It sees the situation quite naturally, albeit in a thoroughly uncritical fashion, "as the form in which its own authentic immediacy becomes manifest and . . . does not even attempt to transcend it."[23]

> "Just as the economic theory of capitalism remains stuck fast in its self-created immediacy, the same thing happens to bourgeois attempts to comprehend the ideological phenomenon of reification. Even thinkers who have no desire to deny or obscure its existence and who are more or less clear in their own minds about its humanly destructive consequences . . . make no attempt to advance beyond its objectively most derivative forms . . .
>
> Indeed, they divorce these empty manifestations from their real capitalist foundation and make them independent and permanent by regarding them as the timeless model of human relations in general."[24]

[22] Furthermore, "this fragmentation of the object of production necessarily entails the fragmentation of its subject," a dynamic that so distances human beings from control of material life that a person's participation can only become more passive and "contemplative."

> "The contemplative stance adopted toward a process mechanically conforming to fixed laws and enacted independently of man's consciousness and impervious to human intervention, i.e., a perfectly closed system, must likewise transform the basic categories of man's immediate attitude to the world: it reduces space and time to a common denominator and degrades time to the dimension of space."

Id. at 88–89. *Cf.* Bertell Ollman, *Alienation: Marx's Conception of Man in Capitalist Society* (Cambridge, 1976).

[23] Lukacs, *History and Class Consciousness, supra* note 20, at 93.

[24] *Id.* at 94–95.

How exactly does this fundamentally *economic* phenomenon take on such encompassing proportions? In answering this question, Lukacs again simultaneously avers to Marx's notions regarding the spatially expansive tendencies of capitalist production and its logic to submerge the entire social landscape, as well as Weber's contentions regarding the pervasiveness of the cultural logic of

From whence derives the specific relationship between reification—hence commodification, abstract labor, and ultimately capitalism itself—and the neo-Kantian canons of philosophical dualism and formal rationalism? In developing his particular view of the nexus between reification, on the one hand, and dualism and formal rationalism on the other, Lukacs remains close to both Marx and Hegel.[25] Modern philosophy of all stripes, Lukacs points out, arrives on the scene already possessing a framework that presupposes dualism and formal rationality. For despite its ostensible comprehensiveness, philosophy even through Fichte and Hegel confidently refused to conceive as its subject the real totality of social being down to its practical, material bases.[26] Thus, practical questions must be conceded to other, separate disciplines or else consigned to metaphysical interventions. Such is particularly true of "modern critical philosophy," or "modern rationalism"—as Lukacs variously describes the tradition in modern philosophy growing broadly out of Kant—which is repeatedly marked by the acknowledgment of a realm beyond the faculties of rational inquiry: in Kant's philosophy, the *noumena*, or thing-in-itself.[27] In one key way, this formulation directly contemplates a refusal to probe the content of reason and a refusal to construe philosophical questions in eminent, totalistic terms. For not only does the Kantian *noumena* (and its analogues) reduce the question of rationality to purely philosophical terms, it also inaugurates (or, more accurately, sustains) a fundamentally dualistic conception of being and so by sleight

---

capitalism. *Id*. at 95–96. Indeed, to a considerable extent Lukacs' entire argument on reification might be understood, as one Lukacs scholar puts it, as a deep synthesis of Hegel, Marx, and Weber centered around the question of reason, its forms, and its historicity. Weber's theory of rationalization is appended to Hegelian and Marxian notions about the material content, the dialectical structure, and the dynamic historicity of human existence. But in the balance, Weber is subjected to the implications of his own critique. Andrew Feenberg, *Lukacs, Marx and the Sources of Critical Theory*, 63–78 (New York, 1986).

In any case, for Lukacs the "distinction between a worker faced with a particular machine" and any other agent in modern society–entrepreneur, bureaucrat, philosopher is "purely quantitative." Lukacs, *History and Class Consciousness*, *supra* note 20, at 98. Interestingly (and here is where their relationship is perhaps most interesting), Lukacs *explains* key aspects of Weber's model of modern life, including the institutions of bureaucracy and legal formalism, in terms of the reification dynamic. Moreover, for Lukacs, "the problems of consciousness arising from wage-labour [are] repeated in the ruling class in a reified and spiritualized" form. *Id*. at 97–100.

[25] Hegel, critiquing Kant's emerging legacy, argued repeatedly that philosophical dualism as well as the non-eminent portrayal of reason were no more than a mark of the immaturity of philosophy and human society in general. In Hegel's words, in fact, it is the "sole interest of Reason to suspend" the subject-object dynamic. G. W. F. Hegel, *The Difference Between Fichte's and Schelling's System of Philosophy*, 90–91 (H. S. Harris & Walter Cerf trans., Albany, 1977). For his part Marx saw these phenomena as reflections of the inability of conventional critique, segregated from *praxis*, to resolve any questions of philosophical truth. *See, e.g.*, Karl Marx, *The Economic and Philosophic Manuscripts of 1844*, 143 (Martin Milligan trans., New York, 1964).

It is perhaps worth noting that this process is developed at length and from a similar perspective by Alfred Sohn-Rethel, who discerns the origins of scientific abstraction as well as epistemological thought itself in the development of abstract labor. Alfred Sohn-Rethel, *Intellectual and Manual Labour: A Critique of Epistemology* (London, 1978).

[26] Lukacs, *History and Class Consciousness*, *supra* note 20, at 109–110, *passim*.

[27] *Id*. at 113–14.

of hand reduces to philosophical truth the practical reality of reification in modern life.[28]

What has all this specifically to do with Weber, a man who so vehemently disclaimed any real interest in philosophy? In Lukacs' view, Kant himself is at least to be applauded for equivocating on matters of dualism and formal rationality.[29] Not so, Lukacs argues, of the main-line neo-Kantians, for whom the most problematic of Kant's tendencies are generally the most ardently embraced.[30] Not so of Weber either, of whose neo-Kantian tendencies Lukacs is intensely, albeit rather obliquely, critical.

For a time before Lukacs' embrace (*circa* 1918) of Marxism and Weber's final repudiations of socialism and his commitment to the Great War, Lukacs enjoyed a very close friendship with both Max and Marianne Weber. Max Weber actually mounted a rather active, albeit unsuccessful, campaign to secure Lukacs' *habilitation* and his introduction to elite intellectual circles. The published papers of both Lukacs and the Webers evidence numerous interactions of this quite personal kind.[31] As we have just seen, Lukacs shows considerable reliance on Weber's own scholarship in compiling this critique.[32] In light of these factors, as well as the fact that Weber's neo-Kantianism is of the most eclectic, ostensibly non-philosophic kind,[33] it seems understandable why

[28] On this point, *see, e.g., id.* at 121–22. In one of many passages that express this determination, Lukacs notes that dualism, or antinomy as he here calls it, arises not from

"the inability of philosophers to give a definitive analysis of the available facts. It is rather the intellectual expression of the objective situation itself which it is their task to comprehend. That is to say, the contradiction that appears between subjectivity and objectivity in modern rationalist formal systems, the entanglements and equivocations hidden in their concepts of subject and object, the conflict between their nature as systems created by 'us' [human beings] and their fatalistic necessity distinct from and alien to man is nothing but the logical and systematic formulation of the modern state of society."

Id. at 128. *See also id.* at 134.

[29] Significantly, Lukacs does applaud Kant's acknowledgment of the practical, "active" dimensions of the quest for philosophical truth. And yet, even in this move Lukacs finds a failure to advance beyond a merely formal invocation of the power to transcend practically the opposition, for example, of form and content. Instead, such power is radically subjectified and formalized in a way that renders even more permanent and comprehensive the essential dualism of Kant's framework. In a word, Kant construes even praxis strictly within a framework that maintains the distinction between the knowable and the thing-in-itself and that leads back to the "limits of abstract contemplation." *Id.* at 124–25.

[30] Lukacs' critique of the Kantian tradition is at its most vigorous vis-à-vis the likes of Rickert, Lask, and Windelband. Among these thinkers, as for Weber, dualism and antinomy take clear form in the embrace of value-neutrality and the epistemological framework, and formal rationalism is presented in unadulterated form. *Id.* at 150–53.

[31] Evidence of such engagements is laid out in sometimes amusing detail in Lukacs' collected correspondence, as is Lukacs' curriculum vitae, which contains a testamentary appeal to Weber. Georg Lukacs, *Selected Correspondence* (New York, 1986). On Lukacs' relationship to Weber, see also Mary Gluck, *Georg Lukacs and his Generation: 1900–1918*, 149–50, 163–64 (Cambridge Mass., 1995).

[32] On Weber's influence on Lukacs, *see, e.g.*, Eva Karadi, "Ernst Bloch and George Lukacs in Max Weber's Heidelberg," in *Max Weber and His Contemporaries*, 499 (Wolfgang J. Mommsen & Jurgen Osterhammel eds., London, 1987).

[33] On Weber's complicated relationship to other representatives of neo-Kantianism, *see, e.g.*, Oakes, "Max Weber and the South-West German School," supra note 6.

Lukacs appears rather hesitant, especially early on, to subject his pre-deceased friend to the full force of his critique.

In his *Destruction of Reason* (1955), Lukacs eventually does subject Weber to an uncompromising, if not dogmatic and overdrawn, critique that ascribes to Weber rather overtly irrational views which Lukacs very directly connected to Weber's imperialist politics.[34] But it is in an earlier and more sophisticated work, *History and Class Consciousness* (1922), that Lukacs' critique of Weber is most persuasive. Here, while actually seldom mentioning Weber and paying even less attention to the particulars of Weber's politics, Lukacs unmasks and critiques the logic of Weber's sociology. Again, the central themes of this critique are dualism and formal rationalism. Like Marcuse after him, Lukacs takes issue with Weber's ultimate conclusion that formal rationality, whether legal or otherwise, marks the apogee of social and legal rationality. With Weber's dualism, this determination serves to validate capitalism as such and to affirm its reifying dynamics: abstract labor, the commodity form, and so forth. In Lukacs' view, Weber's approach guarantees that his sociology exhibits a conservative and a-historical quality, as it forecloses any interest in or possibility of moving beyond the given forms of modern society whilst nonetheless building its claims upon rarefied visions of the past. Much more so than Marcuse, or any other critic of Weber for that matter, Lukacs understands Weber's problematic intellectual character as a product of Weber's reified consciousness, as a product of Weber's inability to transcend a logic imposed on him with apparently overwhelming force by his social context.[35]

An apparent deficiency of Lukacs' critique is its relative neglect of the way Weber's neo-Kantianism relates to his politics. It is primarily in a conceptual and anecdotal way that Lukacs really engages Weber. Such is true even of his otherwise problematic argument in *Destruction of Reason*. A more practical inquiry into the specific details of Weber's imperialism—one that does much to bolster Lukacs' critique—is made by Weber scholar, Wolfgan Mommsen.

Throughout his career Weber was an intensely political thinker who, albeit with characteristic hesitation, was not above entering practical political disputes. Through his entire life, Weber retained a very real commitment to German imperialism and to the associated agendas of German nationalism and power politics.[36] In Mommsen's view, Weber's imperialism is not ancillary to, but in fact "embedded in" his overall view of world history and organically connected to his commitment to liberalism. For Mommsen, "There is in fact a fairly intimate connexion between Weber's scholarly work and his political creed; in

---

[34] Georg Lukacs, *The Destruction of Reason*, 605, 616–19 (Peter Palmer trans., Atlantic Highlands, N.J., 1981).

[35] For a general account of Lukacs' critique of Weber, *see, e.g.*, David Plotke, "Marxism, Sociology and Crisis: Lukacs' Critique of Weber," 20 *Berkley J. Soc.* 181 (1975/1976).

[36] On the evolution of Weber's imperialist and nationalist politics, *see* David Beetham, *Max Weber and the Theory of Modern Politics* (London, 1974).

a way they are even two sides of the same coin."[37] Accordingly, Weber is typically seen as a "liberal" imperialist, a term which refers more to the domestic political aims of the policies in question than to their preferred means of execution. In a closely related sense, Weber's imperialism was throughout a pragmatic and tentative set of commitments, always oriented toward Weber's contingent but ultimately undiluted faith in (or, better said, acquiescence to) bourgeois society as well as his investment in the ideal of the nation state and the interest of the German state.[38]

Of what exactly did Weber's imperialism consist? Certainly, Weber's imperialism finds its clearest intellectual articulation in his inaugural address, which features sometimes blatantly racialist and Darwinist rhetoric about the German people's "struggle for existence" and for "elbow room," and overt appeals to power.[39] And it is here that Mommsen discerns at its most obvious the organic relationship between Weber's imperialism and his scholarly framework, as well as between Weber's imperialism and his overarching pessimism about the world in general.[40] But Weber was more than theoretical about his support for imperialism. The inaugural address itself is specifically directed at questions of German foreign policy. Likewise, Weber's imperialism appears later in his support for German involvement in the Great War. While in certain ways Weber was simultaneously quite wary of the perversion of German war goals and critical of its strategies and tactics, Weber ultimately saw the war as a "great and wonderful" thing. Furthermore, according to Mommsen, among others, Weber was actually deeply distressed that he could not himself fight for Germany.[41]

Another way that Weber's imperialism found practical expression was in his antipathy to socialism. It was in large part because of the anti-imperialist and anti-nationalist tendencies of the proletariat that Weber rejected socialism.[42] Similarly, Weber's imperialism also expressed itself in his rejection of social critique rooted primarily in economic analysis. With its tendency to emphasize proletarian interests, to legitimate the claims of the lower classes, and so to transcend national interests, "political economy" revealed itself as a great enemy of the German people.[43] Weber decries the infection of law with economic

---

[37] Wolfgang J. Mommsen, *The Age of Bureaucracy: Perspectives on the Political Sociology of Max Weber*, xiv, 25 (Oxford, 1974).

[38] *Id*. at 26.

[39] Wolfgang J. Mommsen, *Max Weber and German Politics 1890–1920*, 38–48 (Chicago, 1984).

[40] *Id*. at 80–84.

[41] *Id*. at 195. *Cf.* Diggins, *Max Weber, supra* note 1, at 184–93.

[42] Mommsen, *Max Weber and German Politics, supra* note 39, at 88–90.

[43] In this spirit, Weber concludes that,

"[T]he deadly seriousness of the population problem prohibits eudaemonism; it prevents us from imagining that peace and happiness lie hidden in the lap of the future, it prevents us from believing that elbowroom in this earthly existence can be won in any other way than through the hard struggle of human beings with each other."

Max Weber, "The National State and Economic Policy" in K. Tribe (ed.), *Reading Weber*, 188, 196–97 (London, 1989).

concerns.[44] Against this, Weber insists, "There is only one *political standard of value* which is supreme for us economic nationalists, and it is by this standard that we also measure the classes which either have the leadership of the nation in their hands or are striving for it."[45]

Mommsen, too, touches on the specific organic relationship between Weber's imperialism and his neo-Kantianism. We have already seen Lukacs' argument that neo-Kantianism is implicitly conservative. Mommsen's inquiry into Weber's imperialism finds that it is premised precisely on a thoroughgoing embrace of the notion of permanent conflict. " 'Struggle,' for him, was not only an unavoidable element of social life, but was desirable in principle, whether it took the form of open disputes, economic competition, or biological or other 'selection.' "[46] For Weber, Mommsen says, it was "futile to assume, that a social and political order could be devised in which recourse to force would become less and less necessary, in particular with regard to economic life."[47]

What precisely is, then, the relationship between Weber's imperialism and his comparative law? In light of the critiques offered by Marcuse, Lukacs, and Mommsen, it seems clear that the connection between Weber's imperialism and his comparative methods comprises something far more subtle than the shallow racial and economic ideologies of, say, Roosevelt or Rosenberg. To be sure there are definite strains of this sort of thing in Weber: the blatant Eurocentrism of Weber's legal sociology is easily evident, after all, in a normative hierarchy that lurks just beneath the surface of his "objective" typology and flows right out of his Freiburg Address. But there are also facts that contradict and complicate a straightforward indictment of Weber on such charges.[48]

Much more useful is to see Weber's neo-Kantianism as, in one sense, the vital medium that connects his politics of imperialism to his sociology of law and ultimately his comparative framework. Notably, and this is where Lukacs is especially

---

[44] *Id.* at 196–97.
[45] *Id.* at 202. Weber also writes, for example, that,

"Our successors will not hold us responsible before history for the kind of economic organization we hand over to them, but rather for the amount of elbow-room we conquer for them in the world and leave behind us. Processes of economic development are in the final analysis also *power struggles*, and the ultimate and decisive interests at whose service economic policy must take place are the interests of national *power*, where these interests are in question. The science of political economy is a *political* science. It is a servant of politics . . . And for us the *national state* is not, as some people believe, an indeterminate entity raised higher and higher into the clouds in proportion as one clothes its nature in mystical darkness, but [is] the temporal power-organization of the nation, and in this national state the ultimate standard of value for economic policy is reason of state."

Id. at 198–99.
[46] Mommsen, *Max Weber and German Politics, supra* note 39, at 114–15. *Cf.* Mark Warren, "Max Weber's Liberalism for a Nietzschean World," 82 *Am. Pol. Sci. Rev.* 31, 37 (1988).
[47] Mommsen, *The Age of Bureaucracy, supra* note 36, at 29.
[48] For a brief account of Weber's political ambivalence, one that emerges from an account of Weber's travels through the United States, *see* Wolfgang J. Mommsen, "Weber in America," 69 *American Scholar* 103 (2000).

interesting, this connection need not ever be consciously established, but instead can constitute itself quite unconsciously. In another, related sense, Weber's imperialism, his neo-Kantianism, and his sociology and comparative law project can be seen as an organic, interdependent whole, from which one can only contingently identify a primary component. Either way a definite link is evident between Weber's politics, his legal sociology and comparative framework, and his neo-Kantianism, a link that is ideological in the truest, most indelible sense of the word. To put it crudely, the relationship among these aspects of Weber is in no way accidental.

V. WEBER AND MODERN COMPARATIVE LAW

Few if any modern comparative law scholars apply Weber's complete typology in an unqualified way to contemporary issues.[49] But this chapter's critique of Weber's comparativism makes clear that the most problematic aspect of his project is not the comprehensive application of his theory, but rather its inner logic, and in particular a neo-Kantian tendency toward dualism and formal rationalism, and eventually conservative, a-historical, and altogether reified inquiry. These tendencies are quite evident in modern categorical comparative law scholarship. For this reason, the critique of Weber can speak quite broadly to the discipline's contemporary character.

Perhaps the most obvious Weberian trait in modern comparative scholarship is one ubiquitous in contemporary legal scholarship: an affinity for formal rationalism. Indeed, where comparative law scholars make any specific appropriation of Weber this almost invariably involves the use of his categories of legal rationality. Comparative law scholarship of this sort is quite common.[50] As Marcuse's and Lukacs' critiques of Weber indicate, an incipient conservatism inheres in this approach, for normative endorsement of formal rationalism as the apogee of social and legal reason is latent in the notion that a meaningful distinction, even of an ostensibly neutral, descriptive kind, can be drawn between formal and substantive rationality in the first place. Even by

---

[49] An obvious reason for this, aside from the obsolescence of many of Weber's empirical points, are the inaccuracies that have since been revealed about them. Among many critical works of this stripe, *see, e.g.*, Tony Dickson & Hugh F. McLachlan, "In Search of the 'Spirit of Capitalism': Weber's Misinterpretation of Franklin," 23 *Sociology* 81 (1989); Harold J. Berman, "Some False Premises of Max Weber's Sociology of Law," 65 *Wash. U. L. Q.* 758 (1987); Guenther Roth, "Political Critiques of Max Weber: Some Implications for Political Sociology," 30 *Am. Sociological Rev.* 213 (1965).

[50] There are contemporary comparativists who are directly influenced by Weber. Among them, *see, e.g.*, Albert H. Y. Chen, "Rational Law, Economic Development and the Case of China," 8 *Social & Legal Stud.* 97 (1999); Assaf Likovski, "Protestantism and the Rationalization of English Law: A Variation on a Theme by Weber," 33 *Law & Society Rev.* (1999); K. Peter Takayama, "Rationalization of State and Society: A Weberian View of Early Japan," 59 *Sociology of Religion* 65 (1998) (focusing in large part on legal developments); Ronen Shamir, "Formal and Substantive Rationality in American Law: A Weberian Perspective," 2 *Social & Legal Stud.* 45 (1993).

objectively assessing legal systems on the basis of Weber's categories of ratio-nality, those who build on Weber's categories risk assuming a perspective that, because of its formal and subjective character, inherently denies the possibility of any more eminent forms of rationality either being manifest or latent in the subject, trivializes the historicity of reason and the bases of that historicity, and tends, for lack of a more critical concept of reason, to miss the deeper irra-tionalities inherent in ostensibly rational institutions. The end result of follow-ing Weber can very likely be, as it is with him, a perspective that is both overly pessimistic and myopic.

An example of Weberian dualism appears in the discipline's claims of prac-tical relevance grounded in value-neutral methods, something one often finds couched in rhetoric about the purposes, functions, and usages of comparative law.[51] This approach presupposes at least a fairly rigid distinction between academic and instrumentalist inquiry, hence between objective and subjective modes of critique. Lukacs, as we have seen, would at the outset ascribe this practice to a reification of the subject-object problem, in Weber's own terms a concession to the cultural hegemony of formal rationalism. A very practical liability of this practice is to ignore (despite frequent claims to the contrary) the inevitable inter-penetration of subjective and objective issues at all stages of social inquiry. Doing so has the potential to obscure, or even falsify, the normative, political character of, in this case, comparative inquiry. More prac-tical still is the implicit affirmation of dualism, not just in the abstract, but with regard to the every-day lives of comparative scholars; the scholar is able, like Weber, to alternately hide behind the supposed neutrality of academic inquiry and the subjective license of non-academic commentary. As was clearly the case with Weber, the result in either case is to facilitate easy justification of the sometime cynical, often oblivious roles of comparative law and com-parative law scholars in the critique and affirmation of the world's legal sys-tems.

Another, perhaps more problematic, way that Weber's neo-Kantian tenden-cies are appropriated into modern categorical comparative law is in the found-ing of comparative methods on concepts like "legal families," and "legal traditions." Categorical methods of this kind are absolutely endemic to tra-ditional works in the field. Such is the methodological basis of the main intro-ductory treatise in the field, Zweigert and Kötz's *Introduction to Comparative Law*.[52] Among many other notable adherents to this method are Pierre Arminjon, Boris Nolde, and MartinWolff, Max Rheinstein, René David and John Brierley, A. G. Chloros, John Merryman, and Mary Ann Glendon, the lead

---

[51] *See, e.g.*, Zweigert & Kötz *supra* note 48, at 14–22; Kia Schadbach, "The Benefits of Comparative Law: A Continental European Perspective" 16 *B. U. Int'l L.J.* 331 (1998); Eric Stein, "Uses, Misuses and Nonuses of Comparative Law," 72 *Nw. U. L. Rev.* 198 (1977).

[52] Zweigert & Kötz, *supra* note 48.

author of the main primer on comparative law.[53] Furthermore, the lead case-book in the field advances a categorizing methodology.[54]

Categorization as such is not necessarily problematic, and nothing in the fore-going critique of Weber is intended to suggest as much. But what Weber's approach does reveal are the tendencies toward reification that inhere in overly rigid categorization. In Weber's case, this dynamic took form first as a tendency to trivialize the nuances and subtleties among legal families, as it were. Such is surely a persistent risk in modern categorical comparative law. But, as we have also seen with Weber, a still more problematic and insidious aspect of categori-cal comparative law is a tendency to deny the dynamism and historicity of legal forms. Where it follows Weber's penchant for vigorous formalization and ide-alization, modern categorical comparative law is all but certain to reduce itself to a recitation of facts, norms, and static relationships and to disengage itself from important, often quite normative insights into the future of law on every level of inquiry. As with Weber, the ultimate danger of such an approach is its tendency to comprise a theoretical affirmation of the status quo while perhaps never even acknowledging its political character.

Undoubtedly, every scholar cited above for relying on typological methods claims to be sensitive to these difficulties. Glendon's "nutshell" for example, expressly cautions students to be especially alert to the false implications of cat-egorization.[55] Notably, too, a somewhat younger set of comparativists, includ-ing Ugo Mattei and Mathias Reimann, have moved beyond confessions of unease and undertaken steps to purge this method of its problematic implica-tions.[56] Others have explicitly challenged the inconsistency of traditional methods with identity-based, non-Eurocentric, and feminist agendas.[57] Even more promisingly, some comparativists have begun to question the foundations of categorical comparative law as such. George Fletcher has recently spoken, for example, of the importance of linking comparative law to a subversive "sense of

[53] *See*, *e.g.*, Pierre Arminjon, et al., *Traité de Droit Comparé* (Paris, 1950); René David & John E. C. Brierley, *Major Legal Systems in the World Today: An Introduction to the Comparative Study of Law* (3rd ed., London, 1985); Mary Ann Glendon, et al., *Comparative Legal Traditions* (2nd ed. St. Paul, Minn., 1999); John Henry Merryman, *The Civil Law Tradition: An Introduction to the Legal Systems of Western Europe and Latin America* (2nd ed., Stanford, 1985); Max Rheinstein, "Comparative Law—Its Functions, Methods and Usages," 22 *Ark. L. Rev.* 415, 416 (1968); A. G. Chloros, "Common Law, Civil Law, and Socialist Law: Three Leading Legal Systems of the World" in *Comparative Legal Cultures* 83 (Csaba Varga ed., Aldershot, 1992).

[54] Rudolf B. Schlesinger, *Comparative Law: Cases, Texts, Materials* (5th ed., Mineola, N.Y., 1988).

[55] Glendon et al., *Comparative Legal Traditions*, *supra* note 53, at 13–14.

[56] *See*, *e.g.*, Ugo Mattei, "Three Patterns of Law: Taxonomy and Change in the World's Legal Systems," 48 *Am. J. Comp. L.* 5 (1997) (attempting to reformulate this method to transcend its Eurocentric tendencies); Mathias Reimann, "Stepping Out of the European Shadow: Why Comparative Law in the United States Must Develop its Own Agenda" 46 *Am. J. Comp. L.* 637 (1998).

[57] *See*, *e.g.*, Gunter Frankenberg, "Stranger than Paradise: Identity & Politics in Comparative Law," 1997 *Utah. L. Rev.* 259 (1997); Brenda Cossman, "Turning the Gaze Back on Itself: Comparative Law, Feminist Legal Studies, and the Postcolonial Project," 1997 *Utah. L. Rev.* 525 (1997).

our own contingency."[58] Moreover, Annelise Riles has, in an even more theoretical vein, written of the need to reformulate comparative inquiry to incorporate "a passion for looking forward, an empathy for differences but also for similarities, a faith in the self-transformative task of learning, and an interest in the form of knowledge itself."[59] And in a similarly refreshing way, the discipline has begun again to think seriously about the need to augment its work with that of other disciplines and so to transcend the legal parochialism that inheres in categorical analysis.[60]

Despite these welcome challenges, though, the immediate prospects for comparative law transcending the problems anticipated by and, to some extent, inherited from Weber, seem dim. One great problem in this regard is that unreconstructed categorization simply retains considerable hegemony, as does the appeal of Weber's underlying notion of rationality. Another more difficult problem is that where it challenges this hegemony, the discipline has not yet managed to develop a framework that consistently grasps the dynamism and historicity, or even the overall complexity, of legal norms and relationships in a comparative context. In other words, while the discipline's emerging unease about categorical comparison is quite welcome, in the long run it is crucial that the discipline eschew completely inquiry premised, like Weber's, on underlying neo-Kantian assumptions: dualism, formal rationalism, and the attendant tendencies toward static categories, rigid dichotomy, a-historical analysis, and the like. How can this be accomplished without destroying the comparative aspect of comparative law? I tentatively identify three basic operations essential to avoiding the difficulties of Weberian methods: the first operation involves rejecting formal and subjectivist conceptions of rationality for critical ones that are keyed to the dialectical interplay of subjective and objective, and formal and substantive, dynamics both in fact and as latent potentials within legal systems. The second operation is to embrace dynamism, historicity, and contingency of comparative subjects in the formulation of categories for comparative analysis. The third operation is to replace value-neutrality with value-transparency, a move that is entirely consistent with modern norms of academic objectivity and that, at a minimum, entails an acknowledgement that all comparative law scholarship and every scholar are fundamentally political. While merely identifying these operations clearly does not suffice in itself to constitute a new framework for comparative law scholarship, and is not intended as such, it seems essential to preserving the discipline's coherence and, frankly, its progressive potential. Whether the discipline survives such changes seems to me almost irrelevant in comparison.

---

[58] George P. Fletcher, "Comparative Law as a Subversive Discipline," 46 *Am. J. Comp. L.* 683 (1998).

[59] Annelise Riles, "Wigmore's Treasure Box: Comparative Law in the Age of Information," 40 *Harv. Int'l L. J.* 221, 229 (1999).

[60] *See, e.g., id. passim*; Jennifer Widner, "Comparative Politics and Comparative Law," 46 *Am. J. Comp. L.* 739 (1998).

VI. CONCLUSION

Is Weber's legacy then useless to modern legal comparativists beyond the ability to provide a set of negative examples? Not entirely. While the preceding account speaks very critically to Weber's legacy, it also, I believe, uncovers a deeper value in Weber's work, one that has lain hidden in the shadow of conventional tendencies to appropriate his work and so define his relevance. In particular, Weber's comparative law displays tremendous value in its refusal to conceal the immediate, manifest limitations of every legal tradition and every authority structure that has yet seen the light of day. To a world in which scholars and lay-people alike are increasingly disposed to satisfy themselves with some particular status quo—indeed to paint this or that legal order, traditional or modern, western or southern, in less than critical colors—this insight provides an indispensable foundation for effective inquiry. As we have seen, Weber's approach was surely conservative, but at least in an oblique and cynical way. Similarly, Weber deserves continued appreciation for locating questions of rationality at the center of comparative inquiry. Of course he shows a dubious ambivalence about the meaning of rationality. But Weber at least insists on operating within its framework, on considering at least some of reason's permutations, and in the balance doing much to expose the real impediments to a true rationalization of modern law and society. In this respect, Weber offers an important corrective to comparative law scholars who would release the discipline completely from any normative tethers whatsoever. The same can be said of Weber's overall methodology. While clearly defective, at least is has the benefit of being systematic and rigorous. Such is often sadly lacking among modern efforts in the field.

Part II

The Critique of Classicism

Fig. 1 Hermann Kantorowicz
(Reproduced by kind permission of Frank Carter)

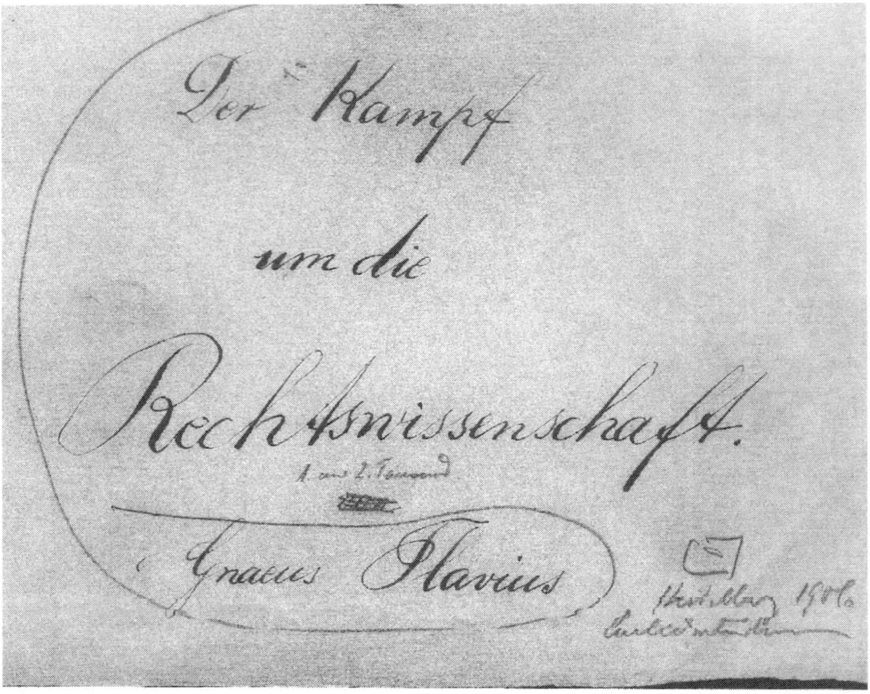

Der Kampf

um die

Rechtswissenschaft.

Gnaeus Flavius

Heidelberg 1906.

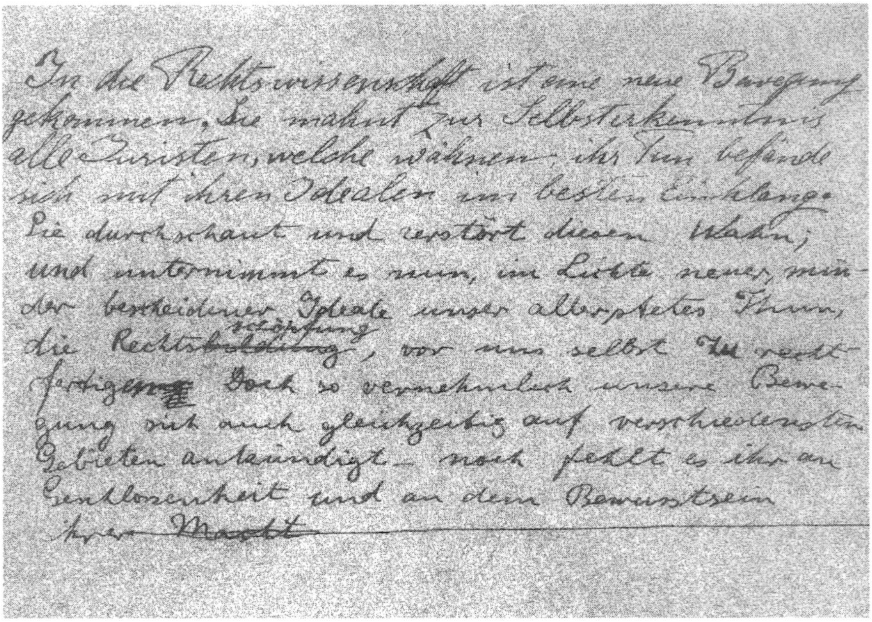

In der Rechtswissenschaft ist eine neue Bewegung gekommen. Sie mahnt zur Selbsterkenntnis alle Juristen, welche wähnen, ihr Tun befände sich mit ihren Idealen im besten Einklange. Sie durchschaut und zerstört diesen Wahn; und unternimmt es nun, im Lichte neuer, minder bescheidener Ideale unser altverpöntes Thun, die Rechtsschöpfung, vor uns selbst zu rechtfertigen. Doch so vernehmlich unsere Bewegung sich auch gleichzeitig auf verschiedensten Gebieten ankündigt – noch fehlt es ihr an Geschlossenheit und an dem Bewusstsein ihrer ~~Macht~~

Fig. 2. A Page from Hermann Kantorowicz's manuscript of *Der Kampf um die Rechtswissenschaft*

Macht. Deshalb sei hier der Versuch ge-
~~macht~~ wagt, alle ihre besten Kräfte ~~in einer~~ zur Einheit
~~Ganzheit~~ zusammen~~zufassen~~, ein Ver-
such der bewusst hinweggeht über alles,
was die einzelnen Schriftsteller von
einander scheidet, eine Ganzheit, die Einheit
nicht erwartet, als das System auch
nur eines von ihnen oder als das
Programm ihrer aller anerkannt zu
werden, und daher unter eigner Ver-
antwortung auftritt.

   ~~Begriffliche~~ Klarheit bis ins letzte
darf nicht gefordert werden; noch keine
junge Bewegung hat genau gewusst,
was sie gewollt, genau gewollt, was
sie erreicht hat. ~~Die werden Klärung eines~~
das Werk der geplanten rechtsphilosophischen
Zeitschrift und anderer eigner wie fremder

Arbeiten bleiben, von denen viele, wie wir
wissen, schon bereitstehen. Auch wolle man
nicht von einer Schrift verlangen, die
das weiteste Feld in der kürzesten Zeit
durcheilen muss, dass alles bedächtig begrün-
det und allseitig entwickelt sei, wir
müssen uns begnügen, auf das von der
Feder der Gesinnungsgenossen schon geleistete
und noch zu erwartende zu verweisen,
und nur da etwas ausführlicher geworden,
wo wir Eigenes und Neues zu bieten
hatten z. B. in der Auffassung des Natur-
rechts, in der Hervorhebung des indivi-
duellen und der voluntaristischen Momentes,
in den logischen und theologischen
Erörterungen. Endlich sei anderen

Arbeiten bleiben, von deuen viele, wie
wir wissen ~~heut stehen~~. Endlich ~~es anderen~~
überlassen im einzelnen die Verdienste
anzuzeigen die Dieser und Jener im
Reich der hier dargestellten Gedanken
als Urheber zu beanspruchen hat.

 Möge diese Schrift neue Streiter
werben für den Befreiungskampf der
Rechtswissenschaft!

~~Straßburg~~, den Februar 1906

Rethinking Hermann Kantorowicz: Free Law, American Legal Realism and the Legacy of Anti-Formalism

VIVIAN GROSSWALD CURRAN*

A BIOGRAPHICAL NOTE

Hermann Kantorowicz was born in 1877, the son of a cultivated and scholarly merchant father who seems to have remained an inspiring presence throughout his son's life.[1] A brilliant student and thinker, Kantorowicz plunged German legal theory into disarray and conflict with the pseudonymous publication in 1906 of his short book, *Der Kampf um die Rechtswissenschaft*,[2] in which he

---

* My thanks to Professors Bernhard Großfeld, Annelise Riles and James Whitman for reading earlier drafts of this chapter, and for their very helpful comments; to Professor Gerhard Hoogers, Mary Rumsey, the U.N. library in Geneva, and the Peace Palace Library in Holland for assistance in providing me with materials by Carl Schmitt; to Frank Carter, the son of Hermann Kantorowicz, for allowing me to publish the photograph which appears here, and for providing me with priceless anecdotes about his father; and to Peter Kent, a descendant of Hermann Kantorowicz from whom I have received numerous documents previously unknown to me, including correspondence by Radbruch, and who put me in touch with Kantorowicz's son. To my great astonishment, Kantorowicz's son assures me that the middle name "Ulrich," in the title of Muscheler's biography of Kantorowicz, *see infra* note 1, as well as in countless scholarly references to him, was not authentic, that Kantorowicz himself occasionally published with the letter "U.," when urged to refer to a middle initial, but that the "Ulrich" in fact is apocryphal. I therefore have deleted "Ulrich" in these pages, except where quoting others' use of it.

[1] Karlheinz Muscheler has written an informative intellectual biography of Kantorowicz, in which all of the biographical facts alluded to in this essay can be found in much expanded form, along with an overview of Kantorowicz's legal theory. See Karlheinz Muscheler, *Hermann Ulrich Kantorowicz: Eine Biographie* (Berlin, 1984). Kantorowicz was also one of the German émigrés to whom a chapter has been devoted in a recent book about the influence of German refugees on legal developments in the United States, an influence particularly marked in the field of United States comparative law. See Thomas Reiser, "Hermann Ulrich Kantorowicz," in Marcus Lutter et al. (eds), *Der Einfluß deutscher Emigranten auf die Rechtsentwicklung in den USA und in Deutschland*, 365–381 (Tübingen, 1993). Monika Frommel, a German legal scholar who has written extensively about Kantorowicz, made the following partially biographical contribution about Kantorowicz: Monika Frommel, "Hermann Ulrich Kantorowicz (1877–1940): Ein streitbarerRelativist," in Thomas Blanke et al. (eds), *Streitbare Juristen: Eine andere Tradition*, 243–252 (Baden-Baden, 1988). In addition, one of Kantorowicz's sons, Tom Carter, is currently writing a memoir of his father.

[2] Gnaeus Flavius (pseudonym for Hermann Kantorowicz), *Der Kampf um die Rechtswissenschaft* (Heidelberg, 1907) (1906).

coined the term, and both developed and advocated the concept of "free law." Like Gustav Radbruch, his close friend and occasional protector, Kantorowicz was deeply interested in (although not entirely uncritical of) the English common-law legal system, and so acquired a comparative perspective in law even before his years of exile.

Kantorowicz's political inclinations towards socialism, in combination with his Jewish heritage and non-traditional theoretical views, impeded his success in finding university positions even in Weimar Germany.[3] After a long struggle, and in large measure thanks to the intervention of Radbruch, Kantorowicz received his "call" ("*Berufung*") to join the law faculty of the University of Kiel in 1928, when he was 51 years old,[4] but his career in Germany was soon terminated by the advent of Nazism.

His political undesirability caused him to figure among the first wave of professors to be dismissed, an apparent calamity that today may well be seen as having been a blessing in disguise, since it prompted him to leave Germany in 1933, when emigration was still relatively easy.[5] He was able to reestablish a flourishing professional life in the few remaining years of his life.[6]

He first spent a year in New York, at the New School of Social Research, which had established the University of Exile to assist scholar refugees from fascism.[7] During that year, he also participated in teaching seminars at Harvard Law School with Roscoe Pound, and at Columbia Law School with Karl Llewellyn, whom he had known in Germany.[8] In 1934, Kantorowicz left the United States to make his permanent home in Cambridge, England, where he remained until his death in 1940, at the age of 63.

OVERVIEW

Hermann Kantorowicz's *Freirecht*, or "free law" theory variously has been called the inspiration for American legal realism and a culprit for the legalization

[3] For an outstanding account of the career paths and difficulties encountered by academics of Jewish origin in Weimar Germany, see Fritz Stern, *Einstein's German World* (Princeton, 1999).

[4] *See* Muscheler, *Biographie, supra* note 1, at 98.

[5] Bernd Rüthers notes that on April 13, 1933, the *Deutsche Allgemeine Zeitung* reported the dismissal of fifteen professors, including Radbruch, Kelsen and Kantorowicz. *See* Bernd Rüthers, *Entartetes Recht; Rechtslehren und Kronjuristen im Dritten Reich*, 131 (München, 1989).

[6] Muscheler notes, however, that after emigration, Kantorowicz lived in financial insecurity for the rest of his life. The professional offers he received from abroad probably saved his life but apparently were remunerated miserably. *See* Muscheler, *Biographie, supra* note 1, at 107.

[7] For more information about the University of Exile, see Gerald Gunther, *Learned Hand: The Man and the Judge*, 443–444 (New York, 1994).

[8] Indeed, it was in the course of his seminar with Llewellyn that Kantorowicz presented his criticism of American legal realism that later took written form under the title, *Some Rationalism About Realism*, about which more will be said in the following pages. *See* Hermann U. Kantorowicz, "Some Rationalism About Realism," 43 *Yale L. J.* 1240 (1934). For a discussion of German influences on Llewellyn, see Michael Ansaldi, "The German Llewellyn," 8 *Brook. L. Rev.* 705 (1992); William Twining, *Karl Llewellyn and the Realist Movement* (London, 1973); and James Whitman, "Commercial Law and the American *Volk*: A Note on Llewellyn's German Sources for the Uniform Commercial Code," 97 *Yale L. J.* 156 (1987).

of Nazi terror. Those descriptions are not inherently contradictory or mutually exclusive, since legal theory in the United States took a critical turn against legal realism after the Second World War for some of the same reasons that caused German jurists to accuse Kantorowicz (and others) of having laid the ground-work for enabling Nazi terror through law.

As will be explained more fully below, free law theory represented a radical departure from centuries-old traditional German legal theory. Like Rudolf von Jhering before him, Kantorowicz recognized the primordial and creative role of judges in deciding cases for which codified law fails to prescribe an answer. Kantorowicz privileged judicial decision-making, and developed a theoretical apparatus designed to balance the inchoate nature of tasks that fall to judges against articulated judicial obligations in performing them. Thus, he strove to systematize the judicial decision-making process in those cases situated within gaps of enacted law. By developing rules for free law adjudication, he sought to eradicate judicial abuse without denying or devaluing judicial discretion.

This essay will focus on Kantorowicz's ideas from two angles, the first of which to my knowledge has not been explored directly by legal scholarship to date, and the second of which has a long history of scholarly debate. The first is his relation to American legal realism as reflective of an unarticulated, under-lying civil-law perspective.

Kantorowicz openly took issue with American legal realism in his article, *Some Rationalism About Realism*, published in 1934, and written during the year he spent in the United States after fleeing Germany and before moving to Cambridge, England.[9] My suggestion in this essay is that Kantorowicz's differ-ences with American legal realism emanated from his fundamentally civil-law conception of law, a conception not shared by the American realists, who, as Professor Merryman has pointed out, generally were uninterested in compara-tive approaches.[10] Kantorowicz did not seem to have considered systemic dif-ferences between the civil and common law as the source of his disagreement with American legal realism. I believe, however, that those differences not only colored his reactions but that their formative, albeit unperceived, role illumin-ates aspects of both American legal realism and German free law.

The second focus of this essay is whether Kantorowicz's free law theory or movement was a causal factor in the often rabid injustice perpetrated by the German courts during the Nazi period. Both of these issues are related to each other. By examining Kantorowicz's criticism of American legal realism, one can glean the extent to which his conception of law was civilian in nature. I hope to demonstrate that those same civil-law aspects of the conception that formed the underpinnings of Kantorowicz's legal theory, underlying even his advocated *departures* from traditional civil-law practices and ideations, illuminate the unwarranted character of the accusations leveled against Kantorowicz since the

---

[9] *See* Kantorowicz, *Some Rationalism*, *supra* note 8.

[10] *See* John Henry Merryman, "Comparative Law Scholarship," 21 *Hastings Int'l. & Comp. L. Rev.* 771, 781 (1998).

Second World War, because the civil-law components of his theory were irre-concilable with the attributes his accusers associated with his views.

My discussion of free law's effect on the Nazi judiciary features within the more general and much-debated issue of legal positivism versus naturalism, and legal formalism versus anti-formalism. The arguments for and against the com-plicity of legal theory or methodology with the betrayal of principles of justice that the German courts perpetrated in the name of law from 1933 to 1945 have been debated and explicated in great and even excruciating detail for more than half a century. Scholars such as Bernd Rüthers have been arguing for many years against the post-war reaction of condemning legal positivism as the culprit responsible for the Nazi-era German court decisions, and indeed have shown that the German judicial approach during that time was far from positivistic.[11] My own view is that the exculpation of positivism can be extended to exculpat-ing legal methodology more generally. While judicial methodology is not com-pletely unrelated to substantive outcome, by itself it has not been a primary force in determining the judicial resolution of cases. The dual consequence is that, while methodology is not responsible for injustice, by the same token methodological reform cannot promise to offer a reliable solution to the prob-lem of judicial injustice.[12]

Current scholarship continues to reiterate and revive charges that target methodology, and, more specifically, to assert claims against the work of Kantorowicz that I consider unjustified and misleading. Consequently, it may be useful still today to examine the evidence, and to explore whether the phenomena

[11] *See* Bernd Rüthers, *Die unbegrenzte Auslegung: Zum Wandel der Privatrechtsordnung im Nationalsozialismus* (Tübingen, 1968) and Rüthers, *Entartetes Recht, supra* note 5. *See also* Peter Caldwell, "Legal Positivism and Weimar Democracy," 39 *Am. J. Jurisprudence* 273, 276 (1994) ("[A]s Franz Neumann and Ernst Fraenkel showed, National Socialism did not counteract the ten-dency to 'deformalize' law through the use of 'general clauses' instead of specific statutes, but actu-ally strengthened it"); *accord*, Walter Ott & Franziska Buob, "Did Legal Formalism Render German Jurists Defenceless During the Third Reich?," 2 *Soc. & Legal Studies* 91 (1993). For Frantz Neumann's concurring views on this matter, originally published in 1937, *see, e.g.,* Frantz L. Neumann, "The Change in the Function of Law in Modern Society," in William E. Scheuerman (ed.), *The Rule of Law under Siege: Selected Essays of Frantz L. Neumann and Otto Kirchheimer*, 101–141 (Berkeley, 1996). For an analysis of the antiformalist approach to law advocated by a prin-cipal figure in Nazi legal scholarship, see generally William E. Scheuerman, *Carl Schmitt: The End of Law* (Lanham, M.D., 1999). Not all of the scholars noted above made the extension from debunk-ing the myth of Nazi positivism to separating judicial methodology from substantive outcome. Rüthers' own conclusions from his study appear not to coincide entirely with my own, in both *Entartetes Recht*, as signaled by Christian Joerges, "History as Non-History: Points of Divergence and Time Lags Between Friedrich Kessler and German Jurisprudence," 42 *Am. J. Comp. L.* 163,187, n. 107 (1994); and in *Die unbegrenzte Auslegung, supra*. The overall thrust of Rüthers' thesis, how-ever, seems to me to be generally consistent with my skepticism of the relevance of the posi-tivism/naturalism issue to the injustice wrought by the Nazi-era courts.

[12] For a discussion of my views on the role of legal methodology during the Nazi era, see Vivian Grosswald Curran, *Fear of Formalism: Indications from the Period in France and Germany of Judicial Methodology's Impact on Substantive Law* (Cornell Int. L. J. (forthcoming)); and in par-ticular in the context of Vichy France, see Vivian Grosswald Curran, "The Legalization of Racism in a Constitutional State: Democracy's Suicide in Vichy France," 50 *Hastings L. J.* 1 (1998); for a thorough examination of the legal world in Vichy France, including a discussion of the role of pos-itivism, see Richard H. Weisberg, *Vichy Law and the Holocaust in France* (Amsterdam, 1996).

at issue were connected by causation or, rather, by a particular confluence of circumstances that *grosso modo* amounts to the linkage of happenstance, refuting the likelihood of a compelled or inevitable connection bridging the long and varied path from the legal theory Kantorowicz promulgated in 1906 to the substance of the judicial decisions rendered by German courts under the Third Reich.

The issue itself is of crucial importance inasmuch as unjustified conclusions may influence judicial methodology in damaging ways. In the United States, moreover, the question of appropriate judicial conduct and initiative is currently being debated in earnest.[13] Putting the issue in a reasonable perspective thus may have particular importance for the United States, where the debate about judicial interpretation has never been settled, even theoretically, and generally may be said to have remained at a more primitive stage of theoretical discussion than in the civil-law world.[14] Part of the discussion in these pages must be situated within the framework of the lengthy debate about positivism, and indeed very much hopes to contribute to it, but assumes the reader's acquaintance with the debate, and does not undertake to reiterate or summarize it.[15]

FREE LAW AND AMERICAN LEGAL REALISM

In his article criticizing American legal realism, Kantorowicz acknowledged that he had been considered a progenitor of the movement.[16] Rather than dissociating

---

[13] *See* Antonin Scalia, *A Matter of Interpretation: Federal Courts and the Law* (Princeton, 1997); Kent Greenawalt, *Legislation: Statutory Interpretation: 20 Questions* (New York, 1999); Melvin Aron Eisenberg, *The Nature of the Common Law* (Cambridge Mass., 1999); William N. Eskridge, Jr., et al., *Legislation and Statutory Interpretation* (New York, 1999); and William J. Brennan, Jr., "Reason, Passion, and 'The Progress of the Law," 10 *Cardozo L. Rev.* 3 (1988).

[14] *See* Vivian Grosswald Curran, "Romantic Common Law, Enlightened Civil Law: Legal Uniformity and the Homogenization of the European Union," 7 *Col. J. Eur. L.* 63 (2001).

[15] *See generally* the debate between Professors Hart and Fuller. H. L. A. Hart, "Positivism and the Separation of Law and Morals," 71 *Harv. L. Rev.* 593 (1958); Lon L. Fuller, "Positivism and Fidelity to Law—A Reply to Professor Hart," 71 *Harv. L. Rev.* 630 (1958); H. L. A. Hart, *Essays in Jurisprudence and Philosophy* (Oxford, 1983). For a summary of the debate in Germany, including references to much of the germane scholarship, *see* Markus Dirk Dubber, "Judicial Positivism and Hitler's Injustice," 93 *Col. L. Rev.* 1807 (1993).

[16] With characteristic modesty, Kantorowicz did not claim to have been the initiator of the free law movement, attributing its conceptual antecedents to Jhering, its development in France to Gény, and referring to its prominent followers in Germany and Austria as Ehrlich, Fuchs, Kohler, Mayer, Radbruch, Sternberg and Zitelmann. *See* Hermann Kantorowicz, "Some Rationalism About Realism," 43 *Yale L. J.* 1240, 1241 (1934). Gustav Radbruch stated, however, that Kantorowicz's 1906 book both founded the free law movement and gave it the name by which it was known throughout Germany and abroad. *See* "In memoriam Hermann Kantorowicz," in Gustav Radbruch, *Gesamtausgabe, Bd.* 16, 73 (1988) (*"seine unter dem Decknamen Gnaeus Flavius im Jahre 1906 erschienene Flugschrift: 'der Kampf um die Rechtswissenschaft' begründete die freirechtliche Bewegung und gab ihr sofort diesen Namen, unter dem sie durch Deutschland und durch das Ausland ihren Weg nahm"*). J. M. Kelly attributed the free law movement jointly to a 1903 lecture by Eugen Ehrlich and to Kantorowicz's book. *See* J. M. Kelly, *A Short History of Western Legal Theory*, 359 (Oxford, 1992). Without attributing the entire movement to Kantorowicz, Arthur Kaufmann nevertheless characterized Kantorowicz as "the most brilliant mind of the free

himself entirely from legal realism, he characterized it as a misguided outgrowth of his own insights. Referring to himself in the third person, he wrote that "for the realist exaggerations he is not responsible, although he has sometimes been praised for them. It is disagreeable enough for a man to have to pay alimony for his own illegitimate issue; but he cannot be expected to pay for other men's bastards, and like it."[17]

In a recent article, Stephen Lubben has suggested that Kantorowicz's criticism of American legal realism reflected a shift in his own theoretical outlook, a shift attributed to a *volte-face* on Kantorowicz's part due to the nascent nastiness of Nazi law and judicial conduct already visible in 1933 at the time of his writing: in other words, an alleged reaction by Kantorowicz to grasping free law's dangerous potential, which, if accurate, would have mirrored the sentiment that was to become widespread in post-war Germany, and would have anticipated the very accusations that were to be leveled against him after 1945 by those who asserted that free law played a role in Nazi judicial injustice.[18]

Such a reading of Kantorowicz's 1933 (published in 1934) article is understandable, particularly in light of the fact that one can identify statements in his earlier work that seem less incompatible with legal realism than what appeared in 1934, and also because his article criticizing American legal realism both explicitly and implicitly bears the imprint of his concern about legal developments in Nazi Germany. Despite the seductive ease of explanation offered by the interpretation that Kantorowicz's views underwent a shift with the advent of Nazism, on the whole the argument is at odds with the content of his earlier work.

In particular, when one considers *Der Kampf um die Rechtswissenschaft*,[19] his influential and highly controversial 1906 book in which he famously expounded his ideas of free law, and if one compares it with one of his last publications, the 1934 criticism of legal realism in *Some Rationalism About*

---

law movement" ("*der brillianteste Kopf der Freirechtsbewegung*"). Arthur Kaufmann, "Problemgeschichte der Rechtsphilosophie," in Arthur Kaufmann & Winfried Hassemer (eds), *Einführung in Rechtsphilosophie und Rechtstheorie der Gegenwart*, 30, 146 (Heidelberg, 1994).

[17] Kantorowicz, *Some Rationalism*, supra note 8, at 1242 (footnote omitted that supports his statement of having been praised for a brand of realism that he did not espouse).

[18] *See* Stephen J. Lubben, "Chief Justice Traynor's Contract Jurisprudence and the Free Law Dilemma: Nazism, the Judiciary, and California's Contract Law," 7 *S. Cal. Interdis. L. J.* 81, 94 (1998) (citing as support Edgar Bodenheimer, *Jurisprudence: The Philosophy and Method of the Law*, 117, n. 8) (Cambridge, Mass., & London, 1962). It is interesting to note that the same theory is frequently put forth that Radbruch's alleged anti-positivism in the wake of Nazism represented a radical departure from his pre-war outlook. For a persuasive presentation of the view, dovetailing my own about Kantorowicz, that Radbruch's outlook essentially remained unchanged by the war, see Arthur Kaufmann, "Problemgeschichte der Rechtsphilosophie," 30, 108–115, in *Einführung in Rechtsphilosophie*, supra note 16, at 108–115. *Accord*, Monika Frommel, "Hermann Ulrich Kantorowicz: Ein Rechtstheoretiker zwischen allen Stühlen," in Helmut Heinrichs et al. (eds), *Deutsche Juristen Jüdischer Herkunft*, 631, 638 (München, 1993). For an overview of the German literature on this issue, see Stanley L. Paulson, "Lon L. Fuller, Gustav Radbruch, and the 'Positivist' Theses," 13 *L. & Phil.* 313, 320 (1994), and sources cited therein.

[19] Kantorowicz, *Der Kampf*, supra note 2.

Realism,[20] one finds fundamental consistency between the two expositions. The emphases differ, each work being geared to a significantly different anticipated readership and reflecting differing authorial objectives, but the two texts supplement and enrich, rather than contradict, each other.[21]

Already in *Der Kampf um die Rechtswissenschaft*, Kantorowicz defined free law as that which emerged to fill in gaps in the law; thus, not as the bulk or primary component of law. He made clear that the contribution of free law was not to replace the contemporaneous idea of law, except inasmuch as the prevailing German (and French) legal theoretical outlook denied that enacted law contained any gaps.[22] That free law was no more than a gap-filling measure was given far more emphasis in the later article, where his objective was to underscore his differences with American legal realism. The gap-filling nature of free law was also fundamental in his 1906 writing, but in 1906 his fight was with those who denied that enacted law left, or should leave, any opening whatsoever for the creation of novel law, so in 1906 Kantorowicz emphasized the space in which free law was to operate, rather than the area that surrounded it. He thus de-emphasized that ocean of official law in which a relatively small island of free law was needed.

In his view, American legal realism had lost its perspective because it focused only on the inner circle, eradicating the principal area of legal activity to concentrate exclusively on a space that had been his own focus also, but that never would, could nor should define the totality of the legal universe. Thus, he insisted in his 1934 piece that free law occupied no more than the interstices of formal law.[23] Perhaps most dramatically, he explicitly stated in 1934 (as he did not in 1906) that free law's "validity is far less than that of the formal law . . ."[24] and that "[t]he law is not what the courts administer but the courts are the institutions which administer the law."[25]

It is my view that he did not make such statements as explicitly in 1906 principally because the context of the time and place were such that none among the

---

[20] Kantorowicz, *Some Rationalism*, *supra* note 8.

[21] I do not mean to take the position that Kantorowicz's views of free law remained identical and unmodified over the course of his life. Rather, I argue here that his later work was not substantially inconsistent with his earlier free law renditions; and, more specifically, that political changes in Germany after Hitler's takeover were not the cause of the differences in his 1906 and 1934 presentations of free law, nor did those differences in focus signify his rejection of the fundamentals of free law that he expounded in 1906. While I focus on only two of his writings in arguing against substantial change on Kantorowicz's part with respect to free law, I also believe that other texts he wrote between 1906 and 1934 confirm a fundamental substantive consistency. I do not deal with them in this particular argument, because most, like his 1906 book, pre-date Hitler's advent to power, and I am arguing specifically against the view that his 1934 article represents a change in his legal theory attributable to his own reaction against Nazism.

[22] "*Aus freiem Recht endlich muß das Gesetz in sich geschlossen werden, müssen seine Lücken ausgefüllt werden. Hier stoßen wir auf das Dogma von der Lückenlosigkeit des Gesetzes. . . .*" Kantorowicz, *Der Kampf, supra* note 2, at 14.

[23] *See* Kantorowicz, *supra* note 8, at 1241.

[24] *See id.*

[25] *Id.* at 1250.

anticipated readers of *Der Kampf um die Rechtswissenschaft* would have been remotely inclined even to consider free law as a replacement for enacted law, obviating any need for Kantorowicz to articulate that it was not. The revolutionary impact of Kantorowicz's 1906 writing was to create and further awareness of the legitimate operation of elusive, informal and fluctuating forces within a codified system of law.[26] What he sought to define and advocate was a phenomenon that might be described in Peircean terms as "not rational, yet capable of rationalization."[27] He waged his struggle against the constricting blindness of an academic legal scholarship that was pitted against the recognition of the legitimacy of fluid, dynamic social and even psychological considerations in judicial decision-making, not because he opposed systematization and judicial objectivity, but, rather, precisely because his opponents' stubborn refusal to acknowledge those forces *precluded* the systematization of the latter that Kantorowicz deemed necessary in order to maintain objectivity in judicial methodology, and balance among judicial decisions, enacted law and evolving social needs.[28]

Similarly, Kantorowicz's adamant insistence on systematization was less apparent in 1906 than in 1934. While his theory of free law was no less systematized in 1906 than in 1934, in 1906 he was struggling against what he perceived to be a claustrophobic, absolutist and excessive systematization of traditional code theory, the *Geschlossenheitstheorie* of "the formalistic schools [which] consider the formal law as a closed system free of gaps and contradictions. . . ."[29] By contrast, in 1934 he was seeking to debunk what he viewed as the equally unreasonable and unwarranted disorganization and lack of systematization of the American legal realist understanding of law. Thus, his theory of free law remained largely consistent and constant over the intervening decades, but the strikingly different external contexts which spawned the works of 1906 and 1934 tended to obfuscate the constancy of his view of free law because of the contrasting points he expressed in each.

Kantorowicz's view of free law was ultimately civilian, not only in its adherence to the general view of law as official, with the exception, rather than the norm being that which was not official law,[30] but also in its insistence on systematization and objectivity, in keeping with the civil-law scientization, or

---

[26] The same may be said of his 1928 article, co-authored with Edwin Patterson, in which he wrote that "[f]ree law is of infinitely greater practical importance than formal law, a lawsuit being generally superfluous if the case in question is really determined by genuine formal law." Hermann U. Kantorowicz & Edwin W. Patterson, "Legal Science—A Summary of Its Methodology," 28 *Col. L. Rev.* 679, 692 (1928).

[27] Charles S. Peirce, 5 *Collected Papers*, 119 (1934–48), quoted in Umberto *Eco, Kant and the Platypus: Essays on Language and Cognition*, 101 (Alastair McEwen trans., London, 2000).

[28] He stated his objective as a battle of liberation for legal science: "*Möge diese Schrift neue Schreiter werben für den Befreiungskampf der Rechtswissenschaft, für den Sturm auf die letzte Bastion der Scholastik.*" Kantorowicz, *Der Kampf*, *supra* note 2, at 6.

[29] Kantorowicz & Patterson, *supra* note 26, at 701.

[30] Kantorowicz's concept of "formal" law extended beyond statutory law. *See*, *e.g.*, *id*. at 692–699.

"*Verwissenschaftlichung*," of law associated, among others, with Continental Europe's reception of Roman law.[31] For Kantorowicz, legal science, or "*Rechtswissenschaft*," was "a rational and normative science which tries to transform the given law into a more or less consistent system of rules."[32]

The first criticism he leveled against American legal realism, namely, that the realists mistakenly saw law as "not a body of rules but of facts,"[33] was imbued with the civilian legal mentality, although, significantly, throughout his analysis, he did not attribute the differences between American legal realism and German free law to features distinguishing the common law from the civil law.[34] He did state with considerable insight that "[t]he realist movement could start and progress only in a case law country because there indeed the law seems to be a heap of decisions, and therefore a body of facts."[35] In the next sentence, however, he insisted that the realists were incorrect *even within the framework of the common law*: "But the cases themselves are not binding; they are not the case law; only the *rationes decidendi* are binding."[36]

Kantorowicz criticized the realists' factual conception of law as unwarranted from two vantage points: as an erroneous failure to distinguish facts from law; and as a failure to conceive of law as "an Ought."[37] His ultimate argument as to the American legal realist failure to see that law and fact are distinguishable reflects what may have been his own failure to grasp the profound and necessary interconnectedness of the two in common-law legal systems.[38] He believed that the realists erred in not understanding that *cases* are distinguishable from *case law*, and that the binding nature of precedents is limited to their *rationes decidendi*, abstract propositions of law purified of facts through their formulation as normative principles.[39]

From a more common-law perspective, the very distinction in the common-law legal world between holding and dictum suggests the conclusion that the common-law *ratio decidendi* is not free of factual baggage. Only that portion of the common-law court's decision that relates to the actual, factual circumstances precisely before the adjudicating court can acquire the binding force of

---

[31] *See* Michael Stolleis, *The Law Under the Swastika: Studies on Legal History in Nazi Germany*, 58–61 (Thomas Dunlap trans., Chicago, 1998); Franz Wieacker, *A History of Private Law in Europe*, 7 (Tony Weir trans., Oxford, 1995); and Geoffrey Samuel, "Can Gaius Really Be Compared to Darwin," 49 *Int. & Comp. L. Q.* 297, 305 (2000). For the argument that the civil-law mentality is closely related to Enlightenment modes of thinking, including the Enlightenment's endorsement of reason and scientific method, *see* Curran, *Romantic Common Law*, *supra* note 14.

[32] Kantorowicz, *Some Rationalism*, *supra* note 8, at 1248.

[33] *Id.* at 1240.

[34] *Id.*

[35] *Id.* at 1250.

[36] *Id.*

[37] *Id.* at 1240–1243.

[38] For the converse examination of an American jurist's view of German legal theory, *see* Mathias W. Reimann, "Holmes' *Common Law* and German Legal Science," in Robert W. Gordon (ed.), *The Legacy of Oliver Wendell Holmes, Jr.*, 72, 96 (Edinburgh, 1992) (describing Holmes' rendition of German legal science in *The Common Law* as "dramatically misleading").

[39] *See* Kantorowicz, *Some Rationalism*, *supra* note 8, at 1240–1243.

precedential authority for future cases.[40] From a common-law perspective, the significance of a precedent can never divest itself of the factual trappings that cling to it, define it, situate and lend meaning to it, trappings that may be most remote from the true facts of the parties' lived experiences, but facts nevertheless, inasmuch as they are those circumstances encoded in and by the court record, a narrative which represents itself as truth, and which defines, petrifies and perpetuates as proven facts evidence first deemed admissible, and subsequently deemed credible.[41] No matter the degree of abstraction of the formulation of a common-law *ratio decidendi*, its influence on the future will be diminished and even nullified to the extent that a court in a subsequent pending case finds and defines the facts of the pending case to be different from those of the prior one.

Kantorowicz's summary of the legal force of precedents as uninhibited by factual attributes in common-law theory is thus an argument that bespeaks of both the civil-law conception of law in general, and, more particularly, a civil-law perception of the common law. One can observe a similar civilian outlook today in contemporary Italy's view of precedents: the case law of the Italian court of cassation is transcribed as *massime*, principles of law extracted from the case law but denuded of factual attributes, transmuted into civilian-style normative legal principles, and, perhaps most significantly of all, applicable to future factually similar *as well as to factually dissimilar* cases.[42]

From his initial premise that precedential authority is not factual by virtue of acquiring legal force only after transmutation into normative, decontextualized legal rules, Kantorowicz deduced that the American legal realists were perpetrating a logical fallacy of such magnitude as to eviscerate the very possibility of *stare decisis* and precedential authority. With flawless deductive reasoning, he nevertheless reached a conclusion that might be challenged from a common-law perspective as stemming from a dubious premise: "[T]he whole temple of case law is founded upon a rule and not upon a fact. Those who deny that rules are binding can hardly admit the binding force of precedents, which they profess to worship. Thus they destroy the Law itself."[43]

Kantorowicz similarly chided the realists for what he saw as their failure to understand that judicial authority did not trump legislation, even if one posited that judicial interpretation eventually and ultimately defined the meaning of legislation. He believed that the realists' error in considering the judicial decision

---

[40] For a more detailed discussion of this common-law attribute, inextricably linking fact to law and vice versa, *see* Curran, "Romantic Common Law," supra note 14.

[41] The potential for court renditions that are remote indeed from the parties' lived experiences in no small part is due to the adversarial nature of common-law proceedings, such that the only proffered facts from which the court may select its own, definitive version, are "framed by [the] adversaries who construct narratives to persuade the judge or jury." Martha L. Minow & Elizabeth V. Spelman, "Passion for Justice," 10 *Cardozo L. Rev.* 37, 47 (1988).

[42] *See* Michele Taruffo & Massimo La Torre, "Precedent in Italy," in D. Neil MacCormick & Robert S. Summers (eds), *Interpreting Precedents: A Comparative Study*, 141 (Aldershot, 1997).

[43] Kantorowicz, *Some Rationalism*, supra note 8, at 1251.

to be supreme was evident by virtue of the indisputable fact that "every statute was once a new statute."[44] In a section he called "*Reductio ad Absurdum,*" Kantorowicz again displayed a primarily civilian conception of legal reasoning, ignoring the extreme difficulty that common-law judges experience in undertaking an adjudication that cannot rely on reasoning by analogy to the factually defined, factually situated law of analogous cases, or on the intricate, detailed processes of comparison and distinction that is the common law's *modus operandi.*[45]

Kantorowicz's assertion in typical civil-law fashion did not consider that common-law judges are prone to finding a way to reason by analogy to case law even where a statute is brand new, and has no prior history of case adjudication. One resolution to the dilemma of having no official precedential authority is the frequent common-law judicial custom of relaxing the hierarchical rules of precedential authority and analogizing to cases decided in "foreign" (*i.e.*, other state) jurisdictions in which similarly or, preferably, identically-worded statutes have been enacted and already adjudicated. Although devoid of officially binding legal authority, such "foreign" cases offer the common-law courts the opportunity to engage in the sole reasoning processes that they are adept at implementing.

The same is true for the common-law lawyers who argue a case governed by a new statute. The common-law legal mind is so attuned to conceiving of law and legal reasoning as dependent upon using factually-clothed norms in a process of comparison in which deduction takes the back seat to intricate, *va-et-vient* analogy, that lawyers present the law to judges on the basis of whatever analogies may be argued, straying ever further from theoretically authoritative or cognizable precedents when officially binding case law is scarce or nonexistent.

Judges for their part tend to accept those arguments as the ones most capable of offering legal illumination. If one views analogizing to precedents as the grammar of the common law, in the manner in which semioticians refer to underlying, systematizing grammars of meaning creation and transmittal, then one may perceive the language of analogy, of detailed, concrete, particularized factual patterns, and of law as inextricably embedded in factual settings, as the only language the common-law jurist speaks fluently. Thus, the judicial construction of an essentially fictitious body of technically "foreign" precedents when adjudicating cases governed by new statutes would not be seen from a common-law perspective as an attempt by the courts to undermine legislation, or to assert the judiciary's primacy among the separated powers of government; it would signify, rather, the common-law courts' attempt to understand and decode enacted law by proceeding along the lines it knows best how to follow.

---

[44] Kantorowicz, *Some Rationalism, supra* note 8, at 1251.
[45] *See id.* For a more detailed discussion of this issue, see Curran, "Romantic Common Law," *supra* note 14.

Kantorowicz's criticism that American legal realism neglected to define law as "an Ought,"[46] also may be seen in light of his civil-law outlook; and, more specifically, of the Continental European tradition of codified law as emblematic of the national legal spirit, an embodiment of what should be, from whose tenets the resolution of cases is to be deduced. The common-law tradition stands in contrast to this conception of law inasmuch as its norms are inducible from the multitude of factually-spawned and factually-characterized norms that are the rules of each case, ideally harmonizable into a mosaic of cohesive legal principles in a process of ongoing, *a posteriori* norm construction.[47]

This rendition is a simplification, in the sense that common-law judicial decisions operate under governing norms, but those few, organic norms are not equivalent to the enveloping normative umbrella of Continental civil codes. In his excellent overview and analysis of the problematic of the normative in law, Arnold Brecht compared Kantorowicz's notion of the normative nature of law to the phenomenologist concession that what is ethical or desirable is not universal, "that immediate evidence may differ among individuals and races and may reveal only what is 'good for me.'"[48] Brecht analogized this phenomenologist perspective to what he most aptly called Kantorowicz's "neutral relativism."[49]

Kantorowicz's insistence on a fluid, socially responsive judiciary and the importance of a free law based on innumerable ineffable qualities represented a departure from and a disruption of traditional civil law perceptions, but also simultaneously remained within the civilian legal mentality inasmuch as he sought systematization in a manner not unlike the systematization to which the civil codes of Continental Europe aspire. Codification's aspirations to systematization may seem inherently contradictory to judicial flexibility and freedom, except if one remembers that generality of expression and fluidity in the attribution of novel circumstances to prior norms are an essential part of the modern era of successful codes, from the *Code Napoléon* to the *Bürgerliches Gesetzbuch*, in contrast to prior failed codes such as the Prussian *Allgemeines Landrecht*, which had been unsuccessful precisely due to excessive specification, stemming from the legislative ambition of micromanaging the future.[50] Thus, modern codification contains an inherent tension between, on the one hand, insistence on the dominance and pervasiveness of the textual command, with its corollary self-representation of being a closed, contained system; and, on the other hand, allowance for judicial manœuvering within the room afforded by loosely-expressed textual guidelines.

---

[46] Kantorowicz, *Some Rationalism*, *supra* note 8, at 1243
[47] *See*, *e.g.*, Curran, "Romantic Common Law," *supra* note 14.
[48] Arnold Brecht, "The Myth of *Is* and *Ought*," 54 *Harv. L. Rev.* 811, 825 (1941).
[49] *Id*. at 825, n. 43.
[50] *See* Reinhard Zimmermann, "An Introduction to German Legal Culture," in Werner F. Ebke & Matthew W. Finkin (eds), *Introduction to German Law* (The Hague, 1966); Eugen Ehrlich, "The Sociology of Law," 36 *Harv. L. Rev.* 130 (1922).

Free law for Kantorowicz combined both freedom, as its name suggests—that open space in which and from which justice could be fashioned—with a systematization that offered objectivity without unnecessary constraint.[51] For both Kantorowicz and his contemporary Eugen Ehrlich, the connection and harmonization between these seemingly paradoxical attributes were to be found in the person of the judge. Ehrlich and Kantorowicz stressed the importance of superior judges, both in terms of intellectual capacity and impeccability of character. Being indispensable and inevitable, judicial discretion in their view was to be embraced rather than shunned or, still worse, denied. But in order for judicial discretion to be warranted and to avoid the pitfalls of judicial abuse, the judges, as Kantorowicz put it, "[o]f course [are to be] only the best judges."[52]

That the majority of Germany's judges fell far short of Kantorowicz's standard became clear in the years that followed. Post-war criticism against Kantorowicz has suffered from failing to differentiate between judicial discretion and judicial abuse, and from failing to address the problem of the inevitability of judicial discretion under any legal system. It also fails to offer persuasive arguments to support a conclusion that justice is more likely to be furthered where judicial discretion is eradicated in favor of (presumably) legislative control. The next section addresses Kantorowicz's theory in light of post-war criticism of free law.

FREE LAW AND TYRANNY

Kantorowicz saw no necessary correlation between judicial discretion and judicial arbitrariness. He appreciated the danger of judicial excess that could not be separated from granting discretion to judges, and indeed saw the free law movement as indispensable to creating a system of judicial discretion that constrained judges by requiring an objective, rational and non-arbitrary application of free law. He defined free law as follows:

> "The traditional sources of the law, the 'formal' law, . . . have gaps which must be filled up, must be filled up with law if the decision is to be a judicial decision, and this law must have a general character if equality before the law is to be maintained; the gap-filling material must therefore consist of rules, of rules of law. These are 'free' law in the sense that they are not formal law: they have not been formalized but are still in a state of transition like bills, principles of policy, business customs, inarticulate convictions,

---

[51] For a sense of the degree to which Kantorowicz believed in systematization, *see* Karlheinz Muscheler, *Relativismus und Freirecht: Ein Versuch über Hermann Kantorowicz* (Heidelberg, 1984). For the limits to Kantorowicz's belief in systematization, *see* Frommel, "Ein Rechtstheoretiker," *supra* note 18, at 635.

[52] Kantorowicz, "Some Rationalism," *supra* note 8, at 1244. *See also* Kantorowicz, *Der Kampf*, *supra* note 2, at 42–45; and Eugen Ehrlich, "Judicial Freedom of Decision: Its Principles and Objects," in *Science of Legal Method*, 47, 74 (Ernest Bruncken & Layton B. Register trans., New York, 1969) (1917) ("The principle of free decision is generally not concerned with the substance of the law, but with the proper selection of judges").

emotional preferences. Many of them are formulated for the purpose of a concrete judicial decision by the courts, acting within their discretion, through acts of will and value-judgments, and constitute therefore judge-made law. Their validity is far less than that of the formal law and sometimes nil, but their practical importance is even greater, because where the formal law is clear and complete, litigation is not likely to occur."[53]

Elsewhere, he summarized that "[l]aw is either formal law, i.e., law having undergone and completed a definite process of formation or integration, or 'free law,' i.e., law which has not completed these processes."[54]

In conjunction with his intention of blending objectivity and systematization in free law with its murky, indefinable and fluctuating elements, Kantorowicz stressed that judicial "discretion is not opposed to rules, as is usually said; it is an intuitive way of finding rules. . . ."[55] In his tribute to Kantorowicz after Kantorowicz's death, Radbruch asserted that free law did not endanger certainty or security in law because it remained bound by rules, and therefore could not be characterized as the arbitrary, subjective creation of judges.[56] Free law was a force in mitigating the chaotic and the unpredictable in law. It did not pretend to eliminate either. Its critics often illogically and unwarrantedly equated its *acknowledgment* of the inevitable element of uncertainty, of what escapes foreseeability and regulation, with the *promotion* or *advocacy* of those attributes.

Kantorowicz's theory was a subtle brew of belief in objectivity, rationality and the possibility of neutral justice, with the perception that even at a theoretical level, law was, and had to be, attuned to its place and time. Thus, it never can reach a state of immutable perfection, and transitions at all levels of law, including philosophical underpinnings, ceaselessly affect and transform it.[57] As he put it, "the objective validity of the values does not necessarily imply their universality, *i.e.*, their equally obligatory character for everybody."[58] It is most interesting to consider the approving nature of some of his references to natural law, especially in light of his own "neutral relativism"[59] and post-war criticism, particularly by German jurists advocating a return to natural law principles.[60]

Kantorowicz was an opponent of natural law in the sense of opposing the view that there are immutable, absolutist principles that can be relied on throughout time. Far from condemning natural law wholesale, however, he

[53] Kantorowicz, "Some Rationalism," *supra* note 8, at 1241. For a more detailed, supplementary presentation of both free law and formal law, *see* Kantorowicz & Patterson, *supra* note 26, at 692–699. *Cf.* Oliver Wendell Holmes, Jr., *The Common Law and Other Writings*, 127 (Birmingham Ala., 1982) ("legal, like natural divisions, however clear in their general outline, will be found on exact scrutiny to end in a penumbra or debatable land").

[54] Kantorowicz & Patterson, *supra* note 26, at 692.

[55] *Id.* at 1244.

[56] *See* Radbruch, *Gesamtausgabe*, *supra* note 16, at 77.

[57] *See* "Die neue Auffassung," in Kantorowicz, *Der Kampf*, *supra* note 2, at 10–47.

[58] Kantorowicz & Patterson, *supra* note 26, at 684.

[59] *See* Brecht, *supra* note 48.

[60] For the principal German natural-law proponents after the Second World War, *see* Rüthers, *Die unbegrenzte Auslegung*, *supra* note 11, at 448.

depicted natural law theory in its own socio-historical context, suggesting its propriety for its own time, but also that its time had passed.[61] In particular, he characterized natural law as an idea of law that was independent of state power, an expression of law through its philosophers that could even be considered as a form of free law.[62] Kantorowicz valued natural law for its insight that state power is not the sole source and form of law.[63]

This belief stood in stark and irreconcilable conflict with the Nazi legal theory of *Führerprinzip* that all law emanated from the state, as embodied by the *Führer*.[64] As Professor Whitman has observed, it would be a mistake merely to equate the *Führerprinzip* with the will of Hitler, inasmuch as Nazi legal theory conceived of the principle as one which commanded judges to decide cases as if the *Führer* had pronounced his opinion of the relevant legal issues, regardless of whether he had in fact done so.[65] This interpretive approach is reminiscent of some United States' interpretive theory, as well as of the explicit directive that the Swiss Civil Code gives judges to interpret legislative gaps in the manner they believe the legislator would resolve them.

On the other hand, the *Führerprinzip* remains in conflict with free law by virtue of its tenet that the state was the sole legitimate source of law.[66] One might dispute that assertion by pointing to the explicit references to the German people, the *Volk*, as the source of National Socialist law, in conjunction with the state. In his 1934 *Nationalsozialismus und Völkerrecht*, for example, Carl Schmitt asserted that the new National Socialist legal order was founded on the twin rights of state and Volk.[67] In *Der Führer schützt das Recht*, Schmitt further articulated that the *Volk*'s right to exist was the source of all law.[68] To the extent, however, that the Nazi political system rendered the *Volk* a nullity by depriving the German population of its freedom of political and other expression, and of the right to elect representatives and thereby to influence the legal order, the net result of Schmitt's theory was that the sole source of law in fact

---

[61]   See Kantorowicz, *Der Kampf, supra* note 2, at 10–11. *See also* Curran, "Romantic Common Law," *supra* note 14. For the not dissimilar perspective of natural law by an American legal realist, *see* William Twining, *Karl Llewellyn and the Realist Movement*, 187 (London 1973).

[62]   *See supra* note 2, at 10–11.

[63]   *See id.*

[64]   *See* Arthur Kaufmann, "National Socialism and German Jurisprudence from 1933–1945," 9 *Cardozo L. Rev.* 1629, 1637–1641 (1988). Bernd Rüthers essentially concludes that the *Führerprinzip* was the ultimate, highest legal norm, surpassing all others, of the Nazi-era German judicial methodology. *See* Rüthers, *Die unbegrenzte Auslegung, supra* note 11, at 105.

[65]   The reference to Professor Whitman's statement is from a communication of June 26, 2000.

[66]   Some of free law's critics seem to ignore that free law scholars not only did not exalt the state, but, indeed, saw in free law an *alternative* to state power. *See infra* notes 79–93, and surrounding texts. Okko Behrends attacks free law on the (in my view) entirely erroneous perception of free law as a total surrender to the state. *See* Okko Behrends, "Von der Freirechtsbewegung zum konkreten Ordnungs- und Gestaltungsdenken," in Ralf Dreier & Wolfgang Sellert (eds), *Recht und Justiz im "Dritten Reich"*, 38, 70 (Frankfurt, 1989).

[67]   *See* Carl Schmitt, *Nationalsozialismus und Völkerrecht*, 5–7 (Berlin, 1934).

[68]   Carl Schmitt, "Der Führer schützt das Recht: Zur Reichstagsrede Adolf Hitlers vom 13. Juli 1934," 15 *Deutsche Juristen-Zeitung* 945, 947 (1934) ("*Alles Recht stammt aus dem Lebensrecht des Volkes*").

was the state, as personified by the *Führer*, except in the *Volk's* initial role as alleged inspiration for the *Führer*.[69]

The substantive nullification of the *Volk* as a player or even viable source in Nazi law was evident from the Nazi view that a total fusion of law, state, power and legal legitimacy occurred in the *Führer*.[70] First Schmitt asserted that state and *Volk* had merged in and through National Socialism.[71] He then equated the *Führer* with law itself, such that the *Führer* was not to be deemed to be acting under or according to the law, but, rather, *was* the law.[72] According to this theory, the *Führer* was the supreme judge. Not only was his role that of law-giver and law-decider, but no other judge had the capacity to realize the law ("*Recht*") as well as he.[73] Schmitt's initial statement of the *Volk's* right to life as a constitutive basis of law seemed to fuse with an unchallengeable (and unverifiable) faith of the people in the *Führer* as the immutable source of a unified, gapless politico-socio-legal order in which the *Führer's* supreme, inter-pretive, legitimating and generative power over law and society was part of a closed system with no mechanism for continued responsiveness to the *Volk*.

Thus, to the extent that one interprets the *Führerprinzip* as incorporating the *Volk's* customs and beliefs by virtue of the *Führer's* synechdocic embodiment of his people, as well as by his adoption of the *Volk's* desires in forging the new legal order, one can argue that the *Führerprinzip* extended indirectly beyond representing the state as sole source of law. To the extent, however, that the *Volk* in reality was a sham construct, no legitimizing entity was left other than the all-encompassing state. The fluid Nazi concept was as ineffable as that of the religious trinity, combining glorification of the *Volk*, identification of *Führer* with *Volk*, and submission of all to the one, with quasi-religious pretensions to the sort of total solutions that Kantorowicz was intent on debunking.[74]

One of the difficulties in dealing with fascist legal theory is the gap between theory and practical meaning. The exalted role of the *Volk* in Nazi German legal theory on its face might bespeak of a novel conceptualization of democracy,

---

[69] For confirmation that, after the Nazi takeover, Schmitt abandoned his former advocacy of democracy through representation, see *Zusammenfassung; i.e.*, the German-language summary of the publication in Dutch by H. G. Hoogers, *De Verbeeding van het Souvereine* (Deventer, 1995) (Hooger's German-language summary on file with author).

[70] *See* Schmitt, *supra* note 68. In this article, Schmitt defended Hitler's order to murder Röhm and others. For an analysis of Schmitt's support of the Führer's right to murder, and of Schmitt's role in Germany after 1934, *see* Rüthers, *Entartetes Recht, supra* note 5, at 120–123.

[71] *See* Schmitt, *supra* note 68, at 947.

[72] *See id.*

[73] *See id.*, at 949. ("*Der Führer der Bewegung hat als solcher eine richterliche Aufgabe, deren inneres Recht von keinem anderen verwirklicht werden kann.*") *Accord*, Carl Schmitt, "Aufgabe und Notwendigkeit des Deutschen Rechtsstandes," 6 *Deutsches Recht* 181, 184 (1936) ("*Der Führer ist nicht Staatsorgan, sondern oberster Gerichtsherr der Nation und höchster Gesetzgeber. . . .*"), *quoted in* Rüthers, *Entartetes Recht, supra* note 5, at 109.

[74] *See* Schmitt, *supra* note 68. For Kantorowicz's position, *see* Kantorowicz, *Der Kampf, supra* note 2, at 35. For an additional portrayal from the Nazi legal vantage point of the tripartite fusion, by a law professor at the University of Kiel, the very university from whose faculty Kantorowicz had been dismissed one year earlier, *see* Ernst Rudolf Huber, "Die Einheit der Staatsgewalt," 15 *Deutsche Juristen-Zeitung* 950 (1934).

except that the theory was written at a time in which the *Volk* was not accorded a political voice. The *Volk* was advanced as the source of legitimacy and of law despite being relegated to an existence limited to (and eviscerated by) the quasi-religious identity theory, which allowed it no independence from the *Führer* or, thereby, from the state. While many of the statements of Nazi legal theory have an apparent surface appeal, it seems to me impossible to divorce the texts from their context, not only because in fact the German population had no voice under Hitler, but also, and even primarily, because the Nazi German legal theorists were writing within the context of that situation, in full knowledge, approval and contemplation of that situation.

The concrete basis for concluding that Hitler was fused with and infused by the *Volk* was the flimsy and fundamentally spurious pretense of Hitler's initial and continuing legitimation as the alleged people's choice. Thus, while the exalted role of *Volk* in the writings of Herder and of Savigny seems to me to suggest genuinely interesting, valuable and valid possibilities for legal structuring, it seems to me unjustifiable to try to divorce word from context in the writings of the Nazi legal theorists whose idea of *Volk* allowed for no component of elected political representation.[75]

The Nazi view of law ("*Recht*") was of an order so imbued with the inner logic and consistency of its National Socialist tenets as to be self-contained in a manner reminiscent of the traditional, pre-Nazi civil-law conception of law as gapless and internally consistent. In the words of Carl Schmitt, National Socialist law ("*Recht*") had "its own, inner logic and consistency."[76] Schmitt referred continually to National Socialist *Geschlossenheit*.[77] Free law sought to demythologize just such a view of law's nature and capacity in the context of the traditional civilian conception of law under codified legal régimes.

Just as he had done with natural law, Kantorowicz also explained legal positivism in its historical context, valid as the nineteenth century's needed correction of natural law, but exaggerated and excessive in its devalorization of natural law. According to Kantorowicz, the positivists correctly reacted against the naturalistic flaws of positing law as capable of immutable perfection, and essentially advocating legal stasis.[78] In his view, the positivists erred, however, in portraying natural law only in terms of what it was *not*, only from the perspective of its inability to sustain its promise of universality and perfectibility, an error that consisted in the positivists' overlooking the contribution natural

---

[75] For a discussion of Herder and his legal progeny in terms of the fascist turn of events in Europe, *see* Vivian Grosswald Curran, "Herder and the Holocaust: A Debate About Difference and Determinism in the Context of Comparative Law," in F. C. DeCoste & Bernard Schwartz, (eds), *The Holocaust's Ghost: Writings on Art, Politics, Law and Education*, 399–410 (Edmonton, 2000).

[76] "*[E]s hat seine eigene, innere Logik und Folgerichtigkeit.*" Schmitt, *Nationalsozialismus, supra* note 56, at 18.

[77] He was not alone among Nazi theorists in reanimating, although in a still more encompassing context of total government and communal social existence, the traditional civilian notion of the gapless system. *See, e.g.*, Huber, *supra* note 74, at 950.

[78] *See* Kantorowicz, *Der Kampf, supra* note 2, at 10.

law offered in representing at least one legal alternative to state power. In this vein, Kantorowicz saw free law as the heir to natural law, but transformed by its era: "Our free law thus is natural law—of the 20th century. . . ."[79]

Not only did free law live independently of state-enacted law, but it also was the foundation on which the state built its laws.[80] According to Kantorowicz, official law by and large was taken from that amorphous mass of concepts and circumstances that Kantorowicz defined as free law. Thus, free law may, and often does, metamorphose into official law.[81]

Kantorowicz went beyond debunking the view that enacted law can solve all future cases, as traditional civilian legal theory maintained. He argued additionally that it is not even *theoretically* possible for every kind of legal problem to have a resolution, implying that to suggest the contrary not only is illogical, but also incoherent.[82] Kantorowicz's argument to a significant extent anticipated by about three decades Isaiah Berlin's lifelong thesis that the widespread human conviction of all good things' mutual reconcilability not only is illogical but actually incoherent.[83] This pervasive underpinning of Kantorowicz's legal philosophy also presents a deep contrast with the Nazi-era German view that the *Führerprinzip* did offer a total solution to the dilemmas of judicial decision-making.[84]

According to Kantorowicz, where free law offers solutions in hard cases, the solutions are contextual, and do not pretend to universal validity.[85] Kantorowicz never promoted free law as a panacea, since he believed that some legal dilemmas inevitably would surpass the scope even of free law.[86] Kantorowicz rejected the idea of infusing the subjective wish of adjudicating

---

[79] "*Unser freies Recht also ist Naturrecht—des 20. Jahrhunderts. . . .*" Kantorowicz, *Der Kampf, supra* note 2, at 12.

[80] *See id.* at 14.

[81] *See id.* at 14–15.

[82] *See id.* at 17 ("*In keiner theoretischen, in keiner praktischen Wissenschaft besteht die Ansicht, daß sie je imstande sein könnte, geschweige denn schon jetzt imstande wäre, jedes erdenkliche Problem lösen zu können.*")

[83] *See, e.g.,* Isaiah Berlin, *Four Essays on Liberty,* II (London, 1969).

[84] Nazi legal theorist Carl Schmitt saw in National Socialism and the unbridled power of its *Führer* the guarantee of legal determinacy. *See* Carl Schmitt, *Über die drei Arten des rechtswissenschaftlichen Denkens* (Hamburg, 1934). Schmitt's advocacy of totalitarian oneness extended from the authoritarian power of the *Führer* to prescribed singleness of racial derivation, or racial homogeneity, in society. He extolled a principle of democracy premised and indeed dependent on absence of diversity. *See* Otto Kirchheimer, "Remarks on Carl Schmitt's Legality and Legitimacy," in *The Rule of Law under Siege, supra* note 11, at 64–68. On the Nazi view of law as "nothing but the command of the leader," *see* Frantz L. Neumann, "Change in the Function of Law," in *id.* at 133; and *id.* at 134 (law under Nazi legal theory was solely "a means serving the stabilization of power"). Neumann elucidated the fusion of the political with law in Nazi legal theory. *See id.* at 138. This can be seen already in Carl Schmitt's pre-1933 work, in which he argued both the pervasiveness of the political, and of enmity as constitutive of the political. *See* Carl Schmitt, *The Concept of the Political* (George Schwab trans., New Brunswick N.J., 1966). *See also* Heinrich Meier, *Carl Schmitt and Leo Strauss: The Hidden Dialogue* (J. Harvey Lomax trans., Chicago, 1995).

[85] *See* Kantorowicz, *Der Kampf, supra* note 2, at 16.

[86] *See id.* at 16–19.

judges into the inevitable aporia of law.[87] At the same time, he signaled the limits of logic, which informed free law but did not define it.[88] Kantorowicz criticized contemporaneous Continental European *Geschlossenheit* legal theory for causing the field of law to stand only with religion in its self-representation of being an entirely contained and efficacious system with the capacity to solve all problems. He noted that even mathematics admitted the existence of insoluble problems, despite its rigorous systematization from axiomatic principles.[89]

Kantorowicz's legal theory anticipated much in modernist approaches to law. His view of the contextual nature of free law was related to his insights into the intricate, dynamic relation between law and language. On the first page of *The Definition of Law*, he described language as "the most dangerous enemy of science . . . that unfaithful servant and secret master of thought. . . ."[90] Under the influence of the developing field of semiotics,[91] he coined the term "conceptual pragmatism" for his theory of the creation of legal significance through systems of signs.[92]

A fruitful application of semiotics to law has been in gleaning insights into mutually interactive dependencies among legal constructs, particularly where previously misrepresented relations have solidified in legal theory and often in the public imagination. In this light, Kantorowicz explored the relation between state and law, suggesting that the commonplace view that the state presupposes law needs to be supplemented by the understanding that law can exist in the absence of the state.[93] Kantorowicz believed that the concept of law was foundational, and that of state derivative.

He thus was not of the view that both concepts are equally foundational, such that neither can acquire identity or definition without being perceived in relation to the other. On the one hand, it might be of interest to consider the consequences of analyzing the state as a concept as foundational as that of law. If one were to take the latter view as an axiomatic point of departure, one would be obliged to consider law-generating entities in their statal capacities, and one might gain insights into the nature of states by looking at the functions of groups and entities one otherwise would not have considered analogous.[94] While Kantorowicz's view would not lead to that path, it would entail extensions of the notion of law beyond the limitations imposed when one ties it conceptually

---

[87] *See* Kantorowicz, *Der Kampf, supra* note 2 at 20.

[88] *See id.* at 22–23.

[89] *See id.* at 18–19.

[90] Hermann Kantorowicz, *The Definition of Law* 1 (Cambridge, 1980) (1959). *Cf.* Clifford Geertz, *Available Light: Anthropological Reflections on Philosophical Topics*, 12 (Princeton, 2000) (discussing "[t]he vicissitudes of 'culture'" as "the *mot*, not the *chose*—there is no *chose*").

[91] Kantorowicz referred explicitly to "*semeiology*" as the philosophical basis of his doctrine. *See id.* at 6.

[92] *See id.* at 5–10.

[93] *See id.* at 15.

[94] Such a view of state and law as equally foundational and mutually interactive underlies recent research by Alan Watson and Khaled Abu El Fadl. *See* Alan Watson & Khaled Abu El Fadl, "Fox Hunting, Pheasant Shooting, and Comparative Law," 48 *Am. J. Comp. L.* 1 (2000).

to the notion of the state. The paradigm he suggested has valuable potentials for examining areas within legal studies that previously would have been considered unrelated to law.[95]

Free law offered living, vibrant, state-free, spontaneous assistance to the inevitable dilemmas of interaction between unsuitable or inapposite codified law and judicial decision-making. Although the advantage of free law was its continuous adaptability to current needs, it did not offer a complete solution, for total solutions are of the domain of dream and illusion, not of law or life. In his criticism of the absolutism inherent in the traditional civil-law faith that all cases can be solved through deduction from enacted law, Kantorowicz pointed to the impossibility of verifying the validity of such deductions.[96] Free law offered hope of reconciling life with theory, practical problems with recognized norms, in recognition of the inevitably fluid and elusive components that human nature and evolving societies infuse into whatever systems legal theorists and legislatures may create.

In *Der Kampf um die Rechtswissenschaft*, Kantorowicz referred to himself as a son of the nineteenth century,[97] writing for the twentieth century. As he penned his words in 1906 in Germany, at the dawn of the new century, he believed that his generation of legal theorists had the task of expelling theology from law, of dispelling the ultimately religious view of the legislator as akin to God, with its corollary that all judicial decisions must relate to textual law, to the revelation of the hidden meanings of the legislative intent both concealed from the masses, and revealed to the initiated by the texts of the law, just as for the Church all truths must relate back to holy writings that both mask and reveal divine intent.[98]

KANTOROWICZ'S LEGACY

Kantorowicz died in Cambridge, England in 1940. In his tribute to Kantorowicz, Gustav Radbruch, omitting all reference to his own efforts before the war to assist

---

[95] Indeed, sociologists of law in recent decades have been studying countries such as South Africa in terms of hidden legal structures within decision-making procedures and bodies that have operated outside any official or previously recognized legal framework, among populations technically subject to a European juridical system. One thinks of studies of groups in which elders' decisions are followed. Particularly in societies in which an official legal system prevailed and nominally governed, such dispute resolution mechanisms tended not to be associated with law until legal sociologists began to include them as targets of legal study. *See* Leon Sheleff, "Customary Law as Common Law," in Roberta Kevelson (ed.), *Conscience, Consensus, and Crossroads: Eighth Round Table on Law and Semiotics*, 315 (New York, 1993), *and sources cited therein*, at 326, n.18, *including* Max Gluckman, *Judicial Process Among the Barotse of Northern Rhodesia* (Manchester, 1954); E. A. Hoebel, *The Law of Primitive Man* (Cambridge, 1954); and Bronislaw Malinowski, *Crime and Custom in Savage Society* (London, 1949). As this essay goes to press, I have started to read Professor Sheleff's new book, which treats these issues in a comprehensive and illuminating way. *See* Leon Sheleff, *The Future of Tradition: Customary Law, Common Law and Legal Pluralism* (London, 2000).

[96] *See* Kantorowicz, *Der Kampf, supra* note 2, at 28.

[97] *See id.* at 12.

[98] *See id.* at 35.

Kantorowicz professionally,[99] noted the integrity and intellectual honesty that characterized Kantorowicz, and that often had hurt his career long before the Nazi régime ended it definitively in Germany.[100] According to Radbruch, Kantorowicz had been lacking in the sort of political savvy that would have benefitted his professional life. Radbruch described Kantorowicz as a valiant, life-long fighter, finding the choice of "fight" in the title of his most famous work (*"Der Kampf um die Rechtswissenschaft"*) all the more appropriate, and con-cluding that Kantorowicz also had died as a fighter in a strange land. (In its more powerfully expressed original form, Radbruch's text, in the midst of allusions to Lessing, reads: *"und als Kämpfer ist er gestorben: in der Fremde."*)[101]

Although Kantorowicz did die abroad, it should be remembered also that he died surrounded by admirers in a country which he himself admired greatly. I do not mean in these pages to suggest that Kantorowicz suffered from universal or even general vilification after the Second World War. On the contrary, after the war, colleagues at Cambridge published his small book, *The Definition of Law*, posthumously, as their final and devoted tribute to him, although Kantorowicz's hope of completing a comprehensive account of his legal philosophy, of which *The Definition of Law* was to be a small part, unfortunately remained unfulfilled due to his early death.[102] Radbruch, who became a prominent legal theorist in post-war Germany, in part due to his admirable and exceptional record during the Hitler period, as well as in a logical resumption of his pre-war eminence, also remained steadfastly loyal to the memory of Kantorowicz.[103] Unfortunately, Radbruch's own views sometimes were misinterpreted and represented as a rejection of free law.[104]

Numerous direct post-war accounts of Kantorowicz's legal theory have been both accurate and positive.[105] J. M. Kelly essentially took the position that, with

---

[99] For more on Radbruch's lifelong loyalty to Kantorowicz, *see* Muscheler, *Biographie, supra* note 1. For an account of Radbruch's extreme courage under Nazism, see Kaufmann, *German Jurisprudence, supra* note 54, at 1633 (going so far as to characterize Radbruch as having stood alone among German legal theorists in openly voicing opposition to Nazism as late as 1933.)

[100] *See* Radbruch, *Gesamtausgabe, supra* note 16, at 73

[101] *Id.* at 88. Radbruch's memorial in general renders a portrait of Kantorowicz as combining insuperable scholarly and human characteristics.

[102] Kantorowicz drafted *The Definition of Law* in 1939 as the introduction to what was to have been a three-volume work under the title *Oxford History of Legal Science*. For more information about this project which ended with Kantorowicz's death, see the "Preface" by A. H. Campbell, and the "Introduction" by A. L. Goodhart, to Kantorowicz, *Definition of Law, supra* note 89, at, respec-tively, vii–x; and xi–xxiv.

[103] Among others, Radbruch had been Minister of Justice during the Weimar era.

[104] Even J.M. Kelly, who otherwise presents an eminently accurate account of Kantorowicz and the free law movement, seems to adhere to this view of Radbruch. *See* Kelly, *Legal Theory, supra* note 16, at 361.

[105] Two of Kantorowicz's staunchest defenders in Germany, Gustav Radbruch and Monika Frommel, both object to what they see as the confusion between legal theory (a term I too have used here with respect to Kantorowicz) and legal methodology. They believe that some of the harm done to free law is due to the incorrect portrayal of Kantorowicz as having advocated legal theory where in fact he only addressed legal methodology, an error which in their eyes was to result in substan-tive distortions of Kantorowicz's message. *See* Radbruch, *Gesamtausgabe, supra* note 16, at 77; and Frommel, *Ein Rechtstheoretiker, supra* note 18, at 636.

free law, Kantorowicz sought the equivalent of equity in law, very much in a tradition that had roots in classical antiquity: "The doctrine of the original apostles of free law hardly amounted, in reality, to more than a plea for equitable creativity in the courts, related to the facts of life."[106] Kelly's account is particularly valuable in exposing the contemporaneous problems in judicial decision-making that Kantorowicz sought to alleviate. In recent years in Germany, Karlheinz Muscheler and Monika Frommel have written extensively and highly persuasively about Kantorowicz's work in thorough, illuminating and admiring scholarship.[107] By the time he died, Kantorowicz's reputation had grown into international renown, unlike that of so many less fortunate German jurist émigrés who never reestablished themselves satisfactorily abroad.[108]

On the other hand, free law not only became, but, still more regrettably, also has remained, the target of criticism that arose after the Second World War and besmirched both positivism and anti-positivism, depending on which theory the critic associated with Nazi judicial conduct. Some of the mud seems to have stuck to Kantorowicz, even among those who value the contributions of free law. In recent years, James Herget and Stephen Wallace, for example, have presented a nuanced view, depicting free law authoritatively and informatively.[109] Their conclusion that the Nazis perverted Kantorowicz's ideas on the one hand correctly suggests that free law did not advocate Nazi judicial conduct. On the other hand, their view appears to me to be at least implicitly misleading to the extent that it seems to suggest a link between the two, perhaps akin to the illegitimate child analogy Kantorowicz suggested between himself and American legal realism.[110] Such an analogy between free law and the court decisions of the Third Reich in my view is erroneous because it fails to illuminate the profound incompatibility between free law and Nazi judicial decisions.

In 1989, the German legal scholar Okko Behrends placed considerable responsibility for Nazi judicial terror on the free law school, arguing, among others, that the Nazi courts derived from free law theory a sense of legitimacy for disregarding enacted law.[111] A conclusion that Nazi judicial decisions were outgrowths of the judges' reading of free law theory overlooks, among others, that Nazi law advocated judicial discretion to contravene statutory law, a discretion Kantorowicz emphatically did *not* advocate as any part of free law; and, moreover, that Nazi

---

[106] Kelly, *Legal Theory*, *supra* note 16, at 361.

[107] *See, e.g.*, Muscheler, *Eine Biographie*, *supra* note 1; Muscheler, *Relativismus*, *supra* note 51; Frommel, *Ein streitbarer Relativist*, *supra* note 1; Frommel, *Ein Rechtstheoretiker*, *supra* note 18.

[108] Of Kantorwicz's international fame, Frommel writes that when in 1937 he celebrated his 60th birthday in Cambridge, Kantorowicz knew that his fame was both international and growing. Frommel, *Ein streitbarer Relativist*, *supra* note 1, at 252.

[109] *See* James E. Herget & Stephen Wallace, "The German Free Law Movement as the Source of American Realism," 73 *Va. L. Rev.* 399 (1987).

[110] *See supra* note 17, and surrounding text. I would place Bodenheimer's rendition of free law in the same category, although, writing in 1940, Bodenheimer might be excused for lacking the perspective that another half century's research might have contributed to his assessment. *See* Edgar Bodenheimer, *Jurisprudence*, 174–180 (1940).

[111] *See* Behrends, *supra* note 66.

law advocated this stance *only where judges were dealing with pre-Nazi German statutes*. Nazi law advocated the strictest adherence to the text of the law, however, if (but only if) the law in question had been passed under Hitler. This duality of methodological approach has been analyzed by Arthur Kaufmann, who refers to it as "the complete pragmatism of a two-track strategy."[112] Bernd Rüthers similarly drew attention to this aspect of Nazi-era German judicial methodology, referring to it as "methodological dualism" ("*Methodendualismus*").[113]

If, as Christian Joerges has suggested, free law and sociological jurisprudence may have "played into the hands of Nazi judges,"[114] it was not because those theories were causal factors in Nazi judicial decisions. As Joerges states, in accordance with the conclusions of Bernd Rüthers, Arthur Kaufmann and Michael Stolleis, "National Socialism had no systematic commitment to particular philosophical or other theoretical guidelines."[115] Its only commitment was to a "display of its ideological foundations."[116] Thus, the purported legal theoretical underpinnings of Nazi-era court decisions fluctuated according to how they would affect the ideologically pre-determined outcomes of the cases. The causal factors behind the cases' outcomes were, rather, identifiable from the *unvarying* aspects of the case law, what Joerges calls the German judiciary's "definite reference points;"[117] namely, the "national-racial [*völkische*] ideal, the conception of race associated with it, and the principle of totalitarian leadership [*Führerprinzip*],"[118] not the pragmatically evoked legal theories of the past, called upon selectively to serve ideologically pre-ordained results.

A recent publication, one that precedes the writing of this essay by only two years, disquietingly associates Kantorowicz explicitly with Nazi law: "Regardless of whether or not the Free Law Movement actually advocated the methods used in National Socialist jurisprudence, the result did seem to be a logical outgrowth of the Free Law doctrine."[119] The author further states that "the Free Law Movement played an important part in the Nazi takeover of the German judicial system, and the Movement enabled this takeover to succeed in a way that was not possible in other fascist countries."[120]

---

[112] Kaufmann, *German Jurisprudence, supra* note 54, at 1645. *Accord*, Rüthers, *Die Unbegrenzte Auslegung, supra* note 11, at 77–80; and Rüthers *supra* note 5, at 32–36. Kaufmann's study generously gives the benefit of the doubt to Nazi-era legal theorists by assuming the sincerity of their belief in the legal theories they advocated.

[113] *See* Rüthers, *Die Unbegrenzte Auslegung, supra* note 11, at 177.

[114] Joerges, *supra* note 11, at 172–173.

[115] *Id.* at 175. *Accord*, Rüthers, *Die Unbegrenzte Auslegung, supra* note 11, at 99; 102; Stolleis, *supra* note 31, at 127–144; Kaufmann, *German Jurisprudence, supra* note 54.

[116] Joerges *supra* note 112, at 175.

[117] *Id.* at 176.

[118] *Id.* at 176. *See also* Rüthers, *Die Unbegrenzte Auslegung, supra* note 11, at, *e.g.*, 102; Kaufmann, *German Jurisprudence, supra* note 54.

[119] Lubben, *supra* note 18, at 94–95.

[120] *Id.* at 98. For the contrary argument, using Vichy French judicial decisions as the point of departure, that a legal methodology diametrically different from the German one nevertheless led to similarly unjust substantive outcomes, and, therefore, that methodology's link to substantive judicial outcome is highly dubious and relatively trivial, see Vivian Grosswald Curran, "The Legalization of Racism in a Constitutional State: Democracy's Suicide in Vichy France," 50 *Hastings L. J.* 1 (1998).

In light of the portrayal of free law given above, it seems unduly bitter that a thinker as intellectually courageous, innovative and rigorously honest as Kantorowicz should have become the target of post-Nazi finger-pointing, and perhaps still worse that the taint should remain to this day. As he wrote of himself, Kantorowicz in 1906 indeed was a son of the nineteenth century, his faith still intact in the usefulness of formulating legal theory to serve the ends of justice.[121] Nowhere in Kantorowicz's writing does one find a repudiation of law as normative. We saw earlier that he criticized American legal realists for not characterizing law as "an Ought." In his 1906 book, he similarly stressed the vital nature of the normative, of the "should," the "*Sollen.*"[122] In his posthumously published book, *The Definition of Law*, he wrote that "[t]he whole history of legal science . . . would become unintelligible if law were to be considered as a body of commands of the sovereign."[123] His 1928 publication in the *Columbia Law Review* similarly stressed the importance of the normative.[124]

Kantorowicz's insistence on law as normative was irreconcilable with the explicit repudiation by Nazi legal theory of a normative basis of law. In *Nationalsozialismus und Völkerrecht*, both delivered as a lecture and published as a book in 1934, Carl Schmitt explicitly defined the National Socialist legal order as *dissociated* from the "abstract-normativistic."[125]

In the detritus of law in Germany after the Second World War, the casting of reproach was liberal.[126] While some, like Kantorowicz's lifelong friend, Radbruch, earnestly sought to glean lessons from the horror of the Nazi years, many sought to strew blame on others for their own conduct.[127] Arthur Kaufmann's study, noted above, in conjunction with Mathias Reimann's historical updating of Kaufmann's analysis, traces the role of Nazi legal theorists from before the Second World War to the present;[128] Ingo Müller has thoroughly documented and compellingly demonstrated the collaboration of the

---

[121] For the view that the twentieth-century cataclysms wrought by Hitler and Stalin altered that faith for many in the post-war era, see Vivian Grosswald Curran, "Deconstruction, Structuralism, Antisemitism and the Law," 36 *B.C.L. Rev.* 1 (1994).

[122] *See* Kantorowicz, *Der Kampf, supra* note 2, at 34–35.

[123] Kantorowicz, *supra* note 91, at 35.

[124] *See* Kantorowicz & Patterson, *supra* note 26.

[125] *See* Schmitt, *Nationalsozialismus, supra* note 56, at 5 ("*Daraus folgt, daß das Recht . . . nicht aus einem abstraktnormativistischen und Regelndenken heraus errichtet. . . .*") Schmitt explicitly opposed legal positivism throughout the book.

[126] *See, e.g.*, Kaufmann, *German Jurisprudence, supra* note 54.

[127] *See id.* for the enthusiastic collaboration of German legal theorists with Nazism; and Ingo Müller, *Hitler's Justice: The Courts of the Third Reich* (Deborah Lucas Schneider trans., Cambridge Mass., 1991) for the equally enthusiastic collaboration of the German judiciary. *Accord*, Stolleis, *supra* note 31.

[128] *See* Kaufmann, *German Jurisprudence, supra* note 54; and Mathias Reimann, "National Socialist Jurisprudence and Academic Continuity: A Comment on Professor Kaufmann's Article," 9 *Cardozo L. Rev.* 1651 (1988).

German judiciary in the Nazi period;[129] and, most recently, Michael Stolleis has given a larger overview of the legal picture in the Nazi period.[130]

To blame Kantorowicz in the light of positivism, anti-positivism, formalism or anti-formalism is to force a reductive and distorted reading of the subtle and nuanced understanding of law that his work reflected. It is also, ultimately, and perhaps most importantly, to miss the point that in judicial methodology lies neither the cause nor the prevention of injustice or of judicial inhumanity. The temptation to blame methodology is, among others, the temptation of the enticing illusion that, if a wrong methodology is responsible for substantive injustice, a right methodology may be hoped for as the solution. As Arthur Kaufmann has suggested, echoing Bernd Rüthers' earlier work,[131] one must look beyond the realm of pure law to understand the deficiencies of law during the Third Reich: "The Weimar Republic failed because too few wanted democracy. . . ."[132] And perhaps more aptly still, Ernst Cassirer explained in *The Myth of the State* that values fluctuate, that law in practice inevitably reflects transient institutional and individual values, but it is in those values that the safeguarding of justice ever perilously and ever unreliably remains:

> "The self-preservation of the state cannot be secured by its material prosperity nor can it be guaranteed by the maintenance of certain constitutional laws. Written constitutions or legal charters have no real binding force, if they are not the expression of a constitution that is written in the citizens' minds. Without this moral support the very strength of a state becomes its inherent danger."[133]

Like natural-law proponents, and in stark contradistinction to Nazi-era judges, Kantorowicz rejected the view that state power defines law. Like positivists, Kantorowicz rejected the view that immutable truths with universal and timeless validity constitute the underpinnings of law. He did indeed signal the limits of systematization, and endorsed judicial discretion. To have denied either or both would not have been to further the goals of justice unless in fact judicial discretion were unnecessary and systematization in fact were capable of generating the answers to all legal controversies. Until and unless Kantorowicz's critics can prove the latter, they will not have shown more than that he drew attention to features of law and of life with which societies do better to deal than to deny.[134]

---

[129]   *See* Müller, *supra* note 125.

[130]   *See* Stolleis, *supra* note 31. *See also* Udo Reifner, "The Bar in the Third Reich: Anti-Semitism and the Decline of Liberal Advocacy," in F. C. DeCoste & Bernard Schwartz (eds.), *The Holocaust's Ghost: Writings on Art, Politics, Law and Education* 263 (2000).

[131]   *See* Rüthers, *Die Unbegrenzte Auslegung, supra* note 11, at 98.

[132]   Kaufmann, *German Jurisprudence, supra* note 54, at 1632–33.

[133]   Ernst Cassirer, *The Myth of the State*, 76 (New Haven, 1946).

[134]   Professor Joerges notes that Bernd Rüthers faulted free law for failing to provide an alternative model to creative judges. *See* Joerges, *supra* note 11, at 187, n.107. Such criticism of free law seems unpersuasive in the absence of any evidence that the desired alternatives exist or even can exist. While Rüthers makes occasional statements that suggest a culpable link between legal methodology and substantive judicial outcome, *see, e.g.*, Rüthers, *Die Unbegrenzte Auslegung, supra* note 11, at 97, my reading is that his general thrust is critical of the erroneous tendency to link the two. *See, e.g., id.* at 98–99.

Central and essential to Kantorowicz's legal theory was its pervasive implicit modesty. Kantorowicz proclaimed the gaps and holes, the unevennesses and insufficiencies of law, but he also presented his own theory as necessarily part of that incompletion. He signaled the relativism of legal solutions, the inherent impossibility of universality, whether in normative or temporal terms. His hope for free law was that its self-transformative features would allow it to be used over time, despite changing circumstances, but he made no claims of universality for it either, not even of its extending to all legal controversies. He took pains to convey that legal science is of a different nature from natural science; among others, incapable of producing verifiable results.[135] He remarked that there could be no *normative science*, only a *science of the normative*.[136]

Kantorowicz clearly failed to foresee in 1906 the upheavals in the law of a society that was to be mired in cynicism and degraded by barbarism. He wrote to dispel illusions that had become part of the theoretical mythology of law in Germany and France at the end of the nineteenth century, and to offer an innovative path for legal theorists and judges willing to acknowledge the practical workings of law, and to seek to maximize their effectiveness in implementation by accommodating existing and developing norms. He faced and drew attention to that most difficult and unwelcome realization that jurists (and others) since time immemorial often try to avoid: the lack of a blueprint built into law's foundations, the lack of security for the future that this entails, and the inevitability of hard decision, of struggle, of risk in judicial processes, rather than mechanical adherence to secure and immutable solutions foreseen and foreordained by an all-knowing legislature.[137] He acknowledged explicitly the need for excellent judges, a goal that was not reducible to formulaic precision. That the Nazis' definition of excellence would beckon the scum to the surface does not militate against either the validity or the integrity of Kantorowicz's theory.

He tried to mitigate the effects of the chaotic residues that confront and challenge the courts by developing as much systematization as possible in and from free law, in the aspiration of maximizing neutrality and objectivity. That he did not try to pretend that free law could change the profound nature and problems either of law or of life; that he never set out to establish that free law would or could "save [law's] actors from the discomfort of choice;"[138] that he did not present free law as offering an ultimate, universal solution, reflects the depth of his intellectual honesty and the integrity of his motive. That Germany's courts for a time failed so miserably to meet Kantorowicz's standards had causes other than Kantorowicz's legal theory.

---

[135] Kantorowicz & Patterson, *supra* note 26, at 28.

[136] "*Es gebe keine 'normative Wissenschaft,' sondern nur eine 'Wissenschaft von Normativen.'*" H. U. Kantorowicz, "Zur Lehre vom richtigen Recht," 2 *Archiv für Rechts- und Wirtschaftsphilosophie* 42 (Bern, 1908/09), *quoted in* Frommel, *Ein streitbare Relativist, supra* note 1, at 247.

[137] For a more detailed discussion of this issue, see Curran, *Deconstruction, supra* note 119.

[138] The phrase is Mathias Reimann's. *See* Reimann, "*Holmes*' Common Law," *supra* note 38, at 84.

Fig. 1 John Henry Wigmore
(Reproduced by kind permission of Northwestern University)

4

Encountering Amateurism: John Henry Wigmore and the Uses of American Formalism

ANNELISE RILES*

One of the recurring complaints about comparative law is that it is amateuristic. It is not a new complaint. For decades, now, the same critiques have been heard and still, the old methods—and the old critiques—persist.

Amateurism within the academy is always met with a certain degree of unease. One common explanation presents amateurism, like popularism, as the effect of another era with its own problems and paradigms. Amateurism, in this view, is a feature of the pre-modernist past.[1] The persistence of amateurism in late twentieth century comparative law, long after the infusion of modern social scientific paradigms and methods into other fields of legal scholarship, then, is treated as something of an embarrassment. And yet, alongside other disciplines specializing in comparison from anthropology to comparative literature, amateurism is perhaps comparative law's defining methodological trait.

This essay began with a quite naïve professionalizing ambition for our amateuristic discipline and an equally naïve interest in one of our discipline's greatest promoters, John Henry Wigmore. Intrigued by Wigmore's three-year stay in Japan and of his work toward the translation and editing of Tokugawa Era[2] statutes and case law, I was interested to learn how a young legal scholar encountered a society which, in his own understanding, was entirely foreign to him, and how the experience might have shaped his work as a comparativist. One of the dogmas of modern relativism is that the encounter with difference

* I am grateful to Jane Campion, Aaron Kirk and Beth Olds for archival research, and to Joann Thompson for help in preparing the manuscript. I thank Hitoshi Aoki, Jack Heinz, Juro Iwatani, David Kennedy, Hiro Miyazaki, William Novak and Mathias Reimann for helpful comments on this paper. All translations are my own.

[1] In this view, what looks to us now as amateuristic scholarship was in fact scholarship tailored for the evolutionary ideas that dominated the academy prior to the introduction of modernist social scientific paradigms. *See, e.g.,* Marilyn Strathern, "Out of Context: The Persuasive Fictions of Anthropology," 28 *Current Anthropology* 251 (1987). On modernism in comparative law, *see* Annelise Riles, Wigmore's Treasure Box: Comparative Law in the Era of Information, 40 *Harv. Int'l. L. J.* 221 (1999).

[2] The Tokugawa Era (properly called the Edo Period, 1603–1867) refers to the period during which Japan, ruled by the Tokugawa family, was closed to outside influences.

through the extended experience of a distant society and its legal system changes the person as well as the scholar; that the personal experience of difference directs and refocuses the theoretical project. From this standpoint, Wigmore's extended stay in a non-European country where he learned the language and engaged in serious long-term research might have provided a model from within the tradition for a more rigorous, less amateuristic, comparative law.

However, an inquiry into Wigmore's encounter with Japanese "custom" complicates the familiar trope of the scholar changed by travel to distant places and the encounter with things strange and foreign there. Not only did Wigmore emerge from his sojourn in Japan with most of the same views with which he began, but there was much that I found troubling about both the content of those views and the genre in which they found expression. I came to accept that Wigmore was an ordinary person and scholar, very much a product of his time and social milieu, with some extraordinary abilities, interests and commitments—we might call them professional hobbies—who produced some scattered but remarkable achievements. More importantly, I came to accept the necessity of rethinking my own ideas about amateurism and related professionalizing ambitions.

John Henry Wigmore, Professor and later Dean of Northwestern University School of Law, was the quintessential establishment figure, and he worked hard at it. He was the sort of dean who was adored by alumni,[3] the sort of scholar whose ideal audience was the local bar association, a man who belonged to every club and society, and who meticulously clipped every reference to his activities in the most trivial of newsletters.[4] Although he has been called the father of American comparative law for his work in introducing the discipline to the American academy,[5] his work is rarely read today. In his time, as in retrospect, he was regarded as an eclectic, free-thinking, exceptionally energetic but somewhat distracted scholar whose contribution lay more in his popularization of comparative and foreign law than in the formulation of new paradigms or ideas.[6]

---

[3] The Northwestern Alumni newsletter records an instance in which 400 alumni gathered, and banged on tables as they sang,

"*Oh! Wigmore, Dean Wigmore,*
You're a leader who is tried and true,
Oh! Wigmore, Dean Wigmore,
Old Northwestern Should Be Proud Of You."

"John H. Wigmore Honored by 'World'," *Alumni News*, Northwestern University (January 1930).
[4] *See, e.g.*, Colonel Wigmore Honored by Japan, *The Discus*, Dec. 1935. (On file at Northwestern University Library).
[5] Jerome Hall, *Comparative Law and Social Theory* 10 (Baton Rouge, 1963).
[6] The reviewer of Wigmore's *Panorama of the World's Legal Systems* for the Yale Law Journal wrote:

"If Dean Wigmore's primary aim is to give the general reader a series of interesting, but necessarily rapid and incomplete, pictures of the historical development of the sixteen legal systems of the world then he has undoubtedly been successful. Beautifully printed on excellent paper and

Wigmore's personal blend of idealism and complacency in his life and scholarship might serve as an apt metaphor for the character of our discipline. In his own time, Wigmore's personal views seemed at once revolutionary and reactionary. He was nominated to the World Court for his rare familiarity with foreign law and his visionary commitment to international institutions, but his nomination was later derailed because of his hostility to pacifists and leftists during World War I.[7] He took strong public stances on controversial issues, and yet he knew how to cut himself off from an unpopular position when necessary.[8] In his letter in support of Wigmore's candidacy for the World Court, Benjamin Cardozo put it in flattering but double-edged terms: "He has attained an eminence that would make him lonely, if he were not so obviously human."[9]

Throughout his career, Wigmore enthusiastically, even didactically promoted the comparative method in legal education. With funds raised from local industrialists, he traveled the world collecting legal materials[10] and covered the

enlivened by over five hundred illustrations the books are a pleasure to the eye. These "impressionistic" sketches, full of pleasant gossipy bits and occasional good stories, are particularly easy reading for they do not attempt to deal with any general ideas or principles. . . . If, however, this work is intended as an introduction to the subject of comparative law, then we are doubtful whether it will accomplish its purpose. . . . After having enjoyed the elaborately colored illustrations of the Great Pyramid, the Hanging Gardens of Babylon, the Parthenon, and the Colossus at Rhodes, it may seem ungracious on the part of the reviewer to disagree with Dean Wigmore's view that the pictorial method is of practical value in expounding the science of the law. A student whose zeal must be stimulated in this way, can hardly be worth teaching."

A. L. Goodhart, "Book Review," 38 *Yale L. J.* 554, 554–55 (1929). *See also* Theodore Pluckett, "Book Review," 42 *Harv. L. Rev.* 587 (1929).

[7] For examples of this hostility, *see* John H. Wigmore, "J. H. Wigmore Answers Frankfurter Attack on Sacco-Vanzetti Verdict: A Fair Trial—Facts as well as Law Reviewed by Supreme Court," *Boston Evening Transcript*, April 25, 1927; John H. Wigmore, "Editorial," *The Boston Herald*, May 10, 1927. Roscoe Pound described Wigmore's attack on Felix Frankfurter in this exchange as "a disgrace to legal scholarship." David Wigdor, *Roscoe Pound: Philosopher of Law* 250 (Westport Conn., 1974). Wigmore's approach to the testimony of sexual assault victims in his writings on evidence has been the subject of much-deserved feminist critique. *See* Leigh B. Bienen, "A Question of Credibility: John Henry Wigmore's Use of Scientific Authority in Section 924a of the Treatise on Evidence," 19 *Cal. W. L. Rev.* 235, 237 (1983) ("Under the guise of arguing on the basis of objective, scientific authority, this section of Wigmore's treatise simply states that all females who allege sexual assault should be assumed to be lying, a repressive and misogynist position.")

[8] Consider, for example, Wigmore's stance toward Japan at the outbreak of World War II:

"John H. Wigmore, dean emeritus of Northwestern University Law School, who spent three years in Japan, was compiling a translation of international law for the Japanese government when the Pearl Harbor attack was made. He says the Japs pay no attention to laws, national or international."

"News Brief," *Momence, Ill. Progress Reporter*, March 12, 1943.

[9] Benjamin Cardozo, Statement regarding Wigmore's Nomination to the Court of International Justice (1930) (on file at Northwestern University Library, Box 1)

[10] Wigmore's summer travel schedule for June 12 to August 30, 1905 was typical.

"Route of tickets: 1st cl. steamer, 2nd cl. rail; beginning at Liverpool, thence by Harwich to Rotterdam, thence by rail Amsterdam, Enkhuizen, and Bremen to Kiel; thence by steamer & rail

walls of the law school with pictures of scenes of courtrooms and the world.[11] He corresponded with comparativists from around the world, and his translation and publication of the works of foreign jurists for an American audience is one of his great ignored legacies.[12] He played a key role in the organization and promotion of the International Congresses of Comparative Law of 1932 and 1937.[13] It was rumored that he even maintained a Shinto shrine in his suburban living room.

By Wigmore's own admission, however, during his most ambitious years as professor and then as dean, comparative law remained primarily a hobby—perhaps of the same order as the musical comedy routines and rhymed mottoes he wrote for the school,[14] or his summer holiday travels. Crucially to the future of comparative law in the United States, he left no disciples.[15] Wigmore rather made his scholarly name as an expert in the field of evidence, and his serious and still-popular treatise is a standard performance in that formalist genre that makes only subtle nods to the virtues of comparativism.[16] During this period, he

---

to Kopenhagen; thence by rail & steamer via Malmo, Sassnitz, Stralsund, Greifswald to Berlin; thence via Dresden, to Prag; thence to Krakau; thence via Waag Valley to Buda-Pest; thence to Vienna; thence via Linz to Salzburg; thence via Strassburg, Luxembourg, Namur, to Brussels; thence via Antwerp to Rotterdam; thence via Harwich, London, Oxford, Hereford to Liverpool."

John H. Wigmore, Summer Schedule: June 12 to August 30, 1905 (on file at Northwestern University Library, Box 12).

[11] *Cf.* Riles, "Wigmore's Treasure Box," *supra* note 1.

[12] The scale of this project was truly astounding. Wigmore's Continental Legal History Series and Criminal Science Series translated and published the works of French scholars Jean Brissaud, Joseph Charmont, Paul Collinet, René Demogue, Léon Duguit, Adhémar Esmein, Alfred Fouillée, Eugène Gaudemet, René Garraud, François Geny, Paul Frédéric Girard, Edouard Lambert, Georges Ripert, Raymond Saleilles, and Gabriel de Tarde; German scholars Fritz Berolzheimer, Heinrich Brunner, Arthur Engelmann, Heinrich Gerland, Andreas Heusler, Rudolf Hübner, Carl Koehne, Josef Kohler, Burkhard Wilhelm Leist, Adolf Merkel, Richard Schroeder, Heinrich Siegel, Rudolf Stammler, Roderich von Stintzing, Otto Stobbe, Ludwig von Bar, Rudolf von Jhering, and Heinrich Zoepfl; Italian scholars Carlo Calisse, Giorgio Del Vecchio, Enrico Ferri, Cesare Lombroso, Achille Loria, Luigi Miraglia, Alfred Rocco, Michele Angelo Vaccaro and Icilio Vanni, and many others from Latin America, China, Japan, Eastern, and Northern Europe. *See generally Continental Legal History Series* (Boston) and *Criminal Science Series. See also* Sarah Morgan, Memorial Proposing Dean John H. Wigmore of Northwestern University (Chicago) for the Permanent Court of International Justice 1930 (on file at Northwestern University, Box 10).

[13] *See generally* John H. Wigmore, "Report of Committee of Conference of State Bar Delegates on 1932 International Congress of Comparative Law," 18 *ABA J.* 37 (1932); John H. Wigmore, "The Congress of Comparative Law," 23 *ABA J.* 75 (1937). "Where most of the American lawyers had never been to Europe, they were amazed to discover that Wigmore already knew all the leading European comparativists and spoke to them in their own languages." William R. Roalfe, "John Henry Wigmore: Scholar and Reformer," 53 *J. of Crim. L. Criminology and Pol. Sci.* 277, 296 (1962).

[14] Wigmore's musical compositions are on file at the Northwestern University Library, Boxes 230–31.

[15] *See* Pierre LeGrand, "John Henry Merryman and Comparative Legal Studies: A Dialogue," 47 *Am. J. Comp. L.* 3, 6 (1999).

[16] *See* John Henry Wigmore, *A Treatise on the System of Evidence in Trials at Common Law* (Boston, 1904). For examples of the enduring relevance of Wigmore's treatise, *see, e.g.,* Terance Anderson & William Twining, *Analysis of Evidence: How To Do Things With Facts Based on Wigmore's Science of Juridical Proof* (Boston, 1991); Paul Bergman, "Of Bentham, Wigmore, and Little Bo Peep: Where Evidence Lost its Way, and a Map for Scholars to Find it," 66 *Notre Dame L. Rev.* 949 (1991).

also devoted great efforts to building the law school and solidifying personal and institutional ties to the local bar associations, and in these tasks he proved to be a shrewd and popular politician.[17]

What is perhaps most difficult to come to terms with is Wigmore's dogged amateurism. The mature Wigmore's "pictorial method" of comparative law,[18] in which stories and images, authentic or not, were collected together into popular volumes and "entertaining" presentations, seems quixotic to the point of absurdity. How are we to reconcile the self-image of the serious young scholar, bringing the "science" of Langdellian legal education and its formalist precepts to the periphery of civilization and returning with "data" about strange foreign customs, with the eccentric presentations of the older scholar? Wigmore's encounter with the Orient and later with the academy, therefore, will serve as an example of the place of amateurism in comparative legal method—that side of comparative scholarship that, as in Wigmore's life, postdates and somehow survives the best justifications for the adventure.

Of course, *this* kind of amateurism, a certain studied eccentricity at the level of self and scholarly presentation, is rare in comparative law. But Wigmore's treatment of non-Western legal culture as a source of information about modern law's evolutionary past is more common. The critique that this paradigm inspires from scholars outside the discipline finds some echoes in comparativists' own complaints about the vacuousness of their analytical categories, the casual way in which data is made to fit arguments about the transplantation of legal systems from one society to another, or the lack of commitment to the societies they describe or interest in the messiness of detail.

Since the critique of the amateurism of adherence to outdated paradigms has already been laid out eloquently,[19] this critique will not be the goal of this essay. Let me be more plain: in the vocabulary of this essay, amateurism is not to be taken as a disparaging word. Rather, my interest is in the features of what critics call amateurism, its internal purposes and rationales.

What was the relationship, then, between professional work and hobby? Did the *Treatise on Evidence* occupy an entirely different world for Wigmore from his comparative interests? I do not think so. Rather, I want to suggest that we read Wigmore's approach to comparison as one enactment of the mainstream American approaches to legal thought we term legal formalism. What I have in mind here, however, is not the doctrinal, epistemological or logical dimensions of formalism often discussed by its realist and postrealist critics[20] but rather its performative, and relational dimensions.[21]

---

[17] *See* William R. Roalfe, *John Henry Wigmore*, 105 (Evanston, 1977).

[18] For a further discussion of Wigmore's pictorial method, *see generally* Riles, *supra* note 1.

[19] *See, e.g.*, LeGrand, *supra* note 15; and papers by multiple authors in "Symposium: New Directions in Comparative Law," 46 *Am. J. Comp. L.* 597 (1998).

[20] *See, e.g.*, Jerome Frank, *Law and the Modern Mind* (New York, 1931); Lon L. Fuller, "Positivism and Fidelity to Law," 71 *Harv. L. Rev.* 630 (New York, 1958); Stanley Fish, "The Law Wishes to Have a Formal Existence," in *There's No Such Thing as Free Speech and It's a Good Thing Too*, 141–178 (New York, 1994); Cass Sunstein, "Lochner's Legacy," 87 *Col. L. Rev.* 873 (1987); Duncan

I begin by taking a cue from Wigmore himself: The trail of scholarship and correspondence Wigmore left behind suggests that the comparativist's life project—Wigmore, the Institution, as one colleague memorialized him[22]—hardly began and ended with the four corners of the scholarly text.

AMBITION IN LOTUS LAND

The origins of Wigmore's interest in comparative law are succinctly retold by Wigmore himself:

"At [the time of my studies] the subject of comparative law was not studied at Harvard, except in James Barr Ames' personal researches, omnivorously sympathetic as he was with all aspects of law. . . . In Japan, the comparative point of view naturally emerged. At that time, as today in China, the new Occidental legislation was occupying all thoughts of the Japanese people, including the students, and no interest was shown in their own native institutions. This then seemed strange to me. . . . I was able to discover a great mass of recorded materials showing their indigenous development . . . and hoped on returning to the United States to become a professor of Comparative Law. But President Eliot [of Harvard University] pointed out to me that there was no American interest in that subject, and no opening for it in law schools. In fact, most of the material which I used for my essay in the Harvard Law Review in 1897 on The Pledge Idea, a Study in Comparative Legal Ideas, was found in the great Library of the College and not in the Library of the Law School of that period."[23]

Wigmore's irrepressible excitement about his project, and his resigned bitterness about its marginality in the academy will be familiar to many comparativists today.

In 1889, as a recent graduate of the Harvard Law School, Wigmore sailed to Japan to help establish the Keio University Faculty of Law on the Langdellian model. In Japan, it was a time of "Westernization" in which everything

Kennedy, *A Critique of Adjudication: Fin de Siecle* (Cambridge, Mass., 1997); Fred Schauer, "Formalism," 97 *Yale L. J.* 509 (1988).

[21] *See, e.g.*, Donald Brenneis, "Dramatic Gestures: The Fiji Indian Pancayat as Therapeutic Event," in Stanford Karen A. Watson-Gegeo & Geoffrey M. White (eds), *Disentangling: Conflict Discourse in Pacific Societies*, 214–38 (Stanford, 1990); Robert P. Burns, *A Theory of the Trial* (Princeton, 1999); Kyoko Inoue, *MacArthur's Japanese Constitution: A Linguistic and Cultural Study of its Making* (Chicago, 1991); Elizabeth Mertz, "Recontextualization as Socialization: Text and Pragmatics in the Law School Classroom," in M. Silverstein & G. Urban (eds), *Natural Histories of Discourse* (Chicago, 1997). My aim here is to bring thinking about legal formalism into conversation with broader debates about the performative dimensions of form. *See, e.g.*, Andrew Pickering, "Concepts and the Mangle of Practice: Constructing Quaternions," in Barbara Herrnstein Smith & Arkady Plotnitsky (eds), *Mathematics, Science and Postclassical Theory*, 40–82 (Durham N.C., 1997); Hirokazu Miyazaki, "Faith and its Fulfillment: Agency, Exchange and the Fijian Aesthetics of Completion," 27 *Am. Ethnol.* 31 (2000); Annelise Riles, *The Network Inside Out* (Ann Arbor, 2000).

[22] Albert Kocourek, "John Henry Wigmore: A Personal Portrait," 24 *The Green Bag* 2, 8 (1912).

[23] John H. Wigmore, "Comparative Law: Jottings on Comparative Legal Ideas and Institutions," 6 *Tulane L. Rev.* 48, 48–53 (1931).

Japanese was to be discarded for things foreign, and Wigmore's work was a small part of this project. Wigmore's letters, diaries, newspaper articles and scholarly writings from his three years in Japan are those of an intelligent, ambitious, but otherwise ordinary law graduate, eager to make some "scientific" use of his time in a far away place, but undistinguished in his general outlook from other expatriates of that time. Like most of his fellow citizens, Wigmore believed that the West, as "Japan's adopted parent," had much to teach, and that the Rule of Law should be first among these lessons.

Wigmore was among the second generation of foreigners hired by the Meiji government—so-called "yatoi" (foreign menials) brought in after 1866 to Westernize all aspects of Japanese society.[24] Legal reform was at the top of the government's agenda as part of its bid to satisfy Western nations' conditions for the cession of extraterritorial jurisdiction over their nationals in Japan—a cause of deep humiliation to Japanese elites.[25] The first generation of foreign scholars had translated Western laws and jurisprudence and drafted the new civil codes, but by the time of Wigmore's arrival, that more momentous work was already coming to a close.[26] Wigmore's role, rather, was to be the training of the next generation of Japanese lawyers—and hence he was free to turn to less applied and more scholarly forms of inquiry.

The nostalgia in Wigmore's discovery of Japanese customary law as a scholarly interest, after the modernizing ambitions of codification were largely spent, was no doubt shaped by the commitments of his predecessors. The earlier generation of yatoi had come to see their role as one of preserving the true Japanese character from the desire to destroy all things indigenous in favor of Western trends—of protecting Japan against itself.[27] Upon his arrival in Japan, Wigmore

---

[24] *See generally* H. J. Jones, *Live Machines* (Vancouver, 1980); Ardath W. Burks, *The Modernizers: Overseas Students, Foreign Employees, and Meiji Japan* (Boulder Colo., 1983); Neil Pedlar, *The Imported Pioneers: Westerners Who Helped Build Modern Japan* (New York, 1990). Wigmore was the "foreign menial" of Yukichi Fukuzawa, an academic and educator, and the now mythical founder of the private Keio University. Fukuzawa's picture appears on the 10,000 yen note today.

[25] Wigmore himself was ardently against extraterritorial jurisdiction and wrote a number of editorials and academic articles in Japan and the United States on the subject. *See, e.g.*, John H. Wigmore, "Foreign Jurisdiction in Japan," *The New York Nation*, Jan. 12, 1893; John H. Wigmore, "Carstens and Extraterritoriality," *The Japan Daily Mail*, Nov. 8, 1892; John H. Wigmore, "Code Translations," *The Japan Daily Mail*, Nov. 14, 1892; John H. Wigmore, "Throwing Stones from Glass Houses," *The Japan Daily Mail*, September 2, 1891.

[26] Key figures in this work included the American Erastus Peshine Smith, who worked for the Japanese Foreign Ministry as an advisor on international law from 1871, the Frenchman Georges Bousquet, who established a School of French Law within the Ministry of Justice in 1872, and most importantly, Emile Gustav Boissonade of the Faculty of Law of the University of Paris, who over a period of more than twenty years drafted the Japanese Civil Code on property, the Penal Code, and the Code of Criminal Procedure. *See* Pedlar, *The Imported Pioneers, supra* note 25, at 187–8.

[27] Bousquet interpreted Japanese disdain for their own traditions

"as vanity, an attempt to show Europe a décor of Western civilization . . . Bousquet felt their efforts too grand, too ostentatious, not in keeping with indigenous qualities. This assessment represents a fair consensus of opinion among yatoi. . . ."

Jones, *supra* note 25, at 15.

received the following counsel from H. B. Adams, President of Johns Hopkins University, who had encouraged him to take the position:

"I think the duty of American Educators in Japan should be to cultivate greater stability of character and judgement in the Japanese youth and to preserve a consciousness of historic continuity in the institutions and culture of the Japanese people. The introduction of the historic method of studying law, politics and religion would be the salvation of that revolutionary and iconoclastic race. . . . I believe you could render a substantial service to New Japan by Historical investigations into the social and legal History of Old Japan."[28]

These academic and political motivations served only as background and pretext, however,[29] for a very fantastical adventure. Wigmore's first letter home captures his mood:

"[T]he sail up the bay to Yokohama was like a sail into fairyland. The mountains on either hand were like curious bits of stage scenery, fantastic shapes and picturesque effect of light and shade. The volcano of Oshima could be seen on the left with a crest of smoke, and after the sun had risen, Fujiyama, the great snow-crowned mountain, came into sight far more majestic and beautiful than we had ever imagined. Soon we passed close to the shore, and the little coves, green sward, and fairy trees made one and all of us feel over and over again that it was a journey into fairy land. In the distance the white and yellow bluffs showed in the sun, and all the hills came close to the water's edge. About us were little fairy boats, like cockleshells or walnut boats . . . [Yokohama] is the most picturesque looking town I have ever seen . . . [The natives with] their shock of black hair, usually carefully parted, with their olive complexions, white teeth, and intelligent earnest looks make them very fascinating. The whole affair seemed like a play, from the ship to the hotel. There we found European life again."[30]

For a young lawyer who had struggled to find enough employment to support himself in Boston, part of the excitement stemmed from his newfound status and relevance. His wife Emma wrote of Wigmore's reaction to the crowd of students that greeted them at the train:

"The dear boy was of course unconscious as ever of his own self, and thought only of the mass of youthful faces about him, and set them almost wild by waving his hat and I don't know but that he joined in their cheering."[31]

---

[28] Letter from H. B. Adams, President of Johns Hopkins University, to John H. Wigmore (October 28, 1889) (on file at Northwestern University Library, Box 18).

[29] Wigmore wrote to his mother-in-law en route to Japan that

"[t]he only thing about the coming tasks that has the slightest burden about it looking forward from now is the work of the lectures, but I am not much apprehensive even about this, for I am told positively that no one works hard in Japan, no matter who he is."

Letter from John Henry Wigmore to Mrs. Vogl (October 20, 1889) (on file with the author).

[30] Letter from John Henry Wigmore to Mrs. Vogl. (October 24, 1889) (on file at Northwestern University Library, Box 179).

[31] Letter from Emma Wigmore to Mrs. Vogl. (October 27, 1889) (on file at Northwestern University Library, Box 179).

The privileges of his colonial status, likewise, were avidly consumed in the register of fantasy and amusement:

> "[W]e took our first ride in the *jinrikishas*. We are all delighted with that way of travelling. The men seem so interested in you and are so intelligent that it is like playing, not like sober life at all."[32]

In joining the expatriate community of Japan, Harry and Emma suddenly found access to a social and political circle far beyond their means.[33] This suited Wigmore's ambitions well:

> "What do you think of all the high-and-mightiness in which we have reveled this week? Think of being specially invited to a tea at the British Minister's! Think of inviting Sir Edwin Arnold to dinner and still more, think of him accepting it!"[34]

Wigmore threw himself into the experience of the expatriate scholar. He studied the Japanese language and read every book and article about Japanese legal institutions he could find. He learned Japanese fencing. He played shortstop on Tokyo's first baseball team.[35] Emma wrote that "this trip to Japan seems to be bringing out many strong points which [Harry] never knew he possessed."[36]

Part of the excitement of Japan was the intellectual freedom Wigmore suddenly gained to stray beyond usual disciplinary confines.[37] He wrote articles for *Scribner's* and *The Nation* on topics as distant from law as the architecture of the new parliament building and the latest fashions in dress.[38] He travelled to the countryside to witness elections. He held "interviews" with prominent Japanese intellectuals. He reviewed books on flower arranging and dissertations

---

[32] Letter from John H. Wigmore to Mrs. Vogl. (Oct. 24, 1889) (on file at Northwestern University Library, Box 179).

[33] Harry and Emma Wigmore's letters and diaries from this period give the picture of a couple with few financial resources struggling to save. They emphasize that they shop at length for every household item; they share a home with another teacher and his wife; they sleep under a cotton comforter rather than a silk one and that Emma wears the same dress to every ball.

[34] Letter from John Henry Wigmore to Mrs. Vogl. (November 12, 1889) (on file at Northwestern University Library, Box 179). Something of their ambitions is revealed in Emma's request from her sister in a letter shortly following:

> "In the next mail will you please send me 'Social Etiquette' and 'The Correct Thing', three hair nets for my bangs, and I wish you could spare me one of your cook books. . . . Harry would like to have you send him 1) all of his newspaper cuttings [and] 2) his printed articles."

Letter from Emma Wigmore to Edith Vogl (November 22, 1889) (on file at Northwestern University Library).

[35] Roalfe, *supra* note 17, at 22–24.

[36] Letter from Emma Wigmore to Mrs. Vogl (February 3, 1890) (on file at Northwestern University Library).

[37] Jones comments that for many yatoi, who were in their mid-twenties, Japan afforded an opportunity to explore ideas and projects that were not yet acceptable in the West. A notable example is Edward Morse's work on human evolution and biological anthropology at a time when the subject was highly controversial in the United States. *See* Jones, *supra* note 25, at 74–75; *cf.* D. Eleanor Westney, *Imitation and Innovation: The Transfer of Western Organizational Patterns to Meiji Japan* (Cambridge Mass., 1987).

[38] John H. Wigmore, "Starting a Parliament in Japan," *Scribner's Magazine*, July 1891, at 33–50; John H. Wigmore, "Parliamentary Days in Japan," *Scribner's Magazine*, Aug. 1891, at 243–55.

Fig. 2 Harry and Emma Wigmore at home in Evanston, Illinois
(Reproduced by kind permission of Northwestern University)

on Japanese history, and collected ethnographic information about festival preparations.

In particular, Wigmore was to find his niche among the members of the Asiatic Society, an institution in many expatriate communities in nineteenth century Asia. Here was amateurism at its zenith. Devoted to the study of local "custom," the Society sponsored talks and published papers about Japanese history and ethnology.[39] Under Wigmore's direction, its Committee on Ethnography collected information on customary land tenure by way of a questionnaire distributed to local elites.[40]

The conversion of adventure into academic project began with Wigmore's discovery of the dusty reports of a Ministry of Justice commission on informal dispute resolution and customary law convened twenty years prior, and shortly

[39] The Asiatic Society of Japan still exists today as a club of amateur ethnologists under the titular leadership of a minor member of the Japanese royal family.
[40] In connection with this work, Wigmore wrote

"The plan adopted, we may add, is not a novel one by any means. Only a year or two ago the China Branch of the Asiatic Society sent out a few questions in the same way and upon the same topic; and very gratifying results were obtained. The Ethnological Society of Great Britain has for some years worked in the same way in investigating the sociology of the southern hemisphere. Perhaps the most systematic undertaking of this sort is that of the United States Bureau of Ethnology, which publishes a book containing several thousand questions, for linguistic investigators among the American Indians. . . . it is impossible to study local institutions aright without giving to folk-lore, superstitions, ceremonies, festivals, and such facts a more important place than hitherto."

John H. Wigmore, "The Asiatic Society's Questions," *The Japan Daily Mail*, Aug. 13, 1891.

after the purposeful obliteration of those customary practices by the Meiji government as part of its modernization drive.[41] Wigmore raised funds from the Asiatic Society and assembled a team of translators to edit an English language abridged version of the records of what he poetically called "Justice in Old Japan." He published the first four volumes of materials in 1892.[42]

It was in the course of this adventure, then, that Wigmore invented himself as a comparative legal scholar. The new science of comparative law provided a rationale for what otherwise must have seemed like an odd hobby. Wigmore imagined this hobby as a potential ticket to a teaching position in an American law school upon his return; in his correspondence with Holmes, Brandeis and other legal theorists back home, Wigmore positioned himself as a diligent foot soldier in the often thankless work of mapping out the evolutionary structure of law and of cataloguing its variations.[43]

On the ground, however, the work was considerably less lofty. Wigmore claimed to speak Japanese and he had learned some technical legal terminology, but he did not read or write. He was dependent, then, on a team of young Japanese academics.[44] The correspondence suggests a cagey set of potentially exploitative relationships in which both sides jockeyed for advantage with their eyes on the project's implications for their personal advancement:

"July 17, 1890

Dear Prof. Wigmore:
I am sorry that I can not do the work for you, for the compensation is too cheap, and I can not get anyone instead of me.

Yours truly,
T. Matsumo"[45]

Although during the course of this work, Wigmore clearly developed respect for his Japanese colleagues and for Japan more generally, it must be acknowledged that the inquiry into Japanese legal custom and the experience of collaborating with Japanese scholars ultimately did not shake the foundations of his own beliefs in the way a late modern comparativist might hope it would have done. One of the more interesting examples of the limits of Wigmore's own relativism concerns his own outrage over the treatment of Japanese immigrants in the

---

[41] John H. Wigmore, *Law and Justice in Tokugawa Japan*, xiv (Tokyo, 1969) (hereinafter, "*Law and Justice*").

[42] "John Henry Wigmore Re-Visits Japan," *The Alumni News* (1935). The Japan Cultural Society (Kokusai Bunka Shinkokai) resumed the project in 1967 under the direction of Dr. Takayanagi Kenzo, a law professor at the University of Tokyo, with funding from the Japanese government. *See* Wigmore, *Law and Justice, supra* note 412, at xi.

[43] *See, e.g.*, John H. Wigmore, Letter to Oliver Wendell Holmes (March 30, 1891) (sending materials on land tenure customs in Japan and informing Holmes that he plans to write a treatise on "native Japanese law").

[44] *See* Letter from John Henry Wigmore to Mr. Karusu (Chairman of the Society for International Cultural Relations) (1935) (on file at Northwestern University Library).

[45] Letter from Matsumo to John Henry Wigmore (July 17, 1890) (on file at Northwestern University Library).

United States. During his time in Japan and throughout his life, Wigmore spoke and wrote extensively about the injustice of American immigration policies.[46] Just prior to the outbreak of World War II, he wrote that the legal treatment of Japanese-Americans constituted "racial discrimination," and that anger about American racism was inflaming militarism in Japan in terms that identified with the point of view of his former hosts: "if I were a Japanese, I should have that feeling."[47]

And yet Wigmore's ability to identify with an "other" as a result of his time in Japan did not challenge his own precepts about the central relevance of race in social policy or the categorization of legal systems.[48] Nor did his sympathy toward Japanese-Americans lead him to question racism toward less exotic others. In one early article condemning a federal court's decision barring Japanese from naturalization as US citizens on grounds that they were not "white," for example, Wigmore argued that the judge's logic could not be defended as a matter of ethnology because

> "the term 'white' cannot be systematically applied to any such general theory as that adopted by the learned judge, or on any other general theory; that it is in fact thoroughly inefficient as to the basis for distinction."

At the brink of making the then radical claim that the notion of whiteness was an unsustainable notion, Wigmore, in a classic lawyerly move, then limited his position to the case at hand with the argument that whiteness could be defined "only in contrast with the African Negro" and that, in effect, Japanese were more white than they were black.[49]

The argument captures the at once visionary and complacent dimensions of Wigmore's very ordinary humanism. Ultimately, his views rarely fell far out of step with the American mainstream. In actuality, his more progressive political positions were always somewhat after the fact.[50] Conversely, his more relativist academic inquiries often confirmed highly conservative political views. He encouraged Japan's colonization policy on grounds of Japanese equality with other great colonial powers, for example, and one of his favorite themes was the oddity of procedural safeguards in American criminal trials from an Asian standpoint:

---

[46] *See, e.g.,* Wigmore, *Throwing Stones, supra* note 24; John H. Wigmore, "American Naturalization and the Japanese," *The Japan Weekly Mail*, Aug. 25, 1894.

[47] John H. Wigmore, "Equality of Races," *Asia Mail*, March 1940.

[48] *See generally* Albert Kocourek & John H. Wigmore, *Sources of Ancient and Primitive Law* (Boston, 1915) (using race as a classification system for legal traditions).

[49] John H. Wigmore, "American Naturalization and the Japanese," *The Japan Weekly Mail* (Aug. 25 1894).

[50] The critique of foreign powers' exercise of extraterritorial jurisdiction in Japan, for example, had become the majority view by the time of Wigmore's advocacy. England and the United States abandoned extraterritorial jurisdiction with Japan in 1894, a year after Wigmore's departure, and other European countries followed shortly thereafter.

"In America, the Cleveland and Chicago horse-car strikes of a few years ago offered the spectacle of a whole city's transportation system in the hands of armed law-breakers, with the police divested of the power to use violence to dislodge them. . . . The tenderness of the Anglo-Saxon race towards criminals is certainly the result of a very peculiar attitude of mind."[51]

The picture that emerges from Wigmore's extraordinary life, then, is that of an ambitious, adventurous, and ultimately ordinary man and scholar caught in the political and intellectual milieu of his time, of which the encounter with a distant legal culture undergoing dramatic change was only one powerful trope. What to make of the ordinary comparative experience then? The question redirects our attention to the qualities of the legal ordinary.

LAW AND CUSTOM

The unifying theme in Wigmore's early work is the relationship between new and old, between "custom" and "law", between past and present.[52] His observations about the Japanese Parliament offer a glimpse of his interests, and an example of his eye for detail:

"The costumes, the building, the drapery, the whole scene, were in appearance thoroughly Western, and one looked almost in vain for a touch of the Japanese. But perhaps the sight was on that account more significant in its contrasts with the past. Everyone remembers the killing of Richardson in 1862, the young Englishman who rashly refused to yield the road to the train of the great Daimyo of Satsuma, Shimadzu Saburo, and was literally cut to pieces by the enraged retainers. The redoubtable Saburo has passed away, but down in the front row of Peers, in the very dress of the once-hated foreigners, sit his two sons . . . All through the assembly stood men whose recollections must have been in equally vivid contrast with the scene in which they were taking part."[53]

---

[51] John H. Wigmore, "Outrage by *Soshi*," *The Japan Daily Mail*, Aug. 17, 1891. The only critical commentary on core Western values I have been able to find in Wigmore's entire corpus of writing about Japan is a reflection on the loss of "personal ties" in acts of charity in the contemporary West. *See* John H. Wigmore, "Charity in Old Japan," *Japan Daily Mail*, Oct. 24, 1891, and a number of critical comments about Christianity. See, e.g., John H. Wigmore, "The New Buddhism," *The Japan Daily Mail*, March 31, 1892.

[52] On this point, as on many others, Wigmore had a certain penchant for clichés:

"The old Japanese artists, in their masterly woodcuts, were fond of depicting the celebrated mountain Fuji, one of the nation's (and the world's) scenic gems. The art of the modern photographer, too, may present it to us in another guise. The impressions are different. But the mountain is the same."

John H. Wigmore, *Panorama of the World's Legal Systems*, 525 (Washington D.C., 1936).

[53] John H. Wigmore, "Starting a Parliament in Japan," *Scribner's Magazine*, July 1891, at 47.

As the emphasis on custom would imply, Wigmore writes within an explicitly evolutionary paradigm.[54] For example, "The Pledge Idea,"[55] perhaps his most respected work on the subject of comparative law, uses comparative materials to attempt to trace the evolution of the institution of the pledge in commercial transactions. This evolutionary paradigm provided the justification for the comparison. Tokugawa Japan should be appreciated as a "laboratory" of legal development, Wigmore argued, because of its isolation from outside influences until Commodore Perry's arrival in 1853:

> "The evolution of legal institutions involves the tracing of their growth. But the reciprocal influences of one civilization upon another form usually a complex phenomenon, difficult to trace. Ever since Egypt and Mesopotamia, down through Mediterranean and European history, there have been borrowings and reactions innumerable. To identify a particular institution of a given country as a product of purely local and internal conditions, or to trace its borrowed path through other communities, has been too often the unattained ideal of the evolutionist. . . . Now, in the laboratory methods of natural science, one of the chief methods of tracing causes is to isolate each hypothetical element and to observe its reactions in that isolation under controlled conditions. So, too, in the study of social evolution, the isolation of a community from outside influences furnishes a decisive opportunity to study the indigenous and inherent evolution of an institution. . . ."[56]

The genre of Wigmore's early work, likewise, carefully mimicked that of Henry Maine and his peers. Like Maine, Wigmore offers readers the thrill of a grander, more historical perspective on familiar phenomena.[57] For example, after introducing Japan's contemporary legal reforms, Wigmore describes the many cases throughout history in which one society has borrowed a new set of laws from another, and concludes:

> "We see, then, that the work of Japan is but a drop in the sea, a foot-path in the midst of highways, a single shot in the cannonade of centuries. This is not depreciating the importance of the work for Japan itself; for such a task seldom comes more than once in a nation's lifetime, and for each nation it has a right to be considered as epoch-making.

---

[54] The eminent Japanese jurist Kenzo Takayanagi writes that at the time of Wigmore's work in Japan, legal positivism was by far the dominant philosophy of the young foreign law teachers at the major universities and that natural law was regarded as outdated. This may explain in part Wigmore's support for the project to codify Japanese law: "[Wigmore,] like [Henry T.] Terry, did not uphold natural law . . . Wigmore was historical and analytical. He followed Maine as well as John Austin." Kenzo Takayanagi, "A Century of Innovation: The Development of Japanese Law, 1868–1961," in Arthur Taylor von Mehren (ed.), *Law in Japan: The Legal Order in a Changing Society*, 15–20 (Cambridge Mass., 1963). Wigmore's co-edited 1915 text reproduces no less than six chapters of Henry Maine's *Ancient Law*. *See generally* John H. Wigmore & Albert Kocourek (eds), *Primitive and Ancient Legal Institutions* (Boston, 1915).

[55] John H. Wigmore, "The Pledge Idea: A Study in Comparative Legal Ideas, Part I," 10 *Harv. L. Rev.* 321 (1897); John H. Wigmore, "The Pledge Idea: A Study in Comparative Legal Ideas, Part II," 10 *Harv. L. Rev.* 389 (1897).

[56] Wigmore, *supra* note 23, at 49.

[57] *Cf.* Riles, "Representing In-Between: Law, Anthropology, and the Rhetoric of Interdisciplinarity," 1994 *U. Ill. L. Rev.* 597, 607–20.

But the remembrance that there is in progress a whole world-movement allows us to look with greater calmness on its manifestation in any particular quarter and to judge it more intelligently."[58]

Although Wigmore never overtly challenged the evolutionary paradigm within which he worked, he found in the model a difference of emphasis. Where Maine had emphasized difference—the question of why some societies ceased to evolve while others continued to progress—Wigmore's interest was rather in *commonalities*. Wigmore describes the emergence of this focus from his research in Japan:

> "All along the line, in Japanese legal history, were found institutions analogous to European ones. And yet there had been no possibility of imitation. Thus the problems of the evolution of corresponding legal ideas in independent systems were forced upon the student's attention. . . . Del Vecchio's philosophy of the development of universal innate legal ideas seemed here to be illustrated."[59]

If one compared practices concerning the treatment of earnest-money, for example, "we find a coincidence of custom between Rome and Japan which is not merely interesting but even startling."[60] Banks in seventeenth century Japan, likewise,

> "lacked none of the essential features of our own. They received on deposit, honored cheques, issued notes, negotiated bills of exchange, discounted bills drawn against merchandise, and acted in general as the intermediaries for commercial transactions. The smaller banks were connected financially with the larger ones, just as the country banks are with those of American cities and the provincial banks are with those of London. . . . They had some sort of a clearing-house system, the details of which are not yet clear. In short, there is little in the Western idea of a bank which the Japanese institution did not have or could not easily have assimilated."[61]

This commitment to the discovery of endless examples of "universal innate legal ideas" animates Wigmore's entire project.[62] In reading the evolutionary paradigm backwards in this way, as a celebration of universalism, it was

---

[58] John H. Wigmore, "The Administration of Justice in Japan, Part III," 45 *Amer. L. Reg. & Rev.* 571, 573 (1897).

[59] Wigmore, *supra* note 23, at 49. (Wigmore refers here to Giorgio Del Vecchio's article, "Upon the Conception of a Science of Universal Comparative Law," published as "Sull'Idea di una Scienza del Diritto Universale Comparato," in *Bericht uber den III Internationalen Kongress fur Philosophie* (1909)). Del Vecchio's work was later compiled, translated and published as part of Wigmore's Legal Philosophy Series. *See* Giorgio del Vecchio, The Formal Bases of Law (John Lisle trans., Boston, 1914).

[60] Wigmore, *supra* note 58, at 578.

[61] Wigmore, "The Administration of Justice in Japan," 45 *Am. L. Reg. Rev.* 628, 628–29 (1897).

[62] The direction of the argument is succinctly outlined in the initial chapters of Wigmore and Kocourek's 1915 comparative law textbook: the book begins with a chapter on "evolution of law," then moves to "ethnological jurisprudence," then to "the origin of legal institutions," and concludes with "universal comparative law" (an exerpt of Del Vecchio's 1910 article translated by Kocourek). *See generally* Kocourek & Wigmore, *supra* note 49, at 3–72.

possible to find a scientific argument for his own secular humanism.[63] Comparative law could serve as a mechanism for making these universals apparent:

> "By comparative law . . . is meant the tracing of an identical or similar idea or institution through all or many systems, with a view to discovering its differences and likenesses in various systems, the reasons for those variations, and the nature and limits of the inherent and invariable idea, if any—in short, the evolution of the idea or institution, universally considered."[64]

Wigmore cryptically named this approach "Comparative Legal Corporealogy."[65]

Here we encounter the nexus of Wigmore's universalist philosophy and his "amateurism." The grand equivalences in the passage quoted above, for example, the willingness to see what today's scholars would describe as a uniquely Japanese financial institution as "some sort of a clearing-house system"—seem overdrawn to contemporary scholars outside the legal academy.[66] But this

---

[63] Some of Wigmore's most intriguing writing from his time in Japan concerns his encounter with Asian philosophy and religion. In an article about the similarities between the philosophies of Confucius and Emerson, for example, he wrote,

> "it testifies to the unity of all experience; and there is something in learning that, whatever the difference of epochs and circumstances, the secret of life was the same for the philosopher of an ancient Chinese principality and the thinker of a modern democracy."

John H. Wigmore, "Confucius and Emerson," *The Japan Daily Mail*, Sep. 25, 1891. This was reflected also in his support for the New Buddhism of the time. A Unitarian, Wigmore was highly skeptical of organized religion and was attracted to the philosophical subtleties of that blend of Buddhism and scientific rationalism. *Cf.* Roalfe, *supra* note 17, at 244–47.

[64] Wigmore wrote,

> "For example, in my study of the comparative pledge idea in 1897, I was able to demonstrate that in ten or twelve systems the modern institution of mortgage, in all alike, begins as an absolute transfer; that in etymology the words for pledge, bet, and forfeit are identical; that the idea of a conditional transfer gradually emerges; that if the condition was not fulfilled at maturity, the transferee retained the article without any duty of restoring the surplus value. . . ."

Wigmore, *supra* note 23, at 51. *Cf.* Giorgio del Vecchio, "Science of Comparative Law," in Kocourek & Wigmore, *supra* note 48, at 66:

> "The fact that juridical institutions are subjected to a process of evolution may appear to negate this unity. On the contrary, it provides a new confirmation; since evolution itself manifests a general attribute of humanity which is realized in an analogous manner among the different peoples widely separated in space and time, and having no connection with each other; where, otherwise, to explain these phenomena, it would be necessary to revert to the hypothesis of a common origin of the races which in many cases is not verified, and where, for the rest, it would be insufficient to justify the analogies observed. The same evolution governs the general expression of the ethico-juridical system and special institutions (such as property, the family, etc.). They pass through a series of determinate stages in a definite order and frequently with the most remarkable resemblances; even to the point of the smallest details, and among nations without any historical association."

[65] The term is intended to highlight the way in which different legal systems, like parts of the body, are all part of one whole. *See* Wigmore, *supra* note 23, at 51. Wigmore cites the Japanese scholar Nobushige Hozumi (*cf.* Aoki, this volume) as the only scholar who had achieved what he believed comparative law should achieve. *See id.* at 52.

[66] It is striking that recent work on Tokugawa legal institutions ignores Wigmore's work altogether. *See*, *e.g.*, Herman Ooms, *Tokugawa Village Practice: Class, Status, Power, Law* (Berkeley, 1996).

amateurism is not simply the effect of an argument from another epoch. As we have seen, universalism at the heart of Wigmore's generalisations is *not* Mainian.[67] Nor is this universalism in the kind of natural law philosophy one might associate with modern law's prehistory; Wigmore, after all, was an historically minded positivist. Wigmore's passion for discovering "universal innate legal ideas" is in fact closer to the modern humanism that animates twentieth century cultural relativism, for example. The problem of Wigmore's amateurism, then, is not simply that Wigmore is out of date.

Wigmore's thinking about the relationship of law to social context further refutes our efforts to understand Wigmore as a product of a different epoch. The emergence of context as an organizing device is one of the defining dimensions of modernism across a variety of disciplines, from economics to sociology, to law. One of the ways in which Wigmore is thoroughly modern in this respect is his awareness of the social context of law and of the relevance of social science to the problems he sought to address. As he wrote of the records of Tokugawa legal institutions he collected,

> "In these trial records . . . not only the legal life is pictured, but also the whole domestic, social, agricultural and commercial life. The testimonies of the parties are set forth in great detail, and the daily events of importance in every walk of life are frankly and vividly revealed. . . . There is a treasure house here for the economist and for the social historian. Every aspect of money lending, every trade and occupation, every commercial transaction, every social institution, is set forth in the parties' own stories."[68]

In its insistence that law be understood as "but a part of human life,"[69] Wigmore's work would have resonated with the contextual turn in modernist legal scholarship. Wigmore's favorite metaphor for legal evolution, the movement of planets in a planetary system,[70] likewise, spoke to the interest in relativism and relativity of a new epoch. Although he wrote within an evolutionary paradigm, Wigmore displayed a sensitivity to the relativism of a more modernist age:

> "The combination of ancient and primitive law itself results, in fact, in inconsistency. Barring the controversy provoked by the term "primitive" (for what is the test of "primitive"?) there are examples of ancient law as modern in conception as anything seen in the world to-day."[71]

Yet note that Wigmore's notion of context in a sense gets the modernist move "backwards". Here, it is not that law stands to be interpreted in its social con-

---

[67] He tells us, contrary to the Mainian evolutionary scheme, that a right to private property, for example, existed during the Tokugawa era: "This is worth while insisting upon, for it is an idea not uncommon among foreigners that Old Japan was a feudalism in which no rights of the common people were recognized and respected." John H. Wigmore, "The Administration of Justice in Japan, Part III," 45 *Am. L. Reg. Rev.* 571, 575 (1897).

[68] Wigmore, *Law and Justice, supra* note 41, at xv.

[69] *See* John H. Wigmore, "Problems of the Law's Evolution," 4 *Va. L. Rev.* 247, 261 (1917).

[70] *See id.* at 264.

[71] Albert Kocourek & John H. Wigmore, "Preface," in Kocourek & Wigmore, *supra* note 48, at x.

text, but that law serves as a source of "stories" about the customs of the past, a source of context itself! This captures the intellectual location of Wigmore's work—not behind, or unaware, or even ahead of the paradigm shifts of his era, but consciously carelessly, somewhere else.

As Wigmore's work developed, the genre, if not the argument, underwent a deep transformation. It began with a shift from accounts of particular institutions, such as the pledge idea, to accounts of the character of different legal cultures. Over time, Wigmore added more vignettes, biographies, and photographs which, Wigmore argued, presented a more "realistic" picture of each legal system.[72]

Over the course of Wigmore's career, therefore, the analytical model—the evolutionary paradigm—gradually faded from overt view. In its place, Wigmore foregrounded the details, the anecdotes, the enticement of the facts. In his *Panorama of the World's Legal Systems*, Wigmore describes each of the legal systems he catalogs with particular attention to the character of the institutions, rather than the doctrine per se, and he makes extensive use of illustration. *Kaleidoscope of Justice*,[73] published over a decade later, goes even further. In this book, Wigmore reviews much of the same material as in *Panorama*, but this time he abandons totalizing descriptions of legal institutions altogether and focuses only on stories and images aimed at revealing what he terms " Justice."[74] For example, stories in the chapter on Japanese law include an account of a custom of placing a bell and a box outside the court for commoners to make their pleas directly to the Shogun,[75] and excerpts of documents from a case in which a wife ran away to a Buddhist convent concerning the rights of convents to grant divorces.[76] The documents and the fragments of anecdotes make no claims to be representative of the legal system as a whole, nor does Wigmore suggest what conclusions should be drawn from their perusal.

Although I find Wigmore's turn to images and stories intriguing and even inspiring at points, any effort to take Wigmore's project seriously as an intellectual venture reaches something of a stumbling block. Is this a farce, one might wish to ask of the collections of documents, slides, songs and typologies that appear in his later works? Wigmore's work seems to take to an extreme a dimension of comparative legal work which, as noted at the outset, has been the basis of a good deal of self-loathing within the discipline. As even one of Wigmore's most devoted supporters wrote in a review, *Panorama* "is not a book for experts embodying the author's researches, but it is worth our special notice as a new attempt by a veteran legal writer to popularize the subject for the

---

[72] *See* Wigmore, *supra* note 52, at 3.
[73] John H. Wigmore, *Kaleidoscope of Justice: Containing Authentic Accounts of Trial Scenes from All Times and Climes* (Washington D.C., 1941).
[74] *Id.* at v.
[75] *Id.* at 327.
[76] *Id.* at 339–48.

general public."[77] A reconsideration of Wigmore's contribution to comparative law therefore prompts a further question: How are we to read the many comparative projects and paradigms, such as this one, that seem to flaunt our collective amateurism?

A PERFORMANCE OF GAPS

Towards the end of Wigmore's life, a surprise opportunity for nostalgia presented itself. The Japan Cultural Society invited Wigmore to return to Japan to complete the translation project he had begun forty years before.[78] By the time of his arrival, the work had already begun under the leadership of several Japanese scholars, and although it proceeded under Wigmore's nominal direction, Wigmore's tasks seem to have been limited to final proofreading.[79] The era in which a foreign generalist effortlessly assumed the reins had long passed in Japan. From the standpoint of his Japanese hosts, too, Wigmore the ambitious young scholar had become Wigmore the amateur.

During this return visit, Wigmore delivered a series of "lantern slide lectures" on the subject of comparative law. The lectures summarized his "legal corporealogy" approach, with one twist: Wigmore illustrated his argument with exotic anecdotes and outrageous special effects, including a live physics experiment with the use of a balloon and a gyroscope, and a trick performed with a ribbon and a bicycle wheel.[80] Critics wrote about the performance with a mixture of bewilderment and condescension. I suspect that in an era of realist "fact skepticism"[81] Wigmore's flood of details, and his appeal to the fascinations of natural science, would have seemed in need of serious updating. Yet what I hope to illus-

---

[77] The Japanese reviewer focused instead on Wigmore's service to Japan and on his relationships with Japanese scholars and lawyers. See Shinzo Koizumi, "Dr. John Henry Wigmore: The Panorama of the World's Legal Systems (an abridged translation of a review of the book)," *Chuo Koron* (August 1935).

[78] "John Henry Wigmore Re-Visits Japan," *The Alumni News* (1935).

[79] Wigmore's request to begin the work in Chicago before his arrival in Tokyo was explicitly rejected in terms that made clear the division of labor envisioned by his Japanese sponsors:

> "Your suggestion is very recommendable and I would like to accept it, had it not been for the fear that you might be confronted with the same difficulty Professor Minegishi is now encountering; namely the difficulty of verifying the accuracy of translation of so many peculiar vocabularies and phrases that appear in the MSS. They are not to be found even in the best dictionaries available at present, and only by the service of experts can they be accurately translated. This matter is withholding the rapid progress of the work. Under such circumstances, I would recommend you to let Professor Minegishi proof read the MSS first before you give the final touch."

Setsuichi Aoki, Letter from the General Secretary of the Society for International Cultural Relations to John Henry Wigmore (March 6, 1936). The introduction to each volume makes it clear that the Japanese editors deviated considerably from Wigmore's translation. *See* Wigmore, *Law and Justice, supra* note 41.

[80] John H. Wigmore, "Evolution of Law," *Tokyo Teikoku Daigaku*, Tokyo, 57 (1935).

[81] *See* Wilfrid E. Rumble, *American Legal Realism*, 107–36 (Ithaca N.Y., 1968).

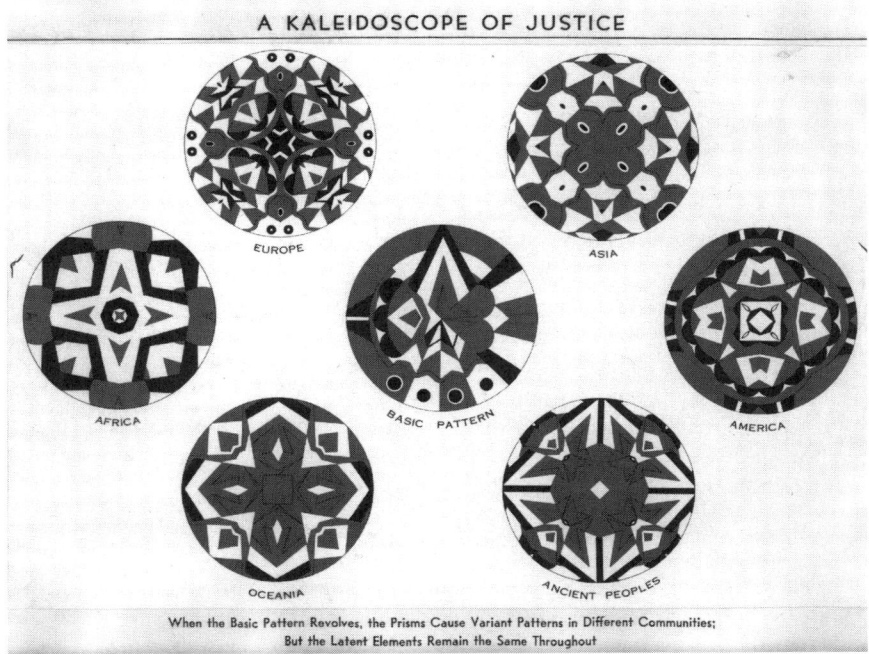

A KALEIDOSCOPE OF JUSTICE

When the Basic Pattern Revolves, the Prisms Cause Variant Patterns in Different Communities;
But the Latent Elements Remain the Same Throughout

Fig. 3   Illustration prepared by Wigmore of his Kaleidoscope concept, as a
prototype for his book, *Kaleidoscope of Justice*
(Reproduced by kind permission of Northwestern University)

trate is that to the extent that these lectures were dismissed for their lack of "new theories" they were profoundly misread. What Wigmore gave his audience, rather, was a virtuoso performance in the American law professor's genre, transposed into comparative legal studies. Indeed, we might read the lectures as an instantiation of Wigmore's entire comparative project: a performative experiment in how law engages.

What did Wigmore's audience have in mind when they dismissed work such as the lantern slide lectures as amateuristic? The reviews repeatedly pointed out that *Kaleidoscope* was simply a collection of stories and images, without more.[82] The text provided no guidance as to the scientific or doctrinal significance of the items collected on the page. Wigmore failed to analyze his material, to produce an argument, in other words. Contrast this failure, for example, with twentieth century social scientific knowledge in the academy in the twentieth century that has served as one powerful model for legal scholarship in the

---

[82]   *Cf.* George F. James, "A Literary Stylist," 32 *J. Crim. L. & Criminology* 275 (1941) (reviewing Wigmore, *Kaleidoscope of Justice*).

post-Realist era (and which I refer to here as modern academic knowledge).[83] Here, the task is to identify and organize a series of facts by adding to these facts a layer of analysis that relates them in an innovative way.[84] Modern academic analysis guides the reader through the experience of the data, and ultimately is what is "gained" from the scholarly experience. The amateurism of Wigmore's comparative legal scholarship, from this point of view, lies in its failure even to attempt an analytical output of this kind. There is no finished product, only a heap of raw material. The text leaves glaring analytical gaps.

Not every modernist read Wigmore in this way, however. Early critics of nineteenth century classicism in the United States and Europe readily recognized Wigmore as one of their own. Edouard Lambert understood Wigmore's project as less normative and programmatic than his own, but nevertheless of great scientific value,[85] and he greatly admired Wigmore's scholarship and his skills as a "propagandist" for comparative law.[86] In particular, Lambert was very much attracted to the presentation of Wigmore's argument:

"Taken as a whole, [the images] constitute for jurists, and especially for legal historians, a living documentation, realistic, moving. This is the transplantation of methods of illustration with images that are beginning to be used in your country for teaching history, but which have never been used on juridical terrain. In the domain of law this is something of very new—like your cards—and something most fecund."[87]

---

[83] I choose the term "academic" to index the opposite of "amateur" because of the confusion that the word "professional" might cause given the association of law schools with professional education. I do not intend to reduce all academic knowledge to a singular type, nor do I mean to imply that law professors could not be modern academics in the sense in which I invoke the term here. Indeed, many of the critical reviews of Wigmore's work, written by law professors, might serve as paradigmatic performances of the academic genre.

[84] *Cf.* Marilyn Strathern, "The Relation: Issues in Complexity and Scale," 6 *Prickly Pear Pamphlet* (1995).

[85] The two exchanged manuscripts and shared information frequently. *See, e.g.*, Letter from Edouard Lambert to John H. Wigmore (July 13, 1925); Letter from Edouard Lambert to John H. Wigmore (October 3, 1929). Lambert campaigned for Wigmore's nomination to the World Court, *see* Letter from Edouard Lambert to John H. Wigmore (April 21, 1930); Letter from Edouard Lambert to John H. Wigmore (April 28, 1930); Letter from Edouard Lambert to John H. Wigmore (May 5, 1930), arranged for the awarding of an honorary doctorate from the University of Lyon to Wigmore, and sought Wigmore's assistance in procuring funding for his projects. *See* Letter from Edouard Lambert to John H. Wigmore (April 20, 1929). (All letters on file at Northwestern University Library).

[86] Letter from Edouard Lambert to John H. Wigmore (April 3, 1930) (on file at Northwestern University Library).

[87] Letter from Edouard Lambert to John H. Wigmore (January 31, 1929) (on file at Northwestern University library). Lambert refers here to Wigmore's notorious Christmas cards, in which he composed personalized poems on scholarly themes. *See, e.g.*, Wigmore, *infra* note 93. In recent years, the visual and entertaining dimensions of modernist science have received some critical attention. *See, e.g.*, James Gleick, *Chaos: Making a New Science* (New York, 1987); Barbara M. Stafford, *Artful Science: Enlightenment Entertainment and the Eclipse of Visual Education* (Cambridge, Mass., 1994); Bruno Latour, "Drawing Things Together," in M. Lynch & S. Woolgar (eds), *Representation in Scientific Practice*, 19–68 (Cambridge, Mass., 1988).

Fig. 4 Wigmore delivers the Lantern Slide Lectures in Tokyo
(Reproduced by kind permission of Keio University)

Roscoe Pound also greatly admired Wigmore's scholarly project and erudition, although, unlike Lambert, he found Wigmore's genre somewhat obtuse:

> "I think Wigmore understands the problem of application of law—the fundamental problem of jurisprudence today—better than anyone in this country unless it is Mr. Justice Holmes. What makes his writing on the subject difficult to understand, perhaps, is that he has not run through the current decisions and compelled himself to look at the problem as it is presented in the everyday workings of our courts. No one is more fertile in good ideas than Wigmore, and really he is worth careful reading and careful reflection after reading, and I guarantee will yield great results when so read and reflected upon. Of course when he is riding on his high horse it is another matter. But many things may be pardoned to one who has achieved what he has in the science of law."[88]

Then, as perhaps now, in other words, Wigmore's work seemed at once relevant to and yet disengaged from his time. In the remainder of this essay, I want to argue that the peculiarities of Wigmore's work are best understood as the influences of American legal formalism.

---

[88] Letter from Roscoe Pound to Henry M. Bates, Dean of the University of Michigan Law School (March 24, 1931) (on file with the author).

At first blush, it may seem counter-intuitive to describe scholarship such as the Lantern Slide Lectures or *Kaleidoscope* as classicist or formalist in the Langdellian mold. To a contemporary reader, the genre of the work—the collections of images, scientific experiments, translations and theories into one all-inclusive text—might bear more resemblance to postmodern scholarship than to the treatises of the late nineteenth century. On a more theoretical level, also, Wigmore readily aligned himself with the Realist *critiques* of classical legal scholarship.[89] The new discipline of comparative law was *de facto* associated with the critique of classical thought in Europe and the United States (*cf.* Curran, this volume). Wigmore's promotion of the discipline would therefore have been widely understood as a challenge to traditional legal scholarship. Like the American Realists, moreover, Wigmore's comparisons emphasized change, discontinuity, conflict and power in the evolution of the legal tradition, and hence his work could be read as a challenge to homogeneic or ahistorical conceptions of legal norms. As Wigmore wrote in 1917,

> "[E]volution of Law, as in other cosmic facts, is always the result of a *conflict of forces*. The situation is very much like that of two men pushing face to face on the pavement, each seeking to pass, or wrestling in a final grip on the mat; in the wrestling match, finally a slight balance of force prevails, and the one man falls on his back, with the other over him as the winner. Then there is equilibrium for a while, but only until the next bout begins."[90]

Nevertheless, in many respects, Wigmore's larger project is archetypically Langdellian. Wigmore shared with Langdell and his followers a "historist" tra-

---

[89] This is particularly evident in Wigmore's correspondence with Holmes, Pound, and other prominent critics of formalism. *See, e.g.*, Letter from John H. Wigmore to Judge Holmes (April 29, 1894) (praising Holmes for "a step which will make the heterodox orthodox" and presenting his own ideas for a new and more functional analytical framework for the law of torts). Wigmore was one of Roscoe Pound's earliest and most enthusiastic supporters, and his own treatise on evidence was criticized for its modernist terminology by the same factions that led the attack on Pound. *See* Wigdor *supra* note 7, at 129. Wigmore's Christmas greeting to Pound in the latter's first year on the Northwestern Law faculty captures Wigmore's unique brand of enthusiasm for the Realist project:

> "All hail the newest star,
> now fixed amidst our constellation!
> A brilliant varied spectrum
> marks your lofty stellar station.
> As sociologic jurist,
> may the message of your pen
> Widely spread a mighty influence,
> from your editorial den!
> When Pharaoh had his Moses:
> *you're* the Moses by whose hand
> Our common law will pass from bondage
> to the promised land."

Id. at 135.

[90] Wigmore, *supra* note 70, at 253.

dition.[91] Although the materials Wigmore collected and exhibited were quite new to legal formalism, the kinds of questions he asked of those materials would have been familiar. One would not expect less from a founder of the Harvard Law Review, and an acknowledged missionary for the case method of legal education invented by Langdell.[92]

Take, for example, Wigmore's "legal corporeology" approach. What renders the term amateuristic to the point of absurdity to modern academic ears is precisely what would have appealed to the Langdellian taste for scientific analogies. Anthony Sebok recently has argued that, contrary to Realist characterizations, Langdellian formalism was committed to the notion of law as organic, living, and hence evolving over time.[93] Langdell's model for legal reasoning, Sebok claims, was biology: the courts were "laboratories," decisions should be thought of as "specimens," and the task was to "select, classify and arrange all the cases which had contributed in any important degree to the growth, development, or establishment of . . . essential doctrines."[94] This attraction to law as a scientific study of organic change pervades Wigmore's project. As Kocourek and Wigmore wrote in the Preface to their early textbook in comparative law,

> "There is a special kind of fascination in attempting here what seems to have been done with great success in the reconstruction of fossil remains of extinct animals. A single bone may lead to the reconstruction of the entire skeleton based on the size, shape, and function of the fragment used as a starting-point. Biological function however is immeasurably more simple than legal function; the one is related to the world of physical phenomena, the other to the world of mental and physical facts."[95]

Thus, although Wigmore clearly felt lonely in the presence of American formalists, and although his work was devalued and even dismissed when he first

---

[91] *Cf.* Stephen A. Siegel, "Historicism in Late Nineteenth-Century Constitutional Thought," 1990 *Wisc. L. Rev.* 1431.

> "Historism conceived law as an evolving product of the mutual interaction of race, culture, reason and events. Moreover, historism taught that objective legal principles were discernible through historical studies, not rationalistic introspection. . . . Historism's central claim was that historical studies reveal objective social norms and moral values. This claim rested upon a host of tenets, the most important of which were (1) that societies, social norms and institutions are the outgrowth of continuous change effected by secular causes; (2) that the universe has an ethical meaning that is accessible to human intelligence; and (3) that societies, social norms and institutions evolve according to moral ordering principles that are discoverable through historical studies."

Id. at 1435 (footnotes omitted).

[92] *See* Robert Stevens, *Law School: Legal Education in America from the 1850s to the 1980s*, 60 (Chapel Hill, 1983) (describing Harvard University President Eliot's congratulations to Wigmore for "having got into a missionary diocese").

[93] *See* Anthony J. Sebok, *Legal Positivism in American Jurisprudence*, 95 (Cambridge, 1998).

[94] Langdell quoted in *id.* at 93.

[95] Albert Kocourek & John H. Wigmore, *Formative Influences of Legal Development*, viii (Boston, 1918).

sought to introduce his former Harvard teachers to the emerging field of comparative law, Wigmore's love of comparison nevertheless built on the formalist sensibilities he had developed as a student. The case method, as developed by Langdell, made liberal use of English cases as a means of identifying through comparative analysis what essential legal principles persisted over time.[96] The Socratic method of classroom dialogue, likewise, was all about comparison: starting from a more or less explicit and absolute notion of the coherence of law and legal decision-making, the notion that "like cases should be treated alike," one compared facts and rules to reach conclusions either about the particular case or the legal principle as a whole. Indeed, the exercise of law teaching was largely concerned with inculcating in students a refined comparative sense.

The difference, of course, was that while the Langdellian formalist compared cases and rules to attempt to make visible a latent system, Wigmore sought to compare systems as total wholes. Indeed, as noted earlier, "legal corporeology" was meant to highlight the contexts of legal rules. Although the relationship of data to analysis in Wigmore's work was thoroughly Langdellian, then the *problem* Wigmore addressed—his subject—was quite different. Wigmore had used formalist knowledge practices against themselves to usher in a new era.

Nevertheless, the strangeness of the biological metaphor to modern ears illustrates how distant Wigmore's work also was from the social scientific approach of Pound and others. The amateurism of Wigmore's work from the social scientific point of view inhered in part in the relationship of facts to theory. By the time of Wigmore's writing, the evolutionary paradigm that sustained this search for generalities would have been already well trodden.[97] Ironically, however, the worn quality of the theory presented Wigmore, with an opportunity: he could take the theory for granted, and indulge, rather, in the detail, the customs, the local facts. For Wigmore, as for Langdell, theory was what one borrowed from Maine and others. What contemporary comparativists would describe as a theory, in contrast, (for example Wigmore's theory about the evolution of the pledge) was for him a *fact* established scientifically through comparative work. In this sense, comparative law was ultimately a localized, factual endeavor, albeit one with theoretical underpinnings and implications.[98]

---

[96] Edwin W. Patterson, "The Case Method in American Legal Education: Its Origins and Objectives," 4 *J. Leg. Ed.* 1, 11 (1951).

[97] *See, e.g.*, Raymond Cocks, *Sir Henry Maine: A Study in Victorian Jurisprudence*, 247 (Cambridge, 1988).

[98] The factual emphasis of Wigmore's project is relevant where the debate over the amateurism of Comparative Law has often been framed as a question of an excess of theory. *See, e.g.*, William Alford, "On the Limits of 'Grand Theory' in Comparative Law," 61 *Wash. L. Rev.* 945 (1986); W. B. Groves, & G. Newman, "Against General Theory in Comparative Research," 13 *Int'l J. of Comp. & App. Crim. Jus.* 23 (1989); Mathias Reimann, "The End of Comparative Law as an Autonomous Subject," 11 *Tul. Eur. & Civ. L. Forum* 49 (1996); Eric Stein, "Uses, Misuses—and Nonuses of Comparative Law," 72 *Nw. U. L. Rev.* 198 (1977).

One way to think about the difference of expectations surrounding Wigmore's work is from the point of view of the relations that intellectual work is intended to generate—the relationship between author and audience, and the extent to which that relationship is mediated by the scholarly text. As Tony Crook has recently argued, for modern academics, textually mediated analysis engenders the social relations that are integral to professional success. A work's audience is the small community of readers who might be enticed to join the author in a debate. Ideas—units of analysis that speak to existing arguments and the communities that stand behind them in the appropriately situated and yet self-differentiated way—engender (academic) persons. To be an academic, then, is to have a stake in being a person in this sense.[99] Yet in Wigmore's most cherished roles as collector, translator, correspondent, critic and editor,[100] the relationality is all within the edited text, not without—among the diverse fragments of essays and illustrations, each with their own diffuse authorship. From the modern academic's point of view, Wigmore's curious failure to analyze his materials, and his disclaimer of an originality that can be situated in relation to the work of others, seems to treat his own relations outside the text, that is, in the community of scholars, as superfluous. We might read the progressive fading of analytical structures in Wigmore's work over the course of his career alluded to earlier in this chapter as a privilege of his amateur status. To topple a predecessor's model or to mount a critique is the ultimate relational, participatory move. Yet to gradually background a model, as Wigmore did with evolutionary theory, is to assert with increasing self-confidence that one has no particular stake in the "debate" per se.

Perhaps this is because for Wigmore the Institution, the darling of the classroom, the law school and the bar association, the global correspondent and world traveler, social relations were elsewhere. Indeed, one difference between the professional and the amateur is that the latter by definition does not live by his or her ideas. Wigmore would have had no need to make himself relevant through his work; he already *was* relevant in every socially and institutionally significant way. Perhaps, then, thinking about interesting questions becomes what we would call a hobby: a privilege of Wigmore's hard-earned position, a chance for adventure, a secret deviance even, but not the source of personal relevance. Wigmore might prompt us to wonder why the effects of scholarship should be judged in only one narrow way.

Wigmore's doggedly amateuristic conceptualization of the scholarly venture was not, and is not, unique, I think, among comparative lawyers. It is no wonder

---

[99] *See* Tony Crook, The Textual Person, paper presented at the American Anthropological Association Annual Meeting, Chicago, Illinois, November 17–21, 1999 (manuscript on file with the author).

[100] One of Wigmore's favorite genres was the book review. In Japan, he summarized the doctoral dissertations of Japanese scholars returning from the West, and he also wrote articles in American academic journals introducing American audiences to the work of Japanese scholars. Later in his career he continued this practice as editor of numerous monograph series.

that Lambert would have drawn a parallel between Wigmore's inventive scholarship and his inventive Christmas cards: The volumes of personal correspondence and frequent visits among comparativists, the international congresses at which it is openly acknowledged that the main attraction is the opportunity to see friends, not to hear academic papers,[101] the several associations, each with their own baroque politics, the committees for the harmonization of legal rules, and the frequent *festschrift* volumes[102] suggest that for this community, the work of relationality lies elsewhere. The community of comparativists is not textually constituted and mediated.

Yet there is more at issue here, I think, than a simple division of intellectual labor into what is professionally significant and what is not. If one remembers that Langdellian formalism was most explicitly a teaching method rather than a theory—that its epistemological, normative and scholarly implications remained largely implicit until they were unearthed in the guise of critique by a later generation—then one can understand the connection between the form of Wigmore's eclectic comparative work and the wider genre of formalist legal teaching. Wigmore was deeply interested in the dynamics of law teaching, and much of his scholarship was presented in the genre of a teaching tool—for academics, law students and the wider community of lawyers. Wigmore's project, as exemplified by texts such as *Panorama* and *Kaleidoscope*, seems reasonable to him, then, just as it seems a bit overdrawn and hence amateuristic to his critics, precisely because it is the formalist genre expanded from the context of teaching to scholarship.

Consider, for example, the casebooks used in legal teaching: If Wigmore would have opposed Langdell's view that the only relevant materials for legal study were legal cases,[103] he clearly shared Langdell's emphasis on the exposure of students to primary materials:

> "For the student, the best results will be gotten by attempting first to master the raw materials of the first volume, in analogy to the case-method; that is to say, by making an effort to reconstruct for himself, from topic to topic, the state of development of the legal institutions among . . ."[104]

---

[101] *See* LeGrand, *supra* note 15, at 22 (quoting John Merryman as saying, "Like most international congresses, these are valuable primarily for the opportunities to meet people and see friends. What the organizers call the "scientific programme" is almost always a debacle.")

[102] *See, e.g.*, Peter Wallington & Robert M. Merin (eds), *Essays in Memory of Professor F. H. Lawson* (London, 1986); Emmanuel G. Bello & Bola A. Ajiboa (eds), *Essays in Honour of Judge Taslim Olawale Elias* (Dordrecht, 1992); David S. Clark (ed.), *Comparative and Private International Law: Essays in Honor of John Henry Merryman on his Seventieth Birthday* (Berlin, 1990); K. Boele-Woelki et al. (eds), *Comparability and Evaluation: Essays on Comparative Law, Private International Law and International Commercial Arbitration in Honour of Dimitra Kokkini-Iatridou* (Dordrecht, 1994); Zoltan Petri (ed.), *Legal Theory Comparative Law: Studies in Honour of Professor Imre Szabo* (Budapest, 1984).

[103] *See* Patterson, *supra* note 100, at 3.

[104] Albert Kocourek & John H. Wigmore (eds), 2 *Primitive and Ancient Legal Institutions* v (Boston, 1915).

The texts used in American law schools in Wigmore's time, as today, are, as their name implies, "materials"—collections of essays and documents. The idea is that the very absence of answers to the text's open-ended questions will stimulate a response from the student and spark a dynamic discussion in class; they are tools for creating a moment.[105] Wigmore and Kocourek epitomise the genre, for example, when they insist that they "have not sought here to solve any problems of their own, or to ventilate any theories" and that "[e]very reader will interpret his own philosophy of history, and construct his own generalizations."[106] Although such a collection and display of disparate fragments is found in some avant-garde forms of literature and art, it probably achieves mainstream status only in American legal teaching tools. Contrast this to the texts used in graduate education in the humanities and social sciences—finished papers and essays that give students an outsider's glance at a very internal debate.[107]

One way of understanding the relationship between Langdellian formalism and the classroom performance is by analogy to Erving Goffman's classic work on the subject of play.[108] Goffman distinguishes the game—the self-contained rules—from play—the experience of performing the rules. In order for games to hold the attention of participants, the outcomes must be both predictable only with reference to the rules, but also contingent.[109] Moreover, the "mutual focused activity" of the game must be delineated from the outside world.[110] The outside world is nevertheless introduced in a controlled or transformed manner (for example in the rule that spouses cannot serve as partners in a bridge game), and ideally, this manner will also serve as a ground for exhibiting skills one has developed elsewhere (as in the importance of memory, or strategy in many games).[111] This is achieved, Goffman argues, through mutually agreed "rules of irrelevance" in which participants promise not to think about certain aspects of their shared experience (for example, the fact that the chess players could

---

[105] I follow here Keith Basso's call to understand "the conditions under which [writing] is selected and the purposes to which it is put . . . in relation to those other channels." Keith H. Basso, "The Ethnography of Writing," in Richard Bauman & Joel Sherzer (eds), *Explorations in the Ethnography of Speaking*, 425, 426 (Cambridge, 1989).

[106] Kocourek & Wigmore, *supra* note 109, at viii.

[107] *Cf.* Mertz, *supra* note 21.

[108] I use the term "formalist" interchangeably with "legal scholar" because as I indicate later, I believe legal knowledge is inherently formalistic as an aesthetic and performative genre, indeed, that this is one of the defining traits of legal thought, whatever its normative or epistemological claims. *Cf.* Anthony T. Kronman, *The Lost Lawyer*, 169 (Cambridge, Mass., 1993) ("For all their fashionableness and novelty, the law and claims of critical legal studies movements are essentially Langdellian in spirit.")

[109] *See* Erving Goffman, *Encounters: Two Studies in the Sociology of Interaction*, 35 (Indianapolis, 1961).

[110] *See id.* at 62.

[111] *See id.* at 33.

remove one another's pieces by simply knocking them off the table) for the duration of the game.[112]

Goffman's vocabulary makes plain, I think, how the classroom experience that Langdell pioneered, and that continues largely to this day, is enabled by the underlying Langdellian epistemology, theory and practice of law. Prowess in the classroom is imagined as a demonstration of lawyerly skill in disguised form. The successful classroom performance, depends on participants' degree of engagement with the performance, and this in turn depends on the existence of a certain element of surprise as to the direction that the event might go. This demands fixed but also subtly porous rules of irrelevance that enable the event to echo the experience of the wider world but also maintain its focused, momentary quality. In the law school classroom it is the precepts of formalism that provide those rules. The complex Langdellian notion of the place of history on the one hand and logic on the other in the science of legal reasoning enables a "vicarious" experience of social life without ultimately undermining the structure of the game itself.

To return to the question of academic relations addressed above, this is possible only because for the formalist legal scholar,[113] the text does not stand for the self in the way it does for the academic, nor does the textual debate stand for the community in which the self is constituted. This is because for the formalist, the relevant site of academic relationality is not the text but the classroom. The site for the formalist's evidence of the self is the classroom performance. The same set of carefully developed peerformance skills are deployed in formal and informal conversations among formalist peers. Whether in the classroom or the faculty lounge, the evidence of academic sociality inheres in the momentary conversation the performance elicits. The achievement of such momentary relationality is dependent on the performer's ability to generate interest at that moment by framing a question or set of materials in a sufficiently focused and yet general way such that a contentious conversation can be generated in a matter of minutes among the members of the audience.

For the formalist, academic reputation is determined by momentary performative skill therefore. Legal knowledge is not ultimately about creating a sustained intellectual debate, and therefore ideas (if defined, as above, as appropriately differentiated but situated units of analysis) are not of primary concern. My point, then, is that formalism cannot be reduced to a theoretical position and an accompanying epistemology. It is first an aesthetic propensity, a genre of self-presentation for the author and the text. From this point of view,

---

[112] *See id.* at 68–77. Patterson argues that one of the goals of the case method is to provide a kind of "vicarious experience" that will "acquaint the student with the contemporary culture in which he lives and in which legal devices are operative . . . By 'culture' I mean nothing more occult than the practices of people in buying and selling, in hiring and firing, in getting houses built and business enterprises financed, in evading or avoiding income taxes, and the like." Patterson, *supra* note 100, at 15.

[113] *See* Goffman, *supra*, note 114, at 19.

I believe we can understand the gaps in comparative legal analysis, of which Wigmore's work offers an admittedly extreme example, as in legal analysis more broadly, as not just a matter of carelessness, but as an outcome, a consequence, of the author's performative goals.

In focusing on the teaching of comparative law, then, I believe that Wigmore ironically found in his own formalist tradition something of enduring interest to a new era of legal scholars. This was true even though the teaching model Wigmore deployed was very much unique to the American legal tradition, and something quite apart from the genre of teaching prevalent in the social sciences that were then serving as the inspiration for legal theory. It is at least suggestive, I think, that realist comparative legal scholars, like the realists more generally, spared the classroom performance from the critique they leveled at the formalist academic text and in fact engaged in the performance to great effect themselves.[114] I suggest this not in the guise of yet another realist critique of law for failing to be social science, but as an effort to understand the unique character of legal knowledge on its own terms.

In appropriating the formalism of legal teaching to scholarship, and hence collapsing the distance between the treatise and the classroom, in other words, Wigmore brilliantly collapses the distinction between performative and analytical genres of formalism. In an era in which the epistemological and political foundations of formalism, as a doctrinal theory, found themselves under attack, Wigmore stretches formalism to the limits of its plausibility. His innovation circumvents the intellectual aridity of analytical formalism, which Wigmore was explicitly against, while preserving the "logical universal form" which Wigmore's inspiration, Georgio Del Vecchio, described as a "necessary condition to experience juridical facts,"[115] by rediscovering formalism's performative

---

[114] On the "practical" question of teaching methods, Pound had very similar ideas to Wigmore's. He wrote to Wigmore in 1905, that the casebook method was far more practical than the social scientific approach in training American law students in comparative law:

"I had inclined to prepare somewhat carefully a small book of extracts illustrating the history of juristic thought and to try teaching from it as an experiment, but I am not at all certain that such a plan would meet the requirements of the situation. Probably the ideal method would be to insist in some way upon adequate economic and sociological training as a prerequisite for admission to a law school. But . . . I fear that a thorough course in constitutional law would tend to dissipate all the results of prior academic training."

Letter from Roscoe Pound to John H. Wigmore (May 11, 1905) (on file with the author).

[115] Del Vecchio, *supra* note 64, at 64. Del Vecchio adds,

"Recognition of this transcendental condition of juridical experience does not diminish the value of experience itself. Rather, it puts experience in its true light and guarantees it authority in its own field. In reality, we are able and ought to borrow from experience as an inexhaustible fountain, knowledge of the content that law has provided in space and time. From what has been just said nothing which credits the study of historical facts in which a juridical character is found is an obstruction to going back in turn to the formal idea of which facts are only the applications and illustrations."

Id. at 65.

side. It was the perfect innovation for an amateur radical and a sometime vision-ary.

I believe we should read this innovation on doctrinal formalism as on par with the analytical *critique* of formalism more famously associated with the realists. Wigmore demonstrated how formalism, as a genre of scholarship and teaching, may be effectively *performed* even when the epistemological or theoretical foun-dations of the performance are entirely at odds with the *beliefs* routinely assoc-iated with a formalistic understanding of law. Wigmore's performative genre of comparative law recreates formalism as the gaps that make play contingent and hence interesting.

In particular the formalist performance genre makes sense of the universalism at the heart of Wigmore's work which, as we saw, also led to dismissals of the work as amateuristic. One of the assumptions that the formalist author/speaker must make in order to generate a momentary debate is that the audience is com-posed of persons with whom one shares a series of assumptions and background knowledge as well as interest and affect. Like students in the classroom in the didactic tradition, the audience is, in a sense, understood from the start. Wigmore extends this notion of "we" not simply within but without, from the relationships of teacher and student or audience to the relationship of the author to his subject. His vision is of a universal set of legal principles and a universal notion of Justice appropriate for an ultimately common humanity. This under-standing in turn assumes access to the minds of other people (imagined to be only superficially different from ourselves).

Yet it is important to understand that Wigmore achieves this success at a moment at which the political, and epistemological foundations of form-alism had been profoundly shaken, only by stretching the formnalist notion of universalism outside the confines of the classroom frame and applying it to scholarship. In the same way he confounds data and audience: his inter-est in the legal profession in different parts of the world as a *subject* for comparison, is one and the same as his interest in rendering comparative law accessible to members of the profession, as *audience*. Popular (read amateuristic) knowledge about law then serves as both the beginning and the ending point of his work, and hence explicitly confounds beginnings and ends. It is the logical equivalent of saying that the questions one asks about legal doctrine in the formalist classroom are indistinguishable from the students who answer them. Herein lies the radicalism of Wigmore's approach.

Wigmore, in other words, demonstrates how formalism enables a particular kind of encounter with difference—a genre of encounter that, in the realm of the comparative disciplines, is probably unique to comparative law. Wigmore's innovation is to push to its limits this dimension of the formalist aesthetic—the possibility that an infinite amount of incongruity and difference can be accomodated without threat to the coherence of the whole. His own reconciliation of his progressive and conservative views and his formalist and realist commitments serves as the ultimate example of how the formalist logic survives challenges to its frame of reference.

CONCLUSION

This returns us to the question of the amateurism in comparative law I raised at the outset. The question of how to handle persons and projects that make our amateurism explicit is a delicate one: At the conference at which this paper was first delivered, a brisk debate erupted as to whether Wigmore could legitimately be considered a "Master" deserving of a chapter in a book alongside Lambert, Rabel, and others. Perhaps the embarrassment stems in part from self-recognition: Although few comparativists today would publish pictorial volumes with romantic titles like *Panorama of the World's Legal Systems*, to a greater or lesser extent, present day comparativists also seem content with the incompleteness of their analysis. To date, there has been little response to outsiders' calls for more rigorous comparative methods other than a sense that "that's just not what we do."

A consideration of Wigmore's life and scholarship suggests that if amateurism is defined as a failure to analyze, then comparative law is inherently amateuristic. It cannot be otherwise as long as our discipline remains comparative *law* that is, a discipline grounded in the culture of legal formalism, rather than comparative politics, literature, aesthetics or anthropology. What I have tried to demonstrate to comparativists more accustomed to thinking of their discipline as the heir to a realist and functionalist critique of classicism, is that the formalist tradition—and particularly the performative formalism of the American law school classroom—has played a productive legitimizing and sustaining role in the discipline, and has also been the source of much of its energy and creativity.[116] Yet, if this is so, we must ask ourselves why the critiques of Wigmore's amateurism never fall upon the formalism of his work in evidence— why the formalism that defines all legal knowledge only looks amateuristic within the context of comparative law where the same analytical moves serve, in other contexts, as the prototype of serious legal scholarship.

---

[116] This proposal will not appeal to today's comparativists. In a recent book, Alan Watson devotes a chapter to an attack on the case method in American law schools:

> "When only a few [cases] are studied, each appears out of context. The casebook does not put any of these into the general framework of the concept . . . to give students the big picture. Students cannot tell how far a quoted case reflects general propositions or whether it stands at the very edge of a doctrine. They have no way of seeing how the law builds up. The role of authority is not clarified. . . . When a case is discussed in isolation, it is often impossible to know which facts are to be regarded as relevant."

Alan Watson, *Law out of Context*, 141 (Athens, 2000).

Watson adds that "the absence of theoretical underpinnings is a fatal flaw in the casebook approach." *Id.* at 143.

One answer, I have tried to show, lies in the necessity of collapsing the distinction between the performative and analytical dimensions of formalism in order to adapt formalism to the modernist comparative project—the project of comparing legal systems rather than tracing the evolution of rules. Ultimately, it is this innovation, *not* a contextual understanding of Japanese or American law, I think, that is the legacy of Wigmore's encounter with Japanese custom.[117] Wigmore's carefree performance of the life of the expatriate amateur remains his prototype of the experience of learning, and hence his experimental model of formalism itself.

Wigmore's work might give the critics of amateurism in comparative law just a moment of pause, then. What is unique about the "amateurism" of legal knowledge, as it has shaped comparative law into a distinctly legal discipline, Wigmore's work suggests, is precisely that, in its analytical incompleteness, it leaves gaps for future analytical work: the comparative text as a set of materials for collective conversation. The "open" dimension of the work serves as a point of entry for the audience, a nexus of mutual engagement. And yet while the notion of the experiment with the open text is as engaging as Wigmore's eclectic materials, Wigmore's life and work as expatriate amateur suggests also the limitations and even the arrogance of the project.

---

[117] Wigmore adds a personal addendum to the preface to *Sources of Ancient and Primitive Law* that makes clear the relevance of his time in Japan to the teaching mission of the volume:

> "Twenty-five years ago, while living in Japan, I became interested in the sources of old Japanese law. On turning over then unpublished materials, I discovered that its institutions, point for point, showed parallel legal ideas, and sometimes (amidst influences totally independent) a striking similarity of development with the Occident. I was led to study these ideas from the comparative point of view. As yet a novice in the world of legal thought, I came under the fascination of what is called comparative law (or, as it may preferably be named, universal legal ideas). And I felt a wish and hope to cultivate that field especially. . . . that early experience convinced me in a personal way that the subject had a real claim upon us and a great future,—immensely greater than the then state of the literature might indicate.
>
> Circumstances obstructed my wish to pursue this task, and it was laid aside as a dream. . . . I obtrude here this personal statement because I have a sentimental interest in thus returning to the science of my early hopes."

John H. Wigmore, "Addendum to the Preface," in Kocourek & Wigmore, *supra* note 48, at xi–xii.

Part III
The Science of Modernization

5

Nobushige Hozumi: A Skillful Transplanter of Western Legal Thought into Japanese Soil

HITOSHI AOKI*

INTRODUCTION

In October 1899, a Japanese legal scholar presented, at the International Congress of Orientalists in Rome, a paper entitled "Ancestor-Worship and Japanese Law," in which he discussed ancestor worship in general and its institutionalization within the new Japanese legal system, particularly in the fields of constitutional and family law. He showed how ancestor worship, one of the most important indigenous traditions of Japanese culture, had been recognized in law and was affecting modern Japanese law.

Five years later, in September 1904, he was invited to the International Congress of Arts and Science in St. Louis. His presentation this time was titled "The New Japanese Civil Code as Material for the Study of Comparative Jurisprudence" and compared, from a wider perspective, various features of the Japanese Civil Code with those of other countries.[1]

The man in question is Nobushige Hozumi (1855–1926), who became the first Professor of Jurisprudence at the Imperial University of Tokyo in 1882.[2] He was the first Japanese legal scholar to appear in international forums and publish papers in English, which are still regarded today as being among the best international references on Japanese law and jurisprudence.

His contribution to the modernization of Japanese law through the transplantation of advanced Western law and jurisprudence was unrivaled by any of

* I express my sincere thanks to Prof. Annelise Riles, Prof. Masaji Chiba, Prof. John Middleton, Ms. Jane Campion, Ms. In Sung Mo and Ms. Hisami Suzuki. Without their kind help, it would have been impossible for me to complete this article.

[1] See Nobushige Hozumi, *Ancestor-Worship and Japanese Law* (4th ed., Tokyo, 1938); Nobushige Hozumi, *Lectures on the New Japanese Civil Code as Material for the Study of Comparative Jurisprudence* (2d ed., Tokyo, 1912). Both papers were later revised and published as books under the original titles.

[2] The present-day University of Tokyo originated from the official schools of the Tokugawa Shogunate, merged as the University of Tokyo under the new Meiji Government, reorganized and renamed the Imperial University of Tokyo in 1886 with four Faculties of Law, Science, Literature, and Medicine.

his Japanese contemporaries. Among other things, he played a pivotal role in drafting, with two other scholars, the new Japanese Civil Code, which finally came into force in 1898. In accordance with Japanese governmental policy, the three scholars mainly referred to the German system (*Pandektensystem*) in drafting the Code. However, Hozumi also had a thorough knowledge of the social evolutionism of H. Spencer, the historical jurisprudence of H. S. Maine, and the ethnological empiricism of J. G. Frazer. Systematic legal thinking and dynamic historical and comparative jurisprudence are thus interlocking in his works.

In his St. Louis address, he characterized the Japanese Civil Code as "a connecting link between the Past and the Present, between the East and the West," standing at the crossroads of historical and comparative jurisprudence.[3] In this chapter, I explore Hozumi's own role as "a connecting link" between the West and Japan through a close reading of another article of his, namely "Tabū to Hōritsu" ["Taboos and Law"]. The article, written under the strong influence of J. G. Frazer, not only illustrates the features of his scholarship, but also contains some critical issues arising from the interaction between Japanese indigenous thought and transplanted Western thought. While treating Frazer's views with due respect and admiration, he deliberately rejected or altered some aspects of them to introduce them smoothly into the soil of Japanese culture. Hozumi's struggle both for and against Frazer brought forth a truly creative work. A close analysis of how and why Hozumi "trimmed" Frazer's work will not only provide interesting materials for the reflection on the method of comparative law but also a possible answer to the contemporary issue of what significance comparative law has to non-Westerners especially.

HOZUMI AND HIS SURROUNDINGS

Let us begin by looking at four pictures. Figure 1 was taken in 1871. On the right, we can see a young samurai wearing a long sword sitting with folded arms. This man is Hozumi who was 16 years old at that time. Figure 2 was taken in 1873, only two years after the first picture was taken. Readers might be surprised to find that the appearances of the boys are totally different here. Hozumi, who is standing in the middle, looks a little embarrassed. He cut his topknot, wore an occidental style uniform with a bow tie, and abandoned his sword that was a symbol of samurai. Figure 3 is a postage stamp issued in 1999 to commemorate the centenary of the Japanese Civil Code. The three men in traditional Japanese clothes were all professors of the Imperial University of Tokyo and they were drafters of the Code. We can see Hozumi in his forties on the right. He does not look embarrassed any more in this picture. On the contrary, his face is full of self-confidence. Lastly, figure 4 was taken in 1924, two years before Hozumi's death. He looks very natural in this picture. At last

---

[3] *See supra* note 1, at 2.

western clothes became him. In my view, these four pictures not only reflect Hozumi's personal history, but also symbolize the path that Japanese law followed after the Meiji Restoration.

Hozumi was born the second son of a middle-class *bushi* [samurai] in the small fief of Uwajima, Shikoku in 1855, at the dawn of modern Japan.[4] Prior to 1871, when the modern system of local government was introduced, the country was divided into fiefs called *han*, each of which was ruled by a *daimyō* [military lord]. Hozumi commenced his studies at a school run by the Lord of Uwajima. As was typical of *bushi* in those days, the main subject he studied was Chinese Literature and Thought. The other subjects were Calligraphy, Swimming, Kendo, Judo, Horseback Riding, Japanese Classical Studies, Military Affairs, and Arithmetic. He spoke no English until he came to Tokyo in 1871.[5]

In 1871, three years after the Meiji Restoration, the new central government ordered each *han* to recommend the brightest youth to be sent to the new capital, Tokyo. The government intended to let them absorb advanced western sciences in order to utilize them as a dynamic force for building a new, modern, and westernized nation. The Uwajima-han selected Hozumi. In the final examination, they tested the candidates' ability to interpret a passage from the Chinese classics. As ridiculous as it might seem when we consider the purpose of the examination, history has subsequently shown that they chose the right candidate. Hozumi left Uwajima for Tokyo by ship in the same year. Disturbed by bad weather, it took more than a month for him to reach Tokyo. Today the same distance can be covered in several hours by air or railway.

The boys in figures 1 and 2 were the elite of the day who had been selected to assemble in Tokyo by the new central government soon after the collapse of the Tokugawa Shogunate. There is a striking change in the clothes, but this change was not due to their personal tastes but rather to Japan's national policy. At that time, the new government issued edicts to cut off topknots (1871) and to abandon swords (1876) in order to hasten westernization of Japanese society; Japan experienced not only a big political change, but also a kind of cultural revolution.

---

[4] In the first half of the seventeenth century, Japan adopted a policy of national seclusion (*sakoku*, meaning "closing the doors of the country"), mainly because the Tokugawa Shogunate regarded Christianity as politically dangerous. With the help of her geographic isolation, Japan was able to maintain this policy for more than two hundred years. Until the mid-nineteenth century, ordinary Japanese had hardly any opportunities to learn about foreign countries and people. Only a limited number of volunteers learned anything of the Western world and sciences. Japanese had been, so to speak, thoroughly isolated from the rest of the world and therefore blind to foreign affairs. In 1853, an American naval officer, Commodore Perry, arrived at Uraga, not far from Edo (Tokyo), with four warships, and requested that the Tokugawa Government open the country. This event shook and awoke the whole of Japan, triggering radical changes in quick succession, during which time the Tokugawa Shogunate was forced to open the nation to the world and, finally, to return political rule to the Emperor Meiji in 1867. Under the authority of the Emperor, a new and young government began to build a modern Japan by importing knowledge, ideas, values, institutions and even everyday etiquette from Western countries such as Britain, France and Germany.

[5] *See*, Shigeyuki Hozumi, *Meiji Ichi Hōgakusha no Shuppatsu*, 3 (Tokyo, 1988).

Fig. 1 Nobushige Hozumi aged 16
(Reproduced from Shigetō Hozumi (ed.) *Hozumi Nobushige Ibunshū*, vol. 1 (1932))

Fig. 2 Nobushige Hozumi aged 18
(Reproduced from Shigeyuki Hozumi (ed.), Meiji Ichi Hōgakusha no Shuppatsu (1988)
with kind permission of the author)

Fig. 3 Postage stamp issued in 1999 to commemorate the centenary
of the Japanese Civil Code

Fig. 4 Nobushige Hozumi in 1924
(Reproduced from Shigetō Hozumi (ed.) *Hozumi Nobushige Ibunshū*, vol. 4 (1934))

After his arrival in Tokyo, Hozumi entered a special school for the elite. This institution was later reorganized into the University of Tokyo, where almost all the important teachers were English, French, German or American and hired by the Japanese Government.[6] It was an Englishman named W. E. Grigsby who first trained Hozumi as a lawyer.[7] His classes were conducted in English.

At that time, Japan had neither a parliament nor a modern systematic corpus of laws—no constitution or civil code, let alone procedural codes or commercial codes. There was in fact a criminal code compiled soon after the Restoration, but its contents were far from modern.[8] For example, crimes were not clearly defined and the punishments tended to be cruel.[9] In addition, the code explicitly ordered judges to qualify criminal acts by analogy when they could not find a section applicable to the offence. Japanese law in the 1870s did not include any of the aspects of legal practice commonly associated with the rule of law, such as the principle of void for vagueness.

Hozumi was sent to England in 1876 to study law. On arriving in London, he enrolled at King's College, University of London and then at Middle Temple, one of the Inns of Court. He qualified as a barrister in 1879. During his stay in London, he devoted his youthful energies to the study of social evolutionism as well as English law, and came to have a strong belief in the universal evolution of law. He declared to one of his Japanese friends that "he would devote all his future life to the study of law's evolution."[10]

In 1880, on his own initiative he moved to Berlin to study German law. In a letter requesting the Japanese Government's permission, he explained his reasons for wishing to move to Germany as follows: (1) he had already obtained "sufficient knowledge of English law to further those studies by himself"; (2) comparative jurisprudence, which he thought necessary for modernizing Japan, was most advanced in Germany while "British people were too proud to learn from the laws of other countries that they unduly looked down upon"; (3) the system of legal education was much more advanced in German universities than in British ones; and (4) as Germany was in the midst of legal reform at that time, it would be most useful for him and Japan to study the German example.[11]

---

[6] *See* Kiyoshi Inoue, *Meiji Ishin* 272–274 (Tokyo, 1984); Tokyo Daigaku Hyakunenshi Henshū Iinkai, *Tokyo Daigaku Hyakunenshi (Bukyokushi)* 41–167 (Tokyo, 1986).

[7] In the Meiji era, many foreigners were hired in arts and sciences. The number of foreigners hired by the Japanese government amounted to more than 500 in the middle of the 1870's including some lawyers. According to a letter of recommendation written by Grisby in 1876, Hozumi had successfully completed the Special Course of Law, which included Public and Private International Law, General Outline of English Law, Law of Contracts including the Laws of Sales and Law of Agency, Constitutional Law, Roman Law – The Institutes of Justinian Book 1 to 3, Philosophy with special reference to Politics, and French. *See supra* note 5, at 144.

[8] *See* Einosuke Yamanaka, *Nihon Kindaihō Ron*, 116 (Kyoto, 1994).

[9] *See* Chihiro Saeki & Yoshinobu Kobayashi, "Keihō Gakushi (Gakushi)," 11 *Kōza Nihonkindaihō Hattatsushi* 207, 211–212 (1967).

[10] *See* Jyoji Sakurai, "Ko Hozumi Danshaku no Omoide," 458 *Gakushikai Geppō* 19, 20 (1926).

[11] *See supra* note 5, at 383–386.

In Berlin, he attended university for two semesters as an auditor. The classes he attended included French Civil Law, German Private Law, History of the Corpus Juris Civilis, Pandekten, Marriage Law, History and Character of the German Criminal Code, On the Death Penalty, Penitentiary Science, and so forth.

On returning home in 1881 after a year's stay in Berlin, Hozumi was appointed associate professor at the University of Tokyo. He became a full professor and dean the following year, despite still being in his twenties, evidence that he had been sent to Europe by the Meiji Government as a young representative of Japan, carrying the future of Japanese law and jurisprudence on his shoulders.

As a scholar, Hozumi published numerous books and articles covering various fields. His method was always empirical, anthropological and comparative, as we will see below. As a teacher, he trained the Japanese elite of the Meiji era, who would go on to build modern Japan as administrative officers, judges, lawyers, statesmen, businessmen, and citizens. As a legislator, he made full use of his knowledge and ability in drafting the Civil Code of Japan. It was a code of national pride that had been developed by the three Japanese professors in picture 3 after the rejection of the first Civil Code drafted under the strong influence of G. E. Boissonade, a French professor employed by the Japanese Government. Hozumi's skill as a legislator was so outstanding that the main part of the code still remains in force a century after its promulgation.

Hozumi was also a statesman who served as an Imperial Nominee to the House of Peers (1890–1892) and then as a Privy Councilor (1916–1926), where he was appointed Speaker in 1925, a year before his death. This aspect of Hozumi's career deserves more than a passing mention. His academic works as a comparative lawyer were supported by his strong patriotism. We should always bear this in mind when reading his articles.

"TABOOS AND LAW"

Now let us turn our eyes to Hozumi's article, "Taboos and Law."[12]

Why did Hozumi choose taboo as his subject? On one level, it was not so strange for Hozumi to pick such a subject, since jurisprudence and ethnology could not be separated as two distinct disciplines in Japan at that time.[13] More

---

[12] *See* Nobushige Hozumi, *Hōritsu Shinkaron* (Tokyo, 1927). The article was first published in 1917 as part of a collection of essays, dedicated to his colleague, Yasushi Hijikata, Professor of English Law at the Imperial University of Tokyo, on the occasion of the twenty-fifth anniversary of his appointment to that office. *See* Hijikata Kyōjyu Zaishoku in Hideo Hatoyama (ed.), *25 Nen Kinen Shihō Ronshū* (Tokyo, 1917). It was a long article of about 150 pages in Japanese, and was later included in Volume 3 of his voluminous but unfinished lifework *Hōritsu Shinkaron* [Theory of the Evolution of Law]. Hozumi published this article rather late in his life. His inclination to the ethnological and historical study had been clear in his early works.

[13] *See* Shinnosuke Sakamoto, "Hozumi Nobuishige to Nihon Jinruigaku no Kigen," 64 *Minzokugaku-Kenkyū* (2000). (Rediscovering Hozumi as one of the founders of Japanese anthropology. To my knowledge, Hozumi was the first scholar to introduce Frazer's work to Japan, although many Japanese anthropologists ignore Hozumi's contribution.)

importantly, in Hozumi's view, at that time there were two different opinions regarding the origin of law. One held that laws are made artificially by high authorities. The other, for example Rudolf von Jhering and Friedrich Karl von Savigny, insisted that law was not made, but rather evolved spontaneously. Hozumi believed the latter to be true and chose taboo as one example to support this general view propounded by the school of historical jurisprudence.

As an ethnologist J. G. Frazer had a very similar view. In the article he contributed to the *Encyclopaedia Britannica*, he remarked:

> "The original character of the taboo must be looked for not in its civil but in its religious element. It was not the creation of a legislator but the gradual outgrowth of animistic beliefs, to which the ambition and avarice of chiefs and priests afterwards gave an artificial extension. But in serving the cause of avarice and ambition it subserved the progress of civilization, by fostering conception of the rights of property and the sanctity of the marriage tie, conceptions which in time grew strong enough to stand by themselves and fling away the crutch of superstition which in earlier days had been their sole support. For we shall scarcely err in believing that even in advanced societies the moral sentiments, in so far as they are merely sentiments and are not based on an induction from experience, derive much of their force from an original system of taboo. Thus on the taboo were grafted the golden fruits of law and morality, while the parent stem dwindled slowly into the sour crabs and empty husks of popular superstition on which the swine of modern society are still content to feed."[14]

It is clear from the references in his article[15] that Hozumi's argument was based on the advanced ethnological arguments of his time.[16] According to Hozumi's grandson Shigeyuki,[17] the shelves of his grandfather's library groaned under the weight of books on ethnology and anthropology, and the margins of books by E. A. Westermarck, L. H. Morgan and J. G. Frazer were filled with notes by Nobushige himself.[18] We can imagine Hozumi's deep admiration for

---

[14] James G. Frazer, "Taboo," in *The Encyclopaedia Britannica* (9th ed., 1888).

[15] *See supra* note 12, at 309, 310, 321, 327, 334, 338, 348, 350, 352, 354, 355, 356, 357, 358, 361, 371, 372, 397, 399, 400, 401, 403, 407, 409, 414, 416, 417, 419, 421, 425, 432 and 442 (citing the following Western books: Brinton, *Religions of Primitive Peoples*; Cherry, *Growth of Criminal Law in Ancient Communities*; Decle, *Three Years in Savage Africa*; James G. Frazer, "Taboo," in *Encyclopaedia Britannica*; James G. Frazer, *Early History of Kinship*; James G. Frazer, *The Golden Bough*; James G. Frazer, *Psyche's Task*; Gennep, *Tabou et Totémisme à Madagascar*; Lubbock, *Origin of Civilization*; W. Mariner, *Account of the Nations of the Tonga Islands* (2nd ed); Matius, *Rechtszustände unter den Ureinwohnern Braziliens*; Steinmetz, *Rechtsverhältnisse*; Sumner, *Folkways*; R. Taylor, *Te Ika A Maui, or New Zealand and Its Inhabitants* (1870); A. S. Thomson, *The Story of New Zealand*; Bail Thompson, *The Fijians*; G. Turner, *Samoa*; Westermarck, *History of Human Marriage*; Westermarck, *The Origin and Development of Moral Ideas*; Yate, *An Account of New Zealand*. Given the academic tradition of the time in Japan of not citing the works of others, Hozumi was without doubt one of the first scholars to write papers in the Western tradition. As we see above, however, he referred to the titles only in most of his citations).

[16] Jun'ichi Aomi, "Keikenshugi no Hōshisō," in Yoshiyuki Noda & Jun'ichi Aomi (eds), *Kindai Nihonhōshisōshi* 394 (Tokyo, 1979).

[17] Shigeyuki Hozumi is a former professor of Western History at Tokyo Kyoiku University and a former president of Daitō Bunka University.

[18] Shigeyuki Hozumi, "Hikaku Hōgaku to Hozumi Nobushige," 21 *Hikaku Hōgaku* 159, 172 (Tokyo, 1987).

those works and his great effort to keep up with the latest western developments.

In the Meiji era, social Darwinism or evolutionism was very fashionable among Japanese intellectuals. Hozumi had come to believe in the universal evolution of law during his stay in London. These thoughts were also propagated by some of the foreign teachers hired by the Meiji government.[19]

The reason Hozumi received evolutionary theories with such enthusiasm must have had much to do with his patriotic concern for the situation of Japan. When he was sent to London to study law, his mission was to absorb western law and legal thought in order to raise his country to the level of "civilized" countries. To do that, it was assumed, it was first necessary for Hozumi to measure the location of Japanese law exactly on the scale of evolution, and then to understand how to raise it to the level of "civilization."

Hozumi's article consists of two parts besides the introduction and conclusion. The first part, entitled Preliminary Argument, is divided into the following six sections: (1) the definition of "taboo," (2) the essence of taboos, (3) the significance of taboos, (4) the types of taboos, (5) the origins of taboos, and (6) the creation of taboos. Such discussions of the problems associated with taboos in general were necessary for Japanese readers unfamiliar with ethnology and the term "taboo" as transliterated into Japanese characters.[20]

The second part deals with more specific problems regarding the relationship between taboos and law. It is necessary to summarize each of the sections of this part, filled as it is with examples,[21] in order to compare his ideas, which I believe to be rather straightforward, with those of Frazer.

Taboos and the Notion of Law

One of the most important requirements for the formation of a nation or legal community is a general habit of subjection to a legitimate authority. When people in the same region begin to form a moral union, their actions tend to be unified to form a system of customs. The belief that a certain act should not be performed and that the infringement of this taboo would invite great disaster gives rise to the common norm of conduct among the people. The sense of law

[19] Ernest Francisco Fenollosa (1853–1908), who had been one of the founders of the Herbert Spencer Club at Harvard, was invited to be the first professor of Philosophy at the University of Tokyo in 1878. His theory was based mainly on Spencer's *Principles of Sociology. See* Shigekazu Yamashita, *Supensā to Nihon Kindai* 123–140 (Tokyo, 1983).

[20] In the Preliminary Argument, Hozumi pointed out that general theory of taboo was also applicable to Japanese examples. One of the examples he cited was the expression *heika*. Heika is the special expression used by the Japanese people to refer to the Emperor. Its original meaning is "under the stairs," indicating insurmountable distance between the speaker and the Emperor. Hozumi believed that this was one of the illustrations of taboos' survival in civilized societies. *See* Hozumi, *supra* note 12, at 308. The expression is still used very often in contemporary Japan.

[21] Hozumi cited numerous examples from East and West, past and present. I omit most of them in this summary.

(*Rechtsgefühl*) comes into existence among the people in this way. The original punishments for the infringement of taboos, formerly sanctioned by priests or chiefs in the form of the payment of redemptions, death penalties or expulsion from the community, were transformed into sanctions of a legal nature.[22]

Taboos and Sovereignty

The solidarity of an organization is maintained by centripetal force, which is strongest when the authority of the chief is "sacred, inviolable and thus unchallenged." To achieve this, the chief needs to make people stand in awe of his superhuman powers. An organization with strong, cohesive internal power can survive, and such power is achieved by attracting people to the chief vertically and solidifying relationships between the members horizontally. In primitive societies, vertical power was most important. Here lies the origin of sovereignty. "A sovereign chief is not always an excellent warrior or a person with superior wisdom or morality. If ordinary people were allowed to approach the chief easily, they might realize how ordinary he in fact was. If his defects were known, his prestige would suffer a severe blow, eventually endangering the solidarity of the society."[23] For this reason, the taboos concerning sovereigns are most commonly found rigidly observed. The inviolability of sovereigns later gave birth to an abstract principle of the inviolability of sovereignty guaranteed by constitution.

The taboos concerning sovereigns can be divided into three types, namely (1) taboos against looking, (2) taboos against touching, and (3) taboos against calling names.[24] Thus, the notion that the sovereign is sacred and inviolable has developed and been maintained with the help of taboos.[25]

---

[22] *See supra* note 12, at 336–340.

[23] *Id.* at 343–344.

[24] *See supra* note 12, at 350. The first type of taboo prohibits someone from looking directly at the sovereign. Such practices are found all over the world. A sovereign was often forbidden to leave his palace and forced to wear a mask or hide behind curtains when granting an audience. In Japan, prior to the Meiji Restoration in 1868, the Emperor shut himself away deep within the palace and met only a few high-ranked officials from behind a bamboo blind. The second type of taboo prohibits touching the sovereign or coming close to him, as drawing near to him would invite divine retribution. The tabooed sphere is usually extended to the entire site of his residence. This is why the Imperial Palace in Japan often carries in its name the character *kin*, meaning "prohibited," *id* at 355. The King's Peace in English law is another example where the taboo against touching was extended to the extreme, *id.* at 358–368. The third type of taboo is derived from the second. The scope of the taboo is extended further from the person to the name. There are three types of these taboos, namely keeping the real name of the sovereign a secret, using another appellation to avoid phonetic collisions with the sovereign's name, and avoiding the use of the same character used in his name or placing it in a special position wherever the name appears in a composition, *id.* at 369–395. Many of these taboos still survive in the Japanese society today.

[25] *Supra* note 12, at 395.

Taboos and Marriage

In primitive societies, religious taboos were the most effective way of preventing adultery and protecting matrimonial fidelity. It was widely believed that breach of this taboo would bring forth a disaster not only to the perpetrator, but also to the whole community to which he/she belonged. The community had to punish the adulterer/adulteress to appease the divine anger and thus avoid the common disaster. This practice of punishment served as a powerful tool to deter adultery and assisted the development of a general respect for fidelity. Later, as public authority developed, the matrimonial relationship was no longer maintained by religious sanctions, but rather by legal ones such as outlawing adultery and making it a cause for mandatory divorce. "As the infringement of the taboo on sex could bring such disasters as famine, epidemic, attacks by furious tigers or big crocodiles, and so forth to the whole community and region, the observance of the taboo was not only a matter of private concern, but also a public preoccupation."[26] If the taboo was violated by adultery or incest, the people needed to perform some kind of ritual to avoid disaster and/or punish the violator to appease the divine anger. It was here that automatic social sanctions against the violation of the taboo appeared in addition to divine retribution. Later, when political organizations and their authority developed in society, observance of the taboos came to be enforced by legal measures, prohibiting consanguineous marriages and treating incest and adultery as criminal offences by legislation. All such institutions stemmed from taboos fostered by superstitions at early stages of their civilization.

Taboos and Property

In primitive societies, there was no concept of private property. People had to protect their possessions and occupations by constant vigilance and reliance on their own physical force. When transcendental power came into force making people respect each others' possessions, the concept of "mine and thine" emerged.[27] It also promoted the evolution of human society and accelerated its material progress. In many primitive societies, it was taboo that served as this transcendental power promoting the notion of inviolable private property. It can thus be said that the exclusive and inviolable possessions or occupations, now protected by law, stemmed from a belief in taboos. Taboos gave birth to the practice of respecting the property of others, which eventually developed into a legal right.

However, taboos were not the only catalyst for modern property rights. The demand for goods necessary for subsistence was another main cause. Any

---

[26] *Id*. at 409–410.
[27] *Id*. at 411.

person wishing to coexist with others is forced to hold on to the things he needs to survive and take every possible measure to secure his possessions. Violation of the possessions would provoke angry retaliation. Fearing such a response, people come to refrain from violating others' possessions and the practice crystallizes after many generations into a full recognition of proprietary rights.

Taboos were thus only one of several causes for the advent of modern concepts of property. Nevertheless, it was the most influential one as the notion of protection of property was most effectively supported by supernatural sanctions.[28]

Taboos and Criminal Law

Taboo is supported by the belief that any violator will suffer the automatic sanction of divine retribution. As the violation was believed to bring disaster to the entire group, however, artificial sanctions in the form of additional punishment were meted out by his fellow men. They might kill and offer him as a sacrifice or ostracize him. The mystical nature of the sanction of the taboo could thus be accompanied by a secular one, and the sanction might come to include both religious and secular meaning. The artificial punishments inflicted by the priest or sorcerer/sorceress can be called "religious" sanctions, while those inflicted by the chief or secular authorities "legal" ones. Once a society had developed sufficiently to have some political organizations, both kinds of sanctions were inflicted cumulatively, although the religious ones were more effective than the legal ones in the early stages.[29]

In their purification rituals for the avoidance of disasters, primitive people tended to offer clothes, food and other items to appease the divine anger, and also gave something to the priest. Where a taboo concerning the chief had been violated, they made an offering to him as well. And if they harmed others by violating the taboo, they paid something as compensation for the damage and attempted to avoid retaliation by the aggrieved. The sanctions against the violation of taboo thus evolved into both criminal penalties and civil compensation.[30]

Conclusion

In sum, taboos are the origin of norms with effective sanctions necessary in an organized human society. They reinforced the psychological cohesive force

---

[28] *Supra* note 12, at 425–426.

[29] *Id.* at 432.

[30] *See id.* at 434. The old Japanese custom of *harai*, where offerings were made to cleanse the violator of contamination, can be understood as one of the purification rituals commonly found in the South Pacific and other regions. It is a prototype of both pecuniary punishment and civil indemnity. *Id.* at 434–440.

among the people negatively but powerfully. From taboos stemmed both the moral conceptions of good and evil and the legal conceptions of rights and crime.[31]

Although Hozumi borrowed many examples and theories from works of the western anthropologists mentioned above, when writing "Taboos and Law" he mainly relied on three works by Sir James Frazer. In the preliminary argument of his article on taboos, his explanations of the etymology of the word "taboo," classifications of taboos, and ways of creating taboos were mainly borrowed from Frazer's article "Taboo" in the *Encyclopaedia Britannica*. Moreover, Hozumi referred to numerous examples which were mostly cited from Frazer's three works, namely the above article, *Psyche's Task* and *The Golden Bough*. The same can be said of the main argument of the article, which contains rich examples.[32] According to my calculations of all the corresponding parts in Hozumi's article,[33] there are about a hundred examples and arguments borrowed directly from Frazer's works.[34]

Apart from the great correspondence of concrete examples, I must emphasize here that the structure of Hozumi's article bears a strong resemblance to much of that of *Psyche's Task*.[35] The four sections in Hozumi's argument correspond to

---

[31] *Id*. at 445–448.

[32] The examples cited are from Polynesia, New Zealand, Borneo, the Malay Archipelago, Africa, Samoa, Melanesia, Greece, Ireland, Jewish Law, the Code of Hammrabi, Laws of Manu, Mosaic Law, Saxon Law, and so on.

[33] *See* Hitoshi Aoki, "Hozumi Nobushige to Sā Jēmusu Furēzā," 115 *Hitotsubashi Ronsō* 62, 75–78 (1996).

[34] In addition to the many examples and arguments borrowed from Frazer, he enriched his article by including numerous ones of his own. For instance, he cited examples from important Japanese classics such as *Manyōshū* [Collection of Ten Thousand Leaves] (an anthology of poetry completed around 759), *Kojiki* [Record of Ancient Matters] (completed in 712), and *Nihonshoki* [Chronicle of Japan] (completed in 720); gave a detailed account of Japanese and Chinese taboos concerning the names of emperors; carefully examined the eighteenth-century Japanese scholar of Japanese Classical Studies, Norinaga Moto-ori's theory on *harai*; and even cast new light on the King's Peace in English law by placing it in the stream of evolution of taboos. Although it is certainly true that all of these, which cover a considerable number of pages in the article, are his original findings, they are used only to verify or reinforce Frazer's hypotheses and not to support his own new ones.

[35] *See supra* note 15. (*Psyche's Task* was first published in 1909 and based on a discourse read at an evening meeting at the Royal Institution in London and lectures later delivered to his class in Liverpool.) The introduction to the book outlines Frazer's aim to show that, whereas we are apt to take a superstition for unmitigated evil, false in itself, or pernicious in its consequences, it has a positive side and deserves to be placed in a rather better light. He proposed to prove through examples that among certain races and at certain stages of evolution some social institutions which we believe to be beneficial have been partially based on superstition. We can see his intention clearly in the fact that he changed the title of the book from *Psyche's Task* to *The Devil's Advocate* when the third edition was published. In addition to the introduction and the conclusion, *Psyche's Task* consists of four chapters: Government, Private Property, Marriage, and Respect for Human Life. The propositions to be proved in each chapter were: (1) Among certain races and at certain times, superstition has strengthened the respect for government, especially monarchial government, and has thereby

the four propositions in *Psyche's Task*. The second section of Hozumi's main argument on "Taboos and Sovereignty" corresponds to Frazer's chapter "Government," the third section on "Taboos and Marriage" to the chapter "Marriage," the fourth section on "Taboos and Property" to the chapter "Private Property," and the last section on "Taboos and Criminal Law" to the chapter "Respect for Human Life."

Readers might think that Hozumi lacked academic originality and he was a mere copier of the western ideas. This criticism would hold true to a certain extent if we are to appreciate Hozumi's works only by referring to present academic standards. But we must bear in mind that in Hozumi's time there were not sufficient Japanese terms corresponding exactly to the notions used in the literature of western social science. Even the most fundamental Japanese terms such as *kenri* (rights) and *shakai* (society) were "invented" in the latter half of 19th century. At that time, it was considered much more creative to translate western theories into Japanese than it is now. We could compare Hozumi to an architect who had to begin by making bricks. Moreover, a closer examination reveals that Hozumi deviated from Frazer's outline in the case of the last section. I explore this interesting issue in the next section.

HOZUMI'S REJECTION OF FRAZER'S THEORY

Although Hozumi gained much from Frazer's theories, there is a remarkable exception in the last section on "Taboos and Criminal Law." While the three preceding sections on sovereignty, private property and marriage correspond almost precisely to Frazer's three chapters, the content of this section does not correspond in any way to the chapter on "Respect for Human Life" in *Psyche's Task*. It is true that Hozumi also used Frazer's examples and arguments in the last section, but many of them were borrowed from the chapter on "Marriage." Why is this so? For what reasons did Hozumi ignore Frazer's last chapter?

If we compare the title "Taboos and Criminal Law" with the tone of other sections, we notice that there is something "unstable" in that title. While sovereignty, marriage and private property can be characterized as values or institutions to be legally protected, criminal law is not an object to be protected, but rather a means of protection. In addition, the main point that the sanction imposed for the violation of the taboo evolved from religious to secular punishment had already been stated repeatedly in the preceding sections. Moreover, in spite of the section's title, Hozumi discusses the origin of civil law damages as

contributed to the establishment and maintenance of civil order. (2) Among certain races and at certain times, superstition has strengthened the respect for private property and has thereby contributed to the security of its enjoyment. (3) Among certain races and at certain times, superstition has strengthened the respect for marriage and has thereby contributed to a stricter observance of the rules of sexual morality both among the married and the unmarried. (4) Among certain races and at certain times, superstition has strengthened the respect for human life and has thereby contributed to the security of its enjoyment, *id.* at 4.

well. In contrast, the subject Frazer chose – human life – belongs reasonably to the same dimension as the other subjects. Frazer's argument seems much more lucid.

I believe it is unnatural for a scholar as competent as Hozumi not to be aware of this—there must have been a substantial reason for his rejection of Frazer's chapter on "Respect for Human Life." By analyzing the reasons why he must have rejected it, we may gain a clearer picture of the relationship between the two scholars.

Simply put, Frazer's argument in the chapter "Respect for Human Life" is that taboos stemming from a fear of ghosts evolved gradually into the legal protection of human life. According to him, the feared spirits were not necessarily those of people who died from unnatural or violent causes, such as a mother who died in childbirth or a man who was slain. Let us select a few examples from among the numerous illustrations in *Psyche's Task*. Australian Aborigines put hot coals in the ears of their departed brother so as to contain his spirit in the corpse for long enough to allow his relatives and other members of the tribe to escape from it. The Tinneh Indians of Alaska greased the hands of a corpse so they could slip through the ghost's greasy fingers and escape when the ghost attempted to grab their souls to carry them off with him. The Lengua Indians of the Gran Chaco in South America lived in great fear of the spirits of their dead. No sooner had a person died than the whole village was evacuated, every hut burnt down, and the property of the dead man destroyed. For these Indians believed that, however good and kind a man may have been in his lifetime, his ghost would always be a danger to the peace and prosperity of the living.[36]

The conception that even the ghost of a beloved family member or a good man could be evil and dangerous was probably beyond Hozumi's comprehension. When he discussed the origin of ancestor worship at the outset of his book *Ancestor-Worship and Japanese Law*, he attributed western scholars' opinions to the dread of ghosts and then confessed:

> "With the greatest deference due to these writers, I cannot persuade myself to accept their view. It appears to me more correct to attribute the origin of ancestor-worship to a contrary cause. It was the love of ancestors, not the dread of them, which gave rise to the custom of worshipping and making offering of food and drink to their spirits. I cannot understand why a primitive people, who must have loved their parents in their lifetime, should have experienced fear of them after their death. I cannot understand why a primitive people should have been so near-sighted and thoughtless as to ill-treat their parents without scruple during their lifetime, and suddenly begin to fear their spirits after their death."[37]

In Hozumi's view, the writers who attribute the origin of ancestor worship to "the dread of ghosts" and to "ghost-propitiation" fail to distinguish between the ghosts to be dreaded and those to be respected. He strongly believed that the

[36] *Id.*
[37] *See supra* note 1, at 9.

ghosts of ancestors were to be respected. This belief must have been formed primarily by the traditional education he received in his childhood as a son of Samurai, and then reinforced by the official political thought of the Meiji government, which also valued ancestor worship very highly, as I discuss later.

Hozumi describes his own personal experience relating to the theory. He recollects a visit to the Lyceum Theatre in London, where he saw Henry Irving play Hamlet, as follows:

"I admired indeed the performance of that famous actor; but when it came to the ghost scene, I was struck with an impression that our actors would perform it in a different way. Hamlet, as represented by Irving, appeared to me as constantly showing signs of fear and dread, not only on account of the horrible story told by his father's ghost – which is but natural – but for the ghost itself. A Japanese actor, if he were to act the part of Hamlet, would certainly show strong marks of love and respect towards the father's spirit, mingled with the feeling of sorrow and sympathy for his father's fate, and of horror and anger at the "foul and most unnatural murder.""[38]

From this episode, we learn that his rejection of Western theories, which ascribed the origin of ancestor worship to the dread of ghosts, resulted not only from an intellectual or scientific reflection, but also from a psychological or even physiological resistance.

This strong attachment to ancestor worship was not a feeling peculiar to Hozumi. It was a widely and deeply rooted feeling among his contemporaries in Japan, with important political significance at that time. After bringing the *Tennō* [Emperor] out of isolation from his palace in Kyoto to the new political center in Tokyo, the Meiji Government aimed ideologically to build a new nation and change the status of the Imperial Family in the process. They wished the Emperor to be father of the nation and consequently installed him as head of state[39] and intended to establish a system to fuse filial piety and loyalty to the Emperor.

Hozumi's younger brother Yatsuka, who also was a professor of The Imperial University of Tokyo, was one of the most ardent advocates of this political thought. In his book *Aikokushin* [Patriotism], Yatsuka remarked:

"What unites a racial group is the authority of the ancestors. The authority of the ancestors does not lie in a promise among equals, so the feeling of veneration is strong and the concept of obedience is profound. In the house, the head of the house, representing the authority of the ancestors, exercises the patrimonial power over the family; in the nation, the emperor, representing the authority of the Sun Goddess, exercises the sovereign power over the nation. Patrimonial power and sovereign power: both are powers whereby the emperor-father protects the children beloved of the ancestors . . . The ancestors of my ancestors is the Sun Goddess. The Sun Goddess is the founder of our race, and the throne is the sacred house of our race. If father and mother are to be revered, how much more so the ancestors of the house; and if the

---

[38] *See id.* at 17.
[39] Inoue, *supra* note 6, at 71.

ancestors of the house are to be revered, how much more so the founder of the country! The position of the head of the house is that of the authority of the ancestors; the throne is the place of the Sun Goddess. Father and mother are ancestors living in the present; the emperor is the Sun Goddess living in the present. For the same reason one is filial to his parents and loyal to the throne; and the national teaching which connects these two is the worship of ancestors."[40]

Thus, as Richard H. Minear summarizes: "Ancestor worship transforms the nature of the power of the emperor-father. This power is not simply force. It is rather the solicitude of a father for his child. Obedience becomes a sacred obligation, the piety of a filial son."[41]

The elder Hozumi did not explicitly advocate such a mythological and eventually chauvinistic theory as his brother. Contrary to Yatsuka's theory that ancestor worship was incompatible with Christianity, Nobushige emphasized their compatibility as follows:

"I look with sincere regret upon frequent conflicts that arise between the missionaries or newly-converted Christians and our people who are ancestor-worshippers; for I am one of those who firmly believe that the practice of Ancestor-worship is not incompatible with Christianity. It is not contrary to the First Commandment, because the ancestral spirit is nothing more than the outcome of the belief in the immortality of soul, and can not be considered as 'gods,' which the 'jealous God' forbids to worship. If Ancestor-worship is, as maintained in this book, the extension of love and respect to distant forefathers, the manifestation of the love and respect in a certain harmless way may be regarded as a realization of the Fifth Commandment to honour the parents; and nothing against Christianity, which is essentially a religion of love."[42]

Although the elder Hozumi was not a narrow-minded chauvinist, as illustrated by the citation above, he certainly was a nationalist. Regarding the emperor-centered political system, the elder Hozumi also praised this national system in his lecture later read in front of the Emperor Taishō by admiring "the strong solidarity of the Japanese nation integrated through the unification of the imperial and the popular ancestor-worship."[43]

Another question arises here: Was Hozumi's adoration of the Japanese political system (*Tennō* system) compatible with his orientation toward western law and his scientific studies of the imperial taboos? From the standpoint of cultural evolutionism, Hozumi regarded the taboo as "a practice of uncivilized and primitive people."[44] To analyze the taboos relating to the Emperor scientifically would have been demeaning to the Emperor. In fact, Ryūichi Nagao has stated that Hozumi "had walked into a dangerous sphere of anthropological study of

---

[40] *See* Yatsuka Hozumi, *Aikokushin* (1897), *cited in* Richard H. Minear, *Japanese Tradition and Western Law*, 73 (1970).
[41] *See id.* at 74–75
[42] *See supra* note 36, at xiii–xiv.
[43] Nobushige Hozumi, *Hozumi Nobushige Ibunshū*, 57 (Tokyo, 1932).
[44] *See supra* note 12, at 303.

the Emperor."[45] Nobuyoshi Toshitani has asserted that Hozumi's evolutionary theory of law was "a heretical doctrine" that conflicted with the orthodox theory that took the inviolability of the Emperor for granted.[46] Did Hozumi not violate the very taboo he sought to describe by examining it too closely? Even if we take into consideration the peculiar situation of the lecture in the Emperor's presence,[47] the question still remains.

By choosing words prudently, Hozumi managed to enable two *prima facie* incompatible standpoints to coexist. For example, in his explanation of the taboo on looking, he stated that the Emperor had shut himself away deep within the palace, but added an important phrase, "until the Meiji Restoration,"[48] to limit the time in which his statement would hold true. In fact, in this respect the Emperor must have lost the character of a tabooed chief especially for Hozumi, who had, as a Privy Councilor from 1916, opportunities to see him daily. Moreover, in this article, Hozumi explicitly classified his country after its adoption of constitutionalism as one of the "highly civilized countries."[49] Remaining taboos were characterized as outdated customs surviving in a civilized society. In short, as far as the article "Taboos and Law" is concerned, Hozumi paid due respect to the contemporary Emperor and the Imperial Family, so we need not be too anxious about Hozumi's apparent critical views on the imperial taboo.

This point becomes clearer when we compare Hozumi's attitude toward the Emperor with the manner in which Frazer described the *Mikado* [Emperor] in *The Golden Bough*. According to Frazer, the Mikado is a typical example of a king who practices magic or conducts religious services:

> "He (Mikado) thinks that it would be very prejudicial to his dignity and holiness to touch the ground with his feet; for this reason, when he intends to go anywhere, he must be carried thither on men's shoulders. Much less will they suffer that he should expose his sacred person to the open air, and the sun is not thought worthy to shine on his head. There is such a holiness ascribed to all the parts of his body that he dares to cut off neither his hair, nor his beard, nor his nails."[50]

And

> "[T]he Mikado's food was cooked every day in new pots and served up in new dishes; both pots and dishes were of common clay, in order that they might be broken or laid aside after they had been once used. They were generally broken, for it was believed

---

[45] Ryūichi Nagao, "Hozumi Nobushige no Hōshinka Shisō," *Nihon Hōshisōshi Kenkyū* 65 (Tokyo, 1980).

[46] Nobuyoshi Toshitani, "Senzen no Hōshakaigaku," 2 *Hōshakaigaku Kōza* 185, at 194 (Tokyo, 1972).

[47] *See supra* note 42. This lecture was read as *Goshinkō-hajime* in January 1919. *Goshinkō-hajime* is a ceremonious lecture in the Imperial Palace at the beginning of the year, where a designated scholar reads his lecture directly to the Emperor who is sitting face-to-face with him.

[48] *See supra* note 12, at 350.

[49] *Id*. at 346.

[50] *See The Golden Bough supra* note 15, at 2–3.

that if anyone else ate his food out of these sacred dishes, his mouth and throat would become swollen and inflamed."[51]

Hozumi totally ignored these descriptions. One of the reasons may be that, as a learned Japanese man, he did not have to use the out-of-date information on which Frazer had relied. In addition, Hozumi must have been convinced of his view that the contemporary Emperor was much more civilized than the magical or religious chiefs in primitive tribes. My guess is that he could not tolerate Frazer's theory on the fate of a priestly king who was to be slain (!) when his magical powers waned.

How then did he understand, for example, the official rituals dispensed by the Emperor and the Imperial Family under the modern constitution? By Hozumi's time, it was well understood that they were not mere survivors or relics of another age. On the contrary, they were given fresh and strong legal support by The Imperial Household Ordinance Relating to Festivals in 1902, which contained detailed regulations regarding the holding of ceremonies in the Imperial Household.[52] Under this Ordinance, thirteen Great Festivals were to be hosted by the Emperor himself and eight Small Festivals by the chief Ritualist on behalf of the Emperor. Remarkably, this general scheme survived within the democratized legal system after the Second World War: some Great Festivals as national holidays and many others as domestic ceremonies of the Imperial Family.[53]

For example, in the Festival of the Feast of the New Crop of Rice, one of the oldest festivals still celebrated today, the offering of the new rice is made to the First and other Imperial Ancestors and other deities in the Sanctuary of the Imperial Palace. The Emperor, after taking a bath to purify his body, enters the Sanctuary, offers his prayer to the deities, and partakes of the new rice along with them. It is undeniable that the role of the Emperor in the festival closely resembles that of a priestly king among primitive peoples described in *The Golden Bough*. How could Hozumi accept modern legislation giving official support to such religious rituals? Is it not a "regression" from the standpoint of his evolutionism?

The clue to answering this question lies in the key term, "ancestor worship." Hozumi commented on each of these festivals in one chapter of *Ancestor-Worship and Japanese Law*. As the title of that chapter, "The Worship of

[51] *See id* at 131.
[52] *See* Shigeyoshi Murakami, *Tennō no Saishi*, 157–161 (Tokyo, 1977).
[53] *See supra* note 1, at 38–40. Great Festivals include the Festival of the Sacrifice to the Origin; Anniversary of the Accession of the First Emperor and the Foundation of the Empire; Spring Sacrifice to the Imperial Ancestors; Spring Sacrifice to the Shrines of Gods; Anniversary of the Death of First Emperor Jimmu; Autumnal Sacrifice to the Spirits of the Imperial Ancestors; Autumnal Sacrifice to the Shrines of Gods; Festival of Offering the First-Fruits of the Year to the First Imperial Ancestor; Festival of the Feast of the New Crop of Rice; Anniversary of the Death of the Late Emperor; Celebration Year's Festival of the Emperors within Three Generations Previous to the Last Emperor; Celebration Year's Festival of the Late Empress who was the Consort of the Last Emperor; and lastly, Celebration Year's Festival of the Late Empress who was the Mother of the Reigning Emperor.

Imperial Ancestors" indicates, all of the imperial rituals were clearly understood to be ceremonies for the worship of Imperial Ancestors. In Frazer's view, a ritual for the propitiation of the dead is nothing but "a means" of controlling natural phenomena and maintaining the peace of that society. It has few or no ethical implications. They are neutral in this sense. For Hozumi, however, ancestor worship was more than just a means to an end—it was an end in itself.

As can be seen from the following example, Hozumi, being very prudent, chose words describing only the facts without confusing "is" with "ought": "[T]hree foreign elements—Confucianism, Buddhism, and Western civilization—all of which have had immense influence upon our laws, manners and customs, and two of which are diametrically opposed to ancestor-worship, could not make way against, nor put an end to, the wide-spread and persistent faith of the people."[54]

In "Taboos and Law," he never directly asserted that ancestor-worship was a moral good that should not be abandoned. However, behind the statement cited above, we can catch a glimpse of his belief that ancestor-worship is a national virtue in which we should take great pride. In fact, he was a well-known worshipper of the dead, and late in life even performed a grand ceremony for the souls of his childhood teachers in Uwajima as a token of his gratitude. With this strong belief in the worship of the dead, common among ordinary Japanese at that time, Hozumi regarded ancestor-worship as something worthy. This, in turn, resulted in excluding from his sight the primitive aspect of ancestor-worship as a magical means for controlling natural phenomena and thereby maintaining social peace. This must have been the very reason why he could be proud of the legislation on the Imperial Festivals in spite of his belief in evolutionism.

In conclusion, Hozumi verified Frazer's fundamental hypotheses by using many concrete examples found in Japan and other countries. But at the same time, he modified Frazer's theory as to the meaning and function of ancestor-worship for the smooth adaptation of it into the cultural soil of Japan according to his own strong belief in the love of ancestors. In this sense, he was indeed a skillful transplanter of western thought into Japanese culture, with his Occidental mind and Oriental heart. The appearance of Hozumi in picture 3 tells us that even after his head had been westernized, his heart remained traditional.

CONCLUSION: HOZUMI'S MERITS

What, then, were Hozumi's merits as a comparative lawyer? It would not be difficult to enumerate his demerits from the eyes of the present generation. Above all, his belief in a simple and linear evolutionism looks naive. His method of

---

[54] *See supra* note 1, at 2–3.

comparison was not refined. Most of the examples used for illustrating his hypotheses were secondary materials collected arbitrarily from the works of western scholars. Hozumi was certainly an "armchair anthropologist." However, these critical evaluations seem unjust. Whatever else might be said, he was undeniably one of the first Japanese scholars to assimilate Western jurisprudence into the Japanese cultural environment. With the help of comparative and anthropological methods, he made a great effort, as an intellectual representative of Japan, to link his isolated country to the rest of the world. This is, I believe, his greatest merit. Masaji Chiba and Jun'ichi Aomi have also praised his pioneering works full of scientific empiricism.[55]

In Japan, Western law and legal thought were not imposed forcibly. They were received or transplanted voluntarily and selectively by a few ardent Japanese scholars like Hozumi. He made full use of his wide and deep knowledge as a comparative lawyer and played a leading role in seeking out the right path for Japanese law to take. The fact that he never lost his national pride when he stood in front of the overwhelming, majestic Western law and jurisprudence is worth a special mention. Although comparative law was a discipline born in Western countries, it provided him with a strong weapon to assimilate Western law and legal thought into Japan. He used that weapon to the full from his firm standpoint as a Japanese citizen.

Hozumi's empirical and anthropological method had few successors in the next generation. In 1889, the Japanese Government adopted a constitution that, for political reasons, was deeply influenced by the Prussian constitution. After its promulgation, most of the new laws including the Civil Code, the Commercial Code and the Procedural Codes were drafted according to the German style. It was natural that the younger scholars tended to devote themselves to the study of abstract legal doctrines (*Rechtsdogmatik*) under these new Codes. Legal scholars were not sent to Frazer's country anymore. They were too busy studying specialized legal subjects to reflect calmly on the function of taboos in the universal evolution of law.

So it is only recently that Hozumi's anthropological works have been reevaluated positively in Japan. His resurgence is connected with his "culturalist" perspective. Nowadays, more and more Japanese comparative lawyers find it important to study law in a cultural context or to study "legal cultures." Some Japanese universities have started a new course on "*Hikaku Hōbunkaron*" (*Comparative Legal Cultures*), and very recently, Tsuyoshi Kinoshita, one of the leading comparative lawyers in Japan, published a 300-page book under the same title.[56]

At the beginning of this essay, I mentioned that I regard Hozumi as being "a connecting link" between the West and Japan. There we find a problem that is still very serious to non-Western lawyers. Hozumi encountered contradictions

---

[55] *See* Masaji Chiba, *Gendai Hōjinruigaku*, 18–19 (Tokyo, 1969); *supra* note 16, at 399.
[56] *See* Tsuyoshi Kinoshita, *Hikaku Hōbunkaron* (Tokyo, 1999) (regarding Hozumi as "a forerunner" who studied legal cultures with a comparative method), at 22.

within himself in the process of introducing Western law and legal thought. As long as contemporary comparative lawyers have culturalist concerns, such contradictions still cannot be avoided.

There are three ways to resolve these contradictions. The first way is to integrate only acceptable parts from Western law and to shut the door firmly to all other parts that collide with Japanese culture. The second way is to abandon one's own culture and adapt completely to Western culture. The third way is to modify both Western law and our own law to accommodate each to the other.

The way Hozumi chose was, of course, this last one. He did not serve as a passive or inflexible channel for importing Western law but he served as an active and flexible mediator between the West and Japan. Through the examination of Hozumi's work as a comparative lawyer, we come to realize two important functions of comparative law, namely, comparative law as a "link" and comparative law as a "weapon." The former function connects non-Western countries to the well-organized Western law and advanced legal science and enables their assimilation. The latter serves as a tool for empowerment to stand against their violent influx. These two functions have to be understood as integral to one another; they are, so to speak, two sides of a same coin. In the process of comparison, every comparative lawyer is thrown into a more or less painful situation, compelled to reflect deeply on his or her own culture. For this reason, comparative law is a discipline that is essentially subjective.[57]

Hozumi was one of the luckiest comparativists who succeeded in resolving these contradictions despite the difficult political situation of his time. Readers would notice that he is smiling peacefully in figure 4. I believe, as his compatriot, that he must have been satisfied with his own achievement.

---

[57] But this, I believe, does not mean that it is not "inter-subjective."

Fig. 1 Abdel-Razzak Al-Sanhuri

6

Sanhuri and the Historical Origins of Comparative Law in the Arab World (or How Sometimes Losing your Asalah can be Good for You)

INTRODUCTION: THE STAKES IN READING SANHURI

This is an essay written by an Arab student of comparative law. The essay examines the historical context in which Abdel-Razzak Al-Sanhuri (1895–1971), the Arab World's foremost comparative lawyer, himself became a student of comparative law. In other words, this is an inherently chummy essay—it can hardly be defended as a detached exercise in intellectual biography. However, the chumminess is not merely personal. Politically speaking, any contemporary reading of Sanhuri's comparativist legacy is invariably an exercise of choosing ideological sides in a long-standing debate over the nature of Islamic legal reform. Accordingly, the present essay, intended as a biographical sketch of sorts, is also intended as a conscious intervention in this ideological debate. I will offer a particular reading of how Sanhuri became a student of comparative law. In this reading, I will celebrate comparativism as the laudable agent of cultural hybridity. In doing so, my purpose is to provide a critical alternative to the most common reading of Sanhuri today, a widely circulated reading which condemns his scholarship as the dire tool of cultural alienation. I hope the personal and political stakes involved in choosing between these two readings will become clearer as this article progresses.

To elaborate, Sanhuri is perhaps the most celebrated Arab jurist of the twentieth century. As the legendary arch-codifier who drafted many a law for many a newly independent Arab state, Sanhuri constantly appealed to comparative law in his work. In particular, Sanhuri relied heavily on comparativism in pursuing his lifelong project of modernizing Islamic law. His most significant achievement in the field of legal reform is the current Egyptian civil code of 1949.

* I would like to thank Lama Abu-Odeh, Yishai Blank, David Kennedy, Duncan Kennedy, Roy Kreitner, Mustapha Kamil Al-Sayed, and Hani Sayed for very helpful comments on earlier drafts. Jane Campion was so patient in editing this article, I cannot even begin to thank her.

The code, very much the product of a comparativist methodology, was later copied by several Arab countries and went on to become the single most influential legal document in the postcolonial experience of Arab legal systems.

For the Arab legal profession, Sanhuri is therefore something of a vernacular Justinian. As such, his legacy is a highly contested field of many readings; on the one hand, Sanhuri is often read as the "failed comparativist," a protagonist with an unsuccessful project: his reliance on comparative law to modernize the Islamic legal system ultimately resulted in a hybrid civil code which many dismiss today as *un-Islamic*; alternatively, Sanhuri is sometimes read as the "tragic comparativist," a tortured scholar who sincerely tried to modernize Islamic law with all the gusto of a man of faith, but who was at heart a wimpy secularist, too scared to come out of the closet; somewhat related to this reading is Sanhuri the "apologetic comparativist," a compromised legislator who, in disjunctive fits of functionalism, drafted a civil code by cutting and pasting Islamic law to fit the modern conditions of Arab society; but then, by contrast, there is also Sanhuri the "progressive comparativist" who believed in the "social," was conscious of the redistributive potentials of law, and aimed to draft a code that was concurrently modern, Islamic, and socially equitable; finally there is the Sanhuri of the present article: a "legendary comparativist," a cosmopolitan, intellectually courageous jurist who believed in the complex and hybrid identity of modern Arab society, and set out to free its lawyers from the hermeneutical tyranny of religious texts which had ruled their pre-modern profession.[1]

Failed/tragic/apologetic/progressive/legendary, the debate over Sanhuri's legacy is really not a debate over Sanhuri at all. Rather, it is a debate over the ideological stakes involved in choosing between the different projects of Islamic legal reform. By far, Sanhuri's most commonly recognized legacy is that of the "failed comparativist." Today, he is remembered above all as the man who attempted to use a comparative law methodology to modernize Islamic law – and failed at it. The argument goes that Sanhuri's use of comparative law overexposed the "Islamic" in Islamic law to alien sources, compromised its cultural authenticity or *asalah*, and led Arab lawyers into a wilderness of professional alienation from their historical identity. Thus for Tariq al-Bishri, one of the most eminent legal historians in Egypt today, Sanhuri's comparativist-led project of modernization was nothing but a corrosive agent for cultural alienation.[2]

---

[1] For the most comprehensive intellectual biography I know of Sanhuri, *see* Enid Hill, "Al-Sanhuri and Islamic Law: The Place and Significance of Islamic Law in the Life and Work of Abdel-Razzak Al-Sanhuri," 10 *Cairo Papers in Social Science* 1 (1987).

[2] *See* Tariq Al-Bishri, *Al-Mas'alah al-Qanuniyyah bayn al-Shari'a al-Islamiyyah wal-Qanun al-Wad'i*, (Cairo, 1996) [*The Legal Question between Islamic Shari'a and Secular Law, hereafter The Legal Question*]. For a study of Bishri's historiography, *see* Roel Meijer, "History, Authenticity and Politics: Tariq al-Bishri's Interpretation of Modern Egyptian History," in 4 *Middle East Research Associates* (September 1989). *See also* Leonard Binder, "Nationalism, Liberalism, and the Islamic Heritage: The Political Thought of Tariq al-Bishri," in *Islamic Liberalism: A Critique of Development Ideologies* (Chicago, 1988).

As a student of comparative law, I am invested in seeing the discipline used to secure a secular and progressive transformation of Arab law. As such, I find two major problems in Bishri's "cultural" critique of Sanhuri's comparativism. First, Bishri's demand for an authentic alternative to Sanhuri's scholarship turns out, over and over again, to be a politically dangerous position which works to the benefit of an ideologically conservative agenda in legal reform.[3] Second, Bishri's nostalgia for a return to a more authentic cultural past strikes me as an intellectually futile exercise—in the postcolonial world we live in, there is no going back to an untainted pre-colonial home.

Accordingly, the purpose of this essay is to provide a critical alternative to the Bishri-led strand of *asalah*-fetishism in legal reform. For Bishri, a successful project of legal reform is one that preserves (or restores) the *asalah* of the Arab legal system. Bishri critiques Sanhuri's appeal to comparativism in legal reform as the source of cultural alienation: Comparative law is a traumatizing discipline which contributed to the deracination of Arab law and the loss of *asalah* or authenticity from the Arab legal system.

By contrast, my aim in the following pages is to provide an alternative reading of the role of comparative law in Egyptian legal reform, a reading which gives reasons to celebrate the loss of cultural authenticity and to embrace hybridity as an emancipatory way of being in the postcolonial world.[4] I hope to do so by exploring the historical circumstances in which comparative law took root in Egypt between the years 1906 and 1936. In this reading, Sanhuri's comparativism is not, as Bishri argues, an agent of alienation. Rather, I will present Sanhuri's comparativism as the flowering of an intellectual movement which transpired in hybrid space between East and West, a space where the colonized Egyptians exercised significant agency in crafting the discipline of comparative law, where they cynically manipulated the Orient/Occident fantasy of their Western colonizer, and where they transformed comparativism into a rubric for anti-colonial activism and leftist political alliances.

I will proceed as follows. Part II of this essay will provide a general introduction to modernity/tradition discourse. My purpose is to contextualize the scholarship of both Sanhuri and Bishri as two distinct interventions in this century-old discourse, as well as outline the different functions assigned to comparative law by the two authors. Part III will tell the story of how comparative law came to take root in Egyptian academia between the years 1906 and 1936. The aim is to provide an upbeat argument to the effect that Sanhuri's-comparativism-is-not-as-bad-as-Bishri-makes-it-out-to-be. I do that by outlining how comparative law was used as a tool for emancipatory politics. In Part

---

[3] In the words of Leonard Binder, "the prescription offered by Tariq al-Bishri may produce a modified Nasserism—bureaucratic authoritarianism plus Islam." Binder *supra* note 2, at 292.

[4] I owe to Nathaniel Berman the basic impulse to view hybridity and authenticity as compatible world-views. His introduction to the Harvard Law & History Workshop, Spring 1999, of such ideas and materials as Jean Bernabé et al. (eds), *Eloge de la Créolité* (Paris, 1993) was instrumental in demonstrating how other cultures, particularly the *Créoles*, have existentially dealt with questions similar to the ones posed in this article.

IV, by contrast, I argue that both Sanhuri and Bishri actually shared a common nostalgic search for a lost and golden Islamic past. To my mind, this common sense of nostalgia lead them both to invent the very tradition they seek to discover. I illustrate this point by making comparative references to the history of modern Islamic architecture. The purpose of Part IV is thus to argue that Sanhuri's-nostalgia-is-really-just-as-bad-as-Bishri's. Finally, in conclusion, Part V will make a plea against the nostalgia inherent in modern projects of Islamic legal reform, even when such projects refrain from employing comparative law as a critique of modernity/tradition.

THE POSITION OF COMPARATIVE LAW IN MODERNITY/TRADITION DISCOURSE:

Modernity/tradition discourse is perhaps the most enduringly popular mode in which the Arab post-colonial condition is theorized.[5] The discourse is conceptually structured across the polar confines of pre-colonial "tradition" on the one hand, and post-colonial "modernity" on the other. It is chiefly preoccupied with understanding and evaluating the numerous transformations, under the general rubric of "modernization," which have changed life in the Arab world since the mid-nineteenth century. The scope of the discourse is thus understandably massive: it covers everything from law and economics to music, poetry and architecture. Its ideological commitments are equally diverse: under its rubric one finds writers of many creeds, from the fundamentalist-Islamist to the liberal-secularist, all advocating competing approaches to resolving the tension between modernity and tradition. Indeed, while some of its participants reduce modernization to an anathema, others advocate a full-fledged adoption of everything modern.[6] Despite its extremely diverse topics of investigation, the discourse nonetheless enjoys a decent degree of conceptual unity, chiefly derived from its obsession with questions of identity. The basic dilemma addressed by the discourse is fundamentally existentialist, namely whether it is possible to live "authentically" in today's Arab world. The discourse asks whether Arabs can live in *mo'asarah*, i.e. lead a "modern and contemporaneous" life, without risking the loss of their authentic identity? Whether they can retain some of their

---

[5] This view belongs to Al-Jabri, one of the foremost theorists on Arab discourses today. *See* Mohammed Abed Al-Jabri, *Al-Khitab Al-Arabi Al-Mo'aser* [*Contemporary Arab Discourse*] 38–61 (Beirut, 1999).

[6] "Modernity/Tradition discourse" is the most common English title used to describe what is known in Arabic as *Khitab al-Asalah/al-Mo'asarah*. The most comprehensive collection of articles I know of, submitted by some of the most prestigious Arab intellectuals today, on the various strands of the discourse, from culture to law and questions of development, remains al-Sayyid Yasin et al. (eds), *Al-Turath wa Ta'hadiyyat al-'Asr fi al-Watan al-'Arabi aw al-Asalah Wal-Mo'asarah* (Beirut, 1985). Another excellent collection is Adonis et al. (eds), *Al-Islam wal-'Hadathah* (Beirut, 1990). For a neo-Marxist reading, *see* Abdullah Laroui, *The Crisis of the Arab Intellectual* (Diarmid Cammell trans., Berkeley, 1976), especially the chapter on "Historicism and Modernisation." Alternatively, for a more humanist intellectual history, *see* Albert Hourani, *Arabic Thought in the Liberal Age 1798–1939* (Cambridge, 1995).

pre-colonial traditions without missing out on what modernity has to offer? In the words of Albert Hourani, the discourse generally asks "How can [Arab] men and women . . . avoid the two dangers of a stagnant reassertion of an identity inherited from the past, and a cosmopolitan and featureless modernity?"[7] In short, the basic question is whether Arabs today can lead an existence which is both "modern" and "authentic". The question is obviously premised on the idea that "modernization" is invariably an agent of "alienation." More specifically, "modernization" is often equated with "Westernization" and thus viewed as an inorganic process forced upon the Arab world as the aftermath of a colonial encounter which the latter lost. Modernization thus means the loss of "authenticity" in favor of social structures, cultural performances, value systems, and political institutions, which are of alien (read Western) extraction.

The basic jargon of modernity/tradition discourse thus involves such mainstays of existentialist terminology as "alienation" and "authenticity."[8] Another important term, which will be used repeatedly in this article, is "hybridity." Modernity/tradition discourse invariably presents modernization as a process that leads to the distortion of pre-colonial "tradition" or its displacement altogether. In its aftermath, modernization has left a new and semi-Westernized Arab world in which no particular experience is purely modern or purely traditional any more. The discourse does not employ any specific term to describe this post-colonial condition of mix-and-match, hodge-podge existence. To fill this terminological gap, I borrow the term "hybridity" from post-colonial theory in order to describe this phenomenon.[9] With respect to "hybridity," two points should be kept in mind. First, modernity/tradition discourse holds the condition of "hybridity" as significantly incompatible with "authenticity." In other words, to live in a "hybrid" world is to live without "authenticity." Second, while pre-colonial "tradition" often proved inept (and therefore required modernization), it nonetheless enjoyed the authenticity associated with being the organic product of an indigenous context. Whether discussing the modernization of law or architecture, the discourse participants thus agonize over how modernization has *hybridized* Arab society and therefore left it with an enduring existential casualty: cultural alienation.

---

[7] Albert Hourani, *Islam in European Thought* (Cambridge, 1991) at 129.

[8] In that sense, modernity/tradition discourse shares many of the concerns of "existentialism" as a Western philosophical tradition. Nonetheless, there are significant differences, some intellectual and others political. This is a much larger topic than is the concern of the present article. However, for an excellent review of the topic, *see* Robert Lee, *Overcoming Tradition and Modernity. The Search for Islamic Authenticity* (Boulder, 1997).

[9] The term entered post-colonial theory to describe the cultural and racial mixing generated by colonialism. Once an object of censure, hybridity was recuperated by post-colonial theorists, notably Homi Bhabha, as a powerful subversion of colonialism's binary oppositions between colonizer and colonized, civilization and savagery, white and colored. In the era of post-independence, multiple identities and cultural blends were generated and gave new meanings to the old, pejorative term "hybrid." *See generally*, Homi Bhabha, *The Location of Culture* (London and New York, 1994).

The above is a brutal reduction of the main intellectual concerns of modernity/tradition discourse. With respect to the question of law in particular, the above abstract terms take on the relatively more concrete concerns of "legal reform." Since the mid-nineteenth century, most Arab legal systems have gone through a series of reforms that effectively uprooted the pre-colonial "tradition" of Islamic law, and replaced it with a set of "modern" legal transplants borrowed from Western legal systems. Often the Western legal transplant was installed side-by-side with some Islamic doctrine, institution, or other. For example, while Western civil, commercial and criminal codes were introduced into the Egyptian legal system, the codes did contain various doctrines derived from Islamic law. Furthermore, personal status law remained Islamic in origin, but its reform was based on a modernist cut-and-paste methodology between often conflicting schools of Islamic jurisprudence.[10] Additionally, while new secular law schools and a judiciary were established, an Islamic judiciary and law school remained intact for quite some time. The end result is the current legal system: a hybrid mishmash of secular and Islamic jurisprudence, doctrines, law schools, and case law.[11]

The legal order's hybridity has been a continuing source of existential anxiety over the past century. The concern is as follows: If the legal order is hybrid, *i.e.* neither purely Islamic nor purely secular, then it must be inauthentic. This anxiety is best captured in a quote from a short story by the Egyptian novelist Naguib Mahfouz. Describing the "double personality" of a typical city-dweller in Egypt, Mahfouz explores the connection between living in a confusingly "hybrid" world, and the anxiety that one's life is somehow not "authentically" one's own:

> "He leads a contemporary [i.e. 'modern'] life. He obeys civil and penal laws of Western origin and is involved in a complex tangle of social and economic transactions and is never certain to what extent these agree or contradict his Islamic creed. Life carries him along in its current and he forgets his misgivings for a time until one Friday he hears the imam or reads the religious page in one of the papers, and all the old misgivings come back with a certain fear. He realizes that in this new society he has been afflicted with a *double personality*: half of him believes, prays, fasts and makes the pilgrimage. The other half renders his values void in banks and courts and in the streets, even in the cinemas and theatres, perhaps even at home among his family before the television set."[12]

---

[10] For details, *see* Lama Abu-Odeh, "Modernization of Muslim Family Law: The Case of Egypt" (forthcoming, draft on file with author).

[11] For a more detailed discussion of nineteenth century legal reforms, *see infra* Section III, "Modernity and the Jurists."

[12] *Al-Ahram* newspaper, May 17, 1977. The English translation is quoted from Hisham Sharabi, *Neopatriarchy. A Theory of Distorted Change in the Arab World*, 8 (Oxford, 1988). For a literary study of the existential dimensions of modernity/tradition discourse, *see* Issa Boullata, "Encounter between East and West: A Theme in Contemporary Arabic Novels," in Issa Boullata (ed.), *Critical Perspectives on Modern Arabic Literature* (Washington D.C., 1980). A recent and most engaging set of personalized accounts written by several Arab intellectuals to reflect on their own relationship to hybridity and authenticity may be found in Roel Meijer (ed.), *Cosmopolitanism, Identity, and Authenticity in the Middle East* (Richmond, 1999).

The principal aim of modernity/tradition discourse is to address the "double personality" anxieties suffered by the likes of Mahfouz's hero. For over a century now, the discourse has been preoccupied with articulating different responses to the tension between the "secular" and the "Islamic" in contemporary Arab law, where and when it exists, and how it may be best tackled. Tariq al-Bishri is one of the most adept contributors to this discourse. His reading of modern Egyptian (and often Arab) legal history is based on a dialectical relationship between two fundamental concepts: "*al-wafid*" (the "Incoming") and "*al-mawruth*" (basically "that which we have inherited/the Indigenous"), each understood as a source of influence on the Egyptian cultural economy, and its Arab counterpart in general. While *al-wafid* represents cultural sources that are literally "coming from the outside and alienating," *al-mawruth* represents a culture that is literally "inherited from the ancestors" and therefore authentic.[13]

Bishri argues that the history of the Egyptian legal system since the mid-nineteenth century is one of *al-wafid* taking control and disrupting the country's organic legal fabric. This took place in three historical stages:[14] The first stage concerns the condition of Islamic jurisprudence at the turn of the nineteenth century. Although the Islamic legal system was stagnant at the time, Bishri notes, there were indigenous attempts to reform the system "from the inside," *i.e.*, without discarding it altogether in favor of Western legal transplants. These attempts at reform all preceded Western colonization of the region, and were aborted at its aftermath. The second stage is what Bishri dubs the phase of "Western Legal Infiltration." This stage runs roughly from the mid-nineteenth century, when the Ottoman Empire embarked on wholesale transplants of Western codes (commercial, civil, and criminal), and terminates in the first quarter of the twentieth century at the beginning of decolonization in the Arab world. Bishri notes that often these transplants were prompted by a local desire for reform. However, they all transpired at the heyday of Western colonialism, and were ultimately reduced to a legislative expression of Europe's military, economic and social might. The third stage is referred to as the "Codes of the Independence Era." This is a mid-twentieth century phase which essentially comprises the legal documents produced by Sanhuri following decolonization in the Arab world. Bishri notes that Sanhuri's aim was to solidify the political independence of these countries by insuring the "independence of the legal order." To this end, Sanhuri set out to produce new codes to replace the Western legal transplants of the nineteenth century. It is these codes, and in particular Sanhuri's most important achievement, the civil code, which Bishri berates as essentially a culturally alien embodiment of *al-wafid*.

Bishri argues that the major source of inspiration behind Sanhuri's civil code was not the doctrines and jurisprudence inherited from the ancestors. Rather,

---

[13] Meijer, *supra* note 2, at 19.
[14] *See* Bishri, *The Legal Question, supra* note 2, at 5–24; *see also* 39–68.

the code's genealogy lies in an amalgam of three different sources: comparative law, Egyptian case law, and finally Islamic jurisprudence. Sanhuri treated Islamic law as he would any other constituent of comparative law. This, Bishri argues, reduced the civil code to a culturally hybrid legal document of alien genealogy. And the hybrid, as discussed earlier, is by definition inauthentic. Although Sanhuri was trying to ensure the independence of post-colonial Egyptian civil law from its Western antecedent, his project of legal reform caused "not only the independence of the 'self' from its [Western] 'other,' but even the autonomy of the 'self' from itself, or at least its historical 'self,' as a constituent of contemporary collective consciousness."[15] Thus, for Bishri, Sanhuri's civil code is viewed as an agent of contemporary cultural alienation. Sanhuri is dismissed as a failed comparativist: His legal reform project, which heavily relied on comparative law, eventually lead to a hybrid civil code which Bishri dismisses as inauthentic.

Sanhuri, by contrast, had aimed at the exact opposite. Much like Bishri, Sanhuri also wanted to put to rest the existential anxieties of Mahfouz's hero. As a budding student of comparative law under the supervision of the legendary Edouard Lambert, Sanhuri seems to have decided early on that his mission as an *intellectual engagé* was to bring the modern "science" of comparative law to bear on the rich but stagnant tradition of Islamic law. The intended synthesis was a new Islamic law: sophisticated enough on the juristic scale to meet the material challenges of modernity, yet unadulterated enough on the cultural scale to preserve an authentic identity. Sanhuri's instrumental aspirations for comparative law are best captured in the dedication he wrote for *Le Califat*, his doctoral dissertation on how to modernize the Caliphate in Islamic law by appealing to comparative methodology. Having pursued his doctoral studies in France for over five years (1921–26), and preparing to return to his home in Egypt, Sanhuri dedicated the dissertation, with full existential rigor,

> "To all who hail from the Orient and know how to conciliate their religious, national and racial ties with ties to their great homeland: the Orient, and with those ties that connect them to an even greater homeland: Humanity."[16]

Comparative law was expected to smooth the way for such a conciliation.

There is nothing peculiar about Sanhuri's sense of competing "ties," and his attempt to mediate them by appealing to the scientific promises of comparative law. The same experience of internal division between competing attachments to the "East" and "West" has been a common episode in the modern experience

---

[15] *See* Bishri, *supra* note 2.

[16] "*A tout oriental qui sait concilier ses attaches religieuses, nationales et raciales avec les liens de sa Grande Patrie: l'Orient, et avec ceux d'une Patrie plus grande encore: l'Humanité,*" *see* Abdel-Razzak Al-Sanhuri, *Le Califat: Son Evolution Vers une Societe des Nations Orientale* (Paris, 1926). For another personal insight on the subject, written at the beginning of the year when Sanhuri's new civil code was promulgated, *see* Nadia al-Sanhuri, "al-Qadim wal-Jadid" [The Old and the New], 57 *Al Hilal* 6–8 (1949); For a general introduction to the subject, *see* Jacques Berque, *Egypt Imperialism and Revolution* 502–518 (Jean Stewart trans., London, 1972).

of Arab students abroad. These feelings have been most powerfully memorialized in al-Tayeb Saleh's famous postcolonial novel, *Season of Migration to the North*. Much like Sanhuri, the narrator of Saleh's novel is a man who returns to his home village by the Nile after studying for seven years in Europe. After having felt in the West like a "storm-swept feather," he returns home in search of his authentic identity as "a being with a background, with roots with a purpose."[17] However, the belief that his village was the last bastion of pure and uncorrupted tradition is soon shattered as the narrator becomes increasingly aware of his internal divisions between East and West, and his inability to transcend them by taking refuge in familiar locales. Back in his home village, he encounters a man by the name of Mustafa Said. Much like the narrator, Said also led "modern" studies in the West, only to return back home and fail in constructing a compartmentalized existence of East and West by the Nile. Unlike Sanhuri's thesis which is dedicated to those who succeed in conciliating between East and West, Said's diary is dedicated to "'those who see with one eye, speak with one tongue and see things as either black or white, either Eastern or Western."[18]

From the above, it seems to me that in modernity/tradition discourse, one can distinguish between two types of "nostalgia," each signified by the above two dedications. On the one hand, there is Sanhuri's dedication which voices nostalgia for a cosmopolitan condition of "hybridity," while on the other hand, Said's dedication voices an alternative nostalgia for the unadulterated condition of "authenticity." To my mind, Said shares the same kind of nostalgia which underlies Bishri's critique of Sanhuri. Those two types of nostalgia are not without political implications. In the next section, I hope to demonstrate the different modes in which nostalgia can be harnessed to a political agenda. More specifically, I will retell the story of how Sanhuri became a student of comparative law in order to demonstrate how his particular type of nostalgia was instrumental in shaping a variety of emancipatory projects in law. This stands in contrast to Bishri's type of nostalgia, which I argue is both intellectually futile and politically dangerous.

Before exploring the above, I should advertise a personal caveat. In exploring how Sanhuri became a student of comparative law, I am essentially retelling Sanhuri's story as that of an elite Arab student who pursued his doctoral studies in comparative law abroad, and then returned to a hybrid homeland feeling ambivalent about his competing "ties." Given the proximity of Sanhuri's story to where I am presently writing this article, it may very well be that I am projecting my own personal anxieties on to Sanhuri. In an attempt to preempt this not-so-outlandish critique, the most intuitive self-defense for me here would be to expose my authorship. I admit that many of the dilemmas and fears that animated Sanhuri's return home after studying comparative law in France, continue to live through me and other students of comparative law. For example, I

---

[17] Tayeb Saleh, *Season of Migration to the North* (Denys Johnson-Davies trans., London, 1992).
[18] *Id.*, at 150–51.

find that my basic anxieties over how to relate the methodological knowledge acquired abroad to "real" legal questions at home, are an uncanny reproduction of Sanhuri's anxiety over how to translate the newly acquired sociological terminology of his doctoral thesis into Arabic legalese. This is yet another reason not to view this article as a detached exercise in biography.

THE EXPERIENCE OF MODERNITY: *"L'ÉCOLE LAMBERT ÉGYPTIENNE"*[19]

In 1906 Sanhuri was an eleven year old student at a preparatory school in Alexandria. At a certain risk of sounding melodramatic, much was happening that year at the Khedivial Law School in Cairo, which Sanhuri was to join seven years later, and which would influence his future progress towards becoming the Arab world's foremost comparativist. In November of that year, the celebrated French jurist Edouard Lambert was appointed to head the educational institution; as its last French dean, he clashed with the British authorities in Egypt and soon left the country for Lyon. He was subsequently followed there by an increasing number of Egyptian law students, including Sanhuri in 1921. While Lambert described the "double personality" of his Egyptian students as "one half eastern, one half French,"[20] Sanhuri expressed the hybrid genealogy of the same Lambert-mentored group of students by dubbing them *"l'école Lambert égyptienne."* In the following pages I would like to explore the role played by the burgeoning discipline of comparative law in informing the different dimensions of modernity which students and mentor experienced, both in Egypt and France, between 1906 and 1936.

Modernity and the Jurists: Major Legal Preoccupations in 1906 France and Egypt

In order to understand better the historical context of our story, I will start by offering an introductory glimpse of some of the major legal preoccupations which set the trajectory of modern 20th century jurisprudence in Egypt and France.[21]

In 1906 France, an assorted group of dissatisfied legal theorists, whom we may loosely refer to as the *juristes inquiets*, had been engaged for over a decade in a host of critical attacks on classical French legal thought.[22] The central object of

---

[19] "The Lambert Egyptian school." The term was coined by Sanhuri.

[20] *"mi-partie oriental, mi-partie française."*

[21] I use the term jurisprudence in the Anglo-American sense to denote a corpus of legal thought authored by jurists and largely found in treatises and legal opinions. This stands in contrast to the French use of the same term with reference to judicial precedents.

[22] The term *"juristes inquiets"* was coined by Marie-Claire Belleau in her ground-breaking work on the subject, and is itself a borrowing from an expression used by Paul Cuche. *See* Marie-Claire Belleau, "The 'Juristes Inquiets': Legal Classicism and Criticism in Early Twentieth Century France," 2 *Utah Law Review* 379–424 (1987). For a general study of the modern history of legal critique in France, *see* André-Jean Arnaud, *Les Juristes Face à la Société du XIXeme Siècle à nos Jours* (Paris, 1975).

their critique was the legal formalism associated with the late nineteenth century jurisprudence of *l'école de l'exégèse*. In the sphere of private law, this formalism had two primary manifestations. First, it was argued that *l'école de l'exégèse* had erroneously held the civil code as the embodiment of a complete legal system, one in which all analytically derived propositions had been integrated into an internally coherent and gapless body of rules. By contrast, the *juristes inquiets* attempted to demonstrate how *l'exégèse* formalism had overestimated the power of legal abstractions to produce inescapable outcomes, and instead advocated as an alternative a "sociologically" minded jurisprudence. Second, the *juristes inquiets* argued that *l'exégèse* jurisprudence was normatively biased in favor of an individualist legal ethic that, grossly sacrificed the collective interests of the community in favor of ideologically conservative doctrines of law. In response, the *juristes inquiets* advanced the "social" as a slogan and a substantive agenda for dealing with the rampant individualism of private law.

The socio-economic context in which these two emerging critiques took root was one of swelling industrialization coupled with the emergence of a new urban proletariat. To the *juristes inquiets'* mind, the deplorable labor and housing conditions of this emerging class seemed to be legitimated under the contracts, torts, and property jurisprudence of *l'école de l'exégèse*, thus obstructing the road to necessary legal reforms and in the process threatening the entire country with anarchist revolutions.[23] On the level of political alliances, however, it should not be assumed that the "social" was exclusively the cry of a leftist coterie of jurists. Rather, the "social," both as an ideological slogan as well as a political agenda, had come to be associated with diverse affiliations across the political spectrum. From the radical left to the Catholic right, through the communists and the fascists, everyone made occasional appeals to such "social" doctrines as *solidarité* in, or the *moralisation* of, private law.[24]

If we shift our attention to the Eastern shores of the Mediterranean, 1906 in Egypt was a time when the bulk of the country's Islamic legal system had been recently dismantled in favor of imported Western codes, usually modeled after the French example. Islamic law had been critiqued since the last quarter of the nineteenth century as an obstacle in Egypt's quest for present day modernization. Centuries of *taqlid*, or juristic imitation, had reduced the Islamic legal system to a rigid and antiquated labyrinth of complexities. Demands for legal reform abounded and the Egyptian government's reaction was radical. Between the years 1876 and 1906, the country had received a new set of civil, commercial

---

[23] Indeed, according to Arnaud's compelling, if rather dogmatic, analysis, it was the fear of socialism, understood as a form of nihilistic anarchism or unabashed state autocracy, which ultimately animated the *Juristes Inquiets'* scholarship as an "effective barrage against socialist ideas" (*"barrage efficace contre les idées socialistes"*) and subsequently reduced their project to substituting a liberal conservatism (*"conservatisme liberale"*) with their own alternative bourgeois conservatism (*"conservatism bourgeois"*). *See* Arnaud, *supra* note 22, at 125.

[24] *See* Jacques Donzelot, *L'invention du Social* (Paris, 1984). For the private law implications of the social, *see* Duncan Kennedy, "Clauses imposées et clauses intèrdites au profit des parties faibles," Sorbonne Lectures (Jan., 1999) (manuscript on file with the author).

and criminal codes, a reorganized court system, and a new secular law school. The reforms took place on two levels, one "native" and the other "mixed." The former served legal disputes between Egyptians, while the latter involved legal disputes with/between foreign parties and was meant to substitute the prior system of legal capitulations.[25]

We cannot overestimate the significant transformation in legal theory and practice which followed these reforms. An entire system of legal rules, arguments and theories was effectively eroded. Conceptual structures and subsystems previously used for the classification of legal questions were at most transmuted into codified forms of hybrid configuration, and more often than not were discarded all together. But this historical transformation was not limited to the conceptual level of the country's legal consciousness. In terms of the composition of the Egyptian legal elite, an entire class of *ulama* and *fuqaha'a*, or Islamic judges and law scholars, was gradually disenfranchised and lost most of the religious/legal power it had previously exercised in the public sphere. Secular law schools replaced the Islamic Al-Azhar University as the breeding ground of the legal establishment and political leaders, while secular courts progressively encroached on the jurisdiction of *shar'i* courts until the latter were abolished all together.[26]

It did not help that the introduction of the above legal reforms was soon coupled with British military intervention and subsequent occupation of the country in 1882. The argument that Western legal reforms were necessary for the modernization of Egypt was thus soon set in doubt. More and more, the reforms appeared as the product of foreign meddling in the country's internal affairs, as opposed to the flowering of a genuine nationalist movement.[27] Accordingly, by 1906, the major concerns of the emerging elite of Egyptian secular lawyers centered around the elaboration of a nationalist agenda in which the evacuation of the British army of occupation figured hand in hand with the modernization of Islamic law.

In sum, if we were to restate in one sentence the major legal preoccupations of 1906 in the above two legal systems, it would be the need to socialize private law in France, and the need to modernize Islamic law in Egypt.

Lambert at the Threshold of Egypt: A Sketchy Portrait

The story being told here starts in the year 1906 when Edouard Lambert was requested to assume the deanship of the Khedivial Law School in

---

[25] For more on the subject, the classic reference remains Jasper Brinton, *The Mixed Courts of Egypt* (New Haven, 1968).

[26] *See generally* Farahat Ziadeh, *Lawyers, the Rule of Law and Liberalism in Modern Egypt* (Stanford, 1968).

[27] Indeed the reforms had started initially in an attempt to stop such meddling. The "mixed" reforms of 1875 were meant to address the prior state of legal disarray which reigned under foreign legal capitulations. *See* Byron Cannon, *Politics of Law and the Courts in Nineteenth Century Egypt* (Salt Lake City, 1988).

Cairo.[28] It is not clear which branch of the government issued the request and what were the factors that prompted the choice of Lambert to assume the post. However, it seems reasonable to speculate that Lambert's celebrated association with the newly established discipline of comparative law may have influenced the Egyptian government's choice.

In the year 1900, the first *Congrès International de Droit Comparé* was held in Paris, and Lambert had been entrusted by the renowned French jurist Raymond Saleilles to elaborate the theoretical and methodological aspects of the discipline.[29] Saleilles, arguably one of the most influential figures in the *juristes inquiets* movement, had also been Lambert's doctoral thesis supervisor, and initiated the latter to the jurisprudential critique of *l'école de l'exégèse*. Within this loose band of "anxious" jurists, Lambert appears to have been associated by 1906 with a much more radical strand in the common project of critique. This is evident from Lambert's scholarship at the time, with reference to both his methodological outlook and political commitments.

On the methodological level, Lambert's views are best represented in his book review of François Gény's *Méthode d'interprétation et sources en droit privé positif*. Although Gény's treatise is perhaps one of the most influential treatises in defining the methodological preoccupations of the *juristes inquiets* at the time, Lambert critiqued Gény's work as much too restrained in its attack on *l'école de l'exégèse*, as not going far enough in its critique of classical conceptualism, and generally for "not daring, like me [Lambert] to rebel openly against the dogma of law's fixity."[30] All in all, Lambert emerges in this book review with a set of views that situate him methodologically on the more radical extreme of what may be viewed as the centrist *inquiets'* line articulated by Gény at the time.[31]

On the political level, the movement of jurists who critiqued *l'école de l'exégèse* comprised a heterogeneous assortment of ideological affiliations. Within this group, Lambert appears firmly situated on the left of the political

---

[28] Subsequent changes to the name of the law school are an excellent indicator of the different episodes in the history of modern Egypt. In 1914, the name was changed to the Sultanyan Law School, symbolizing the termination of nominal Ottoman sovereignty over Egypt and the emergence of the country as a separate "Sultanate" at the beginning of the First World War. In 1925 the Egyptian University was reorganized, and the law school changed its name to the Royal Faculty of Law, "Royal" to the extent that Egypt had embarked on its "liberal experiment" as a constitutional monarchy. In the wake of the Free Officers *coup d'etat* in 1952 and the abolition of the monarchy, the school assumed its current title of Cairo University Faculty of Law.

[29] *See* Carlos Petit, "From Paris to the Hague. Edouard Lambert and Droit Commun Legislatif," in Claes Peterson (ed.), *History and European Private Law: Development of Common Methods and Principles* (Stockholm, 1997). *See also* Bianca Gardella-Tedeschi, *Anti-formalist Strands in Comparative Legal Theory* (LL.M. dissertation, Harvard Law School) (on file with the Harvard Law School Library).

[30] "*n'ose pas, come moi [i.e. Lambert], s'insurger ouvertement contre le dogme de l'immobilité de la loi.*" Edouard Lambert, "Une Réforme nécessaire des études de droit civil," *XL Revue International De L'Enseignement* 216–43, 230 (1900).

[31] For the later adoption of Gény's views into the mainstream of French private law theory, *see* Paul Dubouchet, *La Pensée Juridique Avant et Après le Code Civil* (Martinique, 1994).

spectrum. Only a couple of months prior to his departure for Egypt in July 1906, Lambert published a contribution to a progressive series of legal research on "*L'Oppression des humbles par le droit et les méfaits de l'indivisualisme.*"[32] In a highly rhetorical lecture delivered on "Class Inequalities and Electoral Politics,"[33] Lambert critiqued the *de facto* frustration of universal suffrage at the hands of "the electoral monopoly of capitalists and mandarins"[34] which stifled the political chances of "progressive political parties,"[35] and the possibility of change in favor of the "proletariats who are its victims."[36] Addressing his lecture to "the majority of my audience, namely laborers and petty employees"[37] Lambert attacked "the heavy legislative machinery"[38] whose actors "generally hail from bourgeois circles."[39] With regards to the latter, Lambert rhetorically asked the following inflammatory question of his audience: "And what have you managed to achieve so far? Nothing!"[40]

While his angry language and emphatic class references may induce in the reader an image of Red-Lambert-the-radical-propagandist, things do not seem to have gone that far. Instead of bringing his talk to a close with a call for revolution, he concluded as a firm believer in the liberal promises of representative government, and argued for the refinement of the electoral system so that his listeners might find themselves "on the road to successfully resisting all the forces of oppression which [they] face under the present organization of capitalist society."[41] Naturally, all these references alienated Lambert from the *noyau dure* of the Lyonaise bourgeoisie.[42]

Lambert in Cairo

It was with the above methodological and political commitments that Lambert accepted the deanship of the Khedivial Law School, and moved to Cairo in the fall of 1906. Personally, after my research for this essay, I still find it rather puzzling why an up-and-coming French comparativist like Lambert would agree to

---

[32] Edouard Lambert, *The Use of Law in Oppressing the Powerless and the Ills of Individualism* (Paris, 1906). For a full bibliography of Lambert's scholarship, *see Introduction à l'Étude du Droit Comparé: Recueil d'Études en l'Honneur d'Edouard Lambert*, 7–10 (Paris, 1938).

[33] "*Les Inégalités de classe en matière d'electorat politique.*"

[34] "*le monopole électorale des capitalistes et des mandarins.*"

[35] "*des parties d'avant garde.*"

[36] "*les prolétaires qui en sont victimes.*"

[37] "*la majorité de mon auditoire, ouvriers ou petits employés.*"

[38] "*la lourde machine legislative.*"

[39] "*généralement issus de milieux bourgeois.*"

[40] "*Et qu'avez-vous obtenu jusqu'ici? Rien.*"

[41] "*sur la voie de ceux qui peuvent vous permettre de résister victorieusement à toutes les forces d'oppression que l'organisation actuelle de la société capitaliste fait peser sur vous.*"

[42] The "*noyau dure*" reference belongs to Lambert's grandson, Denis-Claire Lambert, who in a private interview in Lyon in February 1999, elaborated on how his grandfather had been ostracized by the Lyonnaise bourgeoisie, a notoriously close-knit social class.

teach law at a colonial outpost, and a British one no less. An answer of sorts may be found in the Egyptian context at the time. When Lambert arrived in Cairo, the modernizing elite of Egypt had long entertained a particularly hearty fondness for all things French. This fondness, paradoxically rooted in an act of military aggression (Napoleon's invasion of Egypt, lasting 1798–1801), produced a strong commitment to modernize the country after the French model. Egyptian students had consistently been sent to France on government scholarships since 1828, and French technocrats were concurrently imported to help in building a modern Egyptian state. The first batch of Egyptian students returned home in 1831 after studying "natural law, international law, public law, political economy, statistics, and administration," and soon began to translate selections of French codes and legal textbooks.[43] Naturally, when Egypt started reforming its legal system in the 1870s, the codes, the courts, and the law school were all modeled after the French example. The country's subsequent military occupation by the British in 1882 only served to intensify the Egyptian elite's commitment to doing things the French way.[44] Thus, when Lambert was offered the deanship of the Khedivial law school in 1906, he was succeeding to a public post that had seen uninterrupted occupation by French jurists since the school's establishment in 1868.

If the above partly explains why the Egyptians would select a Frenchman for law school dean, it does not explain why Lambert in turn accepted this post. Reconstructing from his later reflections on his Cairo *séjour*, an intuitive account may be located in the not-so-unusual occurrence of a marginalised jurist taking his scholarship to a marginal law school: In 1906, the *juristes inquiets* were largely on the defensive as a peripheral movement in French legal thought. The young Lambert was heavily involved in a curious new discipline called comparative law, and he lectured on his views on the subject from the academically peripheral auditoriums of Lyon. To look at the story from this rather unflattering perspective, accepting the deanship of the Khedivial Law School appears to have been a utilitarian decision on Lambert's part—the anti-colonial sentiments, which later colored his tenure in Egypt, more an afterthought than a deciding factor.

More specifically, Lambert had wanted to enlist the new discipline of comparative law in the budding *juristes inquiets'* critique of classical legal thought, by applying its sociological insights towards formulating a sophisticated anti-formalist alternative to *l'école de l'exégèse*. By moving to Egypt, he was to find himself "swiftly relocated in a milieu which proved to be one the very first locations of comparative law experimentalism . . . and one of its best fields of

---

[43] Ziadeh, *supra* note 26, at 19.

[44] This curious rapport continues to pose its peculiar repercussions to this day. A case in point is the much celebrated bicentennial commemoration of Napoleon's invasion of Egypt, a year long series of events that were sponsored in 1998 by the ministries of culture in both Egypt and France. For more on the subject see Robert Solé, *L'Egypte Passion Française* (Paris, 1997).

application."[45] To Lambert, Egypt thus posed the world's first juristic laboratory, a space where comparative law might be observed in action.

Two particular facets of the Egyptian legal system seem to have attracted his comparativist fancy like no other. First, Lambert was interested in studying the tradition of Islamic law which he had described in pronounced sociological terms in his 1902 treatise on *La Fonction du droit comparé*. The exotic image of Islamic law as the "substantively irrational" Other of Western law in the East was quite popular at the time, and Lambert was largely following the definitions of such scholars as Weber and Goldziher. Second, coming to Egypt would allow Lambert to study the case law of the Mixed Court in which he was very interested for similar methodological reasons. Established in 1875 as part of the Egyptian program of "legal reform," in the Mixed Courts were staffed by judges from Egypt as well as 16 other Western countries, who applied Mixed Codes that were largely modeled after the French example with minor influences from Islamic law. More interestingly, the Codes recognized the existence of gaps in their doctrinal structures and instructed the judges to fill them by resorting to equity. Such legal realism was unheard of at the time, and the fact that the codes were interpreted by a judicial body with varied training in diverse legal traditions made the Courts appear as a cosmopolitan workshop constituting "at that moment in time one of the best fields of experimentalism for the science of comparative legislation."[46]

Accordingly, Lambert expected the study of both Islamic law and the case law of the Mixed Courts' to furnish him with invaluable comparativist energy to rejuvenate the ossified body of French private law. Comparative law insights from Egypt would assist him in formulating his critique of how *l'ecole de l'exégèse* had contributed to the stagnation of the French legal system in general. But Lambert's utilitarian impulse is not without intellectual undercurrents; the sensibility which led him to set sail for the East in search of comparative energy to rejuvenate Western legal theory was an expression of a larger intellectual movement at the time, a *modernist* movement whose most notoriously subversive manifestation is found in the "primitive" influence on arts and literature in the twentieth century.[47]

As stated earlier, the Egypt of 1906 for which Lambert set sail had been a *de facto* British colony for over twenty years (although it remained under nominal Ottoman sovereignty until the outbreak of the First World War in 1914). But

---

[45] *"subitement transporté dans un milieu qui avait été l'une des premièrs terres d'essai du droit comparé . . . l'un de ses meilleurs champs de demonstration."* L'Institut de Droit Comparé de Lyon, *Liste de ses Publications Antériures à*, 3 (Lyon, 1936).

[46] *"en ce moment le meillier champ d'expérimentation dont dispose la science de la législation comparée."* Edouard Lambert, "Introduction" in Mahmoud Fathy, *La Doctrine Musulmane de l'Abus des Droits: Etude d'Histoire Juridique et de Droit Comparé*, at xxxiv (Lyon, 1913).

[47] *See* Robert Goldwater, *Primitivism in Modern Art* (Cambridge, Mass., 1986). For a brilliant study of legal modernism and its connections with modernism in the arts, *see* Nathaniel Berman, "Modernism, Nationalism, and the Rhetoric of Reconstruction," in Dan Danielsen & Karen Engle (eds.), *After Identity: A Reader in Law and Culture* (New York ,1995).

while the British had physically occupied the country, the French were intellectually spread far and wide as "mentors by choice" to the modernizing Egyptian
elite. The Khedivial Law School in particular, with its uninterrupted tradition
of French deans, had become the hotbed of modern Egyptian nationalism.
Indeed, the foremost hero of the nationalist movement at the time, Mustafa
Kamil Pacha, was a graduate of the Law School, and, for him most of his followers, to be an Egyptian nationalist meant to be a francophile. The Egyptian
nationalists' attraction for France was as much an expression of their faith in the
liberal ideals of the French revolution as it was a calculated policy by the nationalists to manipulate Franco-British colonial rivalries in their favor. To embrace
the French intellectually had thus become a successful anticolonial strategy by
which the nationalists carried out their opposition to British rule in the country
(along with courting Ottoman sentiments when France seemed to lag behind in
Egypt's support). The anticolonial success of pitting France against Britain
intellectually is best discerned from the long passages devoted to the subject in
Lord Cromer's canonical book *Modern Egypt*, whose first edition, incidentally,
was published the same year Lambert became dean of the Khedivial Law
School. In that book Cromer, who had been the British High Commissioner to
the country and its *de facto* ruler since 1883, attempted to explain the failure of
British cultural and administrative traditions to take root in Egypt under his
governance. According to Cromer, the answer was located in an *ad hoc* mixture
of French frivolity and Egyptian glibness:

> "Compare the undemonstrative, shy Englishman, with his social exclusiveness and
> insular habits with the vivacious and cosmopolitan Frenchman who does not know
> what the word shyness means, and who in ten minutes is apparently on terms of inti-
> mate friendship with any casual acquaintance he may chance to meet. The semi-
> educated Oriental does not recognise that the former has, at all events, the merit of
> sincerity, whilst the latter is often merely acting a part. He looks coldly on the
> Englishman, and rushes into the arms of the Frenchman."[48]

As Cromer's chagrined analysis would suggest, rushing into the French arms of
Edouard Lambert was exactly what Egyptian students did at the Khedivial Law
School.

In protest against British educational policies in the country, the first student
strike of its kind had taken place at the Law School in February 1906. The strike
soon extended to secondary school students and threatened to ignite a nation-
wide revolt. The significance of the law students' strike was attested to by

---

[48] Cited in Edward Said, *Orientalism*, 211 (New York, 1994), *see also* 212–16. Cromer's summa-
tion on the French in the Orient is only paralleled by that of the French on the English. Of Cromer's
subordinate and superior respectively, Arthur Rimbaud had commented earlier, during the Mahdi
crisis in the Sudan, "*C'est justement les Anglais avec leur absurde politique, qui minent désormais
le commerce de toutes ces côtes. Ils ont voulu tout remainier et ils sont arrivér à faire pire que les
Egyptiens et les Turcs, reuinés par eux. Leur Gordon est un idiot, leur Wolsely un âne, et toutes leur
entreprises une suites insensée d'absurdités et de déprédations.*" See Lytton Strachey, *Eminent
Victorians*, 257–58 (London, 1999).

Cromer's personal intervention in the matter. A compromise was finally reached and the government promised to take note of the students' grievances. In response to the strike, as well as later criticism of British policy in Egypt following the *Denshway* incident, Saad Zaghlul Pacha was appointed as minister of education in October 1906. During the same month of Zaghlul's appointment, Edouard Lambert was made dean of the Khedivial Law School, and, upon assuming his post, Lambert directed paramount attention towards addressing the student grievances which had shaken the Law School prior to his tenure. Law students seem to have been generally angered by the "infantile curriculum" introduced by British educational experts. More specifically, the students were exceptionally alarmed by the British approach of "Indianising" the law school curriculum, *i.e.* of introducing the same Common Law reforms in Egypt which the British had previously introduced in India. Lambert unequivocally sided with his Egyptian students on both accounts, and soon became astoundingly popular at the law school. During his tenure as dean, Lambert introduced the curricular changes demanded by the students, and repeatedly clashed in that respect with Mr. Douglas Dunlop, the British advisor to the Egyptian ministry of education and the man whose policies had been responsible for the law students' strike of February 1906.[49]

Lambert's popularity with Egyptian law students reached its height in July 1907, when he finally resigned from his post as dean of the law school in protest against British educational policies in the country. The reasons behind Lambert's resignation were set forth in an article he later published in the Parisian newspaper *Le Temps* and were reproduced in Arabic in *Al-Liwaa'*, the often-banned newspaper of Kamil's nationalist party. The article largely reads as an impassioned anticolonial manifesto against British educational policy in Egypt, and its publication in France owes much to Kamil's association with the anticolonial circle of Parisian intellectuals. Reading through the article, it soon becomes evident that Lambert had forged a strong emotional bond with the Egyptian nationalist cause, and particularly with Zaghlul in whose defense he ultimately submitted his resignation. Lambert's actions are quite significant given that Zaghlul was soon to become the foremost hero of Egyptian nationalism following Kamil's untimely death. The following is a short excerpt from Lambert's article:

"I have left the post [of dean] with a sense of sorrow that nearly tore my heart in two. Remaining in Egypt was no longer possible for a man like me who dedicated his life to education, for I could not possibly retain my post unless I were to become a mute instrument in the hands of a wicked policy which threatens the good relations between the Egyptian and European peoples. A year before my arrival in Egypt, the administrative powers of M. Grandmolin, who preceded me as dean of the law school, had been usurped by Mr. Douglas Dunlop, the British civil servant who is in *de facto* control of the Egyptian ministry of education . . . I have not succeeded in escaping the

---

[49] *See* Abdel-Rahman Al-Rafi'i, *Mustafa Kamil* (Cairo, 1950).

same fate [as M. Grandmolin] . . . Mr. Dunlop has blindly fought the progress of French education at the law school . . . he stopped the appointment of new professors in the French section in anticipation of its eventual elimination, fired its old and competent professors . . . and appointed instead young English professors who have barely graduated from law school . . . This reactionary policy in education has . . . led an elite and educated group of law school students to join the anti-British forces and caused the transformation of the law school into a stronghold of Egyptian nationalism, a place where among the four hundred students one barely finds ten who do not subscribe to the nationalist ideals of Mustafa Kamil Pacha . . . Mr. Dunlop dealt his ultimate blow to my integrity by attempting to enlist me in his schemes against the nationalist minister of education, Saad Zaghlul Pacha, whom the British authorities had appointed under the pressure of public opinion . . . I finally decided to return to my country after I had exhausted all avenues of defending the students and faculty of the law school from the injustices of Mr. Dunlop."[50]

Lambert's resignation was immediately accepted and a new English-Canadian dean was appointed in his place the next day. Lambert, somewhat bitterly, described Mr. Hill, the new dean "as best summed up in the words of Sir Eldon Gorst [the new British High Commissioner], namely that 'Mr. Hill is an ignorant man, amenable to being lead, and therefore all the more congenial to our policies.'"[51] Thus Lambert became the last French dean of the Khedivial Law School, and his resignation and departure for France caused an outcry from both French and Egyptian nationalists.[52] In the following years, he was followed to France by over fifty of his Egyptian law students, forming the core of what Sanhuri was later to call "*l'école Lambert Egyptienne.*"

The Egyptians in Lyon: Mentoring "*l'Elite Dirigeante*"[53]

Upon his return to France, Lambert assumed once again his original post as professor of civil law at the University of Lyon, only to find himself "at the head of a large adopted family of Egyptian students, which forced me to abandon my earlier work in order to mentor their studies."[54] If we follow what Lambert wrote about this interlude in his career, it is difficult to resist commiserating with the bewildered man at this turn of events. Suddenly surrounded by a seemingly

---

[50] The English text is my own translation from an Arabic version of Lambert's article in *Le Temps*. See *id.* at 244–49.

[51] *Id.* at 248.

[52] While Lambert was indeed the last French dean of the Khedivial Law School, it should nonetheless be noted that his political collaborator Leon Duguit was later commissioned by the law school in 1925 to reorganise its curriculum during its academic reincarnation as the Royal Faculty of Law.

[53] "The ruling elite." The term was repeatedly used by Lambert to describe his Egyptian students. *See infra.*

[54] "*à la téte d'une nombruese fameille adoptive d'étudiants égyptiens qui m'a forcé à abandonner mes traveaux antérieures pour guider ses etudes.*" Edouard Lambert, "Preface" to El-Arabi, *La Conscription des Neutres dans la Lutte de la Concurrence Économique*, at viii (Lyon, 1924).

unending stream of Egyptian students, many of them shunning the hallowed halls of the Sorbonne in Paris in favor of Lambert's mentorship in Lyon, the piteous professor spent the next seven years reeling under the academic demands of his *"colonie d'étudiants égyptiens."*[55] The descent of Egyptian students on Lambert's academic existence in Lyon continued uninterrupted until it was mercifully, if only temporarily, discontinued by the outbreak of the First World War. Yet despite the slightly distraught terms in which he later recalled those years ("a period in which my scientific output was completely interrupted"[56]) Lambert was nonetheless very proud of his association with his Egyptian students. Something of the political animal, the long term strategist, the institutional network builder, were all awakened in him, and from there mingled with the idealistic promises of comparative law. After all, the Egyptians who followed him to Lyon were not just any Egyptian students—they were the future ruling elite of their country. No one was aware of this crucial fact more than Lambert, and he did not take lightly the prospects of mentoring the elite. Reflecting thirty years after the British had forced him out of Egypt, he insisted that he had always understood his responsibilities towards Egyptian law students as one of "preparing them for the active social and political tasks which awaited them as the future ruling elite of their country."[57]

And so, a newly invented discipline called comparative law suddenly posed as a serviceable tool in the actual struggle of a colonized people to modernize their nation. Political activism thus joined with intellectual evangelism, and comparative law was transformed at the hands of Lambert and his students. Surrounded by an eager Egyptian following in Lyon, Lambert's first strategic step was to provide an institutionalized space in which he and his students could be affiliated, and in which the new discipline of comparative law might be pursued. Towards this end, he submitted a proposal to the University of Lyon for the incorporation of a comparative law institute at the Faculty of Law. However, the French government appears to have been troubled by the anticolonial support which Lambert lent his Egyptian students and which contradicted the official French foreign policy at the time.[58] Accordingly, Lambert's request for the establishment of a comparative law institute was rejected by the government.[59] In an obstinate reaction to the government's decision, Lambert announced in November 1907, four months after his departure from Egypt, the establishment of a special *Séminaire Oriental d'Etudes Juridiques et Sociales* which was "completely independent of funding or

---

[55] Edouard Lambert, "Conférences faites à l'Université Egyptienne," 7 *Revue Al-Qanun Wal-Iqtisad* 169 (1937), at 174.

[56] *"une période d'interruption complète dans ma production scientifique."* *Id.* at 176.

[57] *"préparation aux tâches d'action social et politique qui leur inconberaient plus tard comme membres de l'élite dirigeante de leurs pays." Id.* at 175.

[58] The infamous Anglo-French *"entente cordiale"* had been entered into in 1904, basically giving British colonialism a free hand in Egypt in return for a French free hand in Morocco.

[59] Interview with M. Moriteau, Vice President, Institut de Droit Comparé, Faculty of Law, University of Lyon, Lyon, France (February, 1999).

patronage by the university."[60] The *Séminaire* was thus an essentially informal affair, and Lambert assumed full personal responsibility for its initial contingent of Egyptian students; this was made explicit by the *Séminaire*'s brochure which advertised its legal status as having "its headquarters at Professor Lambert's personal residence."[61]

It took the University of Lyon another fourteen years to transform the *Séminaire* into the more senior status of a comparative law *Institut*. In 1921, Lambert became the head of the *Institut de Droit Comparé*, the very first of its kind to be established in France, a position which conferred on him the reputation of the foremost comparativist in the country. The academic transformation of the informal *Séminaire* into a full-fledged *Institut* was naturally coupled with its opening up to a much larger and diversified body of international students that far surpassed Lambert's initial constituency of Egyptian *protégés*. Nonetheless, the Egyptians continued their northern migration to Lyon, were "always received with warm sympathy," and came to assume a rather privileged position "at a home whose foundations were laid by their older brothers."[62] At his moment of official recognition by the academic circles in Lyon, Lambert made sure that no one would forget the foundational role of his Egyptian students in bringing the new *Institut* about, and, more importantly, in the very genealogy of comparative law as a discipline. The very first to receive his thanks in his inaugural speech were "*les étudiants Egyptiens*" who by laying "the first foundations of the *Institut de Droit Comparé de Lyon*" were "the first instigators of the movement which activated in France the teaching of comparative law."[63]

The Egyptians in Lyon: Politics and Methodology

The *Séminaire*, followed by the *Institut*, provided a space between East and West where "liberal understandings between a professor and his students"[64] would allow for a comprehensive experience of modernity with its French and Egyptian challenges, and their respective methodological, and political implications. I mentioned earlier that one of the most pressing legal challenges of modernity for progressive jurists in France was how to *socialize modern law*, while, in Egypt, the major legal preoccupation rested on the need to *modernize*

---

[60] "*complète independance par rapport à l'université et ne solicite d'elle ni concours pecuniare ni patronage.*" Lambert, *supra* note 55, at 175; *see generally* L'Institut Oriental d'Études Juridiques et Sociales de Lyon. *Séminaire Libre Ouvert aux Étudiants de l'Orient Mussulman, Une Brochure de 32 Pages* (Lyon, Imprimerie du Moniteur Judiciare, 1910).

[61] "*pour siège, le domicile personnel du professeur Lambert et a la même mobilité d'assiette et la même aptitude au déplacement que ce domicile*" Lambert, *supra* note 32, at 175.

[62] "*tojours recus avec la plus chaud sympathie . . . dans une maison ou leurs frères aînés ont creusé les foundations.*" Lambert, *supra* note 46, at xiv.

[63] "*les premières bases de l'Institut de Droit Comparé de Lyon . . . les premièrs instigateurs de movement qui a activé en France l'enseignement du droit compare.*"

[64] "*la libre entente d'un professeur et d'étudiants*"

Islamic law. In pursuit of these two distinct projects, a very imaginative and highly committed attempt was made at forging a Franco-Egyptian alliance between professor and students. The alliance rested on two sets of commitments, one political and the other methodological. On a political level, an Egyptian anticolonial agenda found itself allied with a French socialist agenda in law. On a methodological level, an Egyptian agenda of modernizing Islamic law by appealing to the latest theories of French jurisprudence found itself allied with a French agenda of sociological jurisprudence formulated in rebellion against classical legal thought. Politics and legal methodology thus came together under the rubric of comparative law and formed the core of *"l'école Lambert égyptienne."* Let me try to explain further how the relationship between Lambert and his Egyptian students developed around these two sets of commitments.

First, in terms of political activism, studying under Lambert's supervision in Lyon was in keeping with the Egyptian nationalist tradition of establishing an intellectual alliance with France as a mode of anti-British activism. Lyon provided the Egyptians with a supportive atmosphere in which to pursue their nationalist cause, and Lambert had no scruples that "in pursuing him [to Lyon], his students were motivated by an ardent desire to advance themselves intellectually and scientifically in order to participate more effectively in the development of a stable and modern self government in the social and political aspects of their homeland."[65] Towards this end, an *Association des Etudiants Egyptiens de l'Université de Lyon* was duly established, and various lectures and rallies were organized to enlist French sympathies on the *"question égyptien."* Fortunately, the mayor of Lyon, M. Edouard Herriot, enjoyed excellent relations with Lambert and later on secured the necessary government support for the eventual transformation of the *Séminaire* into an *Institut* in 1921. Herriot appears to have lent considerable support to Egyptian nationalist activities in Lyon. One significant example was a function he sponsored at the *salle bandée* of the *Grand Théâtre de Lyon*, where lectures on the history of the anticolonial struggle in Egypt were illustrated by pictures of Cairo and Mecca.[66]

But the political activism of Egyptian law students in Lyon was not restricted to the nationalist cause; they equally took an interest in the numerous social causes that preoccupied the Lyonnais public at the time. To this end, Lambert made an effort to "provide his students with the necessary tools to participate intimately in the social and political life of Lyon."[67] Sanhuri attests to Lambert's efforts in

---

[65] *"ces étudiants était attirés auprès de moi par l'ardent désir de s'outiller intellectuellement et scientifiquement pour coopérer plus efficacement au développement du self-government et d'une organisation plus stable et plus moderne de la vie social et politique de leur pays."* Lambert, *supra* note 32, at 174.

[66] *Id.* 176, *see generally*, 175–182; *see also Liste de ses Publications*, *supra* note 45, at 4. For a general study of anticolonial activism in France, *see* Jean-Pierre Biondi, *Les Anticolonialistes 1881–1962* (Paris, 1992).

[67] *"leur fornir les moyens de pénetrer . . . dans l'intimité de la société et de la vie politique lyonnaise."* Lambert, *supra* note 32, at 175.

various entries of his private memoirs concerning his study in Lyon, in which he describes his participation in meetings of the French Socialist and Communist parties, as well as numerous labor union rallies. He appears to have been greatly influenced by these meetings. In a number of diary entries, Sanhuri over and over again, describes his commitment to establishing an Egyptian "socialist party of workers and peasants" upon returning to his homeland.[68]

Secondly, Lambert's relationship with his students assumed an equally important form of methodological collaboration. More specifically, Lambert introduced his "*collaborateurs Egyptiens*" to the intellectual backbone of the "social" in legal scholarship. As mentioned earlier, the "social" had become both a slogan and a substantive agenda for fighting the individualist spirit that pervaded French law. As such, the "social" had two manifestations in the field of private law. First, the "social" was understood as a set of sociological insights that are meant to replace the rigid formalism of *l'école de l'exégèse* in favour of a more supple jurisprudence conducive to social change. Second, the "social" manifested itself as a concrete set of socialist doctrines advanced as an alternative to the legal individualism of private law at the time. With an elaborate comparative law focus, Lambert introduced his Egyptian students to the above two manifestations of the "social." On the one hand, the nascent theories of sociological jurisprudence were ambitiously broached from both a civil and common law perspective. The Egyptian students were not alone in their study of sociological jurisprudence, and they were made conscious of this fact. Instead, they found themselves part of a much larger network of methodologically rebellious jurists, a trans-Atlantic alliance of progressive legal thinkers who were busy laying the philosophical foundations of modern Western law in France, England, and the United States. The methodological sources to which they were exposed included the works of Holmes and Pound in the U.S., Pollock and Maitland in England, as well as Duguit and Hauriou in France.[69]

Methodological studies in legal realism were coupled with an equally extensive comparative study of the different strands of "social legislation" that were also emerging in the world at the time. For example, Lambert's *Institut* was responsible for publishing the first French translations of the Soviet Codes of Russia in 1925,[70] as well as the different nationalist-socialist codes of Hitler's Germany and fascist legal reform in Italy (1929). On the common law side of social legislation, the *Institut* sponsored various studies of the legal aspects of the New Deal in the U.S., and particularly of the "current struggle between President Roosevelt's politics and the conservative opinions of the American Supreme Court."[71] Naturally, such studies also included French law for which

---

[68] *See generally*, Nadia al-Sanhuri & Tawfik al-Shawi (eds.), *Al-Sanhuri min khilal Awraqeh al-Shakhsiyya* (Cairo 1988).

[69] *Id.* at vii, *see generally* vi–ix.

[70] Edouard Lambert, *Les Codes de la Russie Soviétique* 45 (Paris, 1925).

[71] "*les luttes actuelles entre la politique du Président Roosevelt et les vues traditionelles de la jurisprudence de la Cour Suprême des Etats-Unis.*" Lambert, *supra* note 32, at 180.

the *Institut* was preparing an *Annuaire de la Vie Sociale* "proposing various social reforms modeled after the political reforms of President Roosevelt."[72] On the level of what may be called international social law, the *Institut* published a regular *Receuil International de Jurisprudence du Travail* in association with the International Labour Organisation.

In all of the above pursuits, political and methodological, which informed the relationship between the future *élite dirigeante* and their French supervisor, Lambert appears to have been deeply, and often exclusively, dedicated to his mentoring responsibilities. Reflecting thirty years later, he commented that the presence of his Egyptian students in Lyon

> "led me to be exclusively occupied with guiding them through their legal and socio-logical studies towards the goals they desired . . . which required me to abandon com-pletely my personal work. Furthermore, teaching at the *Séminaire Oriental* in the period of 1907–1914 led to a complete interruption in my scientific scholarship. But I am extremely hopeful that I will find due compensation in the Egyptian scholarship which will sooner or later issue from the Séminaire."[73]

It is to this "Egyptian scholarship" or "*productions égyptiennes*" that we will now turn our attention.

The Egyptians in Lyon: Intellectual Output

Having sought Lambert's mentoring in Lyon, what did the Egyptians finally write about? The comparative law scholarship produced by Egyptian law students under Lambert's supervision oscillated primarily between two major concerns. On the one hand, several doctoral dissertations were occupied with the modernization of certain aspects of Islamic law such as the doctrine of *abus de droit* (abuse of rights), the political structures of the caliphate, or such general areas of private law as the sources of obligation and testamentary law. On the other hand, a very different set of dissertations dealt with specific questions of Western jurisprudence which preoccupied progressive legal thinkers in France at the time, most notably the role of "standards" in the socialization of French private law.[74]

A state of internal division thus rules over the bibliographic legacy of Egyptian scholarship in comparative law—an intellectual testimony to the hybrid space in which this scholarship was pursued. Finding themselves

---

[72] "*vient d'entrer dans des voies de réformation sociale apparentées à celle que suit la Politique de President Roosevelt.*" *Id.* at 181.

[73] "*me permirent de m'occuper plus exclusivement de guider la formation juridique et la forma-tion de science social des étudiants égyptiens de Lyon dans la direction souhaitée par eux . . . Encore me fallut-il, pour y arriver, abandonner complètement mes traveaux personnels. Aussi la période d'activité enseignante—1907–14—du Séminaire Oriental a-t-elle été une période d'interruption complète dans ma production scientifique. Mais j'esperias bien trouver une compensation dans les productions égyptiennes qui tôt ou tard sortiraient de ce séminaire.*" *Id.* at 176.

[74] See *Liste de Publications*, *supra* note 45.

between the competing legal preoccupations of East and West, Lambert's students continuously had to negotiate their academic engagements between two distinct sets of problems:

> "1. the problems faced in modernizing the ancient institutions of their [Eastern] homeland, and above all the history of Islamic civilization . . . [and] 2. the various [modern] problems of legal thought, political science, and social economy which have preoccupied us here [in the West] without being resolved to date. These very same problems are now making themselves felt in the [Eastern] countries from which my students hail and which have been penetrated by our culture and economy."[75]

There is nothing exceptional about all the above; the competing preoccupations of Lambert's students merely confirm the malaise of "internal division" which is said to trouble the Arab intellectual to this day. What is exceptional, however, is the particular methodological choices these students' adopted in mediating their existential divisions between East and West. Something of a distinct approach to comparative law did gradually emerge at their hands that somewhat justifies conferring the factional title of "*l'école Lambert egyptienne*" on this coterie of students. The hallmark of this approach may be described briefly as a progressive synthesis of method and politics, a synthesis allowing the Eastern project of modernizing Islamic law to coincide with the Western project of socializing modern law. Conducting their comparative studies from a hyper-politicized space between East and West, their overwhelming normative stance was an almost obsessive insistence on the converging socialization and modernization of their research subjects. Under different configurations, depending on their respective academic interests, the push "to modernize" a particular legal field seemed invariably equated with a push "to socialize" its normative repercussions.

It is undoubtedly difficult to grasp the nature of this methodology in the abstract terms above. In order to provide a more telling illustration, the following pages will juxtapose two doctoral projects pursued under Lambert's supervision between 1907 and 1926. More specifically, I will juxtapose the very first Egyptian doctoral dissertation to be published by Lambert's *Séminaire* in 1913, against the later doctoral dissertations of Sanhuri which were published by the *Institut* in 1926. While eight other theses were published during the same period by other Arab students of Lambert, the two dissertations discussed below are perhaps most representative of the unique comparativist projects of "*l'école Lambert egyptienne*" as it gradually developed and adopted its distinct methodological tone.

---

[75] "1. *Les problèmes qui soulèvent la reconstitution des anciennes institutions de leurs pays, et avant tout l'histoire de la civilisation Islamique . . . [et] 2. Les questions de jurisprudence, de science politique, d'économie social qui, agitées depuis longtemps chez nous sans y avoir été définitivement résolues, surgissent aujourd'hui avec l'attrait d'une relative nouveauté, et comme une consequence inevitable de la pénétration de notre culture économique et scientifique, dans les pays auxqueles appartiennent mes jeunes collaborateurs.*" Edouard Lambert, "Preface", to in Mahmoud Fathy, *La Doctrine Musulmane de l'Abus des Droits: Etude d'Histoire Juridique et de Droit Comparé*, iii (Lyon, 1913).

The first dissertation to be published by the *Séminaire Oriental* in 1913 was written by the Egyptian jurist Mahmoud Fathy on the subject of *La Doctrine musulmane de l'abus de droit* and advertised as an *Etude d'histoire juridique et de droit comparé*.[76] In turn-of-the-century French private law theory, the doctrine of *abus de droit* was considered highly controversial. The doctrine represented a significant element in the *juristes inquiets'* agenda for socializing modern law, and was accordingly advocated as the "social" alternative to the rigid individualism which characterised French contract and tort law. Fathy's doctoral dissertation needs to be read in the context of this raging debate. Fathy's comparative study of the French and Islamic versions of *l'abus de droit*, aimed to use comparative law to illustrate how the French conservative critique of the doctrine was not of "any real significance [in shaking] the over-all intellectual strength of the young occidental theory [of abus de droit]."[77] Towards this end, Fathy explored the history of *abus de droit* in Islamic law, argued that the doctrine had achieved high standards of juristic sophistication in the East, and opined extensively on how this juristic heritage might prove to be of assistance in the development of the same doctrine in France.

The central thesis which underlies Fathy's comparative study thus proves to be a transgressive act in flipping the traditionally hierarchical relationship of jurisprudence in the East and West. This takes place as follows: While progressive jurisprudence in the West was attempting to socialize "modern" law by introducing the doctrine of *abus de droit*, the very same doctrine under "traditional" Islamic law turned out to be more "social" than anything the West had known so far. But the progressive potential of Islamic *abus de droit* was hindered by the underdeveloped state of the doctrine and its inability to order normatively the material conditions of modernity. This developmental hurdle required Fathy to "conciliate between Islamic traditions and the commercial, economic and political institutions which have been recently imported from Europe."[78] Fathy's proposal to achieve this "conciliation" was to study "the fundamental notions of occidental science with the key aim of adapting them to the particular requirements of Oriental and Muslim societies."[79]

Two all-important factors emerge from the above formula: "Occidental science" and "Oriental requirements." It is the coming together of these two factors that would allow for the simultaneous socialization of French law and the modernization of Islamic law. In the final analysis, the sought-after ideals of *modernity* and the *social* would ultimately converge under a new comparativist version of *l'abus de droit*. The legal preoccupations of progressive jurists in Egypt and France are thus addressed, and resolved, all at once.

[76] *The Islamic Doctrine of the Abuse of Rights: A Study in Legal History and Comparative Law.*

[77] *"sans importance réelle pour la solidité de la ligne générale d'offensive de la jeune theorie occidentale." Id.*

[78] *"la conciliation des traditions islamiques avec des institutions commerciales, economiques et politiques tardivement importées d'Europe." Id.* at vii.

[79] *"les données de la science occidentale par le point de veu principal de l'application ou l'adaptation aux exigences particulières de sociétés orientales et musulmanes." Id.*

Abrasive as the ambition underlying Fathy's project may be, its decidedly subversive implications should not be overlooked. Comparative law in his hands does not entail a simple and unequivocal transplant from West to East, and the relationship between French and Islamic law is far from a straight-forward hierarchical configuration between active and passive actors. This is best illustrated in the family metaphor he employs to illustrate how the two legal systems relate in the comparative exercise: Islamic law is methodologically underdeveloped, and is accordingly qualified as the *"enfant"*[80] of French law. It turns out, however, that the child is both wiser and more virile than its parent, in other words *l'abus des droits* under Islamic law is far more "social" than its Occidental sire. The father is finally likened to an *"adolescent,"*[81] and Fathy pre-dicts that with the aid of comparative law, this Occidental father will hopefully "grow up" to resemble its Oriental *"enfant."*

If we move on to Sanhuri's doctoral dissertations under Lambert's super-vision, the first thing to notice is that much like Fathy, Sanhuri was also pre-occupied with the two concerns that informed Fathy's scholarship, namely the socialization of modern law and the modernization of Islamic law. But unlike Fathy who attempted to mediate between these two concerns in one dissertation, Sanhuri set out to deal exclusively with each of these preoccupations in two sep-arate dissertations. Sanhuri's first doctoral dissertation published in 1925 was entitled *Les Restrictions contractuelles à la liberté individuelle de travail*, and subtitled a *Contribution à l'étude comparative de la règle de droit et du standard juridique*.[82] The dissertation was a study of "Restraints of Trade" as applied by English courts to labor disputes, and essentially pondered the role of standards in the socialization of modern law where we find ourselves "facing a conflict between the competing interests of individuals and commercial enterprises; or, in other words having to address one of the aspects of this delicate phenomenon: class struggle or the conflict between capital and labor."[83] Sanhuri's dissertation on standards was highly acclaimed and confirmed his political and intellectual alliance with the progressive strand of the *juristes inquietes*; in the preface to the dissertation, Lambert likened its arguments to those made by Emanuel Lévy whose work on the socialist vision of law exposes "the conspiracy of silence [and] shakes our conservative instincts . . . [by exposing] the economic and social realities which are hidden by our legal abstractions."[84] By the same token, Maurice Hauriou, one of the major proponents of the "social" in public law,

---

[80] "child."

[81] "adolescent."

[82] Sanhuri, *Contractual Restrictions on the Individual Freedom of Labor: A Comparative Study in Rules and Standards* (Lyon, 1925).

[83] *"en face d'un conflit entre l'intérêt de l'individu et l'intérêt de l'entreprise; en d'autres termes, on se trouve obligé d'aborder une des faces d'un phénomène délicat: la lutte des classes ou le conflit entre le travail et le capital."* Id. at 5.

[84] *"la conspiration de silence, parce que elle heurtait nos instincts de conservatism . . . [en exposant] les réalités économiques et sociales qui se dissimulent sous nos crépissages d'abstractions logiques."* Id. at viii–ix.

published a special booklet in which he reviewed Sanhuri's thesis and enumerated its contribution to the study of *police juridique* or legal policy.[85] Finally, Lambert appears to have been sufficiently thrilled with Sanhuri's critique of logical abstractions in favor of standards to mention it repeatedly in his correspondence with Dean Pound at Harvard Law School, and he ultimately mailed Pound a copy of the dissertation upon its completion.[86]

By contrast, Sanhuri's second dissertation on *Le Califat*, published in 1926 also under Lambert's supervision, was preoccupied with modernizing the Islamic law of the caliphate and proposed developing the medieval political institution along lines similar to those of the newly established League of Nations in Geneva.[87] Sanhuri thus shifted his attention away from the Occidental debate between rules and standards in the socialization of law, and occupied himself with the Oriental debate over the modernization of Islamic law. The two dissertations were thus meant as an intervention in the two sets of debates which animated legal scholarship in Egypt and France at the time. Sanhuri's discursive division between these two debates is certainly part of the competing "ties" to whose resolution by "every Oriental" he dedicated his dissertation on *Le Califat*. A more rigorous attempt at bringing the resolution of these two sets of debate together in a coherent normative order was made later in 1937 when Lambert and Sanhuri were entrusted with drafting the new Egyptian civil code. Until then, however, Lambert continued to offer as much political as intellectual support to the "social" project of modernizing Islamic law. This support took an all-important, if symbolic, turn when in the 1932 *Congrès International de Droit Comparé* Lambert, somewhat schemingly,

> "took advantage of organizational difficulties in preparing the *Congrès*'s plenary section, which led me [i.e. Lambert] to preside over the majority of the *Congrès*'s sessions . . . in order to furnish the Egyptian Faculty of Law's delegation with enough tools to develop and discuss its opinions and conclusions. I applied some pressure, perhaps exceeding the requirements of neutrality as behoved my position in the *Congrès*, in order to ensure that the following *Congrès* would reserve a position for the study of Islamic law as a source of comparative law."[88]

[85] *See* Maurice Hauriou, *Police Juridique et Fond du Droit, a Propos du Livre d'Al-Sanhoury* (Lyon 1926).

[86] My deep gratitude goes to Marie-Claire Belleau who drew my attention to the Lambert–Pound correspondence. *See generally*, the collection of letters between Lambert and Pound at the Harvard Law School Archives, *The Roscoe Pound Correspondence 1907–1964*, in particular the letter dated October 24, 1923, in which Lambert presents Pound with the scholarship of his *"excellent etudiant égyptien, M. Sanhoury, sur 'Le jugement sur régles et le jugement sur standards,"* and to which Pound replies on November 9, 1923, stating that "I shall await with much interest the work of Mr. Sanhoury on standards. That subject grows in importance with us every day." For a study of the relationship between Pound and Lambert, *see* Dubouchet, *supra* note 31, at 169–188.

[87] Sanhuri, *supra* note 10.

[88] *"profitait d'un faut d'organisation de la section générale du Congrès qui m'avait forcée à présider la plupart des séances . . . pour donner a la delegation de la Faculté de Droit Egyptienne . . . les moyens de développer et de faire amplement discuter ses vues et ses conclusions. J'ai appuyé, peut-être avec plus d'insistance que ne le comportait la neutralité présidentielle, ce vœu déposé par elle 'qu'on réserve dans le prochain congrès une place à l'éude du droit musulman comme source du droit compare."* Lambert, supra note 32, at 183.

Ritorna Vincitor!

Forever conscious of his mentorship association with "a small elite of Egyptian intellectuals,"[89] Lambert poetically reminded his students in Lyon of the "beautiful mission of patriotism which could be accomplished at the hands of a truly Egyptian faculty of law."[90] They were all encouraged to return home and commence teaching in their homeland, "a country where the desire for self-government is fervent, and where the elite are convinced that the most sure road to realizing this desire is through the development of national education in all its fields—and above all in the field of higher education."[91] Lambert had a vision— a dashing mixture of Orientalist fancy and sober network-building: his Egyptian students, back in Cairo, aided by its charming weather, "some of the most seducing in the world," would set off to transform the Khedivial Law School into a progressive, cosmopolitan institution where "different youth, of Persian, Ottoman, Hindu or Chinese origins [may receive] a primary induction in the scientific culture which attracts them towards the cold and bitter lands of the Occident."[92]

The majority of Lambert's students did indeed return to Cairo's seductive weather, and proceeded, undoubtedly aided by an attractive suntan, to oversee "the transfer of the Royal School of Law from English to national hands."[93] Egypt became an independent constitutional monarchy in 1923, the young elite assumed their place in the modern bureaucracy, and by 1936 Lambert's star student Sanhuri had succeeded his mentor to the deanship of the Khedivial Law School—now the Royal Faculty of Law. In his capacity as dean, Sanhuri established a comparative law institute in Cairo comparable to the one in Lyon, and invited his mentor to deliver the institute's inaugural lectures. Having left Egypt in July 1907 after clashing with British authorities in the ministry of education, Lambert thus triumphantly returned to the country for the first time since his departure thirty years earlier. The lectures were delivered in March 1937, and in concluding them Lambert understandably declared Sanhuri to be, "in one word, the man of science best equipped to establish in Cairo an [institute of comparative law] equivalent to the one I established in Lyon."[94]

---

[89] *"une petite élite d'intellectueles égyptiens."* Edouard Lambert, "Preface" to Sanhuri, *Restrictions, supra* note 82, at xx.

[90] *"la belle tâche patriotique [qui] pourrait accomplir . . . une véritable Faculté de droit égyptienne."* Id. at xxii.

[91] *"un pays ou s'éveillait le désir du self-government, et ou l'élite de la population etait convaincue que le plus sûr moyen d'arriver à la réalisation de ce desir était le dévelopment de l'éducation nationale dans toutes ses branches, mais surtout sous la forme de l'enseignement supérieur."* Id. at vii.

[92] *"l'un des plus séduisantes du monde . . . la jeunesse persane ou ottomane, hindoue ou chinoise* [may receive] *l'initiation première à la culture scientifique qui l'attire vers les terres froides et rude de l'Occident."* Id. at xxiii.

[93] *"le passage de l'école royale de droit des directions anglaises a une direction indigene."* Id. at xvii.

[94] *"en un mot, l'homme de science le mieux armé pour réaliser au Caire le pendant de ce que j'ai réalisé à Lyon."* Lambert, *supra* note 32, at 184.

Later that year, both student and mentor were appointed as the only two members of the legislative committee entrusted by the Egyptian government to draft the new Egyptian civil code. The Mixed Courts regime had been abolished by the 1937 International Treaty of Montreux, and the country's legal establishment was seized with nationalist fervor at the restoration to full judicial sovereignty. Lambert and Sanhuri were thus responsible for writing the core document that would be credited with reunifying the universe of Egyptian private law. Their new civil code was promulgated in 1949 and soon assumed a highly illustrious career as the single most hegemonic piece of postcolonial legislation in the modern experience of Arab legal systems. The code was to be copied, usually verbatim, by numerous Arab countries in the wake of their independence movements, and Sanhuri's *Al-Waseet*, his master commentaries on the code, is today probably the most important civil law treatise, which no self-respecting Arab lawyer's library would be without. It is to this code and its double agenda of modernising Islam and socialising modernity that we will turn our attention.

THE RECONSTRUCTION OF TRADITION: THE INVENTION OF ISLAMIC LAW AND ARCHITECTURE

Studying comparative law in the West has often been a prelude to the student's eventual trip back home, an intellectual "return," with newly acquired knowledge, to set the house of the East in order. Such was certainly the case with the majority of Lambert's Egyptian students. The 1910 brochure for the *Séminaire Oriental* unequivocally defined its duty towards its students as "aiding them in the process of adapting the legal and social knowledge they acquired in Europe to the particular needs of their home countries."[95] The Egyptian civil code of 1949 is perhaps the ultimate flowering of this pledge to adaptation. Having studied the "occidental science" of comparative law at Lambert's hands, Sanhuri set out to instrumentalize his Western learning in reconstructing the tradition of Islamic law on such modern lines as is necessary to accommodate Egypt's "Oriental requirements."[96] In June 1938 the Egyptian government exclusively entrusted Sanhuri and Lambert with drafting the new civil code. While Lambert died before the completion of the document, his contribution was nonetheless formally acknowledged in the code's *travaux preparatoires* (preparatory words).[97] In 1949, the Mixed Courts were finally abolished and the new civil

---

[95] "*les guider dans l'adaptation aux besoins particuliers de leurs pays des connaissances juridiques et sociales aquis par eux en Europe.*" *Id.* at 174.

[96] Sanhuri's first formal appeal to redraft the old Egyptian civil code on modern lines using the science of comparative law appeared in "Wojoub Tanquih' al-Qanun al-Madani al-Misri," [On the Necessity of Redrafting the Egyptian Civil Code] 6 *Majallat al-Qanun wal-Iqtisad* 1–142 (1936).

[97] *See also* Lambert's article on the domicile provisions in the civil code "Le Chapitre du domicile dans un projet de code civil égyptien," 2 *Bulletin de L'Institut de Droit Comparé de Lyon* 1–57 (Mars–Juin, 1939).

code became the law of the land. Before the Egyptian senate, Sanhuri over and again boasted his use of comparative law in producing a legal document which he claimed was both "Islamic" and "modern."[98]

It is this civil code, the product of Sanhuri's comparative methodology, which according to Bishri embodies the inauthentic state of Arab legislation. Rather than producing a document which is both modern and Islamic, as Sanhuri claimed in 1949, Bishri argues that Sanhuri's comparativism is itself responsible for his failure to produce an Islamic civil code. In this argument lies the second pitfall in Bishri's critique. His insistence that the code is un-Islamic is premised on the conviction that there is something Islamic out there, something authentic, something which pre-dates the colonial encounter with the West, and, most importantly, something whose authenticity can be captured and refashioned for modern day legislation. Although Sanhuri may have genuinely attempted to modernize Islamic law in Bishri's view, his failure lies in having adulterated the authenticity of Islamic law by exposing it to too many Western influences.

The problem here is that Bishri's nostalgia for a return to a more authentic cultural past is itself an intellectually futile exercise—in the postcolonial world we live in, there is no going back to a precolonial home. In that sense, Bishri's "failed comparativist" opinion of Sanhuri actually shares the very same premise which underlies Sanhuri's comparativism. More specifically, the Lambert/Sanhuri civil code project starts from the same kind of nostalgia for a lost past. This very same nostalgia accounts for the main problem with Lambert/Sanhuri's project: using comparativism to reconstruct the past while preserving its authenticity is an intellectually unpredictable, even often futile exercise, given the modernizing agency exercised in inventing the very past sought by comparativists. In their effort to return to Islamic law, to compare it with modern progressive legislation, and finally to reconstruct it on scientific lines, Lambert and Sanhuri ultimately invented a univocal tradition of Islamic law which glossed over, and eventually silenced, the earlier mutli-vocality of Islamic legal tradition(s). In other words, Lambert and Sanhuri ended up inventing the very tradition which they set out to reconstruct and modernize.

Illustrating this argument would require a detailed analysis of the civil code which far surpasses the scope of this essay.[99] Suffice it to say that the invention of tradition is hardly peculiar to the project of reconstructing Islamic law. Rather, it is symptomatic of an overall *modernizing sensibility* which ordered similar reconstructive projects in Egypt at the time, and maintained a very complex relation to contemporary questions of nationalism.[100] Perhaps the best way

---

[98] For Sanhuri's oscillating opinion on the code's Islamicity, *see* Amr Shalakany, "Between Identity and Redistribution: Sanhuri, Genealogy, and the Will to Islamize," forthcoming *Islamic Law & Society Journal* (Spring 2001).

[99] For a more detailed analysis, *see* Amr Shalakany, *The Analytics of the Social: A Comparative Study* (2000) (unpublished S.J.D. dissertation, Harvard University) (on file with the Harvard Law School Library).

[100] For a comparative study, *see* Eric Hobsbawm, "Introduction: Inventing Traditions," in Eric Hobsbawm & Terence Ranger (eds), *The Invention of Tradition* (Cambridge, 1983). It should be

to understand the code as a document which invented the very tradition it set out to modernize is to compare the code against another famous project of Islamic reconstruction at the time, namely the Cairo railway station. Aside from satisfying my personal fantasies as a frustrated architect, I think the juxtaposition of reconstructive projects in law and architecture can be tremendously insightful in illustrating the agency exercised by Lambert and Sanhuri in inventing the tradition of Islamic law.

Much as with Islamic law, modernity/tradition discourse tells us that an authentic tradition of Islamic architecture existed prior to the colonial encounter and that this tradition was ruptured under the material pressures of modernity. A condition of "aesthetic alienation" ensued and various reconstructive projects have called for a return to the lost tradition of Islamic architecture, that would save it from Western distortions, reclaim its authentic essence, and adapt it to fit the modern conditions of Egyptian society.[101]

Some familiarity with the semiotics of architecture may be helpful here. In his study of the subject, Umberto Eco claims that "besides denoting its function, the architectural object could connote a certain ideology of the function."[102] Eco distinguishes between "primary functions" which denote the *utilitatis* of a building, and "secondary functions" which refer to the symbolic connotations of the same building. In the case of the Cairo railway station, the "ideology of the function" may be amateurishly described as follows: First inaugurated in 1856, the station received a series of successive face-lifts, the most important of which took place during the early twentieth century, around the same time Sanhuri and Lambert set out to draft the new civil code by appeal to Islamic law.[103] In its present form, the station exhibits an exterior architecture that appears for all intents and purposes as authentically Islamic, while functioning on the inside as it would in any other modern city of the world: trains coming and going, cafeterias, news stand, and so on. In this sense, the train station was meant to symbolize the reconstruction of tradition, namely Islamic architecture, in the service of modern transportation, just as much as the civil code was meant to symbolize the reconstruction of another

noted that my argument is not meant as a sweeping truth-claim with universal application to all historiographic engagements. By contrast, my claim is infinitely more modest, and I will be more than satisfied if in the following pages I can successfully introduce the faint suspicion that in the specific projects of the Egyptian civil code and the Cairo railway station, a modernizing sensibility has come to exercise, as well as deny, a great deal of agency in the active construction of the very tradition which it passively claimed to reconstruct.

[101] For a general introduction to the subject, *see* Robert Ilbert and Mercedes Volait, "Neo-Arabic Renaissance in Egypt, 1870–1930," 13 *Mimar* 26–34 (1983). For a more detailed study of the architecture of Heliopolis, a new suburb of turn-of-the-century Cairo, *see* Khaled Asfour, *Dealing with the Incompatible!* (1987) (unpublished M.A. dissertation, Massachusetts Institute of Technology) (on file with Massachusetts Institute of Technology).

[102] Umberto Eco, "Function and Sign: The Semiotics of Architecture," in Neil Leach (ed.), *Rethinking Architecture. A Reader in Cultural Theory* 187 (London, 1997).

[103] *See generally* Lionel Wiener, *L'Egypte et ses Chemins de Fer*, 172 (Bruxelles, 1932). The most comprehensive architectural history of the city remains Janet Abu-Lughod, *Cairo: 1000 Years of the City Victorious* (Princeton, N.J., 1971).

Fig. 2 The Cairo Railway Station in the Early 1920s

tradition, namely Islamic law, in the service of a modern legislation. Both projects are based on the possibility of unmediated access to an *authentic* tradition (Islamic law or architecture) in order to produce its *authentic* modernized reincarnation (be it in the form of the Civil Code or the Cairo Train Station). But a closer examination of both projects reveals that the very tradition of Islamic law and architecture turns out to be a modern invention, no more authentic or unmediated than modernity itself.

Let me explain what I mean by that. In its present form, the railway station was designed by an architect whose career very much mirrors that of Sanhuri. Hussein Fahmy Pacha was an Egyptian student of architecture who was sent by the government to study in France. Following the completion of his studies abroad, Fahmy returned home to embark on a professional career as the Sanhuri of public buildings. When commissioned by the government to design the railway station, Fahmy refused to follow the dominant European styles of the time, and instead insisted on a style that would reflect the authentic identity of Cairene architecture. To this end, Fahmy opted for what became known as the "neo-Mamluk" style, an approach which consciously harks back to the Mamluk buildings which glittered in medieval Cairo and gave it its legendary reputation as the greatest city of the Middle Ages. Also known as "Islamic revival" or "neo-Islamic," the "neo-Mamluk" style owed its creation to the "confluence of various intellectual, architectural, and political currents which developed over the course of the nineteenth century, and allowed it to be regarded as the national style of public buildings in Egypt."[104] By rehabilitating

---

[104] Nasser Rabbat, "The Formation of the Neo-Mamluk Style in Modern Egypt," in Martha Pollak (ed.), *The Education of the Architect*, 364 (Cambridge, Mass., 1997).

the architectural style associated with one of Egypt's most glorious periods in its Islamic history, the neo-Mamluk style was soon adopted in the construction of the various bureaucratic buildings of the modernizing Egyptian state, from ministries and government offices, to libraries, museums and public exhibition grounds.[105] Neo-Mamluk architecture was thus meant to furnish the official architectural style for the ideological project of modernizing Islam—basically the same function undertaken by Sanhuri's code in the field of Islamic law.

As it turns out, the Mamluk style which Fahmy appealed to had nothing to do with medieval architecture, just as Sanhuri's Islamic law had nothing to do with its precolonial ancestor. While engaged in the experimental act of reconstructing the Islamic tradition, both lawyer and architect ended up inventing the very thing they set out to *re*construct. For example, what is univocally known as the neo-Mamluk style, turns out to incorporate various architectural motifs that were never part of the Mamluk tradition to begin with: from Mogul to Ottoman to Moorish and Andalusian, Fahmy's railway station represents a modernizing *bricolage* which transgresses the frameworks of coherence associated with the different schools of Islamic architecture. The same could be said of Sanhuri's code which transgresses the frameworks of coherence associated with the different schools of Islamic jurisprudence from which it adopted some of its legal doctrines.

On another level, in terms of form and representation, neo-Mamluk architecture represents a deep epistemological break within the history of Mamluk architecture. The same may be said of the act of codification, which also signifies the same deep break in the history of Islamic legal thought. The Mamluk architect was a brilliant *bricoleur*, to use Levi-Strauss' terminology, who employed a finite and heterogeneous repertoire of tools to produce "structures that are distinguished by their ingeniously negotiated volumes and façades that simultaneously dominate and accommodate their urban surroundings [especially] by their emphasis on verticality."[106] By contrast, neo-Mamluk architecture draws on the *engineer* at his best pretensions: it builds on a general theory of how to modernize Islamic architecture, where verticality is substituted by the traditional horizontal emphasis of western architectural theory, and concerns for symmetry and axiality overtake the building's design.[107]

---

[105] For a study of various public buildings which adopted the neo-Mamluk style, *see* Tarek Sakr, *Early Twentieth Century Islamic Architecture in Cairo* (Cairo, 1992).

[106] Rabbat, *supra* note 104, at 365.

[107] *See* Mona Zakaraya, "L'inscription du discours occidental dans l'architecture et l'urbanism orienteaux," in Marie-Claude Burgat (ed.), *D'un Orient l'Sutre: Les Metamorphoses Successives des Perceptions et Connaissances, vol 1* (Paris, 1991). It should be noted that there is nothing peculiar about the post-colonial experience of Egyptian architecture. For a fascinating study of hybrid architecture, *see* Patricia Morton, *Hybrid Modernities. Architecture and Representation at the 1931 Colonial Exposition, Paris* (Cambridge, 2000).

CONCLUDING REMARKS: DENIAL IS A RIVER IN EGYPT

I started this essay by arguing that Sanhuri is most commonly read today as a "failed comparativist." In Part II I offered a brief discussion of modernity/tradition discourse, and how Bishri, Sanhuri, and comparative law all fit in. I argued that there are two major problems in Bishri's espousal of cultural authenticity in projects of legal reform. First, his position often legitimates an ideologically conservative agenda, and second, it represents an intellectually futile attempt at recapturing the past. Part III of this article attempted to take up Bishri on the first problem. I offered an alternative account of how comparative law came to take root in Egypt between the years 1906 and 1936. My purpose was to demonstrate how comparativism, far from being an alien tool imposed on the project of Egyptian legal reform, was instead an emancipatory instrument largely crafted by Egyptian law students and employed in the service of progressive legal and political activism. In Part IV I addressed my second critique of Bishri's position, namely his nostalgia for the lost authenticity of Arab law. I compared the civil code to the Cairo railway station, and argued that reconstructing past traditions in a way that preserves their authenticity is an intellectually unpredictable, often futile, exercise. Reconstructive projects of Islamic traditions (whether law or architecture) seem invariably to stumble by inventing the very tradition they originally set out to modernize.

To conclude, I would like to clarify one last point without which I fear my critique of Bishri may be radically misunderstood. When I argue that the modernization of tradition exercises agency in inventing the very tradition it sets out to modernize, I do not mean to suggest that there is some *really* authentic Islamic law out there which Sanhuri and Lambert merely distorted by pursuing a flawed approach. I do not mean to argue that maybe Sanhuri and Lambert should have relied less on foreign law, and more on Islamic law, when they decided to opt for a comparativist approach. In other words, I do not believe that the methodological dangers of using comparativism in the modernization of Islamic law rest in the comparativist's introduction of alien or non-Islamic elements. Rather, I believe a much more serious methodological danger lies in Lambert and Sanhuri's conviction that they might have unmediated access to an authentic tradition which might then become the object of reconstruction. Accordingly, my overriding concern in this article is to deny the possibility of having any such unmediated access to an authentic corpus of Islamic law, without leaving us with any prospect of an authentic alternative. I consciously mean to leave Lambert and Sanhuri in the same position in which Saleh leaves his protagonist, the narrator of *Season of Migration to the North*, at the end of the novel.

As noted earlier in Part II, the postcolonial experience of Sanhuri's return from France to reconstruct Islamic law in Egypt lends itself to juxtaposition against the comparable return of Saleh's narrator, after seven years of study in the West, in existential pursuit of an authentic identity at his home village by the Nile. But Saleh's narrator becomes far more conscious of the futility of reconstructing the precolonial past than Sanhuri, Lambert, and certainly Bishri are with respect to Islamic law. It takes a brush with death, at the conclusion of the novel, to jolt Saleh's narrator out of denying the irretrievable loss of "pure authenticity." The relevant episode in the novel goes as follows: Saleh situates his narrator's village at an all-too-symbolic juncture where the Nile departs from its South-North trajectory and starts flowing from East to West. Swimming from the South to the North banks of the river, Saleh's narrator suddenly finds himself stranded between the two sides, unredeemed, and unable to stand firmly on the fertile ground of either shore. The reader is never told what happens to the narrator at the end of the novel. Instead, both reader and narrator are left suspended between North and South. Darkness descends as the narrator screams for help.

The real methodological danger in any project aimed at modernizing Islamic law is the conviction that one can firmly stand on the fertile banks which so elusively escaped Saleh's narrator. The most significant methodological danger of all is perhaps the inability to recognize that the fertile bank of Islamic law is often itself the comparativist's invention. In other words, there is no way of escaping the West, even in one's own reading of one's Islamic culture. As pointed out by Sharabi, "the kind of knowledge that the Other, the object of western knowledge—in this case Arab society and culture—has of itself is . . . essentially Western knowledge even when it is locally produced."[108]

A debate much like the contemporary debate over Sanhuri's legacy in using comparative law to modernize Islamic law, took place in literary theory over the meaning of Saleh's novel. The above, unresolved reading of the narrator's fate, is only one reading of the novel's conclusion. There are several alternative readings of the novel's conclusion that supply the missing sense of resolution. These readings insist on optimistically fixing the fate of the narrator. They interpret Saleh's last pages "as an affirmation of life, as a resolution of conflicts, as the representation of the final closure of imperialism."[109] But, as Makdisi observes, the novel's "power as an ideological form is, ironically, demonstrated by these critics who try to supply it with a narrative closure that will 'make sense' within a certain ideological framework marked and governed by the existence of fundamental categories and rigid absolutes."[110] The exact fate of Saleh's narrator, whether he lives or drowns in the waters of the Nile, is as irrelevant as whether Sanhuri absolutely succeeded in employing comparative law to resolve the Egyptian legal system's competing "ties" between East and West. Both fates should be left gapingly open in the empowering knowledge that, in the

---

[108] Hisham Sharabi, "The Scholarly Point of View: Politics, Perspective, Paradigm," in Hisham Sharabi (ed.), *Theory, Politics and the Arab World*, 1 (New York, 1991).

[109] Saree S. Makdisi, "The Empire Renarrated: *Season of Migration to the North* and the Reinvention of the Present," in Patrick Williams & Laura Chrisman (eds.), *Colonial Discourse and Postcolonial Theory*, 543 (New York, 1994).

[110] *Id.*

postcolonial world we live in, there is no going back home. This almost fundamentalist resistance to nostalgia on my part is of course largely motivated by my own ambivalence about "going back" after the completion of my comparative law studies abroad.[111]

Glossary:

Al-Wafid: Arabic term. Literally, the "incoming." Used by Tariq al-Bishri to describe cultural sources that are "coming from the outside and alienating."

Al-Mawruth: Arabic term. Literally, the "inherited." Used by Tariq al-Bishri to describe cultural sources that are "inherited from the ancestors" and therefore authentic.

Taqlid: Arabic term. Juristic imitation from medieval Islamic jurisprudence.

Asalah: Arabic term. Authenticity.

Mo'asarah: Arabic term. Contemporaniety, or leading a modern life.

---

[111] I really think Gaytri Spivak does a brilliant job of navigating through what she calls the "nostalgia entertained by academics in the self-imposed exile of eurocentric economic migration";—it does not hurt that she adds: "for I experience it myself." *See generally*, Gayatri Chakravorty Spivak, *Critique of Postcolonial Reason*, 209 (Cambridge, Mass., 1999).

Fig. 1 Ernst Rabel
(Reproduced by kind permission of the University of Michigan
Bentley Historical Library)

7

Sculpting the Agenda of Comparative Law: Ernst Rabel and the Facade of Language

DAVID J. GERBER

The method developed by Ernst Rabel for the comparative study of law has acquired the status of orthodoxy in much of the world. His so-called function/context method has dominated much of the work done in comparative law since the Second World War. Yet what kind of orthodoxy is it? What was he trying to do and how did he seek to accomplish his goals? Answers to these questions illuminate the tensions and forces within comparative law today and suggest paths for its future development.

My central objective in this essay is, therefore, to seek answers to these questions. I try to locate Rabel's project and identify some of the principal factors that influenced his goals and shaped his methods. The aim of this analysis is to set the stage for "rethinking" Rabel's methods and their relationship to the contemporary needs of comparative law.

Language is a prominent theme in this story. Rabel's vision of comparative law was defined by both a distrust of language and the need to use it in particular ways to achieve his goals. He sought to penetrate beneath language to a more "concrete reality," while at the same time focusing much of his professional attention on interpreting the formal and often abstract language of legal texts and on preparing the porous and opaque language of international agreements. This tension is central to his methods—a source of both value and constraint.

Educated in turn-of-the-century Vienna, Rabel shared many of the experiences that sensitized Ludwig Wittgenstein and others of his generation to the inadequacy and deceptiveness of language. These experiences led him to distrust the direct comparison of concepts, doctrines and texts that had been the standard methodology of comparative law. Meaningful comparison could be achieved, he argued, only by reference to the underlying social problems to which the language was related. This was his great insight and the core of the methodology he generated.

Yet Rabel's professional goals and projects shaped the ways in which that methodology was understood and used, and they depended on particular uses of language. In the desperately hopeful context of the 1920s, scholars, politicians, bureaucrats and even some business leaders were seeking words that would somehow protect what was threatened and at the same time save the world from chaos and destruction. It was a heavy burden for language to bear, and the effort to bear it has had a profound effect on the development of comparative legal studies.

I first look briefly at the road that led Rabel to comparative law and some of the factors that shaped both his expectations and the mental tools that he brought to the enterprise. I then focus on his principal writings in comparative law and the forces that shaped them. In the final sections of the essay, I turn to the sources of Rabel's influence and to its roles and potential today.

THE PATH TO COMPARATIVE LAW

Vienna

Born in Vienna in 1874, Rabel was raised and educated in the extraordinarily fertile intellectual milieu that that city produced in the decades bracketing the turn of the century.[1] He was a member of a sophisticated German-speaking urban elite often referred to as the "liberal" upper middle class or just "the liberals." His father was a successful lawyer, and Rabel followed in his father's footsteps by studying law. On one level, then, he grew up securely part of an educated elite in a powerful and apparently stable world capital.[2]

There was, however, a darker side to the picture. During the 1890s, this elite was increasingly attacked by other social classes as well as by nationalist groups in many parts of the Hapsburg Empire who sought more rights and more power within the Austrian system. As such groups grew stronger and bolder, they disrupted Austrian political and social life.

It was a conflict in which language was both culprit and target—a marker of tension, and a focus of resentment. German was the language of dominion and control in the empire. It was the language not only of the liberal elite, but of the aristocracy and of government. Nationalist groups thus focused on achieving respect and status for their own languages. As Carl Schorske has put it,

---

[1] Sigmund Freud was reshaping thought about the human psyche; Gustav Mahler and Arnold Schoenberg were creating new forms of music; Carl Menger and Eugen Böhm-Bawerk were developing a fundamentally new approach to economics; and Ludwig Wittgenstein was preparing to chart a new course for philosophy. For evocations of the Austrian intellectual milieu during this period, *see* Carl E. Schorske, *Fin-de-Siècle Vienna* (New York, 1980); Alan Janik & Stephen Toulmin, *Wittgenstein's Vienna* (New York, 1973); and Mark Francis (ed.), *The Viennese Enlightenment* (London, 1985).

[2] Biographical details of Rabel's early life are sparse. For general biographical discussions that include information on this period, *see, e.g.*, Gerhard Kegel, "Ernst Rabel—Werk und Person," 54 *Rabels Zeitschrift* 1 (1990); Ernst Julius Wolff, "Ernst Rabel," 73 *Savigny Zeitschrift, Röm. Abt.* X–XXVIII (1956) and Max Rheinstein, "In Memory of Ernst Rabel," 5 *Am. J. Comp. L.* 185–196 (1956).

"The liberals had conjured up new forces and new claimants to political participation: Slavic nationalists, Socialists, Pan-German anti-semites, Christian Social anti-semites. They neither integrated these new movements into the legal order nor could they satisfy their demands. The conflicting groups may have had different heavens, but they shared the same hell: the rule of the Austro-German liberal middle class."[3]

Thus social, ethnic and religious resentments were all projected onto the "liberal" class and the linguistic hegemony that defined and represented it.

As a result, members of the liberal class were caught between awareness of these disintegrative forces and the desire to protect their own status and values. The role of language in the conflict also made many among them both acutely conscious of language and dubious about its roles. This conflict and the tensions it produced help us to understand the development of Rabel's aims and methods.

Legal Education

While studying law at the University of Vienna, Rabel came under the influence of Ludwig Mitteis, a leading legal historian, particularly of Roman law. It was an influence that would shape the rest of his life. After he finished his basic legal education, Rabel entered law practice with his father, but he soon decided to follow Mitteis to the latter's new position in Leipzig. He there became a legal historian, receiving his doctor's degree in 1899 and his "*Habilitation*" in 1902.

Years later Rabel praised his master's influence, emphasizing the latter's discipline and methodological precision.[4] "More than anything else . . . his scientific discipline was a model for me."[5] Rabel ascribed much of his own style and method in comparative law to this historical training. The main objective of Mitteis' method was to identify and understand the *functions* of the classical legal doctrines and institutions, and from there it "was only an additional step to apply the same method to the comparison of modern systems."[6]

Rabel as Historian

Rabel achieved renown as a legal historian, primarily of Roman and French law, and this led to a quick succession of calls to German and Swiss universities. In

---

[3] Schorske, *supra* note 1, at 303.

[4] For a recent, detailed study of the Mitteis "school" and its influence on Rabel, *see* Reinhard Zimmermann, "In der Schule von Ludwig Mitteis," *Rabels Zeitschrift* 1 (forthcoming, 2001).

[5] Ernst Rabel, "In der Schule von Ludwig Mitteis," 7–8 *J. Juristic Papyrology* 157 (1954). The collected articles of Ernst Rabel have been published in 4 volumes. *See* Hans G. Leser (ed.), *Ernst Rabel, Gesammelte Aufsätze*: vols. 1 and 2 (Tübingen, 1965); Hans G. Leser (ed.), vol. 3 (Tübingen, 1967); Hans Julius Wolff (ed.), vol. 4 (Tübingen, 1971). Because these volumes are difficult to obtain in the U.S., I have generally cited to originals (some of which, of course, are also difficult to obtain in the U.S., but some of which are not).

[6] Rabel, "In der Schule," *supra* note 5, at 159.

assessing Rabel's professional development, it is important to remember that Roman law played a far greater role in early twentieth century Germany than it does today. It was still seen as an important source of guidance in legal thinking and of solutions to current problems, and this influence was far more direct and extensive than we can easily imagine. Rabel's transition from legal historian to comparatist did not, therefore, traverse as much attitudinal status and institutional distance as such a move would today.

After his call to the Munich law faculty in 1916, Rabel changed his focus from legal history to comparative law. His major writings on comparative law date from the period between 1916 and 1939, when he was forced to flee Germany. Our discussion will focus on these two turbulent decades, and this requires a brief glimpse at the contexts in which Rabel operated.

Contexts

One context was European—the general loss of confidence in European civilization and responses to that sense of loss. The Great War had dissolved confidence in Europe's leadership and in many of the ideals and methods associated with it, creating a powerful tension between dissolution and hope that pervaded the intellectual and political life of the period.[7] At one pole was societal disruption and the fear that it would escalate. In some countries (e.g., Russia and Germany) fundamental changes had actually occurred. In others (e.g., France) changes were less dramatic, but fear that society's bonds were dissolving was widespread, particularly within the middle classes. The other pole saw an extraordinary surge of hope that international institutions could prevent future disasters. During the second half of the 1920s, for example, many placed their hopes in new international institutions, organizations and conferences designed to create a new "world society."

In Germany, defeat and the physical and psychological devastation of war joined with postwar political unrest and disruption to explode even rudimentary expectations of stability for much of the period. Crises and instability were prominent during the Weimar years, as were rancour and distrust of "the West," much of it associated with the handling of reparations issues.

Sharp and generally growing tensions between political groups squeezed Germany's educated elite. As a result of the war and the postwar political turmoil, the "Mandarin" class had lost much of its status and economic security. Its members increasingly identified themselves as victims of political conflict and

---

[7] *See, e.g.*, Paul Fussell, *The Great War and Modern Memory* (Oxford, 1975).

acknowledged the need to band together as a class to protect their interests and regain their lost prosperity.[8]

Rabel's primary professional milieu—the German university—was also riddled with uncertainty and disruption. The war had undermined the exceptionally high status of the professoriate. The postwar currency crisis then further devastated educational budgets, and the weakness of Weimar government prevented significant improvements in the social status or financial situation of many professors.

In the university in Berlin, where Rabel taught after 1926, financial insecurity was accompanied by fears for personal security. Ernst von Caemmerer, later one of Rabel's most influential disciples, reported to me that when he went to Rabel's institute in Berlin in the late 1920s he not infrequently encountered gunfire outside the university—skirmishes between rightwing and leftwing groups.

The intellectual milieu reflected this turbulence. It was a period of widespread experimentation with new perspectives and of frequent battles between those who experimented and those who insisted on the primacy of established methodologies and perspectives. In disciplines related to law such as economics and sociology, the historicism that had helped to shape a vision of Germany's "specialness" had been largely discredited, leaving a widespread sense of uncertainty about the role and characteristics of scholarship.[9]

In law itself, the situation was particularly complex. The German legal profession had spent the last two decades of the nineteenth century preparing a new civil code and the first decade and a half of the twentieth examining the code it had created. This had many consequences, not the least of which was to ingrain text-centered habits of thought. The positivism of the prewar period remained powerful, although it was increasingly criticized in academic circles, where emphasis was shifting toward finding new ways of interpreting the code based on the interests thought to be represented by its language.[10]

Rabel bemoaned, in particular, Germany's loss of intellectual leadership in law. German legal scholars were woefully unaware of and uninterested in what was happening elsewhere, he claimed, and as a result their work was no longer as important as it once had been. This was especially true, he believed, in private law. In that area, he wrote, "we have to regret the 'greatest' backwardness and lack of development."[11]

---

[8] The classic account is Fritz Ringer, *The Decline of the German Mandarins: The German Academic Community, 1890–1933* (Cambridge, Mass., 1969).

[9] For detailed recent discussion of the intellectual developments in law and the social sciences during this period, see Knut Nörr et al. (eds.), *Geisteswissenschaften zwischen Kaiserreich und Republik* (Stuttgart, 1994).

[10] *See gen.* Karl Larenz, *Methodenlehre der Rechtswissenschaft*, 36–117 (5th ed., Berlin, 1983) and Max Rheinstein, "Comparative Law and Conflict of Laws in Germany," 2 *U. Chi. L. Rev.* 232 (1935). *See also* Kenneth Ledford, *From General Estate to Special Interest: German Lawyers 1878–1933* (Cambridge, 1996).

[11] Ernst Rabel, "Das Institut für Rechtsvergleichung an der Universität München," 15 *Zeitschrift für Rechtspflege in Bayern* 2, 3 (1919).

Rabel's Roles

Rabel was active in many arenas. He was not only a university professor and institute director, but also a judge, an arbitrator, and an advisor to German business.[12] In the academic world, Rabel was a rapidly rising "star" when he was appointed professor of law in Munich. He had risen to prominence primarily as a legal historian, but in Munich he quickly achieved prominence in comparative law, a field which was just taking shape. Ten years later his preeminence in that field was confirmed when he was named director of the newly-created Kaiser-Wilhelm Institute for Foreign and International Private Law in Berlin, the most prominent position in comparative law in Germany.[13] This institute had both private and public funding and both private and public goals. It was one of several scientific institutes intended to foster the development of scientific knowledge by German scientists, but it was also intended to provide advice to German industry and government officials in their dealings with the West. It gave Rabel exceptional influence and power within the academic legal profession, and it also tied him to German government and business interests.

Rabel also gained extensive international experience during this period. From the end of the First World War until shortly before he left Germany, he participated actively and prominently in several important international institutions, and his activities there shaped the way he understood comparative law and its potential roles. They led him to an agenda in which "science" was to be applied in practical dispute resolution contexts. According to von Caemmerer, he often emphasized the importance of his broad range of practical experiences in the development of his approach to law.

One of those roles was as a judge/arbitrator. In the early 1920s, he frequently served on the so-called "Mixed Arbitral Tribunal Panels" that heard disputes under the provisions of the Versailles Peace Treaty.[14] These tribunals had jurisdiction over disputes involving pre-war contracts between Germans and others and over harm caused by certain war measures. Each tribunal consisted of three judges: one neutral, one Allied, and one German. The tribunals were highly controversial, particularly in Germany, where rulings, particularly in the early years, were often adverse to German interests and, therefore, often seen as indications that the tribunals were not "fair." In the late 1920s, Rabel was also an ad hoc judge on the Permanent Court of International Justice in several prominent cases.

---

[12] He was a judge on a court of appeals in Basel (1907–1910) and in Munich (1920–1925) and on the Permanent Court of International Justice (1925–1928); he was also a judge/arbitrator on the German-Italian Mixed Arbitration Tribunal (1921–1927). For further discussion, *see* Hans G. Leser, "Einleitung," in *I Ernst Rabels, Gesammelte Aufsätze* XVIII, XIX (Tübingen, 1965).

[13] For descriptions of the institute and its operations, *see* Rheinstein, "Comparative Law," *supra* note 10, at 244–5. *See also* Ernst Rabel, "On Institutes of Comparative Law," 47 *Colum. L. Rev.* 227 (1947).

[14] For discussion, *see* Ernst Rabel, *Rechtsvergleichung vor den Gemischten Schiedsgerichtshöfen* (1923).

Rabel was also heavily involved in international legal unification projects. He was, for example, an active member of the League of Nations' institute for the unification of law in Rome. The most important of these projects was, however, the mandate that Rabel received from the League of Nations to create the basis for a unified international sales law. This undertaking led him to investigate systematically the sales laws of the major trading states. His meticulous and insightful comparison of the world's sales laws was highly praised, and it was the basis for his extraordinarily influential study of sales law, the first volume of which was published in 1936.[15] This work was in many ways a kind of "bible" for the efforts after the Second World War to unify sales law that eventuated in the Vienna Convention on the International Sale of Goods.

LAW, DISSOLUTION AND HOPE: RABEL'S STATED AIMS

When exploring Rabel's aims, we need to locate them in relation to the powerful, almost "messianic" discursive field that dominated thought in international political circles in the late 1920s. During those years, many were desperately seeking to repair the shattered confidence in European institutions and stave off the threats of further dissolution, and they often saw international institutions as the most promising—perhaps the only—mechanism for achieving those aims. There was a profound belief among many of those involved in international institutions that they were "saving the world from destruction," and this desperation-hued hopefulness was a major animating force within many of those institutions.

Consistent with this ethos, Rabel saw comparative law in large terms—as part of the solution to the fundamental problems that were facing Europe, in general, and Germany, in particular. As he put it, "Here is the most important point where the comparative law comes in. We must come back to an international treatment in an international spirit of international problems."[16] To that extent, we need to use a different lens in interpreting his objectives than we would typically use today. I suspect that few of those of us engaged in comparative law research today believe that the future of the world rests to any significant degree on our professional activities. Even if we did, few others are likely to agree.

In locating Rabel's project, we also need to be clear about his conceptualization of comparative law as a subject. He refers to three separate components of the comparative law enterprise.[17] One was historical, the study of how different

---

[15] Ernst Rabel, *Das Recht des Warenkaufs* (vol 1., Berlin, 1936; vol. 2, 1957).

[16] Jürgen Thieme, "Ernst Rabel (1874–1955): Schriften aus dem Nachlass," 50 *Rabels Zeitschrift*, 251, 305 (1986). *See also* Ernst Rabel, "Aufgabe und Notwendigkeit der Rechtsvergleichung," 13 *Rheinische Zeitschrift für Zivil-und Prozessrecht* 279 (1924).

[17] *See* Ernst Rabel, "Das Insitut," *supra* note 11, at 2–3. There were some variations in the descriptions of these components over time. *See, e.g.*, Rheinstein, "Comparative Law," *supra* note 10, at 250.

legal systems evolved, particularly in relation to each other. This was his focus during the first part of his career. A second focused on existing legal systems and differences in how they operated. This was his focus after 1916, and it is the subject of our inquiry. A third bordered on philosophy and sought to see the larger meaning of the other two. Rabel never developed this vague third category.[18] Our subject matter here then is only a part of Rabel's broad conception of comparative law.

Pure Science

Rabel claimed that the central goal of comparative law was "pure science"—the search for knowledge (*Erkenntnis*).[19] It was central in the sense that all else flowed from it: specific uses of comparative law were conceived as "applied" science. But Rabel's references to science are remarkably unspecific. He was never very clear about what he meant by the term, perhaps because it was part of a shared "background understanding" and therefore did not require attention. Often he seems to mean little more than the disciplined, self-conscious, and careful search for knowledge.

For Rabel, the subject of this scientific investigation was the *Rechtssatz* (roughly, legal rule or norm).[20] "Legal comparison means that the legal rules (*Rechtssätze*) of one state (or other law-prescribing community) are analyzed in relation to those of another legal order—or as many such orders as possible—from the past and the present."[21] The basic reference point is the rule or norm itself—not the process of creating, interpreting or applying it.

Applied Science

Although Rabel conceived his comparative law methods as science, his writings repeatedly emphasize their practical utility, and this theme became (and remains) a prominent part of the discourse used by his students and followers,

---

[18] In an article published in 1919, he described this third component as follows: "a component that penetrated philosophy, where historical and systematic legal science, together with legal philosophy, examine the deepest issues of the evolution and impact of law." Rabel, "Das Institut," *supra* note 11, at 2.

[19] For discussion of German legal science, *see*, *e.g.*, Mattias Reimann, "Nineteenth Century German Legal Science," 31 *B. C. L. Rev.* 842 (1990).

[20] The term "*Rechtssatz*" is difficult to translate into English. "Legal rule" is probably the closest translation, and that is what I will normally use here, but the German term does not carry the connotations of narrowness associated with the term in English. The reader should think of it as an "authoritative legal proposition." Rabel himself pointed out that a *Rechtssatz* is not the same as a rule or principle in U.S. law. *See* Ernst Rabel, "Die Fachgebiete des Kaiser-Wilhelm-Instituts für Ausländisches und Internationales Privatrecht (Gegründet 1926) 1900–1935," in Rabel (ed.), *Gesammelte Aufsätze*, *supra* note 12, at 180, 191.

[21] Rabel, *Aufgabe*, *supra* note 16, at 280.

particularly in Germany. This combination of academic and practical concerns shaped his methods and distinguished them from those of his predecessors and competitors. In seeking to be simultaneously both scientific and practical, he sought to stake out a unique position in both the academic and policy/practice communities.

One set of applications related to policy. Rabel wanted to create tools that would make better lawyers and better law. His methods were intended to make lawyers more capable of understanding the foreign legal situations they faced and better able to respond to them effectively.[22] They required students to immerse themselves in the details of specific situations and thereby develop a more effective and valuable knowledge of how such situations were treated in other legal systems.

They were also intended to produce better law. They were to be used, for example, to clarify the concepts of legal language and thereby make that language sharper and more effective.[23] In addition, they were to improve the "store of solutions (*Vorrat an Lösungen*)" to societal problems available to decision makers and thereby lead to better solutions to those problems.[24]

But Rabel frequently also referred to the value of his methods in gaining competitive advantages for Germany, German business and German lawyers. He wanted to make the German practitioner better able to understand the contexts in which he was operating, so that he could "win" his battles with his Western competitors and thus also serve Germany's economic and political interests. In 1919 he wrote "The reconstruction of the fatherland and its strengthening vis-à-vis the outside world require a sharpened perception of the events of the world. The new tasks must also find the lawyers (*Juristen*) armed."[25] There is a strong strand of nationalist pride in Rabel's writings during the 1920s.

LANGUAGE AS BOTH FACADE AND RESPONSE: COMPARATIVE LAW'S METHODS

Rabel's methods reflect these goals. Method, in the broad sense of thinking carefully about how one achieves a set of goals, was important to him. He repeatedly refers to it, those who worked for him often refer to his focus on method, and later commentators have recognized it. We might expect him, therefore, to have carefully and self-consciously elaborated his methodology. He did not, at least in his published writings.[26] Ironically, there is little method in his method.

---

[22]   *See, e.g.*, Rabel, "Das Institut," *supra* note 11, at 25–8.

[23]   *See, e.g.*, Rabel, *Aufgabe, supra* note 16, at 285, where he refers to the "cleansing" or "purification" (*Reinigung*) of legal concepts.

[24]   *Id.* at 287.

[25]   Rabel, *Das Institut, supra* note 11, at 6.

[26]   For extended discussion of Rabel's methodology, see Hans G. Leser, "Ein Beitrag Ernst Rabels zur Privatrechtsmethode: 'Die Wohltätige Gewohnheit, den Rechtsfall vor der Regel zu Bedenken,'" in Hans Ficker et al. (eds), *Festschrift für Ernst von Caemmerer* 891 (Tübingen, 1978).

His "methodology" consisted of little more than a set of general claims about the characteristics of scholarship that would serve the goals he had identified. In style, his methodology is close to the historicist methodology in the social sciences that was prominent in Germany from the 1880s until the First World War.[27] "Method" was there a matter of careful attention to patterns and details in the operation of society and economy. It eschewed—even condemned—theoretical development of methodological principles.

Function and Context: How to do Comparative Law

Rabel's prescription for the comparatist was, in its essence, simple: look at how a problem is solved in two or more legal systems and explore the differences and similarities in the respective treatments of the problem. He summarized his project as follows: "Rather than comparing fixed data and isolated paragraphs, we compare the solutions produced by one state for a specific factual situation with those produced by another state for the same factual situation, and then we ask why they were produced and what success they had."[28] In this basic form, the prescription appears simplistic, but it was a new way of thinking about the field, and there was much embedded beneath the apparently simple surface. Rabel's methodology is today often referred to as the function/context method. This linguistic coding appears to have been done by his students rather than by Rabel himself, but it captures the basic structure of his method.

Function

For Rabel, the essence of his methodology was its focus on the concrete, its drive to get behind the facade of language. In his view, information about a foreign legal system was only valuable in so far as it was contextualized. The written text should not structure the analysis, because conceptual and linguistic analyses of the articulated norms of a foreign legal system had little value by themselves. Taken alone, the formal language of rules and principles explained little about how problems were actually solved in the foreign system, and thus to structure analysis around language was likely to obscure rather than illuminate what was happening. The way to acquire relevant information about a foreign legal system was to ask how such rules and principles related to a specific fact situation. What counted was how the norms were applied. In this sense, he was "stripping the facade" of language away from legal reality. It was a pointed rejection of "speculative" and positivist visions of comparative law, both of which focused on that formal language.[29]

---

[27] For discussion and references, *see* David J. Gerber, *Law and Competition in Twentieth Century Europe: Protecting Prometheus*, 29–31 (Oxford, 1998).

[28] Rabel, *Fachgebiete, supra* note 20, at 187.

[29] *See infra*, text accompanying notes 32–4.

He thus shifted the methodological focus to the specific social functions of rules, which were to serve as the *terra comparationis*.[30] It was the mechanism that allowed meaningful comparison. Each system treated specific problems in specific ways, and thus the starting point of analysis should be the problems themselves. Rabel changed the structure of the analysis, moving the focus from the formal language of the system's rules and principles to the concrete reality (function) to which those rules and principles related. Note, however, that his objective was still to understand how the rules worked. The difference was that now rules were studied in relation to a specific problem rather than as the center of the investigation. It was a fundamental shift of conceptual field.

Context

The function/context label suggests that function and context are separate and independent analytical functions, the former to be performed before the latter. In Rabel's writings they are not so clearly distinguished. The conceptual boundary is far more fluid. For him, both components of the analysis flow from the same basic methodological injunction to look at how systems handle specific problems. The analyst has to understand the function—the concrete reality—to which legal norms relate, but she can do so only by looking at what they do in context. Cognitively, the two operations are intertwined.

Nevertheless, "context" did come to be treated in later writing as distinct, and analytically the distinction has value. Rabel insisted that in order to understand how each system treated a particular problem and thus produce an adequate and effective comparison, one had to investigate the entire context. The scope of the analysis was thus—in principle, at least—virtually unlimited in scope.

Curiously, however, Rabel provided little guidance for analyzing context. The analyst was supposed to look at all the factors that influenced the norms and procedures that addressed a particular problem, but Rabel did not concern himself with how this was to be done. Presumably he thought this was just a matter of looking for factors that might influence the application of the norms involved, but the omission is striking. What should the analyst be looking for? Are there patterns of decision making that help interpret particular decisions? Rabel's methodology is silent on such questions. The value of context is affirmed, but it is left largely unattended.[31]

---

[30] One might expect this move to have been tied to developments in social science or to the influence of social science, but I have found little evidence that Rabel paid much attention to social science developments.

[31] One clue to interpreting the role of context was Rabel's perception of the need for reciprocating movement between the specific and general. This was a prominent trope in academic circles of the period. Context was the broader lens, function the narrower one. The comparatist should use the narrow lens of function to see the specific problem to which norms were related, but he had to use the broader lens of context to make the comparison. The interaction between the two perspectives legitimated the analysis.

This lack of attention may relate to the institutional embeddedness of Rabel's methodology. From his early writings on comparative law, he conceived comparative law as an undertaking of large proportions in which many specialists would be responsible for amassing great amounts of knowledge relating to specific situations. It involved massive data-gathering. His comparative law institute in Munich moved in this direction, but it was at the Kaiser Wilhelm Institute in Berlin that he created what he claimed was needed—a large, well-endowed facility with large numbers of specialist researchers and extensive research materials. This institute was the centerpiece of his career.

Shaping Factors

Rabel defined his own methods in contradistinction to the two methods that were most prominent in the field at the time, claiming that both were inadequate to the tasks of the day. One was a kind of speculative jurisprudence of comparison.[32] He believed that comparative law had been too abstract and too philosophical. Scholars had looked at general features of large numbers of systems and drawn general conclusions about the relationships among them. This produced compendia in the style of the "laws of the world," but Rabel saw it as having little value in the "real world" of law. For him, comparison was only useful if it was "grounded" in the realities of the way legal systems actually solved problems.[33]

He was at least as adamant that comparative law was of little value if it merely compared statutory texts. To know the text of a statute was generally of little value if one did not know how the courts and other legal professionals were likely to interpret and use it.[34] Today this point seems trivial, at least to academic legal comparatists, but at the time much of what was called comparative law work was done in that vein. In contrast to this arid and potentially misleading textual orientation, Rabel set out to base his comparison on "living law."

Rabel viewed his methods as essentially—even radically—new. He acknowledged that a few other scholars had worked in the same direction, notably the Frenchman Édouard Lambert.[35] In this context, however, he did not refer to scholars other than his former teacher Ludwig Mitteis as authority or acknowledge their influence on the development of his comparative law methods.[36] Given the importance of context in his methodology, one might suppose that he would refer to social scientific literature, but he seldom did.

[32] For discussion, *see, e.g.,* Rheinstein, *Comparative Law, supra* note 10, at 234.
[33] Recall that he envisioned broader philosophical study of comparative law as a distinct third component of the comparative enterprise that could be usefully engaged in only after adequate development of the functional, doctrinal issues. *Cf. supra,* text accompanying note 17.
[34] Rabel, *Aufgabe, supra* note 16, at 282.
[35] *Id.* at 4, n.5.
[36] For discussion, see *supra,* text accompanying notes 4–6.

At one level, Rabel's goals—both private and professional—shaped his methods. On the professional level, for example, the many legal unification projects in which he was involved created incentives to amass large amounts of information about the treatment of specific problems in specific countries and then create treaty language that would encompass the solutions of the systems involved. His method was particularly well-suited to that enterprise, and it seems likely that the development of the methodology was intentionally designed for that type of use. His methods also answered the many choice of law issues that Rabel confronted in his judicial and arbitral roles. In these contexts, he had to decide which norms were applicable to which specific fact situations, and his method identified the relevant rules and principles. One further example relates to the practical needs of the German businesses and cartels that were desperately competing for international business during the 1920s (and who were in part funding Rabel's institute). For them, the earlier forms of comparative analysis had little value, but Rabel's methods provided specific answers to the specific contract, tort and other private law issues they faced. For these types of functions, Rabel's methods were beneficial and attractive.

These methods also provided benefits for Rabel personally. For example, his emphasis on "rending the veil" of language positioned him as an exceptional intellect who had penetrated the appearances of life to reveal its core and enhanced his status within intellectual circles. Furthermore, as an intellectual in a time when intellectuals had lost some of their status and much of their economic security, his methods helped to make him and his field "relevant" and hence valuable to those outside the university without abandoning the standards of academic discourse. They made Rabel an intermediary between the academic world and the needs of German business and politics, and they attracted the support of both.

In this brief essay, I cannot examine in detail the intellectual influences on the shaping of his methodology. It is important to note, however, that the idea of penetrating "beneath the surface" of conventions and language to a more concrete realm of "phenomena" was a prominent theme of the period. This was, for example, the basic thrust of the highly influential writings of the philosophers Edmund Husserl and Martin Heidegger. Rabel's methods can also be seen as part of a broader movement in law that focused on the "purpose" behind statutory provisions as a tool for interpreting and applying them.[37] Finally, Rabel's extensive study of U.S. law apparently led him to emphasize the importance of case law and the need to attend carefully to the details and contexts in which legal rules operated.[38]

---

[37] *See* Leser, *Beitrag*, *supra* note 26, at 905. This "movement" began with the influential writings of Rudolf von Jhering in the late 19th century and continued with the "Tübingen school" of "interest jurisprudence" in the early 20th century. For discussion, see Larenz, *supra* note 10, at 43–58.

[38] *See* Ernst Rabel, "Deutsches und Amerikanisches Recht," 16 *Rabels Zeitschrift* 340 (1951).

THE ROAD TO ORTHODOXY

My primary aim in this essay is to shed light on Rabel's methods, but the path that led to the successes and the eventual orthodoxy of those methods cannot be separated from the project itself. It provides the perspective from which we today look at Rabel's project, and thus we need to sketch it, albeit briefly.

Rabel's methods must have been "heady stuff" for his students. In the contexts of the Weimar period, they must have found it exciting to be part of an "intellectual breakthrough" that also promised a new kind of relevance for their academic efforts. It cast them as the "new breed" that dealt with reality rather than with the arid speculations of academic theorists or the equally dry parsing of statutory language. It made legal science intellectually challenging as well as immediately relevant to groups outside the academy such as businessmen and politicians, and this, in turn, also provided pecuniary and status-enhancement incentives. Little wonder that they were enthusiastic about it.

After the war, the popularity of the method grew even greater, although Rabel himself played only a marginal role in postwar developments. As a converted Jew, he had been forced to emigrate to the United States in 1938, and he chose never to return permanently to Germany. For his earlier efforts and influence he was honored with prizes and visiting professorships there, but he was not again a direct personal force in German comparative law. His methodology acquired the status of orthodoxy there because devoted students of Rabel such as Ernst von Caemmerer and Gerhard Kegel acquired leadership positions in comparative law in postwar Germany and continued to rely on Rabel's methods and discourse, and because they received support from other former students such as Walter Hallstein who became important political leaders. These former students formed a leadership community for which Rabel's methods served as the intellectual core and which has been passed on to subsequent academic generations with little apparent diminution in force.

Rabel's methodology also achieved a kind of orthodoxy in United States academic comparative law circles after the war.[39] Again, however, it was through his disciples and their influence rather than through his own influence. Rabel was sixty-five when he came to the U.S. in 1939. He knew English, but apparently he was not particularly comfortable with spoken English. He did research at Harvard Law School and the University of Michigan, but he was too old to become a faculty member. Although he managed to publish widely in leading journals, he remained a marginal and relatively isolated figure.

However, several of his closest disciples became leading figures in comparative law in the United States after the war. These included, in particular, Friedrich Kessler, who became professor of law at Yale Law School, and Max

---

[39] For extended discussion of Rabel's influence in the United States, *see* David S. Clark, "The Influence of Ernst Rabel on American Law," in Marcus Lutter et al. (eds), *Der Einfluss deutscher Emigranten auf die Rechtsentwicklung in den USA und in Deutschland* 107 (Tübingen, 1993).

Rheinstein, who was professor of law at the University of Chicago Law School. Many of the members of this group kept close ties to their counterparts in Germany, exchanging visits, sending students to each other, and participating in joint projects. Again, Rabel's methodology served as the intellectual bond of their expanded community.

IMPLICATIONS FOR LOCATING CONTEMPORARY COMPARATIVE LAW

This brief look at Rabel's aims, the methods he developed to achieve them and some of the factors that influenced both aims and methods helps locate comparative law today. The lenses that he fashioned have shaped our knowledge and our agendas, and thus we need to look both at what those lenses include and what they exclude. We can then ask how those characteristics correspond to today's needs.[40]

Lenses: Components of the Knowledge Field

Artifacts

One prominent characteristic of the knowledge produced by these methods is that it relates primarily and often exclusively to the *artifacts* of decision-making rather than to the *process* of creating those artifacts. His methods direct attention to rules and principles and propositions of law—products. They provide a means of identifying these products, abstracting them from the system in which they operate and then comparing the normative constellation of one system with another.

Focus on Detail

The knowledge produced by this method is necessarily detailed. Rabel focused on specific life-situations, comparing the ways in which different legal systems treated those situations. This requires attention to the details of those situations as well as to the details of the normative constructions being applied to them.

Particularism

Such knowledge is also particularist. By that I mean that it is largely independent of and unrelated to other knowledge; it is isolated. The method focuses the attention of the user on a particular problem and produces knowledge about that particular problem. This is not the province of theorizing, pattern identification or generalizations.

---

[40] For additional discussion of some of these themes, *see* David J. Gerber, "System Dynamics: Toward a Language of Comparative Law?," 46 *Am. J. Comp. L.* 719 (1998).

Statics

Finally, the knowledge is largely static. It relates to a specific normative configuration at a fixed point in time. The method creates a careful still photograph, a snapshot. It does not capture change over time, except incidentally. The knowledge produced has a specific temporal location; change is not its concern.

Such knowledge has great value. It answers often highly important questions. It correctly insists that in order to gain knowledge of a foreign legal system's laws, one needs to focus on how that system solves concrete problems at a specific moment. Skill in identifying and analyzing these normative treatments— whether for scholarly purposes or in the context of a judge's, arbitrator's or legal practitioner's decisions—is the basic skill of a comparatist. Effective use of the method requires patient, careful analysis.

What the Lenses Exclude from our Field of Vision

But these lenses also tend to exclude much from our field of vision, and much of what they exclude is of growing importance. In discussing what is excluded from a category, one necessarily has to be selective, but I here note several elements that are particularly significant for assessing the contemporary role of Rabel's methods.

Process

As noted, those methods generally pay little attention to the processes that create the artifacts of law. Who made the decisions that yielded a particular legal rule? Which factors influenced the decision-making process? Such questions are not the focus of the inquiry. In some cases, contextual analysis might touch upon them, but answering them is not the primary objective. Rabel himself considered issues of process important, but the methods developed by him provide little incentive to explore them carefully. In general, the focus on artifacts tends to marginalize process issues. There is little incentive to investigate how a particular solution was achieved; the issue is the solution itself.

Theory, Patterns and Relationships

The method also excludes knowledge about connections between individual applications of the method. It does not relate knowledge resulting from one application to knowledge derived from other applications of those methods. There is no common theoretical or conceptual framework for organizing knowledge and relating discrete pieces of information to each other. Indeed, theory— the conceptual structuring of knowledge—is largely absent from Rabel's knowledge field.

Dynamics of Systems

Rabel's methods produce little information about the dynamics of systems. They do not ask how a system has developed over time or what factors have influenced change. They are not directly interested in questions about how a problem was handled yesterday or what factors might be at work to change how it will be handled tomorrow. In this sense, the specific temporal location of the knowledge produced often obscures the relationship of that specific location to other points in time—past or future. Moreover, the method produces little knowledge of the "personality" of a legal system. Such a system is examined in relation to its production of particular artifacts, but the dynamics of how and why it operates as it does are of little direct concern. Here again Rabel appears to have been personally interested in some of these issues, but the methods create few incentives to pay attention to them.

Communication Issues: Transferring Knowledge

The knowledge produced is also minimally transferable. The methods neither provide nor utilize a language that is designed to convey information about the objects under investigation. Moreover, there is little incentive to transfer the information the methods produce. The knowledge produced by one application is likely to have little value for other potential users of the method, and they are therefore not likely to seek it. If knowledge does not have significance beyond its own specific context, only those who are interested in that context—here, the specific normative arrangement—have incentives to seek it.

Public Law and Procedure

The dominance of Rabel's methods has also tended to exclude issues of public law, procedure and regulation from comparative law study. There are many reasons for the private law bias of comparative law, but the structure of the dominant methodology undoubtedly plays a role. The process of identifying a concrete problem and then looking at how each legal system involved in the comparison treats that problem is relatively straightforward in private law areas such as contract or tort law. Contracts and injuries are part of an identifiable "concrete reality" to which each system must address answers. Contract law, for example, must address the issue of what makes the contract binding, what happens when there is no "meeting of the minds" in the contracting process and so on. Having done so, one need only look at the respective doctrinal treatments of the problem. The analysis may be complex, but the factual situation provides an identifiable structure outside the framework of legal concepts. In public and procedural law, on the other hand, application of Rabel's methods tends to be more problematic.[41] For example, although procedural systems have some common elements, there is often no specific "life-situation" that can be extracted from the procedural context and compared to the same life-situation in another procedural system. Procedural systems create their own "reality" based on interrelated concepts and institutions. To that extent, the "concrete reality" that is necessary for applying Rabel's methods is missing.

Contemporary Needs

This sketch of the knowledge field produced by Rabel's methods helps to locate comparative law and suggests directions for further development of the discipline that Rabel played such a key role in establishing. Legal practice and scholarship today often call for knowledge and skills that Rabel's lenses do not capture or capture only to a limited extent and that therefore have little or no place in the field of vision of those who rely exclusively on those lenses. The increasing globalization of economic activity, for example, increases the need to understand the processes of communication among legal professionals and to enhance the capacity of those professionals effectively to interpret conduct and decisions across the boundaries of legal systems. As the speed and density of communication flows increase, the patient and detailed analysis of specific normative configurations needs to be combined with skills designed to recognize patterns in legal information and language, to perceive obstacles to effective communication among legal actors, and to discern the dynamics of the legal processes that produce a system's rules, principles and procedures. For achieving each of these objectives, the role of language will have to be central.

CONCLUDING PERSPECTIVES

Born of a desire to use comparative law to avoid the horrors of war and the terrors of social disintegration, Ernst Rabel's comparative law project was initially overwhelmed by the forces against which it was ranged. Once these forces were spent or destroyed, however, his project acquired an extraordinary degree of influence. In Germany, the United States and many other countries, his conception of comparative law became the standard vantage point for thinking about what comparative law was and how it should be done.

His methods represented an exceptionally important conceptual breakthrough, and we dare not forget how important they have been and continue to be. They provide a powerful tool of analysis that has been used to create an extensive and invaluable body of comparative law materials dealing with how legal systems treat specific problems.

---

[41] For an effort to apply these methods to procedure, *see* David J. Gerber, "Extraterritorial Discovery and the Conflict of Legal Systems," 34 *Am. J. Comp. L.* 745, 748–67 (1986).

Yet the success of those methods and their status as orthodoxy has also constrained. As with any orthodoxy, his methods have sometimes served as an end rather than a means to an end, thereby limiting intellectual inquiry instead of expanding it. In the role of orthodoxy, the creative tension of the methods has itself sometimes been obscured.

In creating a methodology for comparative law, Rabel sought to make comparative law "realistic." His central message was that the words of the law—its texts and the languages of those involved in it—can obstruct our view of what is actually happening. Therefore, Rabel claimed, we must penetrate behind language to the concrete realities of what is actually done.

Yet language is also the principal source of the information we seek, and thus understanding how it is used to convey and conceal information and to shape the interpretation and application of both concepts and facts is fundamentally important. It is central to our enterprise. Here, however, Rabel provides us with little guidance. In his concern with penetrating the facade of formal legal language, he paid little heed to the problems raised by actually using language to acquire and transmit the knowledge he was seeking.

We need to distrust and be skeptical of language, but we cannot afford to ignore it. I submit, therefore, that a prominent item on the agenda of comparative law should be to find ways to integrate language issues into its goals and methods. In doing so, comparative law's methods would move closer to achieving the lofty objectives that Ernst Rabel set for it.

Part IV

Mid-Century Pragmatism

Fig. 1 René David

8

René David: At the Head of the Legal Family

JORGE L. ESQUIROL

René David is one of few jurists known the world over. In the field of legal comparativism, his name figures prominently among its masters. Yet the reason we remember him, for organizing the world's legal systems into family groups, is exceptionally ordinary. Even in his own time it was not new. Still, David dedicated much of his professional life to refining and disseminating the concept. He described his legal families as a learning tool, a way in which to classify large amounts of material and complexity into broad categories. Much like a spreadsheet or a sven diagram is used to present minutiae in a conceptual manner, David's work has come to stand for the notion of families of law, and the interrelatedness of their members.

The apparent simplicity of David's scholarship is precisely what makes it a cornerstone of comparative law. He himself made no gesture to the grandiose nor did he claim any breakthrough in legal understanding. More simply, he advocated the furtherance of mere common sense. As such, his work did not inspire fierce reaction or impassioned objection from critics. One could disagree over some particular about a familiar legal system. Or, one could possibly make some argument for one family grouping rather than another. However, his work of classification was sufficiently neutral, sufficiently an extension of ideas past, that it stirred no great controversy. From the perspective of his contemporaries, it either elicited satisfaction as yet another ordering of diverse law, or it was greeted with relative ennui at its inconsequentiality.

While at first blush this may appear quite unflattering, it is really one of the sustaining strengths of René David the comparativist. The elaboration of ideas, in a form readily acceptable and automatically capable of becoming background fact, is surely a form of mastery. This accomplishment produces neither novel technique nor a shift in paradigms. Nonetheless, intellectual projects reflecting common understanding may be as much if not more influential than a highly trumpeted departure from established conventions. Taken more critically, the aesthetics of common sense or backgroundness are also deliberate devices, deployed to launch ideas or programs, which are not actually neutral or apolitical. The strategic use of this discourse is quite effective to empower ideas by treating them as uncontroversial. In fact, it may be the very way backgroundness is always reproduced. This doubled mode of writing—innovative conventionalism—is one of the achievements of René David. Far from banal or passive, David's professional life was aflame with institutional projects and academic concerns as he actively advanced his projects, wrote numerous books and articles, and extended his ideas across countries and languages.

This biographical sketch focuses on David's conceptual life. Briefly put, the jurist's life-long work championed the practice of legal comparativism from an anti-formalist perspective. He refitted its methods, grounded in earlier natural law and positivist theories, onto a more sociological framework. His opus not only rendered comparativism more defensible by upgrading its theoretical premises, but it also placed it at the center of legitimating the legal system. Offering a way to re-affirm the coherence of law as a type of science, comparative law provided the device for sustaining the higher authority of law above mere national politics. Comparative law, like legal process or policy science ideas in the Anglo-American context, was for David a way to uphold law's primacy at the centre of to national governance.

It should be noted that what I identify here as David's projects are not, of course, presented by him as such. Instead, his statements about his work repeatedly refer to more modest objectives of enhancing knowledge about law and improving the legal system. Yet he was actually quite aware of deeper motives. In his memoirs he writes: "The work so accomplished did not however have, in my mind, the simple goal of information; it would not obtain all its meanings if it did not open on to concrete conclusions and lead jurists to revise their manner of seeing the law, its elaboration and its application. To give value to the practical interest of comparative law, I was required to combat the commonly admitted views and show their falsity." [1] While he mistrusted theoreticians and loathed dogmatism, systems and fanaticism,[2] he recognized his own penchant for professional projects, order and organization. In his autobiography, David sums up his life as "a life in which nothing extraordinary happened, but just the same was very varied, fertile with funny events and incidents, which by the by lends for useful reflection."[3] David admits he was greatly influenced by his father,[4] and his own family played a prominent role in his life. His career as a law professor was in large measure based on his father's unfulfilled goals.[5] The elder David hailed from rural France, le Jura, and rose to success as a doctor of laws in Paris, becoming the Judicial Administrator to the Seine Civil Tribunal. Born in 1906, David was deliberately succinct about his early life: "It is in this

---

[1] René David, *Les Avatars d'un Comparatiste*, 262 (Paris, 1982). All translations from original French and Spanish language sources are mine.

[2] *Id.* at 10 ("Whatever it may be, I instinctively mistrust systems, the views of theoreticians, pseudo-science. For me there is not an appropriate model for all and for all times: I hate all that is dogmatic, the spirit of system and fanaticism.")

[3] *Id.* at 5.

[4] *Id.* at 13.

[5] *Id.* at 7.

100% French environment, Catholic but without fanaticism, traditionalist but liberal, united by a same feeling of duty and a same conception of life, that I was raised." When it came to his sentimental life, however, the great expositor of legal families was quite reticent, as he put it "for diverse reasons, but above all because I am incapable of speaking of it."[6]

For 25 years David taught at the law school of the University of Paris. Faced with the restructuring of his institution after 1968, he left for the University of Aix-en-Provence where he ultimately retired in 1976.[7] David was the picture of a sensible and steadfast legal craftsman: laboriously sifting through the pieces of the puzzle. He brought to bear upon his work the moral relativism of the era, and he labored over the historical and sociological elements underpinning national legal systems.[8] He regarded all of these as grist for the comparativist's mill. Yet, his comparativism is neither relativist nor all-encompassing; quite the contrary, David's primary objective was defining the parameters of what he understood as meaningful comparison.[9] Uncovering the meaning, or put differently, the function that David assigned to comparativism, is key to appreciating his otherwise conventional, conceptual apparatus. It is precisely this meaning for comparative law which identifies his larger institutional objectives. Another prefatory word about David's idiosyncrasies are in order. Despite his vast academic enterprise, he never presented himself as a lofty scholar. Quite the contrary, his career is filled with anecdotes of a self-effacing and even ironic perspective on himself. An example sheds some light on his personality. When discussing his petition to join the bench of the European Court of Justice, which he ultimately withdrew, David spoke of his reasons for applying. In the first place he wanted to valorize comparative studies. Serving on the court would demonstrate their practical utility. Just as important, though, were his hopes of getting the family dog out of their Paris apartment.[10] This story and others like it in his autobiography speak of a firmly grounded pragmatism. Not surprisingly, David's intellectual projects were similarly unpretentious. This essay traces three of these professional projects, especially his designs for comparative law.

Running through David's work is a concern for legitimating the authority of law. By David's era, natural law justifications for the legal system and for specific laws were mostly discredited. Mainstream scholars were unconvinced of the power of reason or divination to craft definitive legal rules. Positivist theories, by comparison, also faced growing skepticism over their claims to provide

---

[6] René David, *Les Avatars d'un Comparatiste,* at 12.

[7] *Id.* at 156–58.

[8] *Id.* at 10 ("The world is no longer the same: one cannot live, think, act like it was reasonable to do fifty years ago. Did this relativism predispose me to become a comparatist, or does it have to do with my becoming one? It is difficult to answer this question; it is probable that the profession confirmed and increased a natural tendency within me from the beginning.")

[9] *Id.* at 141. (David came to teach comparative law at the University of Paris, according to him, "because no one else wanted to," and it tempted him the most).

[10] *Id.* at 151.

complete and clear resolution of all legal issues which may arise. Equally plaus-ible alternative interpretations and the unavoidable limitations of legislative drafting rendered positivist claims difficult to fulfill.

David drew on a different source. His grand scheme, in the final analysis, but-tressed the workability of positivist legal systems, although he was no ordinary positivist himself. He structured a method in which positive law would be sup-plemented, so as to fulfill its claims to completeness and clarity. Comparative law was the key. It would provide an outwardly non-political, supplemental source of law. Within purportedly like societies, the basis of David's definition of legal families,[11] he upheld the notion of a common law rising above matters of local politics or nationalist idiosyncrasies. At the same time, David's proposal acknowledged the possibility of radical differences existing across legal sys-tems—a mainstay of anti-formalist thinking. Such differences were accommo-dated by grouping them within separate families of law. His scheme was ultimately a way to salvage France's great contribution to the modern legal world. The first part of this chapter focuses on the workings of this central tenet of David's scholarship.

A second and related preoccupation of David's is the Cold War. For him, comparative law could be a tool for finding common ground with political and economic enemies. Even when confronted with opposing governing systems, according to David, law can in many cases be seen as sustaining a common link. In this way, a certain rapprochement would be possible and law would lead the way.

Especially in David's later work this question of world peace occupies center stage. Here legal families play a role, but David downplays their distinctness, at least in the case of the Soviet family and the Western family. Divisions between the Soviet Union and the West are minimized in favor of finding commonality on the terrain of law. Commonality, though, is sought less in terms of positive law and more in terms of legal issues which all societies must perforce resolve.

Finally, David was instrumental in launching the harmonization of private international law, particularly in the field of the law of sales. In a way, this lat-ter project was the practical implementation of the ideas he developed in his scholarship. While his academic writings on comparativism and legal families promised a way to defend the legitimacy of national laws, his efforts to promote Unidroit were the culmination of this vision.

Harmonization, pursued correctly, presented for David the ultimate step toward the goal of maintaining international harmony. David offered a tempered

---

[11] David is, of course, intimately familiar with alternative classifications schemes, based on vary-ing criteria. He cites predecessors such as Sauser-Hall, Levy-Ullman, Clovis Bevilaqua and Martínez Paz. His critique of these is twofold: they were guided by preconceived ideas whose scientific character was not sufficiently established, and their authors did not consistently abide by the same criteria throughout. *See* René David, *Traité Élémentaire de Droit Civil Comparé: Introduction à l'Étude de Droits Étrangers et à la Méthode Comparative*, 222–3 (Paris, 1950); *see also* Hiram E. Chodosh, "Comparing Comparisons: In Search of Methodology," 84 *Iowa L. Rev.* 1025 (1999) (cit-ing numerous comparativists both before and after David deploying the artifice of legal families).

approach to projects of legal unification. Only in legal fields where considerable harmonization had taken place already would it be productive to implement the unification or uniformity of positive law. Not all legal fields would thus be immediately subject to unification. More important than the harmonization of specific rules for him was the harmonization of technique and legal consciousness, made possible through his program of comparativism. Nonetheless, while cautious of its methods and its use, David was a significant contributor to the contemporary unification of international sales law.

I. SALVAGING LIBERAL LAW

David's central preoccupation was defending the legitimacy of law. He employed comparativism as a means to counteract critiques levied against both positivism and naturalism. In brief overview, he built on the—by then hardly controversial—notion that law derives from society and from social interaction. He directed his comparative energies toward identifying like societies, forming the basis for his legal families, and he prescribed an agenda for comparative law practice. He argued that any national system could justifiably draw on a related system's law, not based on faith in positivism or the identification of a natural system at work, but simply because they shared a common source. In this way, the laws, juristic opinions, case law and legal materials of other nations were available to supplement revealed discrepancies and absences within any specific national, positive law system.

The following sections detail the scheme conceptualized by David and the less obvious effects its analysis lays bare.

A. Comparative Law in New Garb

By the mid-twentieth century, the work of founding the discipline of comparative law had been for the most part accomplished by such figures as Edouard Lambert and Harold Gutteridge. The issues facing David, as a rather young comparativist, were very different: the most central concern was to defend the enterprise of comparativism, and its positivist underpinning from attack by mid-century antiformalists. To take up the banner of comparativism required a prefatory apology as to its theoretical bases. It was to this task which René David's first major treatise turned.

The bulk of David's scholarly production redefines, builds and defends the practice of comparativism. During an era in which the discipline had begun to fade, David re-defined its reason for existence. The framework for comparative law practice is painstakingly sketched by David himself in two substantial treatises both published for the first time in the middle of the twentieth century.[12] The theoretical blueprint that animates David's proposal requires a little more effort to decipher.

David first convinced the French Ministry of Education to require all law schools to teach a course on the major contemporary legal systems. He focused his own energies on writing "the book that could serve as the basis for comparative law studies."[13] His treatises therefore were meant to provide the operating instructions for the comparative law practice of the time. As the pages below describe, his comparativism was not merely a project of cultural enrichment. It responded to a vital need to defend the pre-eminence of law and legal governance. Comparativists were to be the avant-garde of this enterprise.

David was also the academic anchor of two significant pedagogical organizations. The first, the International Committee for Comparative Law, was funded by UNESCO in 1949 and came to comprise no less than fifty separate national subcommittees. Its founding board consisted of such figures as Ernst Rabel, John Hazard, and even Harold Gutteridge, who by then was in ailing health. Its objective was to promote an international community of jurists who would have a role in governance. With a cadre of academics positioned in universities throughout the world, David's designs for comparativism would no longer be just a law professor's daydreams of power. The International School of Comparative Law was established in Luxembourg with similar objectives in 1957. Spearheaded by David's longtime friend and collaborator, Felipe de Solà Cañizares,[14] the curriculum modeled David's plan for comparative law practice for both students and law professors.[15] This institution actually produced the comparativists that David imagined in his treatises, practitioners capable of summoning cross-national legal authority in cases of disagreement over the meaning of national law.

In the next few paragraphs is a succinct analysis of the function comparative law plays in David's conceptual framework. It traces the somewhat subterranean intellectual map that formed the basis of his work, and that he refined throughout his life. Moreover, this conceptual grid continues to shape the discipline of comparative law.

---

[12] David, *supra* note 11, at 224; René David, *Les Grands Systèmes de Droit Contemporains: Droit Comparé* (Paris, 1966); *see also* Christopher Osakwe, "Book Review" of *An Introduction to Comparative Law* by K. Zweigert & H. Kötz, 62 *Tul. L. Rev.* 1507 (1988) (noting that in addition to the book reviewed, the other leading European textbook on comparative law is René David and John E. C. Brierley, *Major Legal Systems in the World Today: An Introduction to the Comparative Study of Law* (2nd ed., London, 1978) [translated from R. David, *Les Grands Systemes de Droit Contemporains: Droit Comparé* (first ed. 1964, 1966). *See also* third English language edition 1985).

[13] David, *supra* note 1, at 144.

[14] Felipe de Solà Cañizares was a Catalonian exile from the Spanish Civil War living in France. He was David's principal collaborator, dedicated primarily to the administrative and institutional sides of their common projects. He was also a scholar and author of several books on comparative law. He died in 1965. *See* René David, *Le Droit Comparé: Droits d'hier, Droits de Demain. Economica*, 30–38 (Paris, 1982).

[15] David, *supra* note 1, at 147–49.

Clearly, David saw himself as working within a tradition begun by others.[16] David took pride in occupying the chair once belonging to Raymond Saleilles and Henri Levy-Ullman, pillars of an earlier generation.[17] He derived much sustenance from such figures as Lambert and Gutteridge and openly acknowledged: "My model was rather Edouard Lambert, however much I may have mistrusted the somewhat chimerical tendencies to which his natural tendencies took him."[18] He met Harold Gutteridge in Geneva in the 1930's at a drafting session of the International Convention on Bills of Exchange. Gutteridge invited him to Cambridge, where David spent two years, 1933 to 1935, at Trinity Hall and confirmed his vocation as a comparativist.[19] Later in 1949, while at the University of Paris, David had Gutteridge's seminal work on comparative law translated into French, one year before David's own first treatise was to appear.[20]

David defined his work in relation to Lambert and Gutteridge and saw them as allies engaged in a common project.[21] At first blush, it may appear that the alliance related merely to the advancement of comparative law as a discipline worth continuing. Or it may appear to be merely professional self-interest in perpetuating a common métier. Yet again, David's enduring identification with his own masters may be seen as simple loyalty to ensure that they were not misinterpreted or remembered in ungenerous terms.

More important to David than other concerns, however, was that mainstream legal theory had changed greatly between the early 1900's and David's era. At a minimum, the great challenges posed by antiformalists during the first half of the twentieth century required some response. As a result, the old masters' theoretical backdrop alone was insufficient to sustain David's work. Consequently, David was preoccupied with more than setting the record straight or even vindicating his old teachers once more. He did not concern himself with defending a particular comparativist school per se. David's sense of alliance with his predecessors was rather reflected in their common use of comparative law to reinforce a system of national positive law. The old masters, in broad and general terms, invoked comparativism as a way in which neutral and objective law was knowable and achievable. It is this latter aspect of their project that David rescues and with which he aligns himself.

Still, he had to respond to the supervening questions raised by antiformalists. He thus re-formulated the old masters', by then questionable, theoretical platform

---

[16] Notably, among his intellectual predecessors, David cites Rudolf von Jhering with approval. See e.g. David, *supra* note 1, at 258.

[17] *Id*. at 259. (As to their work, he commented: "I rendered homage to the efforts accomplished by these illustrious predecessors, and appreciated their work, but it did not seem to me to have the necessary breadth nor above all the success it deserved").

[18] *Id*. at 259.

[19] See H.C. Gutteridge, *Comparative Law: An Introduction to the Comparative Method of Legal Study & Research* (Cambridge, 1946); *see also*, David, *supra* note 1, at 28–48, 145–46.

[20] David, *supra* note 1, at 28, 38, 146.

[21] *See e.g.* David, *supra* note 14, at 10–29.

in order to deflect his own contemporary critics. He constructed a position which attempts to fend off the pitfalls of doctrinaire positivism on the one hand and idealist naturalism on the other. Only by dodging the obvious pitfalls acknowledged by the legal academy of his day would it be possible to construct a legal program capable of attracting adherents. By the mid-twentieth century, it was necessary for David's work to incorporate the antiformalist truths of his time, in order to keep his enterprise afloat.

To put this in an historical context, comparative law owed much to natural law theories. Natural law, while spanning a broad range of theoretical constructs, typically claimed to stand for one correct, or more correct, answer based on an overriding absolute, for example, reason, God, or nature. Under a natural law conception, comparative law served as the academic basis to assert which legal solutions constituted natural law and which did not. One important proof was the recurrence of particular legal solutions across national legal systems. Indeed, one of the justifications for the comparisons of different legal systems was precisely to identify the one natural or universal law. Just as reason or theological divination functioned as methodologies for arguments based on natural law, comparative law came into being as another such legal methodology. It thus relied on and advanced natural law thinking.

In their heyday during the 1900s, legal positivists also exploited comparativist technologies. Placing their faith in comprehensive codes backed by the legitimacy of a sovereign law-maker, positivists hoped to perfect the technical aspects of law. Textual comparison was a way of extending the reach of codification throughout the world. At the same time, it promised to refine and perfect the legal enactments of states already devoted to positivist science. David placed Lambert in this positivist camp. His comparative work, David believed, ultimately placed undue emphasis on legislation as the source of law, and comparative law as a mere tool for perfecting its texts.[22]

Critics contended that positive law was incapable of encompassing a range of unanticipated and unanticipatable situations, which would then require some extra-textual means for their resolution. The need for recourse to some other means of decision-making would defeat the positivist claim to completeness. For more radical critics, this deficiency was not limited to the margins but actually reflected a central flaw of positivism. In other words, almost all legal questions are susceptible to an ambiguous reading under the codes and while positivist theorists offered some self-sustaining text-based responses to their critics, these were never completely satisfactory.[23] Additionally, by David's time, this supplement or gap-filling function could not be seriously assigned to

---

[22] *See* David, *supra* note 1, at 263.

[23] Some common legitimating theories of positivism, only by way of example, argue: that positive law demonstrates a "coherence" from which code silences may be filled; another is that ambiguities may be disentangled by the structure of other "analogous" provisions. There are various other fairly standard reactions (not within the scope of this account) to the critiques of positivism which attempt to respond without resorting to legal naturalism.

natural law theorizing which was incapable of providing convincingly singular rules of decision.

Thus, by the middle of the twentieth century, both paradigmatic conceptions of law were problematic. Naturalism was debunked as incapable of accessing metaphysical truths. Positivism was perceived as riddled with inconsistencies and silences that undermined its claims to both completeness and uniformity. Thus, if comparative law was strictly a methodology of naturalism or positivism, then it would be rejected along with these theories. Of course, one could imagine that cross-system comparisons could be undertaken regardless of the underlying theory, but while this is surely true, the question then remains, to what end? David's importance lies in providing an answer to the question of comparativism's practical use post-formalism.[24]

David acknowledged his antiformalist leanings. Indeed, he attributed his particular conception of law in part to his study of the workings of common law, while in Cambridge:

> The law, the rules posed by jurists no longer seemed to me as having a sacred character; I was, more than before, and more without doubt than many French jurists, disposed to see things from a more practical point of view, worrying less about the purity of concepts, taking more into account empirical considerations, and giving priority to justice over law. I am not, in so doing, isolated from French jurists; I have only adhered to a tendency that, in France, encounters much resistance from more classical and conservative elements of the juridical world.[25]

Legal theory based on empiricism, or more specifically for David, social contingency, raises the question of comparativism's utility. The value of comparing phenomena, deriving from social and historical particularity, may be defended as simply cataloguing collections of legal coincidences and divergences, since it is no longer about demonstrating superior drafting technique or much less, overarching truth. In very obvious ways, accepting social relativity and historical contingency, however, opens comparativism to critiques of dilettantism or meaningless curio.

The notion of legal exchanges, across members of a circumscribed legal family, is David's response to such charges. His first treatise sets out five distinct legal families: Western law (including the Romano-Germanic group and Anglo-American law), the Soviet family, the Islamic family, the Hindu family, and the Chinese family.[26] These groupings, according to David, were drawn on the basis of observed ideological similarities characterizing their underlying societies.[27]

---

[24] David launches his classification scheme convinced of the notion that: "It is not possible, we have seen, to distinguish among laws (legal systems) by considering exclusively the nature of things, and the diversity of rules that it imposes." David, *supra* note 11, at 223.

[25] David, *supra* note 1, at 47.

[26] David, *supra* note 11, at 224–25.

[27] *See id.* at 223–4. (David based his classification scheme on two criteria: differences of ideology which depend on religious and philosophical beliefs as well as political, economic and social structures; and differences of technique as developed by jurists. In his first treatise, David considered only ideological differences as running deep. Technical differences were a matter of happenstance (more

Notably, he identified three salient characteristics of the Western family: liberal democracy, capitalist economy, and Christianity. The legal family functioned for David as both a substitute for natural law reasoning and an improvement on positivism.[28] Comparativism also substituted the ordering function provided by natural law arguments. That is, while naturalism evaluates national law against some universal ideal, David juxtaposes national law with "related" systems within the same family:

> I do not hardly believe that society can ever be founded exclusively on love and charity. The first Christians may have had this vision, while waiting for an imminent end to the world, and certain ones may continue to dream of it. Man being what he is, such an ideal can not be but that of a limited community, one whose type is the family: its achievement is problematic in societies of larger size.[29]

Thus, while universal truth or a uniform law worldwide were not easily defensible, a common law of related societies was more sociologically and historically plausible. As such, the members of one legal family become the sources for supplementing the shortcomings of any one national code.[30] The case is made by David in the following way:

> Among certain countries there exists, concerning law, a community particularly close in terms of tradition and principles, which makes the law of those countries belong to one same system and solutions valid in one can, considering particular circumstances, be invoked in another with a comparable value, if not an equal one, to that which it would have if, it had been proclaimed in this [second] country. So long as two laws [legal systems] come from a common source, . . . they are not absolutely, one in relation to the other, foreign.[31]

Specific inconsistencies are resolved and silences are filled with foreign law, albeit foreign law that is produced by and common in a closely-related society.

---

of an obstacle to legal unification than anything else.) In his second treatise, David treats differences of ideology and differences of technique on a par. As such, he sets apart the Common Law (previously the Anglo-American group, reflecting purely technical differences, within Western law) as a separate family. Nonetheless, he re-affirms the significance of speaking of a Western legal family, encompassing both. In this later work, he identified only three major families: the Romano-Germanic, Common Law and Socialist law. He cited four other families as well, pertaining to the laws of the rest of the world. *See* David and Brierley, *supra* note 12.

[28] Reflecting on his work, David avows: "Comparative law studies had a fundamental double role to fulfill: re-give law a universal dimension which is proper to all true science, and restore the idea of a jus gentium that one knew erstwhile, and which had become more necessary than ever in the conditions of the modern world." David, *supra* note 1, at 258.

[29] *Id.* at 267.

[30] By contrast, legal systems part of a different legal family do not offer the same expanded sources of legal development. For example, of Soviet law, David states: "Soviet and bourgeois jurists cannot . . . ever come to an agreement on principles; and a worthwhile comparison between the Soviet and bourgeois laws can only take place on the technical level." David, *supra* note 12, at 165–6.

[31] *See* David, *supra* note 11, at 81.

B. Putting Antiformalism to Work

Another aspect of David's work is his peculiar use of the concepts of history and society. David himself advances an antiformalist conception of law, that is society-based with an emphasis on the sociological and historical aspects of legal development.[32] He saw one of his principal tasks as "denouncing the hypocrisy" of positivism.[33] Rather than returning to some natural law argument for liberal law, he instead undertook a society-specific explanation. His grounding of law in social phenomena offered a mode of ready legitimation. Of course, David did not invent sociological approaches to law, far from it. Rather, by David's time, sociological or material conceptions of law, had come to be associated and damningly tainted by Nazi nationalism and Soviet Marxist abuses. The distinctiveness of David's approach is to hold national, society-specific law to a higher, transnational level of account. Law is conceived as the material production of societies, but the society in question consists of the transnational legal family. Comparative law thus provided the device by which national law can be invested with a broader compass.

Practically, David's proposal relied on an expanded set of sources of law. Under traditional positivism, law was restricted to national codes and legislation. The work of judges was mere application, and the work of legal scholars to elucidate the necessary meaning of the text or prepare the work of legislators. David, by contrast, was an unabashed realist with respect to law-making.[34] He went as far as affirming in 1950 that:

> It is extremely difficult, in French law, as in other foreign law to distinguish the cases where case law and legal scholarship make more precise existing law and those cases in which they create new law; one cannot in effect, in this regard, stop at formulas that are employed and that tend in general to veil the creative role filled by factors other than legislation.[35]

Thus, for David, this complement to positive law mostly takes the form of acknowledging that case law and legal scholarship are both proper sources of law. Sociological and historical particularity are distilled through these

---

[32] René David, "On the Concept of 'Western Law'" 52 *U. Cin. L. Rev.* 126, 129 (1983) ("I believe we confront the problem of the existence or non-existence of "Western" law in these terms. This problem is closely related to the very concept of law that we entertain, and to the opposition between doctrines of natural law and positivism. . . . At present let us put ourselves in the camp of those jurists, possibly "impure," who perceive in law primarily the expression of a civilization, and . . . that establishes the unity of "Western law. . . .")

[33] David, *supra* note 1, at 263.

[34] René David, *French Law: Its Structure, Sources and Methodology* 162 (1960) (Baton Rouge, 1972) ("Until the end of the nineteenth century, however, the process was used with prudence; it was kept in disguise. No one considered setting it up as a principle of interpretation or openly proclaiming the necessity of abandoning historical interpretation. Then suddenly at the turn of the century, a doctrinal movement began to assert the merits and insist on the legitimacy of teleological interpretation. The names of R. Saleilles, F. Gény, and L. Josserand are most commonly associated with this movement in France. . . .")

[35] David, *supra* note 11, at 125.

means.[36] Additionally, these expanded sources of law are further extended by recourse to the sources of other members of the same legal family. The case is made by David in the following way:

> This use of comparative law is illustrated, in a particularly clear way, by the example of the countries whose civil law is inspired by the Code Napoleon. It seems completely natural that, in those countries, gaps in the law should be filled by observing the solutions of French law and by interpreting the Codes using the commentaries of the Code Napoleon or the civil law treatises written by French authors.[37]

By broadening the field in this way, gaps and inconsistencies in national positive law may be filled by not only looking to other members within one's own legal family, but also by looking beyond a narrow definition of legislation to other modes of law-making.

Taken together, the effort is quite an intervention in the legal politics of his time. It claims no pretension to high theory or even to theory at all. In fact, it is the distinctly cobbled-together quality of David's legal thinking that make his injunctions attractive. In comparative law he finds answers to two questions. Comparative law can be used to solve the incompleteness of positive law in one national system by referring to solutions developed in other national systems.[38] Likewise, by identifying legal families in which legal systems are grouped according to similar societal characteristics, and within which comparativism and legal borrowings are thus presumed to be compatible,[39] David developed a response to the society-specific nature of law.

This last response is particularly useful in that it both sustains the usefulness of comparative law, in line with antiformalist accounts, and it avoids the danger of excessive nationalist particularity. The common unit of account is neither the nation nor race but rather the transnational legal family to which one belongs. David's task, as the architect of this recontructivist proposal for law, is to delineate the membership of specific national systems within distinct family groups.

C. Exporting France

Critiques of David's project and his legal methods have of course been made. Primarily, questions were directed at the consistency of David's classification

---

[36] *Id*. at 124.

[37] *Id*. at 79–80.

[38] *See e.g.* René David, "L'avenir des droits Européens: Unification ou harmonisation," in *Le Droit Comparé: Droits d'Hier, Droits de Demain*, 301 (Paris, 1982) ("If law is not, like it was believed in the 19th century in France, the exclusive creation of the legislator, if judges and jurists contribute to making the law evolve and creating it under the inspiration of sociological, economic, political, and moral theories which have not been formally sanctioned by the state, the road is open to recognize again the anational or 'transnational' character of law").

[39] *See e.g.* David, *supra* note 11, at 301 ("European law will exist once it has become natural, for us, to envisage all questions under the angle of comparative European law: when our judges feel the weight of arguments constituted by a decision rendered in another European country, when the legislator feels obliged to consider, in his work, the law in force in other European countries.")

scheme. Some obvious examples are his classification of the Anglo-American tradition within the same legal family as the continental European tradition.[40] David resolved this continuing dispute by categorizing the difference as one of technique within the same legal family.[41]

Another classification question concerns Latin America. Under David's system, the legal system of those countries fits neither within his Romano-Germanic nor general Western family. In order to make them correspond, David contorted his own elements for membership.[42] He stakes Latin America's European pedigree on one salient factor: the "European" idealism of its national jurists who sustain the ideology of a universal law, in the face of admittedly contrary material conditions.[43] These slippages or contortions of David's own professed methods are clearly a basis for academic concern. However, they can be relegated to questions about the fringes of his general method and his general classification scheme. We could reclassify Anglo-American systems, and Latin America may not fit within the Romano-Germanic category, but these need not be damning critiques of his structure or of a structure of this type. They may point to structural inconsistencies, but they do not challenge the edifice itself. These observations however are revealing of the underlying political motivations or political projects behind the method. Here we begin to gain clues as to David's impetus for this elaborate conceptual structure. No doubt the principal motivation is recreating law as an apolitical field of social governance, basing law on society, identifying like societies, and then drawing on them for legal arguments. Preferred legal solutions may then be cultivated and transplanted across nation-states.

More surprising, however, is the working of David's scheme in relation to his view of French law. In his writings on his own legal system, David tends to ignore the importance of cross-fertilization and exchanges among related kin.[44] If anything, he clearly conveys the image of France as parent rather than a same-generation family member.[45] Further, the relevance of comparative law to the functioning of the everyday French legal system is presented as relatively minimal. Rather than an equal partner in the community of societies that share optimal legal solutions, the structure is envisaged as one in which France

---

[40] David's 1950 comparative law treatise argues for a family of Western law, divided into two branches: French law and the common law. See id.; see also David, supra note 31.

[41] To reinforce his argument, David cites the more "philosophical" perspective of Soviet jurists who catalogue both French law and the common law together as "bourgeois" law. David adopts their reasoning to argue for the common ideology behind a Western law, relegating the differences between common and civil law to ones of mere technique. See David, supra note 31.

[42] See Jorge L. Esquirol, "The Fictions of Latin American Law" (Part I), 2 Utah L. Rev. 425 (1997).

[43] René David, L'Originalité des droits Latino-américains in Centre de Documentation Universitaire, Université de Paris V (Paris, 1956).

[44] See e.g., David, supra note 34.

[45] Commentators of David's comparative method, as well as of the legal family metaphor generally, note that this method typically suggests that productive study should be directed only at the legal parent, and possibly one other elder member, but certainly not at common family members.

predominates. In other words, French jurists are urged to make independent decisions about which legal choices and policy preferences come to be inscribed in law. By contrast, other family members of the Romano-Germanic family—if David's method were to be put into practice—should consult with the policy preferences and cultural options embedded in French law, as the matrix of their decision-making. David was rather forthright about it:

> [T]he new developments that have occurred over the past two centuries in the countries of the Romano-Germanic family have been profoundly influenced by French law, and the best way to understand these other legal systems, as well as those of the socialist countries of Eastern Europe, is still to study initially the principles of French law and the way in which French lawyers reason about legal problems.[46]

In short, implementing the structure proposed by David would have a curious effect. Instead of substituting comparative law or the legal family for outdated natural law theories or positivism's unconvincing tropes, the effect would be to put France in their place. In other words, France would be the model for the Romano-Germanic family: its policy choices, framed as law, would enjoy pride of place within the legal possibilities of related national systems.[47] This objective becomes evident in David's writings specifically on French law and the role of comparativism within his own national setting.[48] It plays an important role in his vast institutional project. It promises legitimacy for liberal law at the price of making France the standard. This enterprise is a monumental effort to revive France's contribution to field of law, of the same stature as taking the Napoleonic Code to the world. This version, however, would export not only the positive text but also national juristic opinions, policy choices and cultural particularities inscribed in French law.

II. SOVIET LAW GOES WESTERN

As the Cold War grew more intense, David dedicated much attention and concern to writing about the laws of the Soviet Union. In the highly polarized environment of the time, the differences between East and West were at the forefront of academic and political consciousness. Differences between economic and

---

[46] *See e.g.*, David, *supra* note 34, at vii.

[47] In principle, David was not opposed to France borrowing from its periphery: "The solutions admitted in one of these countries can serve to clarify the solutions that should be applied in another: in a general fashion, they can be easily adopted there. The study of the Brazilian Civil Code of 1916 or the study of the Peruvian Civil Code of 1938 or the new Italian Civil Code of 1942 can suggest reforms to the French legislator that, in general, do not repudiate the spirit of our law and would be easy to accomplish in the framework of our legal institutions." David, *supra* note 11, at 221.

[48] Indeed, David's acceptance speech upon receiving the Erasmus prize in 1976 denies that this was his objective: "I believed that there (in comparative law) was something very useful for humanity, and I really had the feeling that the way for me to serve science, to serve my country, was not by asking people to copy French law, but it was by working to improve the law in all countries of the world and in particular in Europe." David, *supra* note 1, at 165.

social systems were deemed irreconcilable. Capitalism and communism stood as mortal enemies. Pervasive state planning was perceived as a menace to private action and market economies.

A fundamental element of David's classification scheme was the ideological commonality of family members within any one grouping. Developed in his early work, this ideological component rested upon three pillars for the Romano-Germanic family: capitalism, liberal democracy and Christianity.[49] At the opposite end of the socio-political spectrum David catalogued the Soviet Union as the second principal legal family then existing in the world in his early writings in 1950: "given its socialist structure and Soviet economy, the law of the USSR acquires a profound originality, separated completely from the family of Western law."[50]

The Soviet Union and its zones of influence in Eastern Europe constituted one of five main legal families identified in his comparative law treatise.[51] While David recognized a common background shared by Russian law and the Western family,[52] he did not hesitate to draw a sharp distinction with Soviet law:

---

[49] See David, supra note 11, at 224. David later rejected this narrow formulation in favor of a more inclusive, albeit abstract, definition: "In my Traite, I indicate my belief that it was possible to view that unity (of Western law) as based on a tripartite foundation consisting of politics, economics and mores. . . . I no longer maintain those views. As a matter of fact, the "Western" system embraces nations whose constitutions and political regimes are quite diverse. Moreover, all the nations of the West have in varying degrees entered upon the path of socialism, and I think they can proceed a considerable distance along that road without repudiating their "membership" in the system of "Western" law. Finally, numerous non-Christian countries of Africa and Asia have embraced the system without adhering to the principles of Christian morality. None of these factors is essential. . . . What appears to me today as essentially characteristic of "Western" civilization is the opinion regarding the role in society played by law."); see also David, supra note 32, at 129–130.

[50] David, supra note 11, at 329; see also René David, "Les Données Fondamentales du Droit Soviétique" in René David and J. N. Hazard (eds.), Le Droit Soviétique Tome 1 (Institut de Droit Comparé de l'Université de Paris) Librairie Générale de Droit et de Jurisprudence 180 (Paris, 1954). ("Soviet law: a law that does not want to be associated with any absolute value, a law that is asserted to have no permanent value and which openly declares awaiting and expecting its (own) decline, is evidently something other than our Western conception of law; one can legitimately hesitate in qualifying it as 'law' ").

[51] See also David, supra note 11, at 167 (David concludes in his early work, despite the historical and social continuity of Russian law and Western law: "The construction of a socialist law and the elaboration of this notion are due in consequence, rather exclusively, to Soviet leaders and jurists").

[52] David, supra note 50, at 61, 70 ("In conclusion to this study, it seems possible to articulate the following propositions. Russian law (prior to 1917), under the influence of the Church through the mediation of Greek law, and under the influence of legal scholarship of German and French jurists, did not remain in relation to French law, such an original law (legal system) as is, for example, English law or Muslim law. As a result of its juridical notions, to which it makes appeal, its manner of classifying such notions, its reasoning procedures which, to its jurists, seem the most natural, Russian law resembles French law and is part of the large family of Roman law." "Without at all denying the revolutionary fervor and objectives, one does not hesitate to put the accent, in the U.S.S.R., on the constraints that unite Russia today and yesterday. The expanse of Russia, its ground, its climate, continue in general fashion what they were forty years ago. The Russian soul is, in large measure, the product of these geographic givens, even under the influence of a Christianity which had taken particular forms.")

In spite of all that has been written about its so-called socialization, French law, despite all the changes undertaken, is the law of a capitalist, individualist, liberal society that cannot in any way be compared to the socialist society of the U.S.S.R., and French law, like the laws of other bourgeois societies in Europe and America, consequently remains attached to a system completely different than that of Soviet law . . . A veritable revolution would be necessary, overturning the foundations of our social order and our economic order even, for French law to join Soviet Law.[53]

By 1966, David had softened his tone. Yet he still believed that Soviet law merited being classified as a separate family:

one passes into a new world by crossing the frontier of a country of the socialist camp; the problems are different . . . and the words themselves have a different sense. . . . For these reasons Soviet law must be classed in a different 'family.'[54]

He identified a principle of "socialist legality" as the defining characteristic of the legal family of the Soviet Union and its satellites.[55] Its significance was that law is openly subordinate to a socialist economic order. However, David no longer painted the differences in stark contrast to the West.[56] Indeed, much historical and sociological information fills the pages of his second comparative law treatise which emphasizes the close links to the Romano-Germanic group, within the Western family, prior to the eruption of socialism.

By the 1980's, David was actually arguing for commonality across these erstwhile irreconcilable legal families.[57] He reoriented his socio-legal method to highlight the legal similarities existing among the world's superpowers. By this point in his scholarship, David had in fact begun to reformulate the defining criteria of legal families. His tripartite inquiry based on economics, politics and religion had given way to one principal element: "the role in society played by law."[58] For the Western legal family, the defining characteristic was faith in the rule of law; that is, an overriding belief that disputes in society should be

---

[53] *See* David *supra* note 11 at 333, 335–6, 319 ("Soviet law possesses, by rapport of our French law, particular traits which confer upon it total originality, to such point that it is impossible to attach it, like it would be possible with ancient Russian law, to the system of Roman law, and there is reason to assign it to its proper place within the divisions of contemporary systems of law. The originality of Soviet Law is based essentially on two things: [it] is tied to a different philosophy than that upon which French law and the common law rests; [it] is the product of a new organization of production and is in narrow rapport with the socialist structure of the Soviet economy") *Id*. at 319.

[54] David, *supra* note 12, at 144.

[55] *Id*. at 196 ("The regime established in the U.S.S.R, however, changes the fundamentals of every problem, and the principle of socialist legality proclaimed in this country differs from the principle of the supremacy of law, *i.e.* 'the rule of law,' such as it is found in the bourgeois countries.").

[56] *Id*. at 260. David dices it up in the following manner: "Soviet law . . . inherited the concept of the legal rule shared . . . by the Romano-Germanic family; . . . Soviet law is certainly original with respect to its categories and concepts, for while the form . . . has been retained a total renewal of their substance has been achieved."

[57] René David, "Two Conceptions of Social Order," 52 *U. Cin. L. Rev.* 136, 141–42 (". . . law means unrelieved anarchy.")

[58] David, *supra* note 32, at 130.

resolved by laws and judges as a good in itself.[59] Initially, David's use of this criterion cemented French law and common law under the rubric of Western law. Not long after, however, he expanded the category of Western law to include Soviet law and the laws of the republics of Eastern Europe.[60]

By emphasizing an identical role for law in Western and Eastern Europe, despite the public denouncements of the latter, David was able to argue their commonality:

> The U.S.S.R. and the socialist or people's republics of Europe are still states where the social order is founded on law: a 'principle of socialist legality' is simply decorative bunting. In these countries, many people, in their inner consciences, do not expect any substantial change in this state of affairs within any foreseeable future. Western legal scholars may see in this experience a confirmation of their wisdom: a civilized society cannot live without law, and the disappearance of law means unrelieved anarchy.[61]

The point of this passage is that underlying both Socialist and Western societies is a common legal ideology: specifically, a belief in the rule of law. David's close identification of law across the Cold War divide is quite remarkable.[62] Of course, he recognized great differences in the way the legal systems operated. Contract law, for example, though not vastly distinct in doctrinal terms was construed quite differently in the Soviet bloc. It represented for the most part an exercise in state planning and goal-setting, rather than an exchange of binding promises by arms-length parties.

David dedicated much intellectual energy to elaborating the arguments for placing the Soviet Union within the Western legal family in later writings. His work on the concept of socialist legality, as illustrated in the passage above, dismissed the substantiality of any such concept. David denied any separate value to the socialist end of the locution. Soviet legal ideology became mere false consciousness, rhetoric that the Soviet people could actually see beyond. In its place, a more basic legal ideology was said to exist that was shared with the West: that is the rule of law, tout court. In this way, Soviet law while contradicting some of the earlier defining elements of Western law, could still be included in the same legal family, if only as a wayward son. David concluded that the persistent differences did not exclude it from the same family. Rather

---

[59] *Id.* at 131 ("All we mean to affirm here is the existence, at the present time, of a 'Western' concept of law and its role, extolling the 'Rule of Law.'") This concept is opposed in particular to that of Marxist doctrine, in which law is regarded as a pis-aller, valuable during the transitional period of socialism at most . . .").

[60] David, *supra* note 57 (Western law is contrasted with its foil, Far Eastern law, which emphasizes conciliation and the community over individual rights. Litigation is the last recourse, fomenting divisions rather than resolution.).

[61] *Id.* at 141–42.

[62] Specifically, David in his earlier work highlighted the differences of Soviet Supreme Tribunal which: "indicates to [other] tribunals, in a way which is obligatory for them, how to interpret a certain text of Soviet law in the future; or how to fill a certain gap within Soviet law." David, *supra* note 11, at 324.

the differences signified a betrayal, evidence of a deviation from the true, more indelible family.

Here is a curious turn in the general postulates of David's own comparativist principles. Taken at its extreme, it may erode the usefulness of family distinctions altogether. In effect, all legal systems could be reconceived as emanating from the same legal family, the family of humanity, and their differences as deviations from some core commonality. Such a core would, of course, then require definition: no easy feat if one is to avoid the same dead ends reached by naturalist theories. In other words, an all-inclusive concept of commonality would occupy the same role that natural law thinking had occupied in an earlier era.

The work performed by the concept of multiple legal families is intended precisely to avoid these critiques of universalism. David's scheme accommodated significant differences across legal systems in different families. Potential objections to comparative work or cross-national borrowings could then be rebutted by assertions of a family commonality based on societal similarity. Distinguishing between one family and another is based on differences between legal ideologies. Therefore, if legal ideology no longer accounts for the distinction, and if no other distinguishing feature takes its place, David's own intellectual edifice collapses. The result could only be a return to naturalist thinking, a unitary, core-type referent for law.

This is the high-wire act that David's writings on the Soviet Union entail: arguing for cross-ideological commonality while at the same time avoiding a universalist natural law. An interesting comparison, in this respect, would be Nazi law. Although not excluded from the Western family, David presented it as a deviation from the ideological line of Western law. Indeed, David's insistence on an ideological commonality in his comparative law scheme responds in large part to Nazi atrocities. It offers some measure to hold members of a common legal family accountable, at a minimum, by rooting law in a broader morality or set of principles beyond the nation-state.

In the Soviet case, several practical effects can be envisaged as the motivation for this project. If generally accepted, it could lead to more Western influence over Soviet rule-making. It offers a way to justifiably catalogue differences as deviations from a common set of historical family practices. Ultimately, it prepares the way for incorporating the Soviet bloc back into the Western family of law. Accepting the prodigal child as one's own is a surer route to re-unification than ostracism and demonization would be.

III. UNIDROIT FOR ALL

Throughout his life, David was involved in one way or another with projects of legal unification. His first job was as at the then newly-created International Institute for the Unification of Private Law, which ultimately produced the

Unidroit Principles, discussed further below.[63] Later in the late 1960s and early 1970s, he was appointed representative of France to the United Nations Commission for the Unification of International Trade Law. During his time as chief of the French delegation, David was vested in one central proposition. He wanted to establish the principle that a treaty's substantive rules become international law as a result of mere inaction by contracting states.[64] According to the proposal, conventions would become effectively ratified, in the absence of an explicit rejection by national authorities, through the mere passage of time. David recognized the ambitiousness of his suggestion, but also considered it commensurate with the stature of the specific law then under consideration:

> It was, in relation to traditional methods, a revolution; but it seemed to me indispensable to admit if one really wanted to reinstate order to international society. The United Nations and certain other specialized international organizations should be charged with the Universities' former task; it belonged to them to declare the 'common law.'[65]

His proposal was ultimately dropped from the final version of the Vienna Convention of 1980.[66]

Another major project of legal draftsmanship was his Civil Code for Ethiopia. David was practically the sole redactor of that country's core codification, coming into effect in 1960. It would come as no great surprise that it was modeled closely on the Napoleonic Code.[67] As a practitioner of comparativism, David knew little about Ethiopia,[68] its language, or its culture and only visited the country for brief periods:

> Residing in Ethiopia on a permanent basis would have been, despite however much I was tempted, an error: Paris offered the resources in documentation and the possibility for contacts and discussion which I would have never found in the Ethiopian capital.[69]

---

[63] *See* René David, *Le Droit du Commerce International: Réflexions d'un Comparatiste sur le Droit International Privé* (Paris, 1987). David was the first secretary general adjoint of the organization. *See also*, René David, "Le Droit du Commerce International: Une nouvelle tâche pour les legislateurs nationaux ou une nouvelle 'lex mercatoria,' " in *New Directions in International Trade Law* (Dobbs Ferry, 1977).

[64] *Id.* at 66–67.

[65] David, *supra* note 1, at 152–55.

[66] *See* René David, "Renaissance de l'idée de jus gentium," in *Le Droit Comparé: Droits d'Hier, Droits de Demain* 325 (Paris 1982).

[67] David muses that he would have preferred to draft a more flexible, less technical manual which would be given the force of law. The concern was the lack of juristic skill available in the country to implement a classic-type code. However, he notes that the Ethiopian Emperor who commissioned the work wanted a modern code—and so he provided one. David, *supra* note 1, at 171.

[68] David himself admitted: "I knew nothing about Ethiopia. The first thing I undertook was to instruct myself on the country, its history, its mores. I read everything that was published in Western languages on the subject, and I took two years of Amharric language in the School of Oriental Languages. Studying this language was not unuseful, even if I never was able to understand or speak well enough." *Id.* at 170.

[69] *Id.* at 169.

Indeed, the draft code was written in French and then translated: only one other member of the drafting committee spoke French. Under David's scheme, extensive research is required in first designating family groupings and for understanding non-related legal systems. Within one's own legal family, under this same scheme, positive law is highly interchangeable without much extensive investigation. For him, Ethiopia was essentially configured as part of the Western legal family as a result of centuries of Christian domination and the lack of a religious or sacred character in its native customs. David noted that there were no protests against his code: "If there is still some attachment to the Ethiopian customs it is a matter of sentiment or self-interest."[70]

This mode of work is somewhat striking when considered in light of David's views on expanding the scope of comparativism to sociological and historical elements. As an heir to legal historicism, one might expect David to be skeptical of large-scale projects of unification and codification. His conceptual premises lean in the direction of a more fluid and more textured notion of legal development. Similarly, his grouping of legal families is based on deep societal distinctions, which would raise doubts about the sameness of Ethiopia and the possibilities for unproblematic unification.

Indeed, David did harbor misgivings about legal unification.[71] He understood it as an inherently political act.[72] Furthermore, he was discomfited by wholesale attempts to make diverse national law uniform. He expressed his concerns in terms of different national legal techniques, incommensurate legal consciousness from one national system to another, as well as the varying degrees of effectiveness of a uniform law in different societies.

Nonetheless, a significant part of David's work was dedicated to projects of codification and specifically to legal unification.[73] He believed that unification was inevitable, due to practical considerations, and the real question was how and not if it would be done.[74] David managed this apparent inconsistency between his legal theory and his academic practice by prescribing his own formula for unification. His prescription was closely tied to the project of comparativism discussed above:

"The presentation of legal rules is made according to a limited number of models in the world. In this more or less conscious way, the legislators of different countries have adopted certain models; the model of continental European codes; the model of

[70] David, *supra* note 32, at 511.

[71] *See* René David, "L'avenir des droits Européens: Unification ou Harmonisation," in *Le Droit Comparé: Droits d'Hier, Droits de Demain*, 297 (Paris, 1982) ("I always experience a certain apprehension, I avow, before the size of the work that would constitute, in a general way, the unification of European law. It is only in the areas where the terrain appears particularly suited, and where an important practical interest is in play, that there is reason . . . for this ambitious project.")

[72] René David, "Les méthodes de l'unification," in *Le Droit Comparé: Droits d'Hier, Droits de Demain*, 316–17 (Paris 1968) (1982).

[73] Indeed in his first comparative law treatise, he asserted that the principal interest of a comparative method, at the time, was to promote the development of international commerce and to reinforce peace. David, *supra* note 11, at 217.

[74] David, *supra* note 72, at 304–318.

Soviet codes, the model of common law countries. In asking that there be established, in the heart of each of these legal families, or for certain areas by accord among them or among certain ones of them, 'bodies of model law,' we ask only, in effect, that the reality of contemporary juridical orders be expressed with more clarity."[75]

In effect, his efforts were aimed at forestalling initiatives for more radical, and according to him superficial, forms of unification.[76] Rather than strictly uniform laws, he advocated a more gradual harmonization of the law of a certain field.[77] It would entail a more substantial and protracted exchange between legal systems before the stage could be set for more pervasive uniformity. In the meantime, he was not averse to national adaptations of international models. Thus, the differences between national systems would be acknowledged, and at the same time the general ends sought could be accomplished. Desired outcomes to particular issues may be thus made uniform while the legal means may vary from country to country. He also believed that certain areas of law were more susceptible to harmonization than others. These would have already experienced an aggressive process of cross-fertilization and comparative analysis. Commercial law, for instance, was the main field in which David believed efforts at streamlining were well-directed.[78] This notion would be especially important to justifying harmonization across different legal families. In its absence, harmonization would need to be effectuated through a more openly political process of settlement and accord.

David's teachings came to fruition in the elaboration of the Unidroit Principles of International Commercial Contracts, completed in May of 1994: four years after his death.[79] The decades-long enterprise was promoted by the International Institute for the Unification of Private Law, an independent inter-governmental organization, founded in 1926 upon the initiative of the Italian government, and where David first began his career.[80] He came to preside over its working group of ten jurists from different countries ultimately responsible for the document. Unidroit is not an international treaty or a model law, rather it is a separate body of harmonized contract law. It comes into operation when selected as the

---

[75] *Id.* at 309.

[76] *See* David, *supra* note 1, at 298 ("Legal unification is an extremely difficult task, and [mere] enthusiasm could not replace either science or work. We should distrust enterprises which would lead to superficial success. In the interest of unification itself we should consider with reserve projects which are too ambitious . . . and prefer . . . more modest projects but which would permit real progress.")

[77] David argued that unification and harmonization were not different, thus entailing a choice between them. Rather, he described unification as one possible form of harmonization. And, what was clearly desirable (at least for European law) was harmonization. His own preference for the latter, however, tended decidedly against simply making laws more uniform. *See id.* at 296.

[78] *See id.* at 297.

[79] *Le Monde* (June 13, 1990).

[80] Interestingly, David began his professional career and first undertook comparative studies in 1930 as a French representative to the Society of Nation's International Institute for the Unification of Private Law. Related to that time, David confesses: "The Institute gave me sufficient to do so I would not at any moment feel without work; but it left me great liberty, the international unification of private law not appearing like a job requiring inconsiderable haste." David, *supra* note 1, at 27.

governing law by contractual parties. Drawing on the concepts of the Western legal family, this code seeks to replace varying national legislation as the law of international sales. Its rules of contract, no less than a treaty or model law, strive for uniformity and regularity in the law of international transactions.

This type of exercise, although at first blush inconsistent with an unbridled socio-historical perspective on law, is actually quite coherent with David's model of comparative law. In fact, it is directly in keeping with his vision of legal families. It is a work of intra-family comparativism par excellence. Additionally, it is not in furtherance of a particular national system. It stands for the construction of a transnational private law. The end product is quite proximate to the national systems which vigorous comparative practice, according to his own formula for comparativism, would produce over time. The project of Unidroit was, for David, merely a formalized rendition of the natural development of international sales law, in which the Western legal family had already led the way. The process was conducted by jurists making the selections and deciding on the particular mixes of cross-fertilization.[81] It claims to be strictly non-political and technical as opposed to the divisiveness of international conventions and national legislation.

In any case, Unidroit represents the tangible achievement of David's intellectual vision. Similar regimes in other substantive areas of law would surely have occupied his attention had he lived longer. This exercise of unification however has the effect of obscuring the interests and competing programs inherent in law-making. This obscuring aspect is exacerbated by the exclusive environment of juristic law-making. While these practices would no longer be defensible on the stated basis of naturalism or positivism, as discussed at length above, David repackages it in the frame of a sociologically originated set of legal models or families constituting a handful of possible alternatives. Within the legal family, a common law is produced through the work of comparativism. Across these, one model may predominate in a given area of law.[82] It is these latter situations which are then ripe for unification, under David's matrix. Apart from the conceptual apparatus, perceived in David's work, a particularly illuminating remark of his sheds light on his perspective:

> After a period of eclipse, due to the pessimism engendered by two atrocious world wars, the generous universalism of the year 1900 is incumbent if one intends to create the desirable harmony of a world that henceforth knows itself as one.[83]

---

[81] David considered there to be two dimensions to the harmonization of laws: legislative and scholarly. He values scholarly writing more: "The doctrinal (legal scholarship) aspect is in my eyes essential, . . . an inter-European juridical harmony depends on . . . us . . . It will exist when we are penetrated by the feeling that a European law exists . . ."). *Id.* at 301

[82] See David, *Réflexions supra* note 63, at 34 ("When a number of states, of large importance for international commerce, are in accord on an edict, having commerce in view, on substantive norms which in their eyes conform to the interests and justice of all, would it not be reasonable to see in the dispositions in question the expression of a jus gentium according to justice and to apply these rules outside of the circle of contracting states?")

[83] David, *supra* note 72, at 316.

IV. CONTINUING INFLUENCE

More often than not, René David's name is cited in comparative law textbooks as a passing reference—no more than a place marker to note the discipline's historical pedigree. The one-line mention typically conveys no more than the simple idea of legal families for which he has come to be remembered. However, this notion of legal families is not reducible to the mere commonplace that national legal systems share similar elements across countries. The logical extension of this platitude would be, also unremarkably, that family affinity depends on the elements chosen to identify family characteristics. And, sure enough, David is not the only legal scholar who has ordered the world's legal systems according to a specific trait or set of traits. Other comparativists have varied the factors to come up with different groupings. Taken by itself, this idea of classification is but a wooden reflection of the vast program which David sketched out for comparativism.

Regardless of the merits we perceive for it in the world now, or even historically, one of the marks of accomplishment of his system is that it made common sense. It was not rejected outright as anachronous with legal theory of his time, nor with many legal theories in our own time. On the contrary, it was accepted as plausible; no small feat for a reconstructive project with the ambition of re-invigorating liberal law. In our generation, we are for the most part only aware of the technical apparatus surrounding David's intellectual project. Absent from our active consciousness is the impact and institutional meaning of continuing to conceive of legal systems as containing pre-figured characteristics beyond individual human agency, characteristics which are then shared by related systems.

Deploying this artifice, David sought to re-invigorate the role of legal positivism in the mid-twentieth century. He constructed the apparatus primarily as a reaction to the prevailing critiques of his time. He worked around the obvious failings of previous legal ideas to fashion a program capable of withstanding immediate rejection and capable of attracting adherents. His reformulation of the sociological conception of law is an important element. The role he sought for comparative law in offering information about related legal systems is another. More important, for us, are the rough edges we find in his work, where his conceptual apparatus does not neatly fit his institutional objectives. It is precisely in areas, such as reconciling Soviet Law or fitting Latin America within the Romano-Germanic family, that the true meaning of David's comparative work is observed.

In a subtle and understated way, René David was able to launch new ideas in the mode of explaining how things work. Obtaining acceptance of profoundly controversial ideas in this manner is without doubt the mark of a disciplinary master. Thus, his name need not be remembered as simply a perfunctory footnote to the discipline's predecessors. Nor need it be read as a slightly embarrassing version of comparative law, hopelessly outdated and outmoded. On the contrary, David stands as a prominent intellectual interlocutor—one whose ideas should not be accepted as just obvious. Instead, his projects and projects like his should be seen for what they are. Arguing for a transnational law removed from the reach of local actors, even while he argues for its social specificity, ultimately mystifies law and legal practices. Orienting legal technique in different societies to replicate the policy choices of France may very well be unwise for those other societies. Limiting control over the distributional impact of international private law rules under the guise of technical unification disenfranchises those who are thereby most disadvantaged. These are all political positions promoted through institutionally-entrenched practices presented as neutral, as common sense. Just like David, their consolidation as obvious or background fact makes them that much harder to resist precisely because we often do not know what they really represent.

Fig. 1 R.B. Schlesinger (1908–1996)
(Reproduced by kind permission of the University of California, Hastings)

Fig. 2 Rodolfo Sacco
(Reproduced by kind permission of the C.T.N.—Universita degli Studi di Trento.
Photo by Paolo Chistè)

9

The Comparative Jurisprudence of Schlesinger and Sacco: A Study in Legal Influence

UGO MATTEI*

INTRODUCTION

This chapter is an exercise in comparison. It seeks to compare two recognized masters of our field, Rudolf B. Schlesinger[1] and Rodolfo Sacco.[2] The proposition that it wishes to test is the following: structural comparativism, (*à la Sacco*), an approach to comparative law which focuses on the structure and the relationship of the different components of legal institutions (legal formants), can be interpreted as a postmodern European development, whose roots can be located in the U.S. and traced to the work of Schlesinger and of American legal realism. In the passage from American modernism to European postmodernism resides the key to understanding the relationship between Schlesinger and Sacco as well as their continuing influence on contemporary comparative jurisprudence.[3]

In my opinion, comparing legal phenomena is a complex exercise that should include the following activities.[4] First, a comparison has to gather and describe analogies and differences. Second, it has to view the objects of observation in relationship to each other to detect transplants, rather than reinventing the wheel. Third, a comparison has to develop a theory to explain the observations. Finally, comparison might derive some normative lessons from the process of observation and explanation.

The quality of each of these processes can be evaluated from a scholarly perspective. The more the data gathering is based on primary sources the more

---

* I wish to thank Annelise Riles, Steven Schlesinger, Fay Freed, Rodolfo Sacco, Elisabetta Grande, Anna di Robilant, Filippo Sartori, Andrea Pradi, David Kennedy, Duncan Kennedy, Pier Giuseppe Monateri and Mauro Bussani for participating in the process leading to this paper.

[1] Rudolf B. Schlesinger (1909–1996), Late Professor of Law Emeritus, University of California, Hastings College of the Law; Late William Nelson Cromwell Professor of International and Comparative Law Emeritus, Cornell University.

[2] Rodolfo Sacco (b. 1923) Professore Emerito di Diritto Civile, Università di Torino.

[3] This idea is developed in Ugo Mattei & A. Di Robilant, "The Art and Science of Critical Scholarship. Post-Modernism and International Style in the Legal Architecture of Europe," 75 *Tulane L. Rev.* 1053 (2001).

valuable it is. The more there is evidence of a process of contamination by means of thorough historical inquiry the more convincing will be the "transplant hypothesis." The more broad and far-reaching the theory one is able to develop to explain the data, the more valuable and interesting the contribution to our understanding will be. The more convincing the policy advocated, the more worthwhile it would have been to have spelled it out. This basic recipe is of course compatible with the idea that the questions we ask determine the answers that we might receive and, as a consequence, the very choice of the objects to compare is not in itself a neutral exercise.

Usually one compares "the law" in country A with "the law" in country B. The object of observation is complex because the law is by no means a static monolithic unitary phenomenon but is the aggregate of a variety of formants.[5] Comparing two scholars might appear a simpler enterprise, one that significantly reduces the scope and variety of the formants that are involved. However, just as when one compares one decision of the California Supreme Court with one decision of the German Constitutional Court, it is necessary to situate the objects of comparison contextually.

Comparing Schlesinger with Sacco is no easy task. To begin with, because of the tenor of this book it is not enough to compare their work. There is a need to compare them as people in order to ascertain the impact their lives had on their work. This requires a sociological and anthropological inquiry, a consideration of their personality as well as the institutional constraints and incentives under which they have acted.

Second, because of the quantity and the importance of their published work, because of the lengths of their lives (they both published extensively for more than 50 years) and because of their major impact in the construction of our field, the story that I am going to tell will be a story of legal influence, of the major and potentially unique impact they had on the path of the law (or at least on our understanding of it) on both sides of the Atlantic Ocean.

Following the methodological steps that I have outlined, this chapter proceeds as follows. Part 2 details relevant data. Part 3 runs the transplant test[6] discussing the relationship between common core research, the most enduring legacy of Schlesinger,[7] and legal formants the manifesto of Sacco's school.[8] Part 4 attempts to explain the relationship between the two methods as an evolution

---

[4] *See* J. C. Reitz, "How to do Comparative Law," 46 *Am.J. Comp. Law* 617 (1998) (attempting to give a modern normative theory of comparative law).

[5] *See* Rodolfo Sacco, "Legal Formants. A Dynamic Approach to Comparative Law," 39 *Am. J. Comp. L.* 1 (1991).

[6] *See* Alan Watson, *Legal Transplants. An Approach To Comparative Law* (1974) (on the major role of borrowing in the marketplace of legal ideas). On legal transplants as a methodology for comparative law, *see* William Ewald, "Comparative Jurisprudence II. The Logic of Legal Transplants," 43 *Am J. Comp. L.* 489 (1995).

[7] *See* Ru dolf B. Schlesinger (ed.), *Formation of Contracts. A Study in the Common Core of Legal Systems* (1968)

[8] *See* Rodolfo Sacco, "Legal Formants. A Dynamic Approach to Comparative Law," 39 *Am. J. Comp. L.* 1 (1990)

from a modernist to a postmodernist approach in Western jurisprudence. Part 5 encourages the demise of the residual legacy of positivism as a necessary step in the development of comparative jurisprudence.

DATA GATHERING

My data are first hand. They are based on years of personal friendship with both Schlesinger and Sacco. I was a student of both and I have been successor to both of them, in the Chair of Comparative Law at Hastings and in that of Civil Law at Turin respectively. Since Rudolf B. Schlesinger is no longer with us, I have used a two hundred page memoir the Schlesinger family has been kind enough to make available to me.[9] Together with the time we spent together, I received from Rodolfo Sacco a five page personal history that he considers relevant in the development of his scholarly personality.

Schlesinger

Rudolf Schlesinger's life spans the tragedy of last century.[10] Born in Munich to a wealthy Jewish family, the son of a lawyer and the relative of bankers, the young "Rudi" grew up in an exceptionally happy family background, with loving responsible parents. He was never spoiled but neither was he deprived.

His exceptional intellectual gifts, his healthy self-esteem and his warm and curious humanity evolved very early. He was always the best student (only one girl in primary school provided competition!) and his results were sometimes real records (many times he was among the very top in the history of the prestigious educational institutions he attended). He was gifted in sports (a good tennis player, cyclist and hiker), handsome and clearly successful with the opposite sex. His success story continued throughout law school in Munich. He lived for a year in Geneva, he managed to graduate at the very top of his class and to continue on his path for a doctorate, although Nazi law precluded him from taking the exams necessary in Germany to practice as an attorney. Short trips to Switzerland, Italy and the Dalmatian coast, trained him to be curious about and

---

[9] I actually edited the published volume. *See* Ugo Mattei and Andrea Pradi (eds), *Rudolf B. Schlesinger, Memories* (2000).

[10] Articles on Schlesinger in English by F. Juenger and in German by H. Kötz are available in Marcus Lutter et al., *Der Einfluss Deutscher Emigranten auf die Rechtsentwicklung in den USA und Deutschland* (1993). *See also* Richard Buxbaum & Ugo Mattei, "Rudolf B. Schlesinger, 1909–1996," 45 *Am. J. Comp. L.* 1 (1997); U. Mattei, "The Copernican Revolution in Legal Scholarship. In Loving Memory of Rudolf B. Schlesinger," 20 *Hastings Int. & Comp. L. Rev.* 23 (1997); A full bibliography of Schlesinger is also available in the *Festschrift* Issue of the *American Journal of Comparative Law* presented to him in 1995. *See* Richard Buxbaum, "R. Schlesinger. A Tribute" 43 *Am. J. Comp. L.* 217 (1995). Finally one can consult B. F. Willcox, "Rudolf B. Schlesinger. World Lawyer," 60 *Cornell L. Q.* 919 (1975) (being the symposium issue on the occasion of his retirement from Cornell).

understanding of diversity. He was always interested in the arts. His memoir does not show any particular political passion, however. As one who was privileged and free from frustration, we can perhaps locate him moderately to the left of the political spectrum, possibly influenced by his father, himself a social democrat busy as an attorney helping weaker, less fortunate people. However, these are only personal assumptions.

Nazi power, however, was beginning to strike the Jewish community hard. While the Schlesingers were still living, as were most German Jews, anxiously denying the real measure of the tragedy that would shortly follow, he was advised by his doctoral supervisor (the well known German commercial law scholar Professor Müller Ehrzbach) that in a matter of weeks it would not be possible for any Jew to obtain a doctorate from a German university. At this point, he had not written a word of his dissertation. Working harder than he ever did before he was able to complete his thesis and to obtain the title of doctor, with the kind of recognition that was granted to only a handful of people in the twentieth century.

As Nazi brutality spread, Schlesinger found himself working as a lawyer for the bank that many years before had been funded by his ancestors. The bank had mostly Jewish clients and Schlesinger's work as a legal adviser could be seen as that of a formalist, strictly interpreting the flood of discriminatory legislation in order to allow clients to save some of their capital against Nazi rapacity. Perhaps it was in this capacity that he understood the real nature of legal formalism: an exercise in dissimulation and of hiding the ball, sometimes aiding a good cause, but in normal circumstances denying legitimacy and open, democratic decision making.

The decision of whether to stay or abandon Europe was tabled for quite a long time in Schlesinger's family. It was taken rather late, right after Kristallnacht, after his father had already been disbarred, friends and relatives arrested and the hope of saving any of the family wealth had already vanished. Because of rather fortunate circumstances—his father was a U.S. citizen by birth—although he had never actually lived in the U.S. Schlesinger was able to claim citizenship and a passport to freedom at the very last minute before final irremediable catastrophe. The Schlesinger's boat left Europe in December 1939.

His arrival in New York was indeed a new start; no money, no job, and two elderly parents to care for. However, Schlesinger was bright, young and charming. On the professional side, he found a rather attractive job teaching teenage girls at an élite high school in New York City. Shortly after that he enrolled at Columbia Law School, worked hard, became Editor in Chief (the first and perhaps only non-native English speaker) of the *Columbia Law Review*, graduated at the top of his class, and won a prestigious clerkship with Judge Lehman at the New York Court of Appeal. He worked at a major New York law firm and after declining an offer to become partner, found his way into academia getting a teaching job at Cornell Law School in 1948. In due course he was appointed to the prestigious Cromwell Chair in International and Comparative Law. He turned down offers from several other prestigious schools he visited, and became involved in some important law reform projects. He continued to travel extensively within the U.S. and Europe. In 1975 he took Emeritus status from Cornell and joined the Hastings faculty where he retired in 1995 just one year before his death in 1996.

During a journey in California he re-encountered his wife to be Putti (herself the escaped daughter of German Jewish bankers and young sister of one of Schlesinger's best friends from Europe). Together, they were to live a very intense and happy married life; they had three children and travelled a great deal, mostly in Europe and the U.S. His memoir is full of accounts of wonderful vacations, evidence that he was not a workaholic incapable of having fun. If one can attempt an evaluation from outside one would say that Schlesinger was exceptionally endowed with emotional intelligence. He was an accomplished man in every way, able to live a remarkably happy life given the circumstances.

The importance and durability of an academic's legacy to a scholarly community provides a measure for evaluating their work. In Schlesinger's case, one could simply say that he was the founder of comparative law in America. It is true that a number of major comparativists, mainly from Europe, were active in the U.S. during the last century. Some of them, like Ernst Rabel[11] and Stefan Riesenfeld,[12] although considered founding figures, left their most important legacy in the domain of international law. Others, like Max Rheinstein,[13] trained some major contemporary figures in our field such as Mary Ann Glendon[14] and John Langbein,[15] but had more narrowly defined specializations, and have not attached their name to a defining work in the field.

In the case of Schlesinger, the nature of his scholarly output justifies the major visibility he has been able to achieve. An early introductory book, published as early as 1950,[16] (squarely in the Cases and Materials tradition of American legal education), whose sixth edition appeared in 1998, made him "the man with the book" from the very beginning of his academic life. This book has been, and still is, the best selling teaching tool in American law schools: Schlesinger's long-lasting intellectual legacy therefore being, for most American lawyers, the author of the only reading they have done in comparative law ever. Moreover,

---

[11] *See* Chapter 7, this volume.

[12] Stefan Riesenfeld (1908–1999), trained in Germany and Italy, died as a Professor of Law Emeritus at Boalt Hall School, while still active as a Professor of Comparative Law at Hastings College of the Law. See the chapter devoted to him in Lutter, *supra* note 10.

[13] Max Rheinstein, himself a German Professor, was long active in America as the Director of the Institute of Comparative Law at the University of Chicago. *See* A. Sprudzs, *Max Rheinstein's Writings, A Bibliography* (1968).

[14] Professor of Law at Harvard and co-author of standard teaching tools in the domain of Comparative Law including *Comparative Legal Traditions in a Nutshell* (1982) and Mary Ann Glendon et al., *Comparative Legal Traditions* (2d ed., 1994).

[15] Professor of Law at Yale and author of some very influential pieces of comparative law such as "The German Advantage in Civil Procedure" 52 *U. Chicago L. Rev.* 823 (1985) and John Langbein, *Comparative Criminal Procedure. Germany* (St. Paul, 1977).

[16] Rudolf B. Schlesinger, *Comparative Law. Cases, Text, Materials* (1950).

being for many years the only author of a comprehensive work in the United States has allowed Schlesinger to capitalize on much of the worldwide influence and fame that comes to a scholar from being a leader in a leading legal tradition.[17] Indeed, both because of the subject matter and because of the major interest attracted abroad by U.S. law in the post World War II period, for many (perhaps most) European lawyers (not only specialized comparativists) Schlesinger was, ironically, the best known name in American academia. This exceptional intellectual visibility was not only due to the rather fortunate circumstances that determined his publication of the first Case Book of Comparative Law in history.[18]

Also in the domain of legal research, Schlesinger has been a creative and influential innovator. In the early sixties, at Cornell, he launched and carried out, with exceptional organizational and fundraising skills, a collective enterprise, known as the Cornell Common Core Project whose results have been published in two monumental volumes on the issue of the formation of contracts.[19] The importance of this contribution, however, goes well beyond the comparative study of contract law. The "Cornell Project" has been a turning point in comparative law methodology in at least two respects.

First, it has been the application in legal scholarship of that same factual approach (or case method) that in the domain of legal anthropology was developed by, among others, Bronislaw Malinowski, Karl Llewellyn and Adamson Hobel earlier in the last century and which is regarded even today as a most productive tool of anthropological research.[20] The leading comparative law method, until the Cornell Project, was little more than the mere juxtaposition of rules (black letters) from a variety of legal systems. After Cornell, it was possible for comparative law to claim scientific status as an exercise in rigorous comparison of analogies and differences in the law in action. "Common core research"—an effort to observe in different legal systems functional analogies hidden by formal differences—is regarded today as one of the classic methodologies of comparative law.[21]

Second, the Cornell project has been a remarkable effort in collective scholarly cooperation. Because of the subject matter, and the variety of data in need of collection, it is difficult for comparative law to be carried on as a solo exercise in scholarship. As in other areas of social sciences, most important results can stem only from collective efforts that are in need of a methodology to be productive.

---

[17] See Ugo Mattei, "Why the Wind Changed. Intellectual Leadership in Western Law" 43 *Am J. Comp. Law* 199 (1994).

[18] From the memoir, we know that Schlesinger was not planning to publish his teaching materials. It was a colleague at Cornell who gave the mimeographic copy to an agent of Foundation Press visiting the campus hunting for books. Schlesinger apparently learned of the book only when it was at the galley stage!

[19] Schlesinger, *supra* note 6.

[20] *See* Elisabetta Grande, "L'Apporto dell' antropologia alla conoscenza del diritto. Piccola guida alla ricerca di nuovi itinerari" 14 *Riv. Critica Diritto Privato* 467 (1996).

[21] Most recently *see*, George Berman, "The Discipline of Comparative Law in the United States," *Rev. Int. Droit Comp.* 4, 1046, n. 16 (1999).

Such a methodology was provided at Cornell: the questionnaire, painstakingly discussed and eventually produced by specialists of different legal systems (later called upon to answer to it). The aim is to reach (hypothetical) factual situations as free as possible from local qualifications and biases. If the questionnaire is able to reach this factual ground, it will then be possible to test the actual solutions that different legal systems offer to such legal problems. In the process of preparation and discussion of the questionnaires, scholars involved develop a genuine comparative sensitivity that they will certainly continue in their solo, more traditional, scholarly exercises. This is what has happened to the participants of the Common Core Project at Cornell. The project involved and deeply influenced some of the major foreign scholars who were in turn founding the field in Europe.

The methodology developed at Cornell lives on in Europe today. Almost two hundred scholars are active today in the collective effort to unearth the "common core" of European private law. The methodology tested for the first time at Cornell by Schlesinger has found, almost forty years later, a very practical domain of application (the building of European private law)[22] and has already had a relatively significant impact on the development of the culture of European private law.[23]

Sacco

The other Rudolf was born in 1923 in the small town of Fossano, in the southern part of Piedmont in Italy.[24] Son of a successful attorney—who later became a Popular Party (Christian Democracy) senator—and a remarkably intellectual mother, he grew up in a very formal and austere family environment that placed primary importance on intellectual development. He was the very best student throughout his education, and was particularly fond of history and maths. He grew up under a fascist regime, which meant, among other things, the complete impossibility of traveling abroad because of its autocratic policy.[25]

September 8, 1943, possibly the most dramatic moment of Italian history, surprised the second year law student.[26] Sacco had actually been persuaded by his mother to follow the legal path and to give up his early vocation as a professional

---

[22] *See* Mauro Bussani and Ugo Mattei (eds.), *Making European Law. Essays on the Common Core Project* (2000).

[23] On the "Common Core of European Private Law Project" in which Schlesinger served as an honorary editor (succeeded by Sacco) *see* Mauro Bussani & Ugo Mattei, "The Common Core Approach to European Private Law," 3 *Colum. J. Int. L.* 339 (1997). The first book in the series is R. Zimmermann & S.Whittaker, *Good Faith in European Private Law*, in Mauro Bussani and Ugo Mattei (gen. eds), *The Common Core of European Private Law* (2000).

[24] Published information on Sacco's life and a full bibliography can be found in the two volumes of festschriften presented to him, in the classic European tradition, on his seventieth birthday at a ceremony at the University of Turin attended by more than 400 people. *See* P. Cendon (ed.), *Studi in Onore di Rodolfo Sacco* (1994).

[25] *See* Ricordi di Rodolfo Sacco, (unpublished 2000).

[26] Italian legal education is an undergraduate education.

historian (his first published work is on history).[27] With the Italian government's surrender to the Allies, the King and most of the political leadership escaped the Country, and Italy was literally divided into two. The north was subject to a brutal German regime that controlled the puppet government of Mussolini and consequently to relentless and equally brutal Anglo-American bombing and destruction, and the south was under the control of the Allies. In between, Rome was declared an open city.

The young Sacco, like many young intellectuals of his generation, became active in the armed resistance against the Germans. As a result of his exceptional military skills, unusual courage and gift for leadership, he soon became the chief of a clandestine resistance group in Val Chisone (the valley leading to the very well known skiing resort of Sestriere). 'Comandante Rodolfo' (this was the battle name under which he is still known today in veterans' circles) was arrested in 1945 and sentenced to death. After 42 days in jail he managed to escape by attacking the guards just a few hours before he was due to be executed. Shortly after he escaped, the war ended. In Italy, the communist organizations took over the celebratory rhetoric of the final victory over German oppression. Non-communist liberal participants such as 'Comandante Rodolfo' were systematically excluded from the political reorganization process. Despite some early political involvement, Sacco returned to his studies, finished law school in just a year, graduated in jurisprudence with the well known civil law scholar Mario Allara, studied jurisprudence with the well known legal philosopher Norberto Bobbio, economics with the famous economist, later to become President of the Italian Republic, Luigi Einaudi, and wrote a thesis on legal interpretation. This early ground-breaking work, published in 1947,[28] already contained the seeds of the most advanced hermeneutic conceptions, later linked to the German legal scholar Joseph Esser.[29]

Sacco began an academic career in civil law at the same time as he began at the Bar. He passed the bar examination with the maximum grade in all subjects (a record that to my knowledge has never been matched) after the grading committee investigated the possibility of plagiarism. Eventually it was realized that if Sacco were to have copied from all the sources he was able to cite verbatim he would have had to enter the examination room with a full library!

An academic career was not an easy choice for Sacco. Italy at that time was dominated by the so called neo-systematic method, a sort of modernized pandectism, if possible even more formalistic than its cultural roots.[30] In jurisprudence the most influential figure was Emilio Betti, a fascist scholar with whom Sacco had a very harsh open debate about interpretation. In civil law, Mario Allara, the Turin law professor who according to Italian clannish rules

---

[27] This is an interesting analogy with Schlesinger. Schlesinger also considered history and maths as career alternatives to law and had been persuaded by family concerns about career possibilities in these domains. *See* Schlesinger, *Memories*, cit.

[28] *See* Rodolfo Sacco, *Il concetto di interpretazione del diritto* (1947).

[29] *See* J. Esser, *Vorverständnis und Methodenwahl in der Rechtsfindung* (Frankfurt, 1970).

[30] For a fascinating portrait of Italian legal science *see* most recently Paolo Grossi, *Scienza giuridica italiana. Un profilo storico 1860–1959* (2000).

of academic recruitment was supposed to help the young Sacco, was only mildly supportive of his antiformalistic approach. Eventually Sacco had to produce a monograph employing the old fashioned neo-systematic approach in order to make it possible for Professor Paolo Greco, a leading commercial law scholar, to help him to win a Chair in Trieste (1956).

He was thirty-two years old at a time when people were used to being appointed in their early to mid-twenties. In 1960 he started to teach at the Faculté Internationale de Droit Comparé, at that time located in Luxembourg and the only place where it was actually possible to develop friendships with colleagues and students from the other side of the iron curtain. Then, in 1961 he was called to Pavia where he taught civil law, started to teach comparative law and served as the Dean of the Faculty.

In 1971, Sacco returned to his Alma Mater, a "must" in the Italian academic *cursus honorum*, with a Chair of Comparative Law. It was only in 1983 that he came to occupy the more prestigious Chair of Civil Law. He retired from Turin in 1999 where he is now an Emeritus Professor, (which in Italy signifies not only retirement, but is also a scholarly recognition to be granted by the faculty and the ministry of the University).

As a very young scholar in the early fifties Sacco had the chance to serve as an assistant to René David[31] at the European Studies Institute in Turin. This made him "very early feel a comparativist, proud to use a method that could substitute the dogmatic formalism as an epistemological tool for legal scholarship."[32] This sentence contains the core of Sacco's academic battle within a legal community dominated by dogmatic formalistic reasoning.

If Schlesinger 'created' comparative law in the U.S. there is no doubt that Sacco did the same in Italy. The major difference that one can detect between the two patterns of academic influence is that in Italy teaching and scholarship are by no means sufficient to gain influence. Moreover, Italy being now a rather secondary jurisdiction in the international scholarly map of academic influence and prestige, reaching visibility at the international level is an almost impossible task for a solitary scholar, particularly if the scholar—as in Sacco's case—does not express himself in English.

Sacco's professional life was dominated by the creation of his school. In fact, most of his personal energy was used for the benefit of former students whom he was able to have appointed professors throughout Italy. About 20 Italian professors were former students of Sacco. Most of these now hold chairs in Comparative Law. One only has to consider that there were practically no such chairs until a few years ago and that the remarkable expansion of comparative law makes Italy a worldwide leader in the field.[33] Sacco's major impact was the

---

[31] *See* Chapter 8, this volume.

[32] *See* Ricordi di Rodolfo Sacco (unpublished, February 2000).

[33] For Sacco's rather proud reconstruction of the state of comparative law in Italy: *see* Rodolfo Sacco, "L'Italie en tete," *Rev. Int Droit Comp.* 131 (1996). For a reconstruction of the state of the art *see also* P. G. Monateri, "Critique et Difference: Le Droit Comparé en Italie," *Rev. Int. Droit Comp.* 989 (1999).

result of a struggle for academic power that occupied most of his professional life and earned him many admirers and friends but also many enemies.

In a recent comprehensive book on Italian legal scholarship, the leading historian Professor Paolo Grossi argues that a master can obtain long lasting influence within Italian scholarship provided he meets three requirements: he must have an intellectual project; he must have a school, *i.e.* a group of scholars, usually former students, carrying on the same intellectual project; he must be able to control a journal or some other scholarly publication of major visibility.[34] There is no question that Sacco's intellectual project has been to make the comparative approach in the law as fundamental as it is in other social sciences, in a scholarly environment possessed by chauvinism, formalism and parochialism. In order to obtain a respectable number of chairs in comparative law and in order to be able to appoint his former students to such chairs he devoted a large part of his academic life to time-consuming academic struggles. The life of the fighter went on from the Piedmontese Alps to the faculty meetings.

His scholarly output, both as an individual author and as a leader of major collective projects has been abundant, although mostly written in Italian. Before the piece that gave him worldwide recognition was translated by James Gordley,[35] Sacco's scholarship in English was practically nonexistent.[36] A few pieces were available in French, and he was already very famous in the organization of comparative lawyers, The International Academy of Comparative Law and the Faculté Internationale de Droit Comparé, but this was not sufficient to make him recognized around the world as a leader in our field beyond such relatively narrow circles. Today translations in English and French proliferate and as a consequence Sacco's international fame has finally spread. Among the most influential of Sacco's work is the *Introduzione al Diritto Comparat*,[37] his monumental book on contract law,[38] the one on possession,[39] the collective work *Digesto*,[40] his Treatise on Comparative Law[41] and that on Civil Law[42] as well as his work on African Law,[43] various articles on Soviet Law, and his book on Comparative Legal Systems.[44]

---

[34] *Cf.* Paolo Grossi, *supra* note 30.

[35] *See* Rodolfo Sacco, "Legal Formants. A Dynamic Approach to Comparative Law," 39 *Am J. Comp. L.* 1 (1991). James Gordley is the Cecil Turner Professor of Jurisprudence at Berkeley and one of the most distinguished comparativists in the international arena.

[36] Only one article, Rodolfo Sacco, "The Romanist Substratum of Socialist Law," 14 *Rev. Soc. L.* 65 (1988) had been translated into English before legal formants.

[37] Rodolfo Sacco, *Introduzione al diritto comparato* (Torino, 1980) (5th ed., 1992).

[38] Rodolfo Sacco & G. De Nova, *Il contratto* (Torino, 1975).

[39] Rodolfo Sacco, *Il possesso* (Milano, 1988).

[40] Rodolfo Sacco (gen. ed.), *Digesto IV ed* (1987–2000) 50 volumes.

[41] Rodolfo Sacco (gen ed.), *Trattato di diritto comparato* (1990–present).

[42] Rodolfo Sacco (gen. ed.), *Trattato di diritto civile* (1992–present).

[43] Rodolfo Sacco et al., *Il diritto africano* (Torino, 1995); Rodolfo Sacco, *Le grandi linee del sistema giuridico somalo* (Milano, 1985).

[44] Rodolfo Sacco and A. Gambaro, *Sistemi giuridici comparati* (Torino, 1996).

Sacco traveled extensively in Western Europe, Africa (mostly Somalia and Morocco), the Soviet bloc (mostly before the fall) and in a more limited way in America. He served as the Dean of the Law School at the National University of Somalia and at the Faculty of Law in Pavia.

On the personal side, it might be relevant to his comparative thinking that he married Lili, an Italian-Moroccan woman with whom he always speaks in French. They have two daughters. Politically it would be fair to characterize Sacco as a conservative who is fiercely antifascist as well as anticommunist. (This attitude towards authoritarian ideology is something he shared with Schlesinger). Sacco practices the Catholic religion. As a person, he can be rather intimidating at first sight of his powerful severity. Nevertheless, he is a very warm human being capable of developing deep passionate friendships with many people.

Encounters

Despite belonging to many of the same circles and sharing a very large number of common acquaintances mostly around the International Academy of Comparative Law, Sacco and Schlesinger practically never met each other, except for one rather insignificant encounter at Pescara, when they were introduced to one another by Gino Gorla, the famous comparativist and Italian participant in the Cornell Project, during the International Academy of Comparative Law conference in 1970.

I was a student of Sacco in Turin in 1980. In his comparative law classes he would mention Schlesinger's Cornell Common Core methodology, which he had reviewed for the Italian *Rivista di Diritto Civile*.[45] A paragraph of the *Introduzione al Diritto Comparato* containing Sacco's most famous article on legal formants is devoted to the Cornell project. I believe that Sacco never studied Schlesinger's *Comparative Law* case-book in depth. When, in 1987, I began to attend Schlesinger's classes at Hastings, I mentioned to him the name of Sacco. I remember Schlesinger telling me: "That man understood more of the Cornell common core methodology than I did." Schlesinger regretted that most of Sacco's work was not available in English. He used to mention one of his own articles on common principles in International Arbitration, which was published in German in 1964. Schlesinger regarded that piece as his best scholarly work, yet it was practically never cited. I remember that conversation providing the incentive to approach Gordley (himself by that time an admirer of Sacco's work) to discuss finding a way to have some of Sacco's work made available in English. When the manuscript on legal formants was ready, I took it to Schlesinger who read it eagerly. He was enthusiastic about Sacco's work, although he did not like the term 'legal formant' and suggested using 'formative element.' I mentioned this to Sacco who overruled the objection. For him the

[45] *See* Rodolfo Sacco, "Un metodo di lavoro nuovo. I Seminari di Cornell," 2 *Riv. Dir. Civ.* 172 (1972).

phrase was a sort of international copyright on the theory since *"formante"* was already widely used and misused in Italy—indeed there is no Italian comparative law work that does not use the word—and "formant" was also used in some French circles. In the supplement to the fifth edition of Schlesinger's *Comparative Law*, published in 1994, a whole paragraph and a large number of footnotes are dedicated to the work of Sacco and the theory of legal formants is expressed with unmatched simplicity and clarity. Nevertheless, Schlesinger could not resist the temptation to rename the formant as formative element.

In late 1992, during one conversation with Mauro Bussani[46] at Schlesinger's home in San Francisco when we were considering launching a European Common Core Project, the issue of the relationship between the method at Cornell and the theory of legal formants arose again. Schlesinger's position was that the methodology of legal formants, in short, of not assuming coherence between the various levels of legal propositions whose aggregate makes the legal rule—was in the background at Cornell, but in a sense was taken for granted and so was never actually discussed. It was difficult to understand whether Schlesinger was minimizing Sacco's contribution to something that did not need to be stated, or whether he was acknowledging a shortcoming at Cornell. What Schlesinger was saying had some truth in it and indeed, one could say the same of the work of the great Gino Gorla,[47] the Italian participant in the Cornell project. On the other hand, I remember thinking that a methodology cannot be approached critically, and cannot be developed if it is not made explicit. A sense of incoherence between legal propositions is a legacy of realism and perhaps of antiformalism in general, but assuming that incoherence is a structural requisite of the different semantic levels of legal propositions is certainly a step that had to be taken. The former is a hunch, the latter a theory.[48]

Afterwards, Mauro Bussani and I agreed that the issue of the extent of the novelty and originality of legal formants (rather than mere restatement of something that was already common currency at Cornell) had to be approached in the institutional framework of the academic lives of Schlesinger and Sacco. Schlesinger was perhaps somewhat more self-effacing that Sacco, because of fundamental differences between the American and the Italian faculty recruitment processes. Schlesinger was not continuously surrounded by admiring crowds of younger academics (such as ourselves!), following him like the apostles.[49] Moreover, Schlesinger never engaged in such time-consuming power

---

[46] Mauro Bussani is Professor of Comparative Law at the University of Trieste in Italy and is co-general editor of the Common Core of European Private Law Project in Trento.

[47] Gino Gorla (1909–1992) Late Professor of Comparative Law at the University of Rome and Late Dean of the Law Faculty at the University of Alexandria (Egypt). His work on Comparative Law, particularly on Contracts and on the role of Case-law in the civil law tradition is considered foundational worldwide.

[48] For a theoretical discussion of legal formants, *see* P. G. Monateri and Rodolfo Sacco, "Legal Formants," in John Eatwell et al. (eds), *The New Palgrave. A Dictionary of Economics and the Law* (London, 1998).

[49] This colorful parallel was used by my friend and Hastings colleague Joel Paul commenting on Sacco's visit to Harvard in 1997.

struggles as Sacco, and this certainly safeguarded his objectivity more than would have been possible otherwise. Finally, we both agreed that when it came to a personal appreciation of the importance and quality of each other's work, the two held each other in high regard. Moreover, despite differences of personality and academic contexts, the two had pretty strong feelings about the importance and quality of their own work.

Consequently at the time we believed that, whatever might have been the ultimate paternity of the fundamental methodology of present day comparativism, Sacco's research on legal formants had to be seen as a step forward in comparative methodology and such a step had to be reflected in the European Common Core Project.

TRANSPLANTS, ORIGINALITY AND INFLUENCE

If at Cornell the theory of legal formants was already being applied, one could deny its originality and autonomy and conclude that Sacco was a mere European follower of Schlesinger. Of course things are not this simple.

Sacco himself publicly acknowledges his debt to Schlesinger, while privately claiming his originality, and therefore makes it difficult to study the transplant. In a book-length interview published in 1992, Sacco declares:

> " I do not believe that I gave anything to comparative legal scholarship. I have been a Mr. Chips of the law faculties, a schoolteacher able to infect others with my enthusiasm. Moreover, I have been a notary that has put things in writing, using some neologisms when necessary—the new things discovered by R. David, R. Schlesinger and G. Gorla. I have been forced to do so because the three masters who taught me what I know curiously, indeed very curiously, have forgotten to spell out at the end of their works the formulas that allowed them to reach the magical results of their researches. They never seemed to have noticed the work of restating their methodology that I have done."[50]

Not surprisingly this is not Sacco's true feeling. When discussing with me the real meaning of his debt to Schlesinger, Sacco told me that theoretically it was rather trivial and perhaps nothing at all. While the Cornell Project had given him a mine of material to support his theory, the theory of legal formants had been conceived previously and independently, because neither Gorla nor anybody else had ever told him what was happening at Cornell and hence he had to wait for the rather late publication in 1968 of *Formation of Contracts*[51] to know about the Cornell method.[52] In Sacco's own words:

---

[50] *Cf.* Rodolfo Sacco, *Che cos' e' il diritto comparato?* 285 (Milano, 1992).
[51] Schlesinger, *supra* note 6.
[52] Personal communication with the author made while walking toward the Turin railroad station to meet his student and my mentor Professor Antonio Gambaro visiting our legal theory workshop from Milano (February 2000).

"In 1970 I met in Italy Rudolf Schlesinger who was in Italy for the Eighth Congress of the International Academy of Comparative Law. I was introduced to him by Gorla. At the time I had not read *Formation of Contracts*. I started to read and I observed that Schlesinger had approached those misleading circumstances that the superficial comparativist usually neglects (different mentalities, different, tacit assumptions) and has found the correct procedure to overcome them. I also observed that the work lead by Schlesinger *confirmed* that the knowledge of a legal system limited to only one formant (statute, case, explicit description of a local academic . . .) could not avoid being unilateral and crippled."[53]

In his last published work, Schlesinger also seems to acknowledge the originality of legal formants compared to the Cornell methodology:

"I strongly believe that the future belongs to that kind of comparison [the integrative]. The obstacles can be and will be overcome by legal scholars who are aware of their existence. The tools that are appropriate for that task are clearly available: All of the obstacles to which I have referred will yield to the factual method pioneered in the Cornell Common Core Project, especially if each legal system's solution of the questions thus posed is explored and determined in the light of the insights regarding legal formants that have more recently been developed by Professor Sacco."[54]

At this point, given the impossibility of ascertaining with historical certainty how much one approach (legal formants) stems from the other (common core), we need to work toward an understanding of the relationship of the two methodologies by putting them in a broader context.

MODERNISM, POSTMODERNISM AND TWO MEANINGS OF POSITIVISM

Sacco's theory of legal formants can be considered an application to the law of a theoretical and methodological line of scholarship known as structuralism, developed in the social and cognitive sciences but also applied to mathematics and biology. Structuralism aims at an understanding of a system by observing the relationship between the elements that make the structure of the system. Beginning in linguistics (with the work of Ferdinand de Saussure, Roman Jacobson, Emile Benveniste[55]) structuralism has found its way into anthropology (Claude Levi Strauss[56]), psychoanalysis (Jacques Lacan[57]), psychology (Jean Piaget[58]),

---

[53] Sacco, *supra* note 9.

[54] More recently, the leading American comparativist George Bermann mentions three distinct "higher profile" methods of comparative law: common core, legal transplants and legal formants, hence agreeing that we are looking at different original theories. G. Berman, "The Discipline of Comparative Law in the United States," *Rev. Int. Droit Comp.* 4, 1046, n 16 (1999).

[55] Ferdinand de Saussure, *Cours de Linguisitique Generale* (Paris-Lausanne, 1916); Roman Jacobson, *Essais de Linguistique Generale* (Paris, 1963); Emile Benveniste, *Problemes de Linguistique Generale* (Paris, 1966).

[56] Clande Lévi-Strauss, *Anthropologie Structurale* (Paris, 1958).

[57] Jacques Lacan, *Ecrits* (Paris, 1966).

[58] *See* R. I. Evans, *Jean Piaget: The Man and His Ideas* (Eleanor Duckworth, trans., New York, 1973).

philosophy (Louis Althusser, Michel Foucault[59]), into semiotics (Umberto Eco[60]), and finally, with Sacco, into the law. Structuralism attempts to develop a scientific method for describing the laws that govern the relationship of the elements of the structure with the system in its totality.

Sometimes structuralism in comparative law is opposed to functionalism. The structuralism-functionalism opposition privileges the relative predominance of the form of the system, and the development of the system as an historical accumulation of meaning, over the aim of the system. Functionalism in the law (as in architecture),[61] on the contrary, stresses the aim of the function of law over its form. In this sense common core methodology can be considered functionalist, because of its emphasis on how solutions to social conflicts (the function of legal systems) are in fact much more common across different legal systems than the method by which the solution is reached (determined by the structure of the legal system as an accumulation of meanings). Functionalist comparative law has its most distinguished proponents in Konrad Zweigert and Hein Kötz.[62] In comparative law, however, the structuralism-functionalism opposition cannot be usefully used in establishing an alternative view of the world. It might at most convey the idea of integrative comparativism (emphasizing analogies) as opposed to contrastive comparativism (emphasizing differences) with all the limits of generalizing this dichotomy stemming from the persistent lack of reliable measurement techniques suffered by the comparative method in social science.[63] In a sense, Sacco's style of structural comparativism does not disregard the function of the law (alternative legal formants may perform the same function in two systems, or different functions might be performed by the same formant). The common core approach, as developed by Schlesinger is also structuralist when, for example, it stresses how procedural institutions and their organization are the truly central aspect of the civil law versus common law opposition.[64] Hence we could not capture the relationship between Sacco and Schlesinger by claiming that the former is structuralist while the latter is functionalist. Accordingly, an alternative opposition to understand the relationship between the two should be looked for; that, rather simplified in the present context, is the contrast between modernism and postmodernism.[65]

In Sacco's work there are seeds of the European postmodern condition, and of the high degree of cultural relativism that characterizes it. Such aspects of the postmodernn attitude, which in the law regards the interpreter as a storyteller,

---

[59] *See* Louis Althusser et al., *Lire le Capital* (Paris, 1965).

[60] *See* Umberto Eco, *Trattato di Semiotica Generale* (Milano, 1975); U. Eco, *La Struttura Assente* (Milano, 1978); Umberto Eco, *Semiotica e filosofia del Linguaggio* (Milano, 1984).

[61] *See* Ugo Mattei & A. di Robilant, cit. *Supra* note 2. (For a detailed discussion and bibliography of functionalism in architecture).

[62] Konrad Zweigert & Hein Kötz, *An Introduction to Comparative Law* (3d ed., Oxford, 1998).

[63] *See* Ugo Mattei, *Comparative Law and Economics* (Ann Arbor, 1997).

[64] *See supra* text accompanying footnote 29.

[65] For a discussion of the many cautions that should be used in handling the modern-postmodern opposition *see* Mattei & di Robilant, *supra* note 2.

and the interpretation as a participatory exercise per se creative of the legal order, cannot be found in Schlesinger's work. Other aspects of the postmodern condition such as the return to form, the free borrowing from a variety of previous styles, the emphasis on the value of localism and diversity, the distrust of functionalism and the disillusioned attitudes in the face of the normative possibilities of the scholar's work in determining change are also entirely absent from Schlesinger's writing while strongly part of Sacco's.

Postmodernism constructs previous movements as an historical past from which to borrow. Sacco views and puts in context Schlesinger's work (as well as that of realism and other schools of thought) as historical experiences with the detachment that can stem only from the sense of being part of a successive movement and of the next generation. It is natural to take freely some elements of historical experience, though the different context and timing make the difference rather radical. Moreover, the relationship with what can be considered *real* changes entirely. Participatory interpretation is stressed, and the interpreter as a storyteller or as a hidden law giver assumes a very central role in the picture.[66]

True, there is in Sacco's work a difference between description and normativity, between the *is* and the *ought*, that is entirely modern and that is wholly refused by the postmodern condition. However, there is a fundamental tension between this modern positivistic conception (perhaps coming from pure formalistic legal theories such as Mario Allara's, his mentor in Turin, or, perhaps from the general structuralist claim of being a scientific method) and the theory of participatory interpretation that he was able to develop very early in his scholarly life.

Because of this fundamental tension, one could deny the postmodern flavor of Sacco's work. Nevertheless, this objection can be overruled, because the broad scope suggested by Sacco's methodology looks at postmodernism itself as a culturally contingent historical movement at play in one context and not in another, and as a consequence makes the storyteller incapable of determining what he is observing.

One should note, however, that the postmodern attitude of breaking with a notion of objective knowledge and of positivistic science has by no means been followed by Sacco's structural comparativism, whose attitude in this perspective seems deeply grounded in mid-twentieth century modernism. Positivism, however, can mean at least two things. The belief in the distinction between the *is* and the *ought* is the sense in which, among social scientists, economics can be considered positivistic. This is the sense in which Sacco can be considered positivist. The belief that only that which is backed by the political force of a state is positivist law, and that therefore the legal order is limited by the domain of

---

[66] See A. Gambaro, *Il Successo del Giurista, Foro Italiano*, p. v, 85–9 (1983).

the state, is the sense of positivism fully developed by Hans Kelsen in continental Europe[67] and by John Austin in England.[68]

Positivism, in this second sense is completely absent in Schlesinger's as well as in Sacco's work probably because of the nature of comparative law as the study of disparate systems. The critique of positivism as state-centrism is well developed in Schlesinger's work and can be regarded as his fundamental contribution to jurisprudence.[69] But participatory interpretation and the seeds of postmodernism as a challenge to the *is/ought* distinction were entirely absent from Schlesinger's work and might be considered the fundamental postmodern contribution of Sacco's structural comparativism in Europe.

Despite this rather important difference, the passage from modernism to postmodernism in comparative law has not changed the direction of the struggle and critique of comparative law against the overwhelming parochialism of legal culture. As discussed elsewhere, I believe that the central contribution of Schlesinger's jurisprudence has been to show that like anthropology, economics, political science, sociology, and linguistics, legal scholarship should proceed first by comparative analysis and only at a later stage, when we have understood the nature of a legal problem, be concerned with the peculiarities of each national legal system. Of course, as most jurists believe even today, the local technicalities of the law affect the solution of a problem at the local level. However, if scholarship is aimed at understanding and explaining legal phenomena it cannot do so if it is focused only on parochial contingencies. Deeper understanding of legal problems is thus precluded from all approaches that remain entangled in local technicalities.

Seen from the comparative perspective pioneered by Schlesinger at the Cornell Seminars, and fully developed in Sacco's Legal Formants, legal positivism is *the enemy* of understanding in the law. It is a reductionist perspective that artificially excludes from the picture the deeper structure of the law (things like legal culture, language of legal expression, revolutionary moments and so on) as well as (in typical postmodern style) the decorative, and symbolic elements of it. Positivism, as a consequence is unmasked as an inherently formalistic approach, in the sense that form prevails over structure in determining the law's domain. It *outlaws* (considers outside of the law) deeper structural aspects such as political power, economic hegemony (including economic efficiency), cultural legitimacy, intellectual prestige, sexual dynamics, race relations and so on. It also outlaws rhetorical elements so important in the legal picture.[70]

---

[67] *See* H. Kelsen, *General Theory of Law and State* (Cambridge, Mass., 1949).

[68] *See* J. Austin, *Lectures on Jurisprudence, or the Philosophy of Positive Law* (R. Campbell ed., London, 1875).

[69] I develop the point in Mattei, *supra* note 9.

[70] *See* Mitchel Lasser, "Judicial (Self-) Portraits: Judicial Discourse in the French Legal System," 104 *Yale L. J.* 1325 (1995); Mitchel Lasser, " 'Lit. Theory' put to test: A Comparative Literary Analysis of American Judicial Tests and French Judicial Discourse," 111 *Harv. L. Rev.* 689 (1998). *See also*, for further steps, A. Di Robilant, "Non soltanto parole. In margine ad alcuni itinerari di Law and Art," in *Materiali per una Storia della cultura giuridica* (2001).

These broader *outlawed* phenomena that in all societies (in different forms) affect social control and controlling processes[71] are simply and arbitrarily considered irrelevant for the lawyer. They are the domains of sociology, anthropology, or of political sciences. The domain of the law is reduced to that of the (more or less legitimized) political production of binding norms and institutions. It is not the job of lawyers to point at other, perhaps more relevant, variables. The lawyers have to point to *legal constructs* that determine legal outcomes. Such legal constructs are locally produced and determined: parochialism is hence justified. This narrow conception of the law as *the political product of the state within a given territory* has also affected American legal realism making it ultimately and paradoxically still a formalistic approach to the law. Even the idea of looking at judges as legislators (Cardozo[72]), at what they do rather than at what they say they are doing (J. Frank[73]), or of recognizing the crucial role of administrative agencies (K.Llewellyn[74]) is not much of a change of perspective from considering *appellate opinions* as the laboratory materials of legal science as Ames and Langdell used to do.[75]

Comparative jurisprudence shows that a full structural understanding of the law does not occur until case law is reduced to just one of the many legal formants (perhaps the American favorite) of the law, itself a much more complex phenomenon. Both formalism and realism, from the comparative perspective, fall short of making us understand the nature of law as a global phenomenon of organization of power, rhetoric, path dependency, and policy.

From American legal realism, Schlesinger took the attitude of looking at what really matters in the law, beyond the rhetoric contained in the law in the books. But from his civilian background, beginning from the clear perception of the crucial role of legal scholarship he refused the narrow realist notion that what matters are only cases or other official decision making processes (such as administrative agencies). On this basis it has been possible for Sacco and the structural school to see the law as conditioned by a much broader variety of factors: the unofficial (not only legal scholarship of course but practices and mentalities in general) and unconscious ones being as important as the official and the conscious. The following stage of this evolution reconsidering the role of legal form is the emphasis on the interpreter as ultimate storyteller participating in the power game of constructing legitimacy. This final step is visible both in comparative law and economics' idea of efficiency as a legitimating process,[76] and in the critique of interpretivism of the recent merger in Europe between crits and comparativists.[77]

---

[71] *See* Laura Nader, *Law in Culture and Society* (Berkeley, 1997).
[72] Benjamin Cardozo, *The Nature of the Judicial Process* (New Haven, 1921).
[73] Jerome Frank, *Law and the Modern Mind* (Gloucester, Mass., 1970).
[74] *See* Karl Llewellyn, *The Bramble Bush* (New York, 1930).
[75] *See* Grant Gilmore, *The Ages of American Law* (New Haven, 1977).
[76] *See* Gambaro, cit. *supra* note 59, and Ugo Mattei, *supra* note 63, at 20 ff.
[77] *See* P. G. Monateri, "Everybody's Talking. The Future of Comparative Law," 21 *Hast. Int and Comp. L. R.* 825 (1998); *See also* the symposium issue of the *Utah L. Rev.* (1997) devoted to new

While in Europe Schlesinger's comparativism planted the seeds of structural comparativism,[78] his intellectual legacy in the general jurisprudence of the United States has been much less recognized. In the United States Schlesinger's jurisprudence has been relatively ineffective (because jurisprudence scholars do not read technical comparative legal work) and very often misunderstood. Possibly Schlesinger's major role in mainstream U.S. comparative law made him responsible (a sort of respondeat superior) for the much criticized telephone book aspects of our discipline that in the last few years have been under fire.[79] There is no question, on the other hand that the major critique of state-centrism and the strongly antiformalistic aspects of Schlesinger's work have been fully appreciated in Europe where Sacco was able to develop, at least in part, his structural methodology based on the building blocks of Schlesinger's work.

approaches to the discipline. For a discussion and evaluation of the relationship between structuralism and critical legal studies in Europe, *see* Mattei and di Robilant, *supra* note 2.

[78] Schlesinger's work in Europe has been extensively cited and I believe that the Volume "Formation of Contracts" has received more book reviews in the old continent (mostly very favourable) than any other book ever published in the U.S.

[79] The most brutal methodological indictment of comparative law is William Ewald, "Comparative Jurisprudence (I). What Was it Like to Try a Rat," 143 *U. Penn L. Rev.* 1889 (1995). *See also* the issue "New Directions in Comparative Law," 46 *Am. J. Comp. L.* 597 (1998) as well as M. Graziadei, *Comparative Law, Legal History and the Holistic Approach to Legal Cultures*, 531 (1999).

Index